WHITE SPACE

WHITE SPACE

Race, Privilege, and Cultural Economies of the Okanagan Valley

DANIEL J. KEYES AND
LUÍS L.M. AGUIAR

30 29 28 27 26 25 24 23 22 21   5 4 3 2 1

Printed in Canada on FSC-certified ancient-forest-free paper (100% post-consumer recycled) that is processed chlorine- and acid-free.

Library and Archives Canada Cataloguing in Publication

Title: White space : race, privilege, and cultural economies of the Okanagan Valley / Daniel J. Keyes and Luís L.M. Aguiar.
Names: Keyes, Daniel J., editor. | Aguiar, Luis L. M., editor.
Description: Includes bibliographical references and index.
Identifiers: Canadiana (print) 20210329866 | Canadiana (ebook) 20210329890 | ISBN 9780774860048 (hardcover) | ISBN 9780774860055 (paperback) | ISBN 9780774860062 (PDF) | ISBN 9780774860079 (EPUB)
Subjects: LCSH: Whites—Race identity—British Columbia—Okanagan Valley (Region) | LCSH: Okanagan Valley (B.C. : Region)—Race relations.
Classification: LCC HT1575 .W55 2021 | DDC 305.809711/5—dc23

Canadä

UBC Press gratefully acknowledges the financial support for our publishing program of the Government of Canada (through the Canada Book Fund), the Canada Council for the Arts, and the British Columbia Arts Council.

Printed and bound in Canada by Friesens
Set in Perpetua and Minion by Apex CoVantage, LLC
Copy editor: Joanne Richardson
Indexer: Emily LeGrand
Cartographer: Okanagan Nation Alliance and Eric Leinberger
Cover designer: Will Brown

UBC Press
The University of British Columbia
2029 West Mall
Vancouver, BC V6T 1Z2
www.ubcpress.ca

To Charles Blair and Arthur Chapman, the two Black Summerland hotel workers who died in 1908 and were memorialized via the naming of N–toe Mountain near Penticton on December 1955, and to the missing children referenced in Volume 4 of the Truth and Reconciliation Report. More work must be done to meaningfully address the ongoing intergenerational trauma of colonization in the Okanagan and beyond.

Decolonize now.

CONTENTS

ACKNOWLEDGMENTS

Typically acknowledgments thank and give credits to the various influential and inspiring persons who helped make a work possible. In the case of this anthology on whiteness, we first need to acknowledge our positions. We are two academics, one ethnicized with economic privileges and the other white with multiple privileges working and living on the Syilx's unceded territories. We would also like to acknowledge people who have vocally resisted and highlighted whiteness in the Okanagan Valley – people like Dr. Jeannette Armstrong, Ben Lee, Dr. David Lethbridge, and others too numerous to name.

It was about 2003 when I (Luís) had a conversation with my colleagues Patricia Tomic and Ricardo Trumper on the patio of the cafeteria of the then Okanagan University College about the blinding whiteness in the composition of the social characteristics of people living in the valley. Luís, Patricia, and Ricardo decided there and then to investigate the whiteness of the Okanagan Valley before it became a thing at UBC Okanagan. The three of us collaborated and went on to coauthor several publications on whiteness and racism before moving on to other solo projects. As far as Luís is concerned, Patricia and Ricardo are largely responsible for his development as a scholar via, among other things, enabling his understanding of whiteness in the valley. Therefore, he would like to thank them for their teaching, encouragement, and contribution to his intellectual growth not only with respect to his understanding of whiteness but also with respect to his understanding of the continuing relevance and function of class in the Okanagan and beyond.

Daniel acknowledges and thanks his colleagues (Maria Alexopoulos, Alifa Bandali, George Grinnell, Alison Hargreaves, David Jefferess, Hussein Keshani and Ruthann Lee, and Kyong Yoon, among others) and former students (Lindsay Balfour, Rina Garcia Chua, Jordan Coble, Lindsay Diehl, Kezia Elaschuk, Taya Jardine, William Jones, Tahira Saeed, Mehnaz Tabassum, Mari Tanaka, Janna Wale, Kelsey Wheelhouse) in and associated with the Cultural Studies Program at UBC Okanagan who have been very much engaged with contesting the textual spectres of this region's white fantasies. He would also like to thank the Okanagan Nation Alliance for providing the map, included in the introduction, and Eric Leinberger for helping to recreate it.

Edited books are never easy and not just because publishers are reluctant to support them. We would like to thank our contributors who stayed with us through this long editorial process. They, along with us, have persevered with this project since we all believe in its necessity. We want to thank them for the collegiality they've shown in producing this timely and necessary book. Meagan Dyer and Darcy Cullen from UBC Press have been very patient with us. We would also like to thank the anonymous reviewers of the manuscript who provided frank, constructive criticism that has helped hone this project. We thank them for helping us shepherd this work to its conclusion.

Finally, we want to thank our families for their love, patience, and support.

WHITE SPACE

INTRODUCTION

Daniel J. Keyes

Typically in western Canada the phrase "the Okanagan" evokes images of a place of warmth, sunshine, leisure, and relaxation. For some it is a sleepy rural valley filled with fruit stands and vineyards, while others tout it as a "silicon vineyard," a high-tech corridor of industry set in a bucolic valley (*Wired* staff 2000). The Okanagan refers to a 120-kilometre-long and 20-kilometre-wide valley located in the centre of southern British Columbia with a population of 362,238 (Central Okanagan 2016; North Okanagan 2016; Okanagan-Similkameen 2016). However, the Okanagan is also a state of mind.

A potential newcomer searching the internet for information on this region would have the above pleasing images confirmed if she landed on okanagan.com. On this website, a ninety-second promotional video begins, accompanied by mellow acoustic jazz guitar over a series of still shots of the valley confirming these pleasant images of warmth, sunshine, leisure, and relaxation (Knowlton 2015). The video's opening shot of the valley includes an image of Okanagan Lake with no development around it and then cuts to a map of North America firmly planting the Okanagan in Canada. A small Canadian flag appears in the top right-hand corner of the screen to secure the Okanagan as part of Canada. There is no attempt to situate the Okanagan as the unceded territory of the Syilx People (Okanagan Nation Declaration 1987; Syilx Okanagan Nation 2021). Figure 1 below shows a map produced by the Okanagan Nation Alliance countering the video's cartography

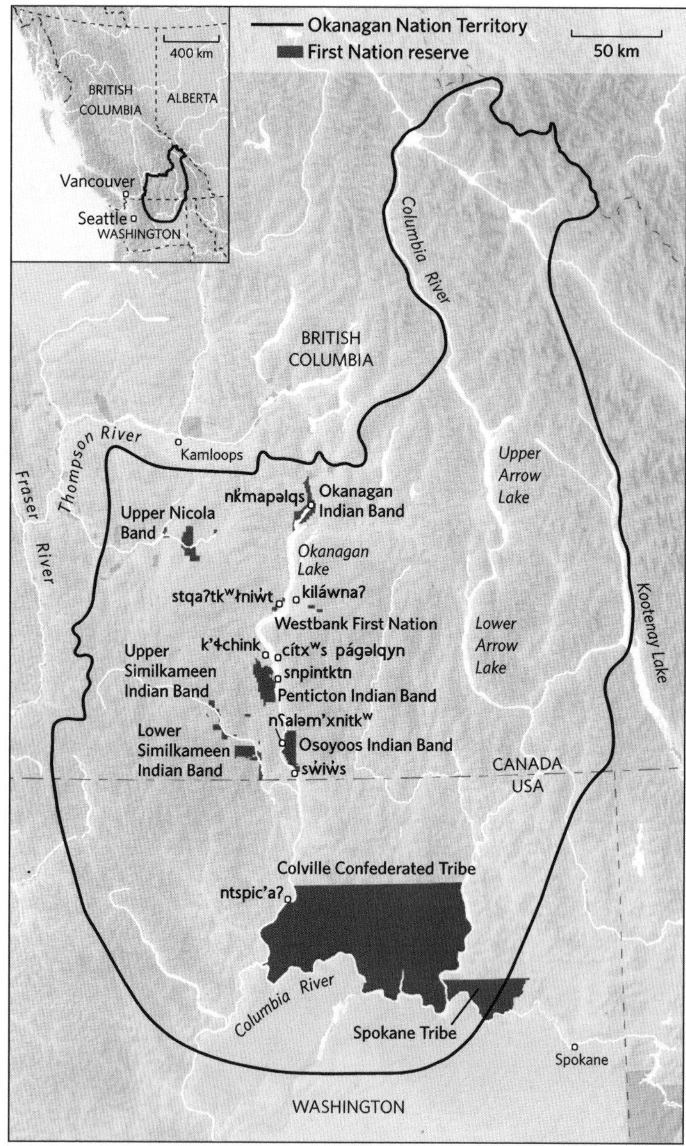

FIGURE 1 Okanagan Nation Territory with the lower third extending into Washington State. | Map by Eric Leinberger, derived from the Okanagan Nation Alliance's (ONA) map of the Syilx Territory. *This map is not inclusive of all Syilx place names, nor are there always English equivalents for specific place names provided. No part of this map may be translated, modified, or used for any purposes, including in a publication, without the express written permission of the ONA.*

by insisting that, since time immemorial, the Syilx people of the Okanagan Nation Alliance have lived in this region.

The remainder of this promotional video sequentially unfolds using the following keywords along with evocative still stock images of the region: Vineyards, Wineries, Sunshine, History, Culture, Nature, Fruit, Beaches, Health, Golf, Resorts, Food, Shopping, Skiing, Fun, Adventure, and, finally, Paradise. This word "Paradise" frames the Okanagan's reality as a fantasy space of leisure where modern urban conveniences like shopping and fine dining are available, and the rural serves as a playground. In this fantasy, the rural is associated not with the labour of cultivating food but with the recreation potential of nature. The Okanagan's rural is a white playground. Absent from this video are labourers and people of colour. The still images offer gender conformity with anonymous white women on beaches, shopping, and exercising on paddleboards while white men appear skiing down hills and riding mountain bikes. The video's pairing of images to keywords flattens the limited diversity of the valley into a spectacle of sanitized white pleasures. For example, excluded from this promotional video's history of the region are the many Chinese labourers who built the Okanagan's Kettle Valley Railway between 1910 and 1915 (Gaffney 2016; Williams 2008). Similarly, the keyword "Culture" appears with the image of a silhouette of a metal sculpture of an Indian Brave on a horse, thus evoking an anachronistic and exotic Indigenous culture. The video does not offer viewers an image of the Westbank First Nation's Sncewips Heritage Museum, which insists that Syilx continue to shape contemporary culture on their unceded lands. This video, and indeed the Okanagan.com website, which offers virtual tours of the region's tourist hot spots, reinforces the visual tropes of the Okanagan as a tidy white fantasy space situated within this rural-urban paradise, so different from diverse urban spaces like Vancouver or Toronto (Hage 2000). This video's fantasy of the Okanagan rests on what human geographer Andrew Baldwin (2009, 530) refers to as a Canadian spatial imaginary "between contingent poles in a national performative logic of space of wilderness/nature and a multicultural urban zone." The website's fantasy of the Okanagan decidedly tilts towards the wilderness/nature pole while offering a sense of a white rural-urban space free of multicultural entanglements. The sole exception to this fantasy is one link buried under the "More" tab titled "Fruit Jobs," which hints at the euphemistically named "temporary labourers," many from the Global South, who come to the valley not to sample fine wine and cuisine but to pick fruit for minimum wage. Their labour supports the tidy white fantasy of bucolic leisure (Tomic and Trumper 2012). The Okanagan state of mind as exemplified by Okanagan.com embodies the fantasy of unquestioned white privilege as natural and inevitable in this rural-urban paradise.

This anthology analyzes whiteness in the Okanagan. Whiteness permeates contemporary representations of the ideal Okanagan life in magazines, maps, posters, institutions, and websites that picture the region as a literal contemporary paradise for white bodies. These texts inoculate viewers against the colonial history of the valley and its neocolonial present by framing representations of the region in white innocence. Neocolonialism refers to societal structures in contemporary settler states that do not appear to settlers as intentionally harmful and assimilative as do old, more explicit, versions of colonialism. Neocolonial attitudes assert that colonialism has waned (e.g., the "Indian" Residential Schools are all closed) and that Canadians should not dwell on the distant past. Neocolonial attitudes argue that Canadian society has moved passed the persistent history and ongoing violence of colonialism. Nevertheless, neocolonialism ignores how settlers continue to reap the benefits of colonialism's legacy by maintaining dominance. Neocolonialism shies away from confronting the structural benefits of land dispossession for settlers.

This anthology dubs representations of the Okanagan that appear on Okanagan.com and elsewhere as fantasies (rather than as realities) in order to contest how Okanagan representations invariably generate and secure for settlers ideal and comforting places for white identity to thrive without apparent challenge. White fantasies obstruct and silence differences and, in so doing, present whiteness as the norm and ideal for the region. Whiteness as an Okanagan fantasy undermines variations in gender, sexuality, age, ability, and, significantly, class by uniformly presenting itself as both an ideal and a norm. Into the second decade of the twenty-first century, over 90 percent of the Okanagan's population identifies as white (Teixeira 2011, 177). This statistic suggests that Okanagan.com's paradise is a fractal part of the Okanagan's fantasy that suppresses the region's colonial past to offer a safe white present for newcomers and permanent residents who identify as belonging to the 90 percent. White fantasy generates norms to mobilize and solidify consent and conformity. This fantasy invariably presents itself as the sole plausible organizing foundation for life in the valley's rural-urban space.

The Okanagan's white fantasy is particular to the Okanagan, despite partaking of elements of Western mass media's normative whiteness (Hughey 2014). Whiteness in the Okanagan has national, provincial, and regional elements that reflect a late nineteenth-century and early twentieth-century investment on the part of Anglo-white settlers in celebrating the fantasy of whiteness (as a bundle of explicit attributes such as entrepreneurial zeal, mastery of the frontier, and implicit attributes such as class, masculinity, and heteronormativity). This fantasy actively marginalizes, silences, and dispossess other cultures and peoples while producing white normativity as a standard against which to measure others as lacking. This anthology's critique of the Okanagan resonates with critical race work that needs to occur in rural-urban spaces in Canada and in other settler nations where similar fantastic projects of place-making perpetuate neocolonial fantasies. It situates whiteness in rural-urban Canada by situating a specific analysis of historical and contemporary whiteness. It cannot argue that the dynamic of whiteness in the Okanagan operates in other regions in Canada, but it suggests that whiteness is an essential element for understanding settler privilege in the rural-urban regions of the country. As a white editor of this anthology, I strive to include perspectives that provide a resolute challenge to the dominance of whiteness while being fully aware that I continue to benefit from my multiple privileges as a tenured academic, settler, and straight white abled man. This anthology's chapters provide readers with the tools for contextualizing and dismantling the appeals of affective whiteness that see 90 percent of the Okanagan self-identify as white (Teixeira 2011, 177), and it makes terms like "settlers" distasteful to many who refuse to admit white privilege. It contributes to the literature on whiteness by tracing how colonialism evolves into neocolonial whiteness and how triumphant liberal whiteness evolves into flexible neoliberal whiteness in rural-urban spaces.

WHY NOW?

White Space intervenes at a moment when the political landscape of Canada grapples with its colonial legacy. Progressive forces like the Okanagan's grassroots organization RAMA (Radical Action with Migrants in Agriculture) challenge whiteness's grasp on Canadian and regional Okanagan identity (RAMA 2019). In the last ten years, nested in national, provincial, and regional remits, progressive attempts to grapple with Canada's legacy as a settler state occur: nationally, the Truth and Reconciliation Commission's ninety-four sweeping recommendations argue for a nation-to-nation reconciliation of relations between First Nations people and the Canadian state (Truth 2015). The implementation of these recommendations remains in question. Provincially, BC NDP premier John Horgan agrees to adopt the 2007 United Nations Declaration on the Rights of Indigenous Peoples on 18 July 2017, which would see nation-to-nation type relations replace the colonial model dictated by Canada's Indian Act (Palmer 2019). In December 2018, ignoring environmental and First Nations concerns, Premier Horgan affirms the continued development of the Site C dam project on the Peace River in northeastern British Columbia, which the previous Liberal government initially approved. Horgan admits failure: "I am not the first person to stand before you and disappoint Indigenous people ... But I am going to do my level best to make amends for a whole host of issues and decisions that previous governments have made to put Indigenous people in an unwinnable situation" (Palmer 2019). The conversation on resource development in British Columbia remains contested, with many First Nations arguing resource development negatively affects their unceded territories while industry asserts the neocolonial view that Crown land should be in the service of wealth development and providing well-paying jobs for Canadians.

Regionally a shift in how the Okanagan acknowledges its colonial history has occurred: in 2015, the then provincial Liberal government renamed southern Okanagan provincial parks with *nsyilxcən* (the language spoken by Syilx, the people of the Okanagan Nation Alliance) names to replace those of prominent settlers (Moore 2015). Upset readers of *Castanet*, a local online news website, vociferously argue that these name changes as reported by the website threaten to violate history and common sense. These recent gestures towards decolonizing Canada, British Columbia, and the Okanagan suggest that whiteness offers flexibility even while maintaining neocolonial dominance.

The Okanagan's white fantasy gains much of its flexibility and agency via its alliance with neoliberal ways of thinking. Neoliberalism, as Aihwa Ong (2006, 1–12) observes, has many variations worldwide, yet the term stands in opposition to classic liberalism. Classic liberalism assumes that state oversight working with the markets improves life for citizens, as opposed to neoliberalism, which assumes that removing the shackles of government oversight and support frees all individuals to achieve their fantasies (Harvey 2007, 2–3). Neoliberalism generally favours economic restructuring over social and environmental welfare and generates a precariat that is unable to compete successfully (Harvey 2014, 91–111). Additionally, neoliberalism in the North American context supports post-racial thinking as it assumes that race and other markers of difference (like class, gender, etc.) are not barriers to an individual's success. The neoliberal self is one who, through hard work, merit, and initiative, succeeds. In the Okanagan, neoliberalism conveniently and consistently denies the privileges of being an Anglo-white settler in a region that persistently endorses and supports Anglo-white settlers over others (Aguiar, Tomic, and Trumper 2005; Aguiar and Marten 2010; Tomic and Trumper 2012; Tomic and Trumper 2016). In the late twentieth century, the valley swung from colonial to neocolonial and liberal to neoliberal. Today, it strives for a cosmopolitan multicultural ideal as a good globally oriented business practice (Momer 2011); yet it consistently fails in this as it defines its global citizens in terms circumscribed by neocolonial and neoliberal principles underpinned by white fantasies. This anthology demonstrates how whiteness subtly maintains and produces exclusions of place well into the third decade of the new millennium in the rural-urban Okanagan.

The following two sections offer first a colonial history of and second the contemporary status of Okanagan whiteness. This parallels the anthology's division of chapters between one section on the colonial past and one on the neoliberal and neocolonial present.

OKANAGAN COLONIAL HISTORY

The dominance of white political, economic, social, and cultural values arrived in the region for the Syilx, the people of the Syilx Okanagan Nation, over the nineteenth century via what Carstens (1991, 30) characterizes as "furs, gold, and souls." For the Syilx, the fur trade in the Okanagan (1811–47) depleted game and spread disease (31). The gold rush of 1858 triggered an influx of miners and violent encounters between miners and Syilx (42–45). In 1859, the provincial government responded to these disputes by creating regulations for adult white male settlers to pre-empt Crown land for agricultural development (Royal BC Museum 2012). Pre-emption ensured that the Okanagan's settlement benefited settlers and dispossessed Syilx. The colonial provincial government offered Syilx reserve land as an afterthought (Carsten 1991, 45). The third element of settlement involved Christian missionaries converting souls to Christianity and European notions of civilization. The missionaries arrived with the Hudson's Bay Company in the 1830s (48). Carstens describes how the "missionaries bent on saving souls" not only drew Syilx away from their traditional beliefs and value system and into the Roman Catholic Christian community but encouraged "a transition from hunter and gathering to agriculture" (50). To varying degrees, the Syilx frustrated these goals. Carstens notes of the Catholic Oblate missionaries: "local mission stations were never established among the native people themselves" (52), with priests primarily supporting settlers. Thus, a system of spiritual apartheid between settlers and Syilx begins in the 1850s, shifting power to settlers.

As early as 1859, British Columbia used pre-emption to award Crown land to settlers for agricultural development (Royal 2012). On 14 April 1861, the first settler pre-emptions in the Okanagan were to a missionary, an ex-miner, and a government official (Carstens 1991, 57). James Douglas, first governor of "Vancouver Island from 1851" and of both Vancouver Island and the mainland "from 1858 to retirement in 1864" (17), conceived of land settlement as open to both settlers and Indigenous peoples. Tennant (1990, 31) indicates of Douglas's plan: "Indians ... are to have access to new rights – the rights of individual British subject to equal treatment under the Crown, including the right to pre-empt unsurveyed Crown lands. Indians are to be treated as though there were immigrants without prior land rights." However, Indigenous people rejected this offer to surrender title for the right to pre-empt. In October 1861, Douglas has William Cox, his gold commissioner based in Rock Creek (located in the Thompson-Okanagan), set aside reserve land for the Syilx "at the head and foot of Lake [Okanagan] totally some twenty square miles" (Thistle 2015, 37–38). In April 1865, following Douglas's leaving office, Judge Haynes, the magistrate for the region and one of the first settlers to take advantage of the pre-emption law (Carsten 1991, 63), reduces these reserves to "just over five square miles" (Thistle 2015, 38). Haynes's rationale for reducing the Syilx land reserve was that the Syilx only briefly remain on reserve land (Carstens 1991, 63).

Douglas's immediate successor, Lieutenant-Governor Joseph Trutch, in the 1870s denies Indigenous title and denies Indigenous people the ability to pre-empt land (Tennant 1990, 42). Legislation passed in 1872 and 1875 excluded Indigenous people from voting on the grounds of race (Carstens 1991, 69; Fisher 1977, 178). The Indian Act, 1876, established the reserve structure for the Okanagan that saw the Syilx on land that could not agriculturally support their numbers. While settler land barons lay claim to vast swaths of the most arable land, frustrating the attempt to transform the Syilx into ranchers (Carstens 1991, 77; Burrows 1986). Thistle (2015, 166) notes that, "by the 1890s, Okanagan Valley rancher Thomas Ellis alone" accumulated "over 30,000 acres" in the South Okanagan. Settlers dismissed opposition to the transformation of the grasslands into pasture with the rationale that "economic growth and the benefits of making the grasslands 'productive' through 'rational land use' and 'range improvements'" (Thistle 2015, xvii) trumps Indigenous concerns over the radical shrinkage of existing reserves.

The case of Cornelius O'Keefe, an Ottawa-born Irish Catholic settler, offers an example of how white settlers thrived under this colonial system, which legitimized the development of the Okanagan in the name of progress. O'Keefe arrived, with cattle, at the head of Lake Okanagan during the gold rush and began to amass land while marrying a Syilx woman named Rosie. He later married a white woman from his hometown near Ottawa, while keeping Rosie and her two children on his ranch. Eventually, Rosie returned to her people (Carstens 1991, 71). O'Keefe's route to power hinged on forging close relations with government officials to enlarge his ranch.

He entertained "the first Lieutenant-Governor of British Columbia, J.W. Trutch ... in the early 1870s. And in 1882 the Marquis of Lorne spent four days at the ranch while he was governor general of Canada. O'Keefe, despite his Roman Catholicism, always had good connections with the largely Protestant establishment" (73). By the 1870s, the Syilx had lost the political ability to reverse or change the course of settlement in the valley, with settlers like O'Keefe and Ellis having consolidated land and power in the name of progress.

The chiefs of the Shuswap, Okanagan, and Couteau/Thompson tribes, in their 1910 letter addressed to Prime Minister Sir Wilfrid Laurier, eloquently argue that it is the Crown's responsibility to deal honourably with First Nations (Louis et al. 2010). The letter diplomatically summarizes the colonial history, seeing the fur-trading period prior to the 1850s as a period of calm and respect between First Nations and whites. The chiefs note that, during the fur-trading era, the "real whites," francophone traders, had fairly dealt with First Nations. They lament the inhospitality of the provincial government and late-arriving Anglo-white settlers and urge Laurier to resolve the treaty process and to address how the reserve system displaced, criminalized, and impoverished Indigenous people. Laurier's government and subsequent governments have not heeded this invitation.

The early twentieth century saw the Okanagan transformed into a modern irrigated agricultural valley with further reductions to the Syilx's reserve land. McFarland (1990, 58) documents the paternalistic shrinking of Okanagan reserve lands that occurred with the Royal Commission of 1913, which principally consulted with the Indian agent and not the Syilx: "the end result for the Okanagan Agency was 18,536.80 acres cut-off and 2,600 acres added in the form of a new reserve." The commission removed land as "not necessary to the Indians" (57). Post-First World War, the provincial government spent over $3 million (1929 dollars) to develop an irrigation system to transform the southern Okanagan desert grasslands into fertile orchards (Murton 2007, 161). Murton describes the influx of settlers and the shaping of dominant Anglo-white culture: "Nearly twenty-five thousand middle- and upper-class Britons emigrated to BC between 1891 and 1921" (29). Despite this tilting of the Okanagan towards Anglo-white settlement, Asian settlers in the early to mid-twentieth century struggled in the North and Central Okanagan to gain a foothold as market gardeners (Kyle 2017).

Kelowna, which is now the major city in the Okanagan, in the 1930s had a population of around five thousand (BC Stats 2019). Huyskamp (2010, 4) estimates that Kelowna's Chinatown peaked in the 1930s at "between 400 and 500." The implementation of the federal head tax on Chinese immigration and the exclusion of immigration for Chinese women and children ensured that, by "the 1960s[,] only about 60 people remained in Chinatown" (5). Despite this presence of a socially segregated Asian agricultural working class, Anglo-white civility dominated the Okanagan in the early to mid-twentieth century (Joy 1982, 150, 190–91). Murton (2007, 29) describes the love of all things British in the Okanagan: "In places such as Kelowna and Summerland, fruit farmers set up clubs and played cricket and football, organized polo matches, established private schools and Anglican churches, conducted fox hunts, and attended the productions of the Kelowna Musical and Dramatic Society." In this period, private education modelled on the private British schools inculcated a class of Anglo children whose parents "were themselves privately educated" (Barman 1984, 33) in Kelowna in the Central Okanagan, and in Coldstream in the North Okanagan (33–35). This pedagogy cemented the notion that the Okanagan was to be developed by an Anglo-white ruling class of orchardists. Once pupils inculcated these values, notions of whiteness were recognized but never admitted as privileging sources of unearned advantages.

This form of white pedagogy constructs discourses and practices, and normalizes white privilege, assuming merit, work ethic, ingenuity, and dedication as the sources of achievement and success. The Anglo-white fantasy of the small-scale gentleman capitalist, minding his own self-sufficient plot of land and growing fruit, gained momentum as the Okanagan was fully transformed by state support for this "Garden of Eden" (Koroscil 2008).

Murton (2007, 22) argues that the provincial government embraced state intervention, assuming that rugged agriculture would cure the ills of urban modernity and generate an "alternative rural modernity." He writes:

> Promotional pamphlets for the [irrigation] project ... emphasized a confluence of nature and the machine. Panoramas of the valley lands were set alongside images of the modern building technology that

> would be used in the valley's transformation and the rural plenty that would follow – trees heavy with ripe, round fruit; families picking together; hillsides covered with crops; and snaking irrigation flumes before Okanagan Lake and the hills of the opposite bank. As the slogan at the end of one text declared, "Where apples grow best, man lives best." (155)

Okanagan.com's video extolling the valley as paradise has deep roots in a belief in Anglo-white technocratic modernity's ability to provide the good life via nature transformed. Belich's (2009, 5) environmental history of England's global explosive colonization asserts: "English-speakers around 1900, or 'Anglo-Saxons' as they tended to call themselves, were awestruck by their own achievements, and preferred to attribute them to virtues rather than vices, and to destiny rather than accident." This entitled attitude pervades contemporary Okanagan representations.

In the twentieth century and more recently, the history of white settlement in the Okanagan is mythologized as white benevolence towards "uncivilized" peoples sitting on a rich and fruitful land but without the ingenuity to make it produce and yield abundantly. Only Anglo-Saxon expertise guaranteed the inherent qualities necessary to ensure that the land prospered. This heritage fantasy of the colonial past remains visible to this day via numerous reports, publications, celebrations, and the historic O'Keefe Ranch, which "tells the story of early BC Ranching and endeavours to preserve the history and culture of the early ranching era for future generations" (O'Keefe Ranch 2019). In official narratives of the Okanagan, with few exceptions, whiteness operates as the founding tradition. Heritage projects continue to hide the violence of colonialism and dispossession while celebrating the figures of the Anglo-white male entrepreneurs. The following section considers how whiteness manifests itself in the contemporary period via the neoliberal racialization of place and space.

CONTEMPORARY NEOLIBERAL CRISIS IN OKANAGAN ANGLO-WHITE IDENTITY

Harvey (2007) defines neoliberalism as an economic model developed in the 1970s that appeals to freedom but inevitably shifts wealth to the already rich. Neoliberalism's core tenet is that there is no alternative (TINA) to its plans to ban unions, privatize social programs, and institute freer trade, which inevitably shifts wealth upwards (Queiroz 2018). Neoliberalism operates as a mode of regulation whereby state and civic institutions discipline workers and citizens to participate in legitimizing and reproducing it. With neoliberalism, discourses valuing individualism, self-care, and entrepreneurialism dominate. Entrepreneurialism embeds itself in the economic restructuring of the Okanagan as neoliberalism charges the state with dismantling social protections while unfolding policies and initiatives favourable to business ventures and interests.

In this context, whiteness holds steadfast, even arrogantly so, displaying its permanency in the everyday culture of the Okanagan Valley. This everyday culture of whiteness is a combination of representation and affect invoking feelings of well-being and independence, as evidenced in the Okanagan.com website and elsewhere. However, life in the Okanagan unravels as the working class endures poor wages in dead-end service jobs, lost between their economic reality and the Okanagan white fantasies of effortless prosperity enabled by entrepreneurialism. Members of the working class struggle to own a house and outdoor toys in the second most indebted city in Canada (Walks 2013). Even with significant economic disruption and challenges to white dominance, the fantasy of whiteness persists, as the example below demonstrates.

In September 2002, the Western Star trucking company closed its Kelowna factory in the Central Okanagan, in one stroke dismissing eight hundred mostly white male workers (Aguiar and Marten 2010, 174 [my coeditor, Luís Aguiar, generously provided this paragraph]). This closure withdrew from the local economy about $400 million per year. As if this direct economic withdrawal were not bad enough, seventy-seven local companies employing over three thousand workers felt the repercussions since they supplied Western Star with various parts for the assembly of trucks. This local economic crisis soon turned into a crisis for the white, primarily male working class of the Central Okanagan. Western Star paid high wages and was unionized. However, in the name of restructuring, the manufacturing plant moved to Portland, Oregon. In the midst of this example of capital mobility, an economic crisis arose concerning the future of high-wage work for white working-class men. The identity and masculinity of white working-class men, who no longer held jobs capable of maintaining an adequate standard of living for themselves and their families, generated a predicament (Pacholok 2009; Parsons et al. 2012). Few local job alternatives that offered comparable wages and benefits were available to those who lost their jobs with the departure of Western Star.

Neoliberal economic policies and practices undermine workers' respect and confidence. To remain globally competitive, companies seek to lower wages and to reduce collective bargaining rights as they strive for flexibility in recruiting cheaper and reliable workers with fewer demands on the bottom line (Tomic and Trumper 2012; Tomic and Trumper 2016). Consequently, workers (young and middle-aged), lacking wages to maintain their standard of living and to support their families, commute to northern Alberta and British Columbia for high-paying jobs in remote areas, where they typically live in bush camps for weeks at a time (Peterson 2014a; Peterson 2014b; Peterson 2014c; Husain and Matheson 2017). At the same time, Okanagan employers recruit what are euphemistically referred to as "temporary migrant workers" from the Global South (primarily Mexico and Jamaica) to assume jobs in construction, farming, and in the front of the house in the fast food industry (Tomic and Trumper 2012). These jobs offer low wages, few benefits, no union contracts, and no chance of Canadian citizenship, despite the fact that, year after year, these workers often work ten months a year in the Okanagan. They have no access to the Canadian labour market as one employer owns them for the length of their contract (Trumper and Wong 2007). Despite this, the region touts itself as a silicon vineyard designed to grow tourism, wellness, and post-secondary education, as is indicated in a high-tech blog written for a healthcare service company (Danielson 2017). While the IT sectors promote a wide-open labour market (Okanagan Partnership 2008), evidence shows that this is more fiction than fact, given the whiteness of the tech sector in the United States and Canada (Aguiar and Marten 2010; Aguiar, Tomic, and Trumper 2005; Wong 1988; Trumper and Wong 2007).

Business writers and business promoters for the region tout Kelowna, the major and central urban centre of the Okanagan, as the most entrepreneurial city in the country (Mann 2015; MacNaull 2016; Central Okanagan Economic Development Commission n.d.). However, in 2016, according to a Bank of Montreal study, Kelowna ranks as the worst place in the country to find a job (Tencer 2016). The fantasy of white entrepreneurialism in the valley ignores the fact that, historically, entrepreneur settlers relied on the state's dispossession and displacement of the Syilx to prosper. Teixeira's research on the contemporary Okanagan reveals how unwelcoming to immigrants the entrepreneurial culture of the valley is in spite of its attempt to brand entrepreneurialism as the identity of the Okanagan itself (Teixeira 2009; Depner and Teixeira 2012).

Whiteness underwrites entrepreneurialism whether it focuses on the figure of the exalted male pioneer of the contact period or today's Okanagan "silicon vineyard" entrepreneur (*Wired* staff 2000). So, while the economy shifts from agrarian to service industries, the figure of the white male entrepreneur remains constant. Today this figure lacks the Anglo-white qualities that informed early twentieth-century gentlemen orchardists of the Okanagan; nevertheless, this figure remains underwritten as a self-assured subject who is clearly the unquestioned master of this land. Kelowna-based entrepreneur Lane Merrifield's promotional video announcing his arrival as a dragon (a panelist who sits in judgment on other aspiring entrepreneurs on the CBC's reality TV program *Dragons' Den*) frames him as a master of the silicon vineyard. Merrifield and partners developed and, in 2007, sold the children's online gaming platform Club Penguin to Disney for $US700 million (Caddell 2018). The CBC promotional video begins with a female voice-over describing Merrifield as a thrill seeker and adventurer marking his own path and marching to his own tune (Dragons' Den 2018). The video presents him as a conspicuous consumer of fossil fuels, riding a motorcycle, piloting a plane, driving an expensive sports car, wake boarding, and, finally, back flipping off a powerboat on Lake Okanagan. In the first segment of the video, only he occupies the camera's frame, conveying the idea of entrepreneurialism as a lonely journey of creativity and discovery, which only the most gifted (white and usually male) can pursue without help or assistance. Near the end of the video, and having displayed the journey to success, Merrifield stands on the rooftop of a business centre he funded, over-looking Okanagan Lake and ready to mentor the next generation of Okanagan entrepreneurs. This video marks the difference the local makes. Here, local neoliberalism is white entrepreneurialism, displaying the individual as conquering the world from the interior of the province while skiing, flying, and motoring – playing – on the way to the top of the global economy (I thank my coeditor for contributing his insightful analysis of the video and neoliberalism below).

However, neoliberalism is not only about economic restructuring: capitalism is inherently prone to crisis. In fact, "crises are essential to the reproduction of capitalism" (Harvey 2014, ix) in that they shift the economic organization of society from one model of profit-making to another. In the Global North, crisis is reoriented to include a thorny racial element intertwined with whiteness. Often, an economic crisis is also a crisis in whiteness. This is because so much of economic expertise and confidence is rolled into the agency of whiteness, be it as entrepreneurialism or in the chest-thumping of dominant masculine Anglo-Saxon economic clout. Whiteness, as the most conscious racial identity, organizes and repositions itself to remain at the centre of racialized and racializing capitalist society (Goldberg 2009). Just as class is central to the reproduction of capitalism, so too is race. In settler nations, whiteness takes advantage of periods of social and economic turmoil to reassert itself at the centre of the reproduction of social life under capitalism (Goldberg 2009; Roberts and Mahtani 2010). After all, with whiteness comes a corresponding entrepreneurial ethos that assumes whiteness unifies a population and coaxes from it a work ethic dedicated to the restoration of order, confidence, and proper placement in the hierarchy of profitability. In the Okanagan, this economic logic ties into multiculturalism and diversity. Local government champions the notion that the Okanagan accommodates racial diversity, adhering to the business-friendly ethos that sees multiculturalism as a key to economic success (Momer 2011). This move to encourage global capital investment by embracing a superficial multiculturalism is neither new nor specific to the Okanagan. Attempts to represent the Okanagan as tolerant and diverse exercise a flat diversity, where a symbolic tokenism regarding national representations of racialized groups frequently lacks authenticity and credibility. A pious, flat diversity maintains the fantasy of Okanagan whiteness as broadly inclusive, forward thinking, and so on, while in fact it is the opposite.

The Okanagan may strive for diversity, yet instances of explicit racism occur: in 2008, and shortly before its inauguration, a Sikh temple in northeast Kelowna was vandalized with hate graffiti, as was the Jewish synagogue in Kelowna (*Daily Courier* 2008; *Castanet* 2008; *Castanet* 2005–08). In 2018, in the North Okanagan, a mural depicting Canada's missing and murdered Aboriginal women was defaced with racist graffiti (Deacon 2018), while a few months later a hand-drawn sign appeared outside the local drive-in movie theatre, complaining: "Stop paying lazy Indians" (Handschuch 2018). Beyond these disturbing and explicitly racist incidents, more subtle forms of racism percolate, underpinned by neoliberalist principles that see white people as benevolent beneficiaries of prosperous modernity living in a bucolic playland. Sarazin, a viticulture student in the South Okanagan who was raised in Bogato, Columbia, explains how Okanagan farmers, who continually praise Mexican labourers as hard workers, generate a dynamic whereby: "essentially what the farmer is actually saying is 'I'm the brains, they're the brawn'" (Sarazin 2016). She points to the precarious economic reality of Mexican labourers who "are not coming to Canada to live like kings upon returning to Mexico … Obviously an individual who accepts work at the risk of the violation of their [sic] human rights is an individual who is living in poverty and desperation. It's time to stop believing in any notion that Mexican labourers are exploiting Canadian minimum wage" (ibid.). Yet the popular neoliberal fantasy of Okanagan whiteness avoids these realities. Instead, it embraces the fantasy of an Okanagan made great by entrepreneurs generating wealth in a rural-urban playland.

Local neoliberalism in the Central Okanagan intertwines with race, as is seen in the flat multicultural rhetoric offered by Liberal member of Parliament for Kelowna Lake Country Stephen Fuhr. His 2018 Canada Day speech, while implicitly critiquing American president Donald Trump's wall-building policy, hailed voters as naturally partaking in a form of rural white Canadian identification: "Although we enjoy our Tim Hortons, maple syrup and our hockey, we are much more than just our 'Canadiana.' It is our method that truly defines us. Our nation chooses to build bridges instead of walls and it is this Canadian approach that will not only drive our success, but propel us into a global leadership position" (Fuhr 2018). According to this logic, multiculturalism and other forms of benevolent global citizenship, despite the dominance of conspicuously settler-coded rural "Canadiana," operates as a flat diversity that ensures the nation's success on the global stage. Fuhr strives to distance himself from the tokenism of white Canadian symbols, yet these symbols appeal to a benevolent white fantasy. The *Celebrate Canada Day Kelowna!* flier for Kelowna's 2018 Canada Day celebration amplifies Fuhr's gesture by detailing various ethnic dancing and foods itemizes a range of performances by Filipino, Serbian, Asian, Polish, Mexican, Irish, and Chinese dancers (Celebrate 2018). Curiously in this program, the Ki-Low-Na Friendship Society, a non-profit First Nations society, offered a blanket ceremony that promised to explain to participants how "colonization of the land we now know as Canada has impacted the people who lived here long before European settlers arrived. Participants will explore the nation-to-nation relationship between Indigenous and non-Indigenous peoples in Canada, how this relationship has been damaged over the years, and how we can work towards reconciliation" (Ki-Low-Na 2018). Resistance to the white fantasy of peaceable Canadian identity that challenges settler resistance to reconciliation and provides meaningful support for multiculturalism has not disappeared in the Okanagan. However, resistance remains the exception to the rule of the Okanagan's white fantasy, which is dominated by populist folksy rural symbols like Tim Hortons, maple syrup, and hockey combined with urban entrepreneurial figures like Merrifield.

Whiteness snugly embeds itself within the neoliberal economy of the Okanagan, where it is all but impossible to raise the abuses of white privilege. Dismantling whiteness in the Okanagan involves changing perceptions. This anthology advances contemporary race and racism analysis to lay bare the neocolonial and neoliberal landscape of the Okanagan in the hope of unsettling "fragile" latecomer settlers who refuse to admit they participate in and benefit from the white fantasy that comprises the Okanagan (DiAngelo 2018). *White Space* requires readers to reflect on Okanagan whiteness as not just "a natural fact" but as an extension of settler fantasies that refuse differences: Who earns advantage by not being able to think of white people as settlers? Who earns advantage by thinking about the development of the Okanagan as a nice, safe middle-class place to live? This anthology seeks to unsettle settler fantasies of the Okanagan to locate an Okanagan aware of its colonial legacy and contemporary oppressive structures.

CHAPTER OUTLINES

Reflecting the contributors' disciplinary specializations, the approaches to whiteness in this anthology vary from spatial, discursive, historical, literary, to auto-ethnographic analysis. No chapters in this anthology directly explore how whiteness intersects with faith. In light of the 27 May 2021 announcement by the Tk'emlups te Secwépemc First Nation of the findings of 215 remains of Indigenous children on the grounds of the Catholic Residential School outside of Kamloops (Casmir 2021) and the burning of two on-reserve churches (Bonneau 2021), this seems a glaring oversight and one that future scholarship and activism beyond this anthology must address. The anthology's chapters attend to the colonial and neocolonial fantasies of whiteness in the rural-urban Okanagan, where whiteness securely persists. *White Space* is divided into two sections. Section 1, titled "Historical Erasures and Re-Inscriptions," locates the Okanagan as a contested space that has systematically sought to erase the presence of others while exalting the Anglo-white settler. First Nations, Métis, African, and Asian settlers are all part of the Okanagan's heritage.

Collectively, Part 1 examines resistance and support for settlers' Okanagan fantasies. Its chapters challenge the exalted narrative of white, predominantly Anglo, settlement. They suggest that Anglo pioneers and their heirs control the spaces and narratives of the Okanagan in ways that insists on erasing the presence of the Other and/or incorporating it into triumphant settler narratives. The first chapter in this section, by Bill Cohen and Natalie Chambers, from a blended Indigenous and settler perspective, draws attention to how what they dub a "whiteout" has sought to erase Sqilxʷ history, knowledge, language, and values. The Syilx, via local Aboriginal ways of knowing and self-education, actively resist this whiteout. They argue that the Okanagan language and worldviews provide an approach to shared responsibilities, diversity, and relational sustainability that may attenuate the effects of the whiteout. Additionally, they celebrate the recent steps by regional publicly funded school districts to support Aboriginal education.

The next two chapters, written by me (Daniel Keyes), focus on white place name making and historiography that serves as an example of the complex colonial and neocolonial moves involved in what Chambers and

Cohen refer to as a whiteout. The first of these two chapters deals with the peculiar naming of a mountain as "N–toe" outside of Penticton in 1955 to commemorate the nearby deaths of two African American men in 1908. In order to practise cultural safety in these two chapters, I redact the n-word rather than use the hateful word itself. I yearn for a parallel style guide for dealing with this term, like my former colleague Greg Younging's *Elements of Indigenous Style* (2018, 62) that guides scholars on respectful usage and as such indicates without redaction the s-word designates "An offensive term for an Indigenous woman." Cornellier (2017, 35) as "a white Quebecois settler" writing about Quebecois literature redacts all uses of the French equivalent of the n-word beyond where he sparing cites in his notes a reference to a book with the title (56). I respect that for some Black scholars context determines use and that the term can circulate within Black communities to heal (Maya 2018), but I agree with Cornellier that settler scholars should use the redacted form. I acknowledge that Volokh and Kennedy from the view of American legal education (2021a, 2021b) argue redaction risks obscuring "the ways in which epithets have been an integral part of the soundtrack of American prejudice" (2021b) and that scholars should not tamper with quotes and references but have duty to not bowdlerize the historical record. (I thank my former dean Wisdom Tettey for guiding me to this source and arguing that I should eschew redaction.) However, in making this choice to redact, I am guided by the Black English-based journalist Onanuga (2014) who advises: "Even though I believe writing out the word in full can be justified in very limited circumstances when quoting someone, there is no denying that it remains deeply offensive to many people." With advice from the editors at UBC Press and advice from Cornellier, Onanuga, and Younging, I use the redacted forms for these two offensive terms while sparingly using the terms in both my own prose and in direct quotes from historical sources and the References.

In the second of these two chapters, I recount how, in 1966, the federal government sought to erase the n-word from all Canadian place names and thus consulted with white local community groups to change the mountain's name. The naming committee selected the name "Nkwala," which belongs to a prominent nineteenth-century Syilx leader (Carstens 1991, 60–63). The committee selected this name partially based on this particular lineage but primarily because Nkwala celebrates the fictional title character from Anglo-Canadian author Elizabeth Lambert Sharp's Governor-General-Award-winning 1958 children's novel. These benevolent and misguided attempts by white local historians, under the guidance of federal and provincial officials, to construct inclusive histories and spaces in the mid-twentieth century are fraught with the erasure of the violence of colonialism on non-white bodies. This naming and un-naming becomes an exercise in pointing to the gaps left by the whiteout of Okanagan spaces.

The next chapter in this section, by Janet MacArthur, focuses on life writing by exploring the disjuncture between the public and private writings of Susan Moir Allison (1845–1937), one of the first settler women in the Okanagan. MacArthur suggests that Allison's experiences in the early contact period with Indigenous people, such as her husband's Indigenous wife, provide her with a deep ambivalence regarding the whiteout's attempt to settle Indigenous people and land. MacArthur argues that Allison ambivalently disaffiliates from the wider colonial project of creating a white ethnoscape in the early twentieth century while still reaping the limited rewards of publishing her pioneer history in the Vancouver *Province* newspaper. MacArthur's and my chapters on the naming and unnaming of N–toe Mountain pivot on this sense of white melancholy, which exalts and ameliorates the violence of the colonial past. These chapters hinge on the sense that settler melancholy, despite its apparent fragility, operates as a durable way of maintaining white heritage fantasies as status quo. The next and final chapter in this section, by Audrey Kobayashi, offers an auto-ethnographic meditation on the erasure of her grandfather's legacy as a Japanese settler. He cleared land for the Okanagan Land Company in a space that now commemorates a white pioneer. She recalls a childhood suffused with anglophile toys, books, and the need to assimilate into an unattainable white space. She argues that today's Okanagan offers an anemic version of multiculturalism that assumes that all non-white newcomers must be able to fit into its tacit white norms. In their chapters, Audrey Kobayashi and Stephen Svenson (author of the last chapter of *White Space*) provide auto-ethnographic approaches to their individual critiques of valley whiteness that differ from the more textual analyses employed in the volume's other chapters. *White Space* is richer for these two perceptive embodied accounts.

The chapters in the second section deal with the Okanagan in more recent and explicitly neoliberal and neocolonial times, where, simultaneously, whiteness is invisible for many white middle-class Okanagan residents and hyper-visible for those who do not signify as white. The first chapter in this section, by Jon Corbett and Donna Senese, titled "Mapping White Consumer Culture: Kelowna's Tourist Maps 1983–99," examines an archive of tourist maps produced by the local Chamber of Commerce. These maps imagine Kelowna as a straight, upper-class, white playground. They depict white women as passive trim figures and white men as fit, active, and rugged. Thus, they erase markers of working-class industry to provide representations of the region that cater to the tastes of a masculine elite leisure class. This chapter, like my chapters on N–toe and Nkwla, demonstrates the maintenance of the fantasy of white space. Whereas my two chapters scrutinize the derogatory inclusivity of naming a mountain N–toe and renaming it Nkwla in the mid-twentieth century, Corbett and Senese demonstrate how, in the late twentieth century, tourist maps sustain a fantasy of white belonging in an emergent neoliberal and neocolonial playground that evacuates working-class labour and Syilx resistance.

The second chapter in this section, by coeditor Luís Aguiar, argues that the fantasies of the Okanagan as presented in media and public art tend to frame the region as a safe playground for the middle class while effacing Others, such as the euphemistically referred to "temporary farm labourers" from the Global South or the Syilx. Where Corbett and Senese demonstrate the whitening effect of media that actively exclude the bodies that do not fit the white paradigm, Aguiar asserts that the contemporary neoliberal Central Okanagan presented in pamphlets, reports, and posters conveys a smug yet faux sense of inclusivity. He analyzes the affective pull of what he dubs "encore whiteness": a version of whiteness that mobilizes feelings like smugness and niceness to maintain white dominance amid a faltering fantasy of middle-class norms. In the next chapter, Shelia Lewis and Lawrence Berg document the perceptions of twelve urban Indigenous women seeking housing in the city of Kelowna and, in so doing, support Aguiar's contention that bodies that do not present as white face discrimination. These women feel they are under constant surveillance, and this makes them acutely aware of their non-white status in the dominant community. Drawing from critical race theories of whiteness, Lewis and Berg argue that the Okanagan's peculiar brand of Anglo whiteness enforces a structural advantage for white residents while diminishing the capacity for Indigenous women to fit into Kelowna's urban space. The ethnographic methodology in this chapter, like that in Kobayashi's chapter, demonstrates the oppressive sense of valley whiteness while asserting that the perceptions of these twelve urban Indigenous women are consistent with the structural barriers that Indigenous women confront across Canada.

The next two chapters use varieties of discourse analysis to examine how white privilege resonates in Okanagan media. The first of these chapters, by Carl James, reflects on the local reactions to the introduction of Jamaican migrants, euphemistically referred to as "guest workers," to Kelowna in 2007. Using media reports and other sources, he discusses what the responses to the presence of Black Caribbean young men in predominately white Kelowna represents. He argues that the supposedly colour-blind discourse of multiculturalism, which underlies Canada's historical policies of controlled immigration of non-white immigrants, and the racial profiling of Black Jamaicans contribute to the policy of, as one local newspaper headline put it, "No Sex, No Pot for Workers" (Nieoczym 2007). This attitude to policing racialized Others as conspicuous outsiders who are not citizens resonates with Lewis and Berg's earlier chapter on Aboriginal women seeking housing in Kelowna. The next chapter, also by me (Daniel Keyes), draws on and supports Aguiar's chapter on encore whiteness in the Okanagan; additionally, it complements Corbett and Senese's and James's chapters, which examine contemporary media representations in the Okanagan. I analyze the precarious neoliberal condition of print and internet journalism in the Okanagan. Additionally, I provide a textual analysis of specific columns, advertising, and coverage of events to argue that print journalism rarely deviates from presenting for its readers a white fantasy of belonging, in which the entrepreneur is the exalted subject of fascination.

In the second to last chapter, Delacey Tedesco explores how Kelowna, as the largest city in the Okanagan, aspires to cosmopolitan world-class stature while clinging to a small-city fantasy that is implicitly white and rural. She maps the contested imaginaries of the city in its fraught colonial history, current policy documents, and public art. She argues that Kelowna's founding and present depends on patrolling racialized borders that persists in a form of mixophobia. Cosmopolitan citizens must challenge this mixophobia. Turning away from the consideration of the urban, the final chapter, by Stephen Svenson, challenges rural valley whiteness from the perspective of a self-described "redneck, hippie intellectual." Svenson describes how travel abroad and post-secondary education make him an outsider to redneck culture. He articulates his unspeakable discomfort with racist jokes and folk wisdom about non-Anglo types, which he experiences as endemic in the valley. Like the chapters by Cohen and Chambers, and Tedesco, he concludes with a qualified optimism regarding the possibilities of challenging the whiteout. While these contributors suggest whiteness's power may be waning, I fear the valley's colonial history, combined with the effects of neoliberalism and neocolonialism, makes it difficult to dislodge the Okanagan's stubborn, persistent, and flexible white fantasies.

REFERENCES

Aguiar, Luís L.M., and Tina Marten. 2010. "Wine Tourism and Post-Fordist Restructuring in the Okanagan Valley, British Columbia." In *Interrogating the "New Economy": Restructuring Work in the 21st Century*, ed. N. Pupo and M. Thomas, 173–93. Toronto: University of Toronto Press.

Aguiar, Luís L.M., Patricia Tomic, and Ricardo Trumper. 2005. "Work Hard, Play Hard: Re-Inventing the Okanagan for the 'New Economy.'" *Canadian Geographer* 49 (2): 123–39.

Baldwin, Andrew. 2009. "The White Geography of Lawrence Stewart Harris: Whiteness and the Performative Coupling of Wilderness and Multiculturalism in Canada." *Environment and Planning* 41 (3): 529–44.

Barman Jean. 1984. *Growing up British in British Columbia: Boys in Private School.* Vancouver: UBC Press.

BC Stats. 2019. *British Columbia: Municipal Census Population (1921–2011).* Accessed July 31, 2019. http://www.bcstats.gov.bc.ca/StatisticsBySubject/Census/MunicipalPopulations.

Belich, James. 2009. *Replenishing the Earth: The Settler Revolution and the Rise of the Anglo-World, 1783–1939.* Oxford and New York: Oxford University Press.

Bonneau, Athena. 2021. Two On-reserve Churches Burned Down on Indigenous Peoples Day in B.C.'s Interior." *Indiginews.* June 21, Accessed June 22, 2021. https://indiginews.com/okanagan/two-churches-burned-down-on-indigenous-peoples-day.

Burrows, James. 1986. "'A Much Needed Class of Labour': The Economy and Incorporation of Southern Plateau Indians, 1897–1903." *BC Studies* 71 (Autumn): 27–59.

Caddell, Nathan. 2018. "Five Questions with Club Penguin Co-Founder Lane Merrified." *BC Business.* 23 June. https://www.bcbusiness.ca/Five-Questions-with-Club-Penguin-co-founder-Lane-Merrifield.

Carstens, Peter. 1991. *The Queen's People: A Study of Hegemony, Coercion, and Accommodation among the Okanagan of Canada*. Toronto: University of Toronto Press.

Casmir, Rosanne. 2021. "Office of the Chief: for Immediate Release." *Tk̓emlúps te Secwépemc/Kamloops Indian Band*. 27 May. Accessed June 22, 2021. https://tkemlups.ca/wp-content/uploads/05-May-27-2021-TteS-MEDIA-RELEASE.pdf.

Castanet. 2005–08. "Jewish Community Center Vandalism." *Castanet Forum Index, Regional Topics, Central Okanagan*. http://forums.castanet.net/viewtopic.php?f=23&t=13972&start=30.

Celebrate Canada Day Kelowna! 2018. "Schedule of Activities, July 12, 2018," *Festival Kelowna*. Accessed July 29, 2018. http://www.festivalskelowna.com/images/docs/cda%20day%20schedule%20letter%20size%202018%202pgs%20-%20final.pdf.

Central Okanagan Economic Development Commission. n.d. "Business Landscape Most Entrepreneurial Region in Canada." COEDC. https://www.investkelowna.com/about-the-okanagan/business/business-landscape/.

Central Okanagan, Regional District. 2016. *Statistics Canada*. Accessed July 3, 2018. https://www12.statcan.gc.ca/censusrecensement/2016/dppd/prof/details/page.cfm?Lang=E.&Geo1=CD&Code1=5935&Geo2=PR&Code2=59&Data=Count&SearchText=central%20okanagan&SearchType=Begins&SearchPR=01&B1=All&TABID=1.

Cornellier, Bruno. 2017. "The Struggle of Others: Pierre Vallières, Quebecois Settler Nationalism, and the N-Word Today." *Discourse* 39, no. 1 (2017): 31–66. Accessed June 12, 2021. doi:10.13110/discourse.39.1.0031.

Danielson, Cindy. 2017. "3 Reasons CoreHealth in Headquartered in Kelowna, British Columbia." *CoreHealth*. 18 April. https://blog.corehealth.global/3-reasons-corehealth-is-headquartered-in-kelowna-british-columbia.

Daily Courier. 2008. "Hate Crimes Unit to Investigate Anti-Jews Graffiti." 24 June. Access July 23, 2020. www.kelownadailycourier.ca/stories_local.php?id=117967.

Deacon, Chantelle. 2018. "Racial Slurs Ruin Mural." *Castanet*, 10 May. https://www.castanet.net/news/Vernon/225986/racial-slurs-ruin-mural.

Depner, Wolfgang, and Carlos Teixeira. 2012. "Welcoming Communities? An Assessment of Community Services in Attracting and Retaining Immigrants in the South Okanagan Valley (British Columbia, Canada), with Policy Recommendations." *Journal of Rural and Community Development* 7 (2): 72–97.

DiAngelo, Robin. 2018. *White Fragility: Why It's So Hard for White People to Talk about Racism*. Boston: Beacon Press.

Dragons' Den. 2018. "Meet New Dragon Lane Merrifield (Dragons' Den Canada)." *CBC Dragons' Den*, 4 September. https://www.youtube.com/watch?v=Dqwjz9clS3M.

Fisher, Robin. 1977. *Contact and Conflict: Indian-European Relations in British Columbia, 1774–1890*. Vancouver: UBC Press.

Fuhr, Stephen. 2018. "Fuhr: Canada Builds Bridges, Not Walls." *Capital News*, 28 June. https://www.kelownacapnews.com/news/fuhr-canada-builds-bridges-not-walls/.

Gaffney, Blaine. 2016. "Kelowna Cemetery First Provincial Site of Chinese-Canadian Monuments." *Global News*, 4 December. https://globalnews.ca/news/3105872/kelowna-cemetary-first-provincial-site-of-chinese-canadian-monuments/.

Goldberg, David Theo. 2009. *The Threat of Race: Reflections on Racial Neoliberalism*. Malden, MA: Wiley-Blackwell.

Handschuch, Darren. 2018. "Another Act of Racism." *Castanet*, 24 July. https://www.castanet.net/news/Vernon/232184/another-act-of-racism.

Hage, Ghassan. 2000. *White Nation: Fantasies of White Supremacy in a Multicultural Society*. New York: Routledge/Annandale, NSW: Pluto Press.

Harvey, David. 2007. *A Brief History of Neoliberalism*. Oxford and New York: Oxford University Press.

–. 2014. *Seventeen Contradictions and the End of Capitalism*. New York: Oxford University Press.

Hughey, Matthew W. 2014. *The White Savior Film: Content, Critics and Consumption*. Philadelphia, PA: Temple University Press.

Husain, Matt M., and Bowen Matheson. 2017. "Relative Deprivation vs. Transition: Rehabilitating Laid-Off Young Oil Workers in Kelowna and Beyond." *Journal of Rural and Community Development* 12 (1): 168–80.

Huyskamp, Ross. 2010. *Report on Kelowna's Historic Chinatown Site*. The City of Kelowna's Community Heritage Commission. 5 August.

Joy, Annamma. 1982. "Accommodation and Cultural Persistence: The Case of the Sikhs and the Portuguese in the Okanagan Valley of British Columbia." PhD diss., University of British Columbia, https://open.library.ubc.ca/cIRcle/collections/ubctheses/831/items/1.0095597.

Ki-Low-Na Friendship Society. 2018. "Blanket Exercise." *Festival Kelowna*. July 20, 2018. http://www.festivalskelowna.com/images/docs/blanket%20ceremony%20poster%20-%20ki-low-na%202018%20canada%20day.pdf.

Knowlton, Trevor. 2015. Okanagan.com: Travel Guide to the Okanagan Valley, Canada – Okanagan Valley, British Columbia. http://www.okanagan.com/videos.html.

Koroscil, Paul. 2008. *The British Garden of Eden: Settlement History of the Okanagan Valley, British Columbia*. Burnaby, BC: Department of Geography, Simon Fraser University.

Kyle, Catherine Jane. 2017. "Lost Landscapes of the Market Gardeners: A Qualitative Historical GIS Examination of the Demise of the Chinese and Japanese Market Gardening Industries in the North and Central Okanagan Valley, British Columbia, 1910s–1950s." PhD diss., University of British Columbia Okanagan.

Louis, Petite, John Tetlenitsa, and John Chilahitsa. 2010. *The Memorial to Sir Wilfrid Laurier, 1910*. Transcribed by James Alexander Tiet. https://www.sfu.ca/~palys/OpenLetterToWilfredLaurier-1910.pdf.

Mann, Heidi. 2015. "Kelowna One of the Top Entrepreneurial Places in Canada." *Accelerate Okanagan*. https://www.accelerateokanagan.com/community/blog/news/kelowna-one-top-entrepreneurial-places-canada/.

MacNaull, Steve. 2016. "Kelowna Ranked Top Place in Canada to Be in Business." *Daily Courier*, 18 October. Accessed August 20, 2017. http://www.kelownadailycourier.ca/business_news/article_f1d42e8e-95b3–11e6-a2c3-d7959537ed80.html.

McFarland, Dana. 1990. "Indian Reserve Cut-Offs in British Columbia, 1912–1924: An Examination of Federal-Provincial Negotiations." MA thesis, University of British Columbia. https://open.library.ubc.ca/cIRcle/collections/ubctheses/831/items/1.0302324.

Momer, Bernard. 2011. *Our City, Ourselves: A Cultural Landscape Assessment of Kelowna, British Columbia.* City of Kelowna, Recreation and Cultural Service. https://www.academia.edu/647691/Our_City_Ourselves_A_Cultural_Landscape_Assessment_of_Kelowna_BC.

Moore, Wayne. 2015. "Parks Take Native Names." *Castanet*, 22 May. http://www.castanet.net/news/Penticton/140517/Parks-take-native-names.

Murton, James Ernest. 2007. *Creating a Modern Countryside: Liberalism and Land Resettlement in British Columbia.* Vancouver: UBC Press.

Nieoczym, Adrian. 2007. "No Sex, No Pot for Workers." *Daily Courier*, 23 September.

North Okanagan, Regional District. 2016. Statistics Canada. Accessed July 14, 2018. https://www12.statcan.gc.ca/census-recensement/2016/dppd/prof/details/page.cfm?Lang=E&Geo1=CD&Code1=5937&Geo2=PR&Code2=59&Data=Count&SearchText=North%20Okanagan&SearchType=Begins&SearchPR=01&B1=All&TABID=1.

Okanagan Nation Alliance. 1987. *Okanagan Nation Declaration.* https://www.syilx.org/wp/wp-content/uploads/2017/01/ON_Declaration.pdf.

Okanagan Partnership. 2008. *Okanagan Tourism Labour Study 2008.* Kelowna, BC: Okanagan Partnership/Service Canada.

Okanagan-Similkameen, Regional District. 2016. *Statistics Canada.* Accessed June 12, 2017. https://www12.statcan.gc.ca/censusrecensement/2016/dppd/prof/details/page.cfm?Lang=E&Geo1=CD&Code1=5907&Geo2=PR&Code2=59&Data=Count&SearchText=Okanagan&SearchType=Begins&SearchPR=01&B1=All&TABID=1.

O'Keefe Ranch. 2019. "OK: Historic O'Keefe Ranch." https://okeeferanch.ca/.

Onanuga, Tola. 2014. "The N-word: Do We Have to Spell It out?" *Guardian.* May 8. Accessed June 12, 2018. https://www.theguardian.com/media/mind-your-language/2014/may/08/mind-your-language-n-word.

Ong, Aihwa. 2006. *Neoliberalism as Exception: Mutations in Citizenship and Sovereignty.* Duke, NC: Duke University Press, 2006.

Pacholok, S. 2009. "Gendered Strategies of Self: Navigating Hierarchy and Contesting Masculinities." *Gender, Work and Organization* 16 (4): 471–500.

Palmer Vaughn. 2019. "NDP Grapples with Pipelines, Consent, and Reconciliation." *Vancouver Sun.* http://ecosocialistsvancouver.org/article/ndp-grapples-pipelines-consent-and-reconciliation.

Parsons, J., Sherry Pacholok, Tara Snape, and A. Gauthier. 2012. "Trying to Do More with Less: The Mothering Experiences of Middle-Income Mothers." *Families, Relationships, and Societies* 1 (3): 361–77.

Pete, Maya G. 2018. "The Nigga Word: A Black Millennial Perspective on Its Healing, Usage, and Continuity." Honours Thesis. Stanford University. https://stacks.stanford.edu/file/druid:dt116dj9345/Maya%20Pete_The%20Nigga%20Word.pdf.

Peterson, Wade. 2014a. "The 1,300 km Commute (Part 1: the People)." *Kelowna Capital News*, 7 February. http://www.kelownacapnews.com/news/244332651.html.

–. 2014b. "The 1,300 km Commute (Part 2: The Community)." *Kelowna Capital News*, 11 February. https://www.kelownacapnews.com/news/the-1300-km-commute-part-2-the-community/.

–. 2014c. "The 1,300 km Commute (Part 3: Getting There)." *Kelowna Capital News*, 13 February. https://www.kelownacapnews.com/news/the-1300-km-commute-part-3-getting-there/.

Roberts, D., and M. Mahtani. 2010. "Neoliberalizing Race, Racing Neoliberalism: Representations of Immigration in the *Globe and Mail*." *Antipode* 42 (2): 248–57.

Royal BC Museum. 2012. "Quick Guide to Pre-Emption and Homestead Records." *British Columbia Archives Research Guide*. http://royalbcmuseum.bc.ca/assets/Pre-emptions_homesteads_quick_guide.pdf.

Queiroz, Regina. 2018. "Neoliberal TINA: An Ideological and Political Subversion of Liberalism." *Critical Policy Studies* 12 (2): 227–46.

Sarazin, Natasha. 2016. "We Show Our Subtle Racism When We Praise Mexican Farmworkers." *Daily Courier*, 12 May. Accessed June 11, 2021. http://www.kelownadailycourier.ca/opinion/article_60ecd166-e7ce-11e5-92c0-47f36bbbefca.html.

Syilx Okanagan Nation. 2021. *Territory*. https://www.syilx.org/about-us/syilx-nation/territory/.

Teixeira, Carlos. 2009. "New Immigrant Settlement in a Mid-Size City: A Case Study of Housing Barriers and Coping Strategies in Kelowna, British Columbia." *Canadian Geographer* 53: 323–39.

–. 2011. "Finding a Home of Their Own: Immigrant Housing Experiences in Central Okanagan, British Columbia and Policy Recommendations for Change." *Journal of International Migration and Integration* 12 (2): 173–97.

Tencer, Daniel. 2016. "Canada's Worst City to Find a Job? Kelowna, BC, BMO Data Indicates." *Huffington Post*, 8 February. https://www.huffingtonpost.ca/2016/02/08/worst-city-to-find-job-canada_n_9189314.html.

Tennant, Paul. 1990. *Aboriginal Peoples and Politics: The Indian Land Question in British Columbia*. Vancouver: UBC Press.

Thistle, John. 2015. *Resettling the Range: Animals, Ecologies, and Human Communities in British Columbia*. Vancouver: UBC Press.

Tomic, Patricia, and Ricardo Trumper. 2012. "Mobilities and Immobilities: Globalization, Farming, and Temporary Work in the Okanagan Valley." In *Legislated Inequality: Temporary Labour Migration in Canada*, ed. P.T. Lenard, and C. Straehle, 73–94. Montreal and Kingston: McGill-Queen's University Press.

–. 2016. *Farm Workers in Western Canada: Injustices and Activism*. Edmonton: University of Alberta Press.

Trumper, Ricardo, and Lloyd Wong. 2007. "Canada's Guestworkers: Racialized, Gendered and Flexible." In *Race and Racism in 21st Century Canada*, ed. S.P. Hier, and B.S. Bolaria, 151–70. Peterborough: Broadview Press.

Truth and Reconciliation Commission of Canada. 2015. *Truth and Reconciliation: Calls to Action*. https://www.documentcloud.org/documents/2091412-trc-calls-to-action.html.

Volokh, Eugene, and Randall Kennedy. 2021a. "The New Taboo: Quoting Epithets in the Classroom and Beyond." *Capital University Law Review* 49.1: https://www2.law.ucla.edu/volokh/epithets.pdf.

–. 2021b. "The Case for Quoting the N-word in University Classrooms: If the Slur is Mentioned in Key Court decisions, It Should Not Be Taboo in Law Schools."

Washington Post May 13, 2021. https://www.washingtonpost.com/outlook/2021/05/13/slurs-classrooms-law-school-taboo/.

Walks, Alan. 2013. "Mapping the Urban Debtscape: The Geography of Household Debt in Canadian Cities." *Urban Geography* 34 (2): 153–87.

Wired staff. 2000. "Hot Times in 'Silicon Vineyard.'" *Wired,* 2 August. https://www.wired.com/2000/08/hot-times-in-silicon-vineyard/.

Williams, Maurice. 2008. *Myra's Men: Building the Kettle Valley, Myra Canyon to Penticton*. Kelowna: Myra Canyon Trestle Restoration Society.

Wong, Lloyd. 1988. "Migrant Seasonal Agricultural Labour: Race and Ethnic Relations in the Okanagan Valley." PhD diss., York University.

Younging, Greg. 2018. *Elements of Indigenous Style: A Guide for Writing by and about Indigenous Peoples*. Edmonton: Brush Press.

Part 1
HISTORICAL ERASURES AND RE-INSCRIPTIONS OF WHITE FANTASIES

CHAPTER 1

EMERGING FROM THE WHITEOUT

Colonization, Assimilation, Historical Erasure, and Syilx Okanagan Resistance and Transforming Praxis in the Okanagan Valley

Bill Cohen and Natalie A. Chambers

Ads in magazines, tv and online social media commercials, and billboards in the sunny Okanagan Valley boast lavish spa resorts, condos, and gated communities adjacent to finely groomed golf courses and endless opportunities to enjoy the great outdoors, ski in the local mountains, play in Okanagan Lake, sunbathe on a sandy beach, or tour a local winery. The Okanagan Valley is one of the hotspots in BC for tourism, residential and business development. The Okanagan watershed and west into the Nicola Valley and east into the Arrow Lakes are also the homelands of the Swknaqínx who are part of a larger interconnected alliance of Syilx peoples whose language is Nsyilxcn (Okanagan Nation Alliance 2021). "Okanagan," or Swknaqínx, as Syilx conceptual metaphor, is a place and people descriptor and connotes looking into the future responsibly. "Okanagan" is the anglicized version of Swknaqínx and in this chapter, Syilx Okanagan, and Syilx will be used to refer to the Indigenous Peoples in whose territory the Okanagan Valley is situated.

The Syilx are the Indigenous Peoples of a territorial ecology that covers approximately 72,000 square kilometres in south central British Columbia and north central Washington. The Syilx are here, and we have not forgotten who we are. Although strands connecting us to our ancestors' accumulated wisdom have been diminished by colonization, settlement, and new formations of colonization, including neoliberal economics and corporatization of our lands, the Okanagan-Syilx are alive and, in the present day, extended family members are proactively resisting erasure by taking control of our children's education and the knowledge to which they have access, and are contributing to curriculum development in public schools. We have not been assimilated. Acknowledgement of the Syilx as human, as a people, has recently become a common practice at post-secondary institutions and high schools with land acknowledgements before meetings and events. Several municipalities in the Okanagan have also made a practice of land acknowledgements before town council meetings. These developments are in response to Truth and Reconciliation Calls to Action (2015a), a commitment by many to Indigenize curriculum, and be more inclusive and tolerant of difference and diversity.

In the present day, past patterns of imperialism, colonization and settlement, patriarchy, intolerance, systemic racism, and racialized othering continue to produce oppression and violence towards Indigenous Peoples and peoples of colour, women, non-binary individuals and other marginalized peoples. Recent events, marches, vigils, and movements such as Red Dress Campaigns, Orange Shirt Day in memory of Indian Residential School survivors, Unity Runs, Black Lives Matter protests and marches, Idle No More (Idle 2021), anti-Asian hate and anti-racism demonstrations, Pride Parades and Rainbow Crosswalks are raising awareness that Canada and other colonial nations are built on racist notions of white supremacy and have benefited from genocide, oppression, and slavery. These are also generations of findings from task forces, royal commissions, special reports, and inquiries, from Dr. Bryce's chilling reports of 1907 and 1922 The Story of A National Crime Being An Appeal for Justice to the Indians of Canada (Milloy 1999, 102) on the appalling conditions of the Indian Residential Schools, to the Royal Commission on Aboriginal Peoples (1996), the Truth and Reconciliation Commission of Canada's Final Report (2015a) and its 94 Calls to Action (2015b), Reclaiming Power and Place: The Final Report of the National Inquiry into the Missing and Murdered Indigenous Women and Girls (National Inquiry into Missing and Murdered Indigenous Women and Girls. 2019), and In Plain Sight: Addressing Indigenous-specific Racism and Discrimination in B.C. Health Care (Turpel-Lafond 2020). In May 2021, the confirmation of bodies of 215 children at Kamloops Indian Residential School who lay in unmarked graves (Casmir 2021) and the murder of three generations of a Muslim Canada family in Ontario in a premeditated attack (Al Jazeera 2021) make it harshly clear that othering, racism, and intolerance are very much part of Canada's past and present.

British, European, American, and Anglo-Canadian settlement in what is now known as the Okanagan began 160 years ago at the Mission near Kelowna. Schooling for settler children and for Syilx Okanagan children began in this era as well (Thomson 1985). In a relatively short time, the sustaining Food Chief based relationships between the Syilx Okanagan and the territorial ecology and homelands of the Syilx Okanagan were replaced by land theft, oppression, displacement to Indian reserves, and forced assimilation policies that attempted to permanently disconnect children from their extended families, cultural identities, reciprocal responsibilities and rights (Sam 2008).

Colonial legislation that mandated the forced removal of Syilx Okanagan children from their families and communities to Indian Residential Schools was just one part of a larger systemic attempt to erase Indigenous Peoples from their traditional homelands. In April 2021, the confirmation of the remains of 215 children at the former Kamloops Indian Residential School brought the degrading treatment of Indigenous children once again into Canadian consciousness. The "discovery" was no surprise to Indian residential school survivors or their families and communities, and indeed, to anyone paying attention. This is underscored by the comments of an editorial written in 1907 after the public release of Dr. Bryce's scathing medical report on the high mortality rates of children who went to the schools:

> His report is printed, many people will scan the title on the cover, some will open it, a few will read it and so the thing will drift along another year. And so with the next year and the year after. So will be the course of events … unless public opinion takes the question up and forces it to the front. Then Parliament will show a quick interest, pigeon holes will give up their dusty contents, medical officers will have a wealth of suggestions and the scandalous procession of Indian children to school and on to the cemetery may possibly be stopped. (Editor 1907 quoted in Malloy 1996, note 89, 331)

Within this context, the confirmation that Indigenous children lie in unmarked graves surrounding Indian residential schools across the nation is a tragic reminder of how widespread public apathy and colonial government's self-serving disinterest continue to fuel and reinforce destructive cycles of colonial and racialized violence. Indeed, many of the Truth and Reconciliation of Canada's 94 TRC Calls to Action (2015b) are concerned with educating settlers about historic and ongoing complicity in supporting racist colonial policies that serve to enrichen the majority while silencing and erasing Indigenous Peoples on our own homelands. However, in Reclaiming Power and Place: The Final Report of the National Inquiry into the Missing and Murdered Indigenous Women and Girls, goes farther stating

> "An absolute paradigm shift is required to dismantle colonialism within Canadian society, and from all levels of government and public institutions. Ideologies and instruments of colonialism, racism, and misogyny, past and present, must be rejected ... The Canadian legal system fails to hold the state and state actors accountable for their failure to meet domestic and international human rights and Indigenous rights obligations" (National Inquiry 2019, 174).

These reports and events demand settlers face the truth that the colonization and whiteout of Turtle Island *is* genocide. So, what will we do about it?

LOOKING THROUGH THE WHITEOUT

The term "whiteout" has been used in whiteness studies to describe the hegemonic impacts of racism on social, cultural, and ecological relations and contexts (Doane 2003, 17). Racialized terms such as "white" and "whiteness" are useful to understand historic patterns of imperialism and colonization that are very racialized; these terms, however, also express aspects of racialized othering and homogenization. A more humanizing discourse acknowledging human diversity will ultimately be more transformative. The goal would be a shift from "white," "whiteness," "Indian," "Aboriginal" etc. to Syilx, Secwepemc, Maori, Irish,

Greek. From the perspective of one Syilx Okanagan educator, it is as if a blanket of residential, agricultural and commercial development, and exploitative resource extraction distorted the natural ecosystems, limiting vision, making it hard to see and to keep good relations with the natural biodiversity of our territory. Animals, plants, habitats, landforms, cultural markers, and story symbols have been diminished. Within seven generations, thousands of years of sustaining cultural and ecological relationships expressed through Syilx Okanagan societal practices have been largely replaced with the English language, Anglo-Canadian white his-story and knowledge, and the institutionalized denial of Syilx existence, sovereignty, and legitimacy.

Syilx Okanagan people have been subjected to an aggressive "assimilation" policy that sought to erase our Syilx cultural knowledge, language, reciprocal relationships and responsibilities, and our rights and title to our territorial lands and resources. Colonial attitudes toward Indigenous Peoples have ranged from the superior and paternalistic doctrines of the Papal Bulls and terra nullius to the misguided and self-serving benevolence of missionaries, to denial, silence or ignorance among younger generations (Crosby 1991; Moreton-Robinson 2004). Within the context of the Indian Residential Schools system, this forced assimilation has only recently been described as cultural genocide (TRC 2015a); however, as Chrisjohn, Young, and Maraun bluntly puts it, "cultural genocide is genocide. Finally, in any intellectually honest appraisal, *Indian Residential Schools were genocide*" [emphasis in the original] (1997, 404).

Many post secondary settler students we encounter as professors struggle to comprehend that colonization, racism, and land theft are perpetuated in the sunny Okanagan in the present day through perpetuation of the British Columbia "land question" and unresolved Indigenous "land claims" that are embedded in colonial mythologies intended to obscure the underlying title held by Indigenous Peoples. As the late Secwépemc leader Arthur Manuel explained: "It is the loss of our land that has been the precise cause of our impoverishment. Indigenous lands account for only 0.36 per cent of British Columbian territory. The settler share is the remaining 99.64%" (Manuel and Derrickson 2017, 25). Given that, in 2008, the federal government issued an official apology to survivors of the Indian residential school system (Canada 2008) and the Final Report of the Truth and Reconciliation

Commission of Canada was released in 2015, it is astounding that in 2021 many settler students continue to know little or nothing of Indian residential school policies that forcibly removed Indigenous children from their families and communities across the country and institutionalized them for nine to twelve months of the year for the duration of their childhood.

Our experiences teaching undergraduate courses with Indigenous content at the UBC Okanagan and Okanagan College have led us to concur with Warry (2008, 14): "Put simply, upon entering university, students know little or nothing of Aboriginal issues and are ill-equipped to filter the many conflicting perspectives and arguments they hear about the challenges facing Aboriginal communities. When they learn more, most are baffled by the government's inability or unwillingness to place Aboriginal issues higher on the political agenda ... This ignorance is widespread." Most adult students appear to have little or no awareness about the Indian Act and that Indian residential school policies were one among many forms of legislation intended to eliminate Indigenous Peoples as distinct and diverse self-governing nations on traditional homelands. Yet, here we are; we all live here, and it is in all our collective children's interests to learn how to live together sustainably. So, what can we look ahead to?

The inclusion of the perspective of a Syilx Okanagan transforming educator in a book whose central theme is white fantasies and neoliberalism brings intellectual and cultural positioning into play. Is white studies the latest intellectual pastime for a privileged, increasingly multicultural elite that has time to reflect upon and pose critical questions about societal patterns, ideology, and hegemony? Is white studies "a relatively meaningless debate on the construction of White identity" (Doane 2003, 17) that does not actually change or transform anything? Or does it have the potential to contribute to the struggle to collectively free ourselves from hegemony and make a more peaceful, and culturally diverse, world with new webs of relationships? In either case, this chapter represents twenty years of our own personal dialogue as partners, parents, scholars and educators, and our voices are those of a Syilx educator, artist and poet, and a white settler woman and educator. We believe it is critical that Okanagan-Syilx knowledge and perspective be included in a work about white settler fantasies in Syilx Okanagan homelands. Contemporary Okanagan-Syilx intervention strategies, informed by traditional knowledge, play critical roles in resisting assimilation, and cultural and historical erasure, while transforming the historical and current conditions that foster "white" hegemony and knowledge reproduction in the Okanagan Valley region. Okanagan-Syilx knowledge can also contribute to creating new relationships informed by respect, diversity, and sustainability, transformative cross-cultural dialogues, and understandings that may lead to a more sustainable and diverse sense of belonging for all in the Okanagan Valley.

THE SWKNAQÍNX, THE SQILXW: THE PEOPLE OF THE STORIES

Swknaqínx, or Okanagan, a conceptual metaphor, suggests the ones who can see and hear far away into the future. The word for our people or ourselves is "Sqilxw, which in a literal translation means the 'dream in a spiral.' We recognize our individual lives as the continuance of human dreams" (Cardinal and Armstrong 1991, 111). Sqilxw as a conceptual metaphor for humans, is that we humans have the mind power to make happen or create into reality whatever we can dream or envision. Unlike salmon, roots, berries, and bears, we humans do not know how to live our lives in ways that contribute to the wellbeing and health of the future peoples and all of the water, earth, plant and animal communities and species and life forces we are part of. When our human lifeways become unbalanced with the health and ability to self-renew of the ecosystems in which we live, us humans have to learn and practice being responsible and restoring and renewing responsible relationships. This way of life is the Sqəlxʷɬcawt. Currently, Syilx language and, subsequently, Syilx worldview, knowledge, culture, and people are critically endangered because of homogenization, assimilation, and exclusion. Fortunately, Syilx Okanagan presence in knowledge and cultural production in UBC Okanagan through Indigenous Studies, the new Bachelor of Nsyilxcn Language Fluency Degree, pedagogical contributions in the Okanagan School of Education, and numerous land-based, Syilx knowledge informed projects are substantial opportunities for renewal and resonance. Our ancestors left us with knowledge, practices, tools, and an understanding of natural laws, thousands of years of accumulated wisdom to enable us to live sustainably, connected within our territorial ecology. Indian residential schools not only disconnected many Indigenous children from respective knowledge and imagination systems, these destructive colonial institutions prevented everyone else from learning from and with Syilx peoples here, and Indigenous Peoples throughout the world. It is up to all of us to reconnect to those strands of knowledge and to create new systems that balance creativity and survival, new understandings and shared responsibilities that express and embody diversity and relational sustainability. The Okanagan-Syilx are the "people of the stories" and, through storytelling and relationship building – by renewing the extended family learning and teaching relationships – the Sqəlxʷɬcawt, human lifeways responsibly and dynamically balanced with the health of the territorial ecology, continue and visions are realized (Cohen 2001).

Within the Okanagan story system, the captíkʷɬ stories are connected to places, resources, and practices within the Okanagan territory. Over thousands of years the knowledge expressed through captíkʷɬ and the medium of the Okanagan language, Nsyilxcn, has nurtured collectively shared sets of values and ethical sensibilities. The land, the tmxʷúlaxʷ, knows us. Our knowledge comes from the tmixʷ, the diverse life-forces of the ecology, which are recorded and expressed in the captíkʷɬ story system that very much involves the spirits of the land and our ancestors talking to us. Our responsibilities as Syilx are to know the captíkʷɬ, the accumulated wisdom the natural communities have shared with us so we would survive. According to the captíkʷɬ, the tmixʷ knew that humans would be coming to the world and determined that they would provide the means for our survival and well-being. Metaphorically, and literally, humans were "torn from the earth" (Okanagan Tribal Council 1993–34, 3). The earth gave birth to us, and our earth mother planned for our well-being, and how she would care for us. Our responsibilities as Syilx Okanagan are to maintain those sustainable relationships, the kinship relationships between a mother and her children. We respect our earth mother because she cares for and provides for us. If we respect and maintain that relationship, then our survival in this land and, by extension, on this planet is more assured.

Mindpower and outcomes expressed in Okanagan-Syilx captíkʷɬ stories are associated relationally with experience and wisdom, and it is clearly understood that we humans have the mind power to move mountains, rivers, trees, and so on. Senklip (Coyote) does this in many stories. If we express that power without responsibilities to the people-to-be in mind, then the captíkʷɬ suggests that we will be caught up in hegemonies of self-importance, and notions of dominance and superiority over others and natural communities, the consequences of moving away from natural laws. Power and wisdom are associated with the ability to put things back because we are part of a larger system of knowledge and creativity. The Syilx concept of kʷulncútn describes the Creator, or all of Creation, which is endlessly moving and changing, and recreating herself continuously. In other words, the earth will regenerate herself and continue with or without humans. Nsyilxcn does not have gender pronouns like English so the authors choose here to counter repressive patriarchal patterns and refer to the Creator or God as her.

Okanagan-Syilx traditional knowledge is expressed in our captíkʷɬ stories, our language, responsibilities and rights are expressed by living Syilx culturally informed lives. This does not mean "going back" in time or rejecting technology or ideas from diverse global cultures. Captíkʷɬ stories make it clear that our world, knowledge, and society are continuously evolving. Senklip (Coyote) is symbolic of mind power, creativity, and vision, and sometimes that gets us into trouble. A recurring theme in captíkʷɬ involves Senklip getting destroyed through foolishness, greed, ambition, ignorance, neoliberal economic policies, and so on. Xwylxʷ (Fox) always gathers up the bits (hair, bone, etc.), breathes into the assembly, steps over it three or four times, and Senklip comes back to life. Fox gathers old knowledge (including attitudes, practices, mistakes, successes, failures, unpleasant bits as well) and breathes new life into what has been gathered to create new knowledge and understanding for current application. Knowledge is understood as a continuously evolving creative, ecological, cultural, and intellectual process. We need, for example, Syilx responsibly positioned scientists and engineers appreciating rather than exploiting tmixʷ. We sometimes act like the destructive part of Senklip, but we are also Xwylxʷ. Our challenge is to collectively create new ways forward so where all tmixʷ flourish.

Within Syilx territory, there is much to learn from each other. This learning is very much connected to larger provincial, national, and international relationships. Everybody is a learner and everybody is a teacher. Syilx webs are reconnections to strands of Syilx knowledge that have been disrupted by colonization, and they are continuations of Syilx knowledge that has informed our cultural survival through resistance to colonization, leading us into the more proactive current era, which has the potential to transform current destructive colonizing relationships. As Smith (2003, 4) writes, Indigenous education and pedagogy, "needs to be transformative because the 'status quo' for most indigenous contexts is not working well and needs to be improved." This continuing knowledge is inclusive of Western and/or scientific knowledge, which complements evolving socially and ecologically sustainable Syilx cultural relationships. This is evidenced by, for example, the return of the salmon to the Okanagan River (Syilx 2021); the development of the Indigenous Studies Program and Syilx Okanagan Canada Research Chair at UBC Okanagan; UBC's strategic plan that commits to "implementing the United Nations Declaration on the Rights of Indigenous Peoples" (UBC 2020); a partnership between Okanagan Indian Band and School District 22 to develop and implement a contemporary Syilx Okanagan Social Studies curriculum mymaytwixʷmntm isqilxwtet Stories of Our Sqilxw Ways (Cohen and Chambers 2016); and the large numbers of school district educators and other residents in the Okanagan Valley who are participating in training sessions with IndigenEYEZ that "uses land-based learning with the arts and best practices in community-building" (IndigenEYEZ 2021) with programs like KinSHIFT (KinSHIFT 2021). These projects have been led or informed by the En'owkin Centre, the Okanagan Nation Alliance, and Syilx Okanagan communities. Despite the ongoing whiteout, a way forward involves collaboration through education – a collaboration that transforms the exploitative ahistorical pattern of development that has characterized European settlement in the valley. We are all responsible for the webs our children will inherit.

SCHOOLING AS A PEOPLE-, KNOWLEDGE-, LANGUAGE-, CULTURE AND DIVERSITY-DESTROYING MONSTER

The recent history of this land that settler peoples have mapped and inscribed as the Okanagan Valley is an ongoing story of the immigration of displaced newcomers and their descendants as well as consistent attempts to replace and eliminate the Syilx Okanagan people, and reshape the tmxwúaxʷ (land/territorial ecology). Immigrants came and continue to come here for many reasons, some fleeing oppression in their ancestral homelands, others, including migrants from other parts of this country, seeking prosperity, new resources, maybe a sunny retirement in the land of lakes and grapes (Aguiar, Tomic, and Trumper 2005). Nevertheless, once here, many newcomers and their descendants who are born in the valley perpetuate the ideologies of colonialism as they make their homes on Syilx Okanagan people's lands. Few are aware of whose land they are on, the Syilx name of the peoples whom they displace, their language and complex epistemologies, and their intimate knowledge of the land and all life on the land.

In the Okanagan, hegemonic colonial beliefs that settlers have put the land to superior use and have the god-given or crown-given right to colonize and claim Syilx Okanagan territory has come to define past and present-day relationships with settlers who reside in the homeland of the Syilx Okanagan peoples. In 2004, through elementary school tours of "historic" Vernon, our children passively learned that local history began when settlers arrived in the mid-1800s. They were confused when we pointed out that the settlers were the newcomers and that their relatives and ancestors, the Syilx peoples, have lived in their homelands since time immemorial. In Grade 9, one of our children was asked to complete a Social Studies assignment in which the students were to pretend they were "captured by Plains Indians ... Describe the people and the camp ... Describe the sun dance." A follow up meeting with the Principal and Teacher resulted in outdated stereotypical resources being replaced with more informed resources.

At home in the Okanagan, tourists and some comment on the unusual-sounding names of places such as Okanagan Lake, Kelowna, Penticton, Keremeos, Kalamalka Lake. These place names are anglicized versions of Syilx place names. Many institutions also take their names from Swknaq́inx – the University of British Columbia Okanagan and Okanagan College are examples. Kelowna is the largest city in the interior and it is where UBC Okanagan is located. Today Nsyilxcn place names mark the roads within the UBC Okanagan campus, for many the first connection with Syilx peoples' distinct language, Nsyilxcən. For the past twenty plus years that we have both taught post-secondary courses with Indigenous content, we inevitably have many settler students in our classes who admit to having lived their entire lives in the Okanagan Valley with no awareness of the

Syilx Okanagan people. The extent of historical exclusion and erasure in the education system and its effect on public conscious is appalling. Following classes about Syilx and Indigenous Peoples, students often display genuine expressions of shock and grief. Many ask, "Is this true?" and "How is it that we did not learn this in elementary or secondary school?" Some express disbelief and denial, and defensiveness: "Nations have been colonized for thousands of years. It's a natural part of progression." Or, as some insist, "colonization is just a part of the history of the world … Indigenous Peoples have to get over it and move on." For many, the realization gradually sets in that they have grown up in Canada, in the Okanagan Valley, in ignorance, and that public education has been complicit in ensuring their ignorance as participants in the ongoing oppression of Indigenous Peoples. Yet here it is within post-secondary educational institutions that so many students learn of this complicity (Jefferess 2014, Berry 2018).

Education – schooling particularly – has been a very destructive, intolerant, homogenizing monster, and it is education that plays a critical role in creating opportunities for both Indigenous and non-Indigenous students to become aware of the whiteout that surrounds and subsumes them: "It [Education] is one of the major sites in which different groups with distinct political, economic, and cultural visions attempt to define what the socially legitimate means and ends of a society are to be" (Apple 2000, 17). Public education is a contested site in which neoliberal and neocolonial agendas resist de-colonizing discourses, and it is a site of struggle to create space for Syilx and Indigenous knowledge and connect students to more responsible place-based applications of Science, Technology, Engineering, Arts and Mathematics.

TRANSFORMING THE MONSTER WHO STEALS CHILDREN

In the Syilx story system, horse and dog were people-destroying monsters that were transformed by Coyote's powers so that they became useful, beneficial, and integral to ongoing Sqəlxʷɬcawt. Schooling cannot be treated uncritically, and for schooling to be effective, beneficial, and compatible with Syilx knowledge and cultural aspirations, it must be transformed by knowledge and pedagogical "tools" from Coyote, Fox, the Food Chiefs, and others symbolic of knowledge relationships into an ongoing, expression of living in dynamic balance with the Indigenous ecological diversity in which we live.

Western schooling has been used by colonial governments as a "people-destroying monster" (Cohen 1998, 34). Schooling, particularly with reference to the Indian residential schools, has been likened to skalula, "the monster who steals and devours children" (Sterling 1997, 183). After the Indian residential school era ended in the interior, from 1970, Syilx Okanagan children were integrated into public schools, but the exclusion of Syilx language, knowledge, and pedagogy continued in the public school curriculum. Since 1975, a culture-based educational movement in the United States and Canada has involved implementing more Indigenous local cultural activities as an "add-on" to the public-school model (Hermes 2005). Critics have noted that this piecemeal approach has not produced any fluent speakers of heritage languages or greater academic success for Indigenous students (243). In the Okanagan Valley, many schools have Aboriginal dance and culture programs. Some have Okanagan language programs, in which students can learn the Syilx language for up to one and half hours per week. These types of programs did not exist in the early 1980s. They are a result of both Indigenous activism and a more inclusive and pluralistic public school system. Public schools have improved Indigenous graduation rates with bridging, self-esteem, and assistance programs, so more Indigenous children can achieve prescribed and imposed learning outcomes. Syilx cultural aspirations for knowledge, however, remain at the margins, and children can go through elementary and high school in complete ignorance that we still exist (Bear 2010). Indigenous education programs should contribute to language and knowledge revitalization rather than continue, in effect, to promote assimilationist policies (Bear 2010). We are still here. In Syilx Okanagan Nation communities, leadership and community members are proactively taking responsibility, and developing schools with extended family relationships, Sqəlxʷłcawt pedagogy and immersion programs. As Regan (2010, 23–24) observes, the journey must embody the destination:

> Failure to link knowledge and critical reflection to action explains why many settlers never move beyond denial and guilt, and why many public education efforts are ineffective in bringing about deep social

> and political change. At the same time, I am mindful that, because radical change is not ultimately in its best interest, the dominant majority is apt to reinforce benevolent imperialism and colonial attitudes, often unconsciously, in ways that are antithetical to decolonization. An unsettling pedagogy is therefore based on the premise that settlers cannot just theorize about decolonizing and liberatory struggle: we must experience it, beginning with ourselves as individuals, and then as morally and ethically responsible socio-political actors in Canadian society.

After all, whose knowledge and language should be taught to Indigenous students in their respective territories and schools? Public and mainstream schools must develop and implement Indigenous and unsettling pedagogical approaches and curriculum content that support non-Indigenous teachers and students from kindergarten to Grade 12 to examine their relationships to this place, the homeland of the Syilx, or with the Indigenous Peoples on whose lands they reside. Indigenous Studies departments, programs, and courses at universities and colleges provide models for resisting the whiteout in three important ways: (1) they are creating spaces for Indigenous knowledge in sites of dominant knowledge reproduction; (2) they are educating the mainstream public about the existence of Indigenous Peoples and the vast diversity of Indigenous languages and cultures; and (3) they are nurturing a new generation of Indigenous and mainstream transforming educators. In so doing, Indigenous scholars, leaders, and allied educators are creating intellectual and transformative spaces with strong ties to communities and territories in daycares, elementary and secondary schools, and universities. They are bringing Indigenous creativity and imagination into the knowledge reproduction aspects of schooling.

Transforming educators create Indigenous intellectual spaces for Indigenous and non-Indigenous students to feel connected to their communities and lands, and to nurture a critical mass of critically conscious Indigenous and Western or world scholars. Such approaches have the potential to create experiences of belonging for all based on truth and reconciliation rather than on lies and the historical omission of Indigenous Peoples' wisdom. As Māori educator Graham Smith (2003, 10–11) notes: "This movement to indigenous theorizing is not a rejection of 'western theorizing' or of non-aboriginal knowledge forms [but is viewed] as the addition of an indigenous set of intellectual 'tools' into the total 'tool-box' of theories generally available in the academy."

CONCLUSION

One hundred and sixty years ago, the building of the Mission in Okanagan territory signified the start of a period of intense whiteout embodied by the attempted systematic erasure of Syilx knowledge, language, cultural memory, title, and rights from the physical, spiritual, and cognitive ecology. However, the Okanagan-Syilx survived and are emerging from the whiteout, and Okanagan-Syilx knowledge is defining Syilx Okanagan educational institutions, including Syilx Okanagan elementary schools and the En'owkin Centre, an Okanagan post-secondary institution. This chapter was first drafted in 2012, and, since then, there have been many changes in the public school system concerning Indigenous Peoples, increasing interest in Syilx pedagogical approaches and curriculum content, as well as in new opportunities for teachers to learn about cultural safety, decolonization and indigenization. Syilx knowledge is, therefore, moving, albeit slowly, into the curricula of mainstream education institutions, such as public schools, UBC Okanagan, and Okanagan College.

A healthy cultural and linguistic diversity can only be achieved by transforming dialogue, respect for difference and diversity, and developed as a shared ethic by Indigenous peoples and non-Indigenous Canadian populations. Diversity and pluralism are necessary to a vibrant larger community, inclusive not only of Indigenous Peoples' knowledge and languages in their respective homelands but also of everyone else who lives here, has come to know the Okanagan Valley as home, and is part of diverse cultural and ecological webs of relationships. Transformation in the public and mainstream school system, band schools, universities, and colleges have the potential to connect new generations to Indigenous Peoples' territorial ecology-based knowledge systems and languages, and achieve Indigeneity, the dynamic balance resulting from pedagogy and praxis tied to place and peoples to be.

Currently, the influx of international students, tourists, new immigrants, and refugees into the Okanagan Valley present opportunities for us to critically rethink who benefits from a continued whiteout. Several years ago, at a multicultural health fair in the North Okanagan, local settler, MLA Tom Christensen, in his opening address asked the entire crowd to stand. He then asked, "If you were not born in Canada, please sit down ... if your parents were not born in Canada ... if your grandparents were not born in ... your great-grandparents ... etc." Within a few generations, the entire crowd was seated, with the exception of the Syilx Okanagan children, parents, and families who had been invited, as well as the other Indigenous guests. It was a transformative moment for the crowd to critically reflect on the whiteout in a public acknowledgment of the history, presence, and continuing reality of the Syilx Okanagan as First Peoples. Our children, in their traditional regalia, sang in Nsyilxcən, songs of welcome to the many newcomers, older generations, and more recent immigrants and refugees to their territory. It is a "new" experience for Okanagan-Syilx children to sing and speak their own Indigenous language, which they have acquired as a second language. Their presence is a reminder to all that the Okanagan-Syilx live here, that this is our homeland, and that our identity, language, culture, and rights continue through our children.

It is apparent we as a larger society, are learning, slowly, to be more tolerant and appreciative of cultural and ecological diversity, are intending to be more inclusive, pluralistic, and sustaining in terms of our cultural and economic relationships with the natural world, so we should understand how past patterns of racism, othering, colonialism and intolerance have been reproduced, and can take new forms. If we are to transform and/or decolonize educational institutions, in our teaching and learning with students, overcome and leave these monsters in the past, or transform these destructive monsters so they are helpful and beneficial to the children now and future generations, we need to identify and understand these monsters. It's a critical time for Indigenous Peoples to contribute knowledge and imagination to the ways we humans live in relation to the water, earth, plant and animal communities that give us everything we need to live well and peacefully. Indigenous Peoples have place-based experiential cultural lifeways that have maintained ecological and economic health, food security, and distribution. In the Okanagan Valley those knowledge relationships, collaborative partnerships rather than unilateral and imposed, start with the Syilx Okanagan. We, Syilx, and the municipal, economic, educational institutions, communities, settlers in our homelands, need to put our knowledge and imagination together to understand the past, collaborate in the present so we can all have a future.

POSTSCRIPT BY BILL COHEN

In discussions with Kamloops Indian Residential School survivors in my family and community about the 215 unmarked graves of children at the school, the event is very emotionally and spiritually jarring and triggering for survivors and our families. Even so, it is clear that we need to remember the 215 kids and all those subjected to the Indian Residential Schools and the larger genocidal project to eliminate Indigenous peoples, while continuing to look out for our children of the Syilx Okanagan, Nlaka'pamux, Secwepemc, and St'atimc nations, and Indigenous peoples in our respective homelands. The women in my home community organized COVID-19 safe ceremonies in Komasket Park at our Indian Residential School Memorial to remember, in our language, the children, families, and Elders, past and present, so we can have a future. A teacher, Paul Britton, from the school district, came with his child to grieve with us, stand with us, and to together create new teaching and learning relationships. Limlmt (respect and appreciation) for joining us.

The task as educators, I believe, is to be as informed as possible to educate those in our learning, teaching contexts and responsibilities so we are contributing to the wellbeing of the future. Reconciliation in the larger context is restoring a dynamic balance between human lifeways and the place-based territorial ecologies' ability to self-regenerate. The tmxʷúlaxʷ, the diverse earth, water, plant, and animal communities which give us everything we need to live well, has proven to work for millennia, so we need to work on our bringing back to life songs, lifeways, and gifts. To get to reconciliation, we must first face the true historic patterns of the colonialism, racialized othering, intolerance, and violence that has occurred and continues. We have all that to understand and transform so we can have respectful, humanizing, and sustaining relationships, and it is a good thing we are emerging from the patriarchal colonial whiteout with much stronger intellectual and creative monster transforming potential. We certainly need this way of pedagogy and praxis.

REFERENCES

Aguiar, L.L.M., P. Tomic, and R. Trumper, R. 2005. "Work Hard, Play Hard: Selling Kelowna, BC, as Year-Round Playground." *Canadian Geographer* 49 (2): 123–39.

Al Jazeera. 2021. Grief, Mourning a Funeral for Muslim Family Killed in Canada. Human Rights News. June 12. https://www.aljazeera.com/news/2021/6/12/grief-mourning-funeral-muslim-family-killed-canada.

Apple, Michael W. 2000. *Official Knowledge: Democratic Education in a Conservative Age*. New York: Routledge.

Bear, Nicholas, A. 2010. *Canada's Colonial Mission: The Great White Bird*. Unpublished paper. https://iportal.usask.ca/action.php?sid=769538126&url=https://web.archive.org/web/20100415162706/http://www.nativestudies.org/native_pdf/canadascolonial mission.pdf&acti on=go&id=31097.

Berry, Carli. 2018. "UBCO Sociology Class Calls on Kelowna Chiefs to Change 'Derogatory' Name: The Sociology Class Sent an Email to the Media Yesterday Afternoon." *Kelowna Capital News* November 30. Accessed June 20, 2021. https://www.kelownacapnews.com/news/ubco-sociology-class-calls-on-kelowna-chiefs-to-change-derogatory-name/.

Bryce, P.H. 1907. *Report on the Indian Schools of Manitoba and the Northwest Territories*. Ottawa: Government Printing Bureau, 1907.

Bryce, P.H. 1922. *The Story of a National Crime Being an Appeal for Justice to the Indians of Canada*. Ottawa: James Hope and Sons, Ltd., 1922.

Canada. 2008. "Statement of Apology to Former Students of Indian Residential Schools: Prime Minister Harper Offers Full Apology on Behalf of Canadians for the Indian Residential Schools System." Crown-Indigenous Relations and Northern Affairs, June 11. https://www.rcaanc-cirnac.gc.ca/eng/1100100015644/1571589171655.

Casmir, Rosanne. 2021. "Office of the Chief: for Immediate Release." *Tk'emlúps te Secwépemc/Kamloops Indian Band*. 27 May. https://tkemlups.ca/wp-content/uploads/05-May-27-2021-TteS-MEDIA-RELEASE.pdf.

Cardinal, D., and J. Armstrong. 1991. *The Native Creative Process: A Collaborative Discourse between Douglas Cardinal and Jeanette Armstrong*. Penticton, BC: Theytus Books.

Chrisjohn, R, Sherri Young, and Michael Maraun. 1997. *The Circle Game: Shadows and Substance in the Indian Residential School Experience in Canada*. Penticton: Theytus Books.

Cohen, Bill. ed. 1998. *mayx twixmntm tl q'sapi lats k'ullmstm i snlkc 'askaxa. Stories and Images about what the Horse Has Done for Us: An Illustrated History of Okanagan Ranching and Rodeo*. Penticton, BC: Theytus Books.

–. 2001. "The Spider's Web: Creativity and Survival in Dynamic Balance [Sqilxwcut model]." *Canadian Journal of Education* 25 (2): 140–48.

Cohen, Bill, and Chambers, N. eds. 2016. *mymaytwixʷmntm isqilxwtet Stories of our sqilxw ways*. Vernon: Okanagan Indian Band.

Crosby, M. 1991. "Construction of the Imaginary Indian." In *Vancouver Anthology: The Institutional Politics of Art*, ed. Stan Douglas. 267–91. Vancouver: Talonbooks.

Doane, Woody. 2003. "Rethinking Whiteness Studies." In *White Out: The Continuing Significance of Racism*, ed. W. Doane, and E. Bonilla-Silva, 3–20. New York: Routledge.

Editor. 1907. "Editorial." *Saturday Night*, 23, November. N.A.C. RG 10, Vol. 4037, File 317021.

Hermes, Mary. 2005. "'Ma'iingan Is Just a Misspelling of the Word Wolf': A Case for Teaching Culture through Language." *Anthropology and Education Quarterly* 36 (1): 43–56. https://search.ebscohost.com/login.aspx?direct=true&db=edsjsr&AN=edsjsr.3651308&site=eds-live&scope=site.

Idle No More. 2021. "About the Movement." *Idle No More*. https://idlenomore.ca/about-the-movement/.

IndigenEYEZ. 2021. "Mission: Strength of the Past; Communities of the Future. *IndigenEYEZ*. https://indigeneyez.com/mission/.

Jefferess, David, ed. 2014. *Settler MelanKelownia: Colonialism, Memory, and Heritage in the Okanagan*. Accessed June 20, 2021. https://fccs.cms.ok.ubc.ca/wp-content/uploads/sites/92/2019/03/Settler-Melankelownia.pdf.

Kinshift. 2021. Breaking Barriers, Build Community, Create Change. *Kinshift.ca* https://kinshift.ca/.

Manuel, Arthur, and Ronald M. Derrickson. *The Reconciliation Manifesto: Recovering the Land, Rebuilding the Economy*. James Lorimer & Company Ltd., Publishers, 2017. https://search.ebscohost.com/login.aspx?direct=true&db=cat08731a&AN=olc.cef75266.e215.45c5.84bd.cc8122c09320&site=eds-live&scope=site.

Milloy, John. 1999. A National Crime. The Canadian Government and the Residential School System 1879 to 1986. Winnipeg: University of Manitoba Press.

Moreton-Robinson, A. 2004. "Whiteness, Epistemology and Indigenous Representation." In *Whitening Race: Essays in Social and Cultural Criticism*, ed. A. Moreton-Robinson, 75–88. Canberra: Aboriginal Studies Press.

National Inquiry into Missing and Murdered Indigenous Women and Girls. 2019. *Reclaiming Power and Place. The Final Report of the National Inquiry into Missing and Murdered Indigenous Women and Girls*. The National Inquiry. https://www.mmiwg-ffada.ca/wp-content/uploads/2019/06/Final_Report_Vol_1a-1.pdf.

Okanagan Nation Alliance. 2021. *Syilx Okanagan Nation Alliance*. www.syilx.org.

Okanagan Tribal Council. 1999. *Kou-Skelowh / We Are the People: A Trilogy of Okanagan Legends – How Food Was Given, How Names Were Given and How Turtle Set the Animals Free*. Penticton, BC: Theytus Books.

Regan, Paulette. 2010. *Unsettling the Settler within: Indian Residential Schools, Truth Telling, and Reconciliation in Canada*. Vancouver: UBC Press.

Royal Commission on Aboriginal Peoples (RCAP). 1996. *Report of the Royal Commission on Aboriginal Peoples*. Ottawa: Minister of Supply and Services Canada.

Sam, Marlowe. 2008. Oral Narratives, Customary Laws and Indigenous Water Rights in Canada. UBC Dissertation. Accessed June 20. https://open.library.ubc.ca/cIRcle/collections/ubctheses/24/items/1.0074307.

Smith, Graham Hingangaroa. 2003. "Indigenous Struggle for the Transformation of Education and Schooling." *Keynote Address to the Alaskan Federation of Natives (AFN) Convention*, Anchorage, Alaska. Accessed June 18, 2021 https://citeseerx.ist.psu.edu/viewdoc/download?doi=10.1.1.603.1987&rep=rep1&type=pdf.

Sterling, Shirley. 1997. "The Grandmother Stories: Oral Tradition and the Transmission of Culture." PhD diss., University of British Columbia. Accessed 18 June 2021. https://open.library.ubc.ca/cIRcle/collections/ubctheses/831/items/1.0054963.

Syilx. 2021. "Our Journey Bringing the Salmon Home" *Syilx: Okanagan Nation Alliance.* Accessed 18 June 2021. https://www.syilx.org/fisheries/okanagan-sockeye/our-journey-bringing-the-salmon-home/.

Thomson, Duncan Duane. 1985. *A History of the Okanagan: Indians and Whites in the Settlement Era: 1860–1920.* [Doctoral Dissertation]. University of British Columbia. https://open.library.ubc.ca/cIRcle/collections/ubctheses/831/items/1.0107160.

Truth and Reconciliation Commission. 2015a. *Final Report of the Truth and Reconciliation Commission of Canada, Volume One: Summary: Honouring the Truth, Reconciling for the Future.* James Lorimer & Company.

Truth and Reconciliation Commission. 2015b. *Truth and Reconciliation Commission: Calls to Action.* Winnipeg: Truth and Reconciliation Commission.

Turpel-Lafond, Mary Ellen. 2021. *In Plain Sight: Addressing Indigenous-specific Racism and Discrimination in BC Health Care, Full Report, November 2020.* Addressing Racism Review. https://engage.gov.bc.ca/app/uploads/sites/613/2020/11/In-Plain-Sight-Full-Report.pdf.

UBC. 2020. "New Indigenous Strategic Plan Establishes UBC's Role in Upholding the Rights of Indigenous Peoples. September 14. *UBC Media Relations.* https://irshdc.ubc.ca/2020/09/13/ubc-launches-indigenous-strategic-plan/.

Warry, Wayne. 2008. *Ending Denial: Understanding Aboriginal Issues.* Toronto: University of Toronto Press.

CHAPTER 2

N–TOE MOUNTAIN

Colouring Hinterland Fantasies

Daniel J. Keyes

Berg and Vuolteenaho's (2009, 7) *Critical Toponymies* insists that place names, also referred to as toponyms, "often appear to people as ideologically innocent rather than power-charged semiotic dynamos for making meaning about places." The naming of a mountain between Penticton and Summerland on 1 December 1955 as "N–toe" Mountain, and its renaming at the request of the Canadian government on 29 April 1966 as "Nkwala," a First Nation word plucked from the title of Anglo-Canadian author Elizabeth Lambert Sharp's (1958) Governor General Award-winning children's novel (Mount Nkwala 2018; Okanagan Historical Society 1966, 144), demonstrates that toponyms are not ideologically innocent; they are vexed by the Okanagan's status as a colonial "landscape of dispossession" (Berg 2011, 17).

Tennant (1990, xi) notes a linguistic shift in British Columbia as the term "white" falls out of favour in official discourse: "Until the late 1940s[,] Whites in the province were eager to distinguish themselves from non-Whites and to protect white political interests, as they did in denying Indian claims, curbing Asian immigration, and prohibiting non-white groups from voting." While one might assume that, mid-twentieth century, the shift in discourse articulated by Tennant would have ushered in a more inclusive, multicultural, and postcolonial era with the expunging of the derogatory toponym "N–toe," this chapter and the next contend that these toponymic shifts reveal how settler heritage assigns, erases, and domesticates for use the absent presence of Others. I have struck through the term "non-white" and will refrain from its use even though the term appears in Tennant's valuable quote above. "Non-white" risks centring and perpetuating whiteness as a type of subject that defines all Other subjects as lacking whiteness. Instead, I use the term "Other" to signal that, historically, settlers have come to class Indigenous people and other immigrants from non-Northern European origins as a way of asserting the superiority of European modernity in the colonial project. In the particular case of the mountain's renaming, this toponymic swapping reveals a colonial melancholy and ambivalence about Others. The phrase "colonial melancholy" is adapted from postcolonial theorist Paul Gilroy, who, working in the British context thinking through the neoliberal nationalist legacy of Prime Minister Margaret Thatcher, coins the term "postmodern melancholy" to describe how England fails to deal with its loss of empire. He diagnoses Britons as melancholics who "come to need 'race,' and even rely upon its certainties as one sure way to keep their bearings in an increasingly confused world" (Gilroy 2003, 33). Essentially, the melancholic figure for Gilroy is one who is blocked from coming to terms with the end of empire but who, nevertheless, remains fascinated with race. This melancholic attitude aptly frames how the toponyms "N–toe" and "Nkwala" persist in articulating race without speaking about whiteness and colonialism. In an active way, these toponyms sidestep the Okanagan as a landscape of dispossession. As Freud (1999, 249) writes of melancholics: "Their complaints are really 'plaints' in the old sense of the word. They are not ashamed and do not hide themselves, since everything derogatory that they say about themselves is at bottom said about someone else." Thus we can see how race operates in the toponyms "N–toe" and "Nkwala" as displacements of an explicit white supremacist past, yet both names continue to tacitly support the colonial melancholic project. Both names operate as what Australian postcolonial theorist Ghassan Hage (2000, 44) names a "spatial management" of a national fantasy for the Other as a way of relegating the Other to a past and asserting white hegemony.

Ultimately, these changes in toponyms operate as a benevolent management of "local" colour within a mapping of the region as an exalted Anglo settler space. The adjective "exalted" is used here and throughout to acknowledge Thobani's (2007, 5) use of the term to indicate how Canadian national identity is framed within an Enlightenment discourse that positions white Canadians as exalted global citizens while others, like Indigenous, immigrants, and refugees, are relegated to an outsider status as troublesome subjects who have "failed" to properly embrace technological capitalist modernity. As I relate below, the vexed naming of this mountain clearly fits within Thobani's idea that frozen African American immigrants and First Nations fail to adapt. Thus "superior" Enlightenment modernity relegates these figures to quaint toponyms rather than positioning them as markers of resistance to the persistence of the colonial project. Melancholia and benevolence are two strategies settlers use to obscure the trauma of settlement with the discourse of progressive modernity.

"Melancholy," as noted by Eng and Kazanjian (2002, 3), has "a long and expansive pedigree dating to classical times" – to Freud's "Mourning and Melancholia" (1999 [1917]) – marking a distinction between how one deals with loss: either the mourner productively admits and reconciles with the lost Others or the "melancholic's sustained devotion to the lost object" is "not only pathological, but also … antithetical to the ego's well-being, indeed, its continued survival" (Eng and Kazanjian 2002, 3). For Freud (1999, 243), "mourning is regularly the reaction to the loss of a loved person, or to the loss of some abstraction which has taken the place of one, such as one's *country, liberty, and ideal* [emphasis mine]." If one reads "mourning" in the strict literal sense of mourning for a recently deceased friend, then reading toponyms as either an act of grudging anti-colonial mourning or psychically stuck colonial melancholy may seem counter-intuitive; however, following Freud's gesture towards applying these terms to national belonging, citizens can mourn for a lost ideal. In this context, the naming and unnaming of the mountain works as a signifier of a lost displaced psychic object that cannot be reconciled with the exalted settler heritage of the Okanagan. The bizarre memorialization of two Black men's death on Christmas Day 1908 ("A Christmas Tragedy" 1909, 1), which become the winking toponyms N–toe in 1955 and Nkwala in 1966, offers examples of the stuck melancholic imagination. As Freud might have it, these toponyms operate as signifiers of lost unarticulated "objects" that might threaten to reveal the landscape of dispossession. If Tennant is correct that mid-twentieth-century British Columbia settlers began to sense the limitation of the white colonial project, then this naming and un-naming is symptomatic of a melancholic refusal to mourn the "passing" of explicit white supremacy. The elliptical narrative of doomed Black men in the Okanagan hints that this landscape of dispossession is an "unsettling" colonial narrative. This chapter and the next aim to unearth this narrative of naming to explore how N–toe and Nkwala reveal a space that remains psychically stuck in a melancholic white supremacist mode.

Theories of mourning and melancholy vary, and I am wary of the limitations of Freud's circular and universalist approach to discourse analysis, yet the compelling work by postcolonial (Gilroy 2003, 2005; Mohanram 2007) and trauma theorists (Mitscherlich 1974) suggests that these terms provide a useful explanatory model with regard to considering how historical consciousness operates. Inflected by Walter Benjamin's (1969 [1940]) "Thesis on the Philosophy of History," Eng and Kazanjian's (2002, 1) notion of the distinction between mourning and melancholy differs from that of postcolonial theorists like Gilroy and Mohanram. Eng and Kazanjian see mourning as moving to completion, while melancholia, with its persistent ambivalent engagement with "the loss of the loved object," offers a continued reworking through this loss whereby the sense of the past is never completed (3–4). I am not convinced that perpetual grief over an incomplete lost object can be productive, and I suggest that approaches to mourning offered by Atwood (2007), Mohanram, and Gilroy, which frame mourning as active, productive, and continuous, provide the better model for excavating the Okanagan's lost object: the landscape of dispossession.

In order to excavate this region's melancholic approach to alterity and place in the Okanagan, I chronologically examine two moments: (1) the death of two Black hotel workers in 1908 and (2) the naming of N–toe Mountain to "commemorate" their memory in 1955, apparently based on a 1948 *Okanagan Historical Report* (note: the title of the *Okanagan Historical Society* changed to *Okanagan History*, so while the print copies of the journal bear the title *OHS*, library catalogues reflect the new name, *Okanagan History*) (Harvey 1948, 213). The next chapter discusses the renaming of this geographical feature as Mount Nkwala (Mount Nkwala 2018) in 1966 to demonstrate how white hegemony has managed this space within a national and regional framework with a possessive investment in managing racialized Others and displacing the Okanagan as a landscape of dispossession.

1908 PRECARIOUS BLACKNESS IN THE OKANAGAN'S HINTERLAND

In the last thirty years, various Canadian scholars (Bristow et al. 1994; Hudson 1996–97; Clarke 1997; Foster 1996; Walcott 1997; Sim 2001; Peake and Ray 2001; McKittrick 2002; and Nelson 2008) signal and contest the erasure of African Canadian spaces within the Canadian nationalist project. Clarke (1997, 35) asserts the traces of Black heritage that have been erased: "the image confronts the consensual understanding of Canada as a white, pristine land settled by pristine whites, with only a few docile First Nations people providing incidences of local colour." In the context of the Okanagan, with the exception of the brief winking in and out of existence of the N–toe toponym, this quote aptly captures how settlers have managed toponyms by naming most features after early settlers and providing a few that record quirky stories about First Nations. Clarke's phrase "incidences of local colour" aptly accounts for how the Okanagan's 1950s hinterland came to name "N–toe Mountain" by including an oblique narrative to mark early colonial traces of Black identity. Following the lead of Tennant, who argues that, post-mid-twentieth century, British Columbia becomes less explicitly white supremacist, one could argue that this toponym nominally demonstrates an attempt by provincial and federal naming authorities and local white organizations to acknowledge Black heritage – for eleven years – under a pejorative. However, the toponym "N–toe" does not rupture the exalted dominant British white narrative of settlement; rather, it operates to inject local "colour." The naming operates like many "othered" toponyms in the Okanagan's settler space as a way of signifying a quirky melancholic history of which little can be learned other than that the "natural" region is inhospitable to Black men. Thus the narrative informing N–toe preserves the traces of Tennant's assumption that, pre-mid-twentieth century, white British Columbians sought to keep intact the exalted colonial fabric of settlement.

The 1955 naming of the mountain "N–toe" memorializes the death of two Black Summerland-based hotel workers, Charles Blair, a cook, and Arthur Chapman, a waiter, who, on Christmas Day 1908, after a few drinks at the bar in Penticton, returned on horseback to their workplace in Summerland, lost their horses, became disoriented, and died of exposure (N–toe

Mountain 2018; N–toe Mountain 2021). The third Black companion of this party, Arthur Wilson, the second cook at the Summerland Hotel, survived. The 1909 textual trail of these men's existence in the Okanagan is limited to two newspaper articles ("A Sad Fatality" 1909, 1; "A Christmas Tragedy" 1909, 1) and the coroner's inquest into Chapman's death (Inquest into Death of Arthur Chapman 1909). Perhaps the status of these men as Black and as hotel employees dictates why there are few primary historical records pertaining to them.

In terms of historiography, the ability to locate evidence of Black settlement in BC's interior is frustrated by the lack of documentation. Ripmeester's (1990, Table 10) thesis, which focuses on the ethnic division of labour for the Kootenay town of Rossland, indicates that the national 1901 census for male labourers by "distribution of ethnic backgrounds" offers four categories: "British Isles," "North Western Europe," "Central and Eastern Europe," and "Asia," leaving a category of "Other" for African Canadians and American immigrants and First Nations. Library and Archives Canada indicates that "many immigrants to Canada came from the United States or sailed from Europe to American ports on their way to Canada. Prior to April 1908, people were able to move freely across the border from the United States into Canada; no record of immigration exists for those individuals" (Canadian Genealogy Centre 2011). American records for this period are also sketchy, with no interior border post recorded (National Archives 2000).

The online British Columbia geographic names database reveals the n-word begins to be approved in the 1930s throughout British Columbia's Interior by the B.C. Gazetteer, the legal notice publication of the government. For example, in 1939 N– Creek appears near Barkerville in the Cariboo (N– Creek 2021a) and another N– Creek in the Kootenays near Cranbrook (N– Creek 2021b) while another N– Creek appears in 1954 in Northwest British Columbia near Telegraph Creek (N– Creek 2021c) with its name changed to Crayke Creek in 1967 (Crayke Creek 2021). A N– Lake appears in the Kootenays in 1939 (N– Lake 2021) attached to the N– Creek (N– Lake 2021). By the 1960s all these place names are changed. For example, N– Bar Creek is renamed after Rossland former mayor Goodeve Creek (Goodeve Creek 2021) while N– Lake is "changed to Negro Lake 3 May 1961" (N– Lake 2021).

The persistence of the n-word as this generic marking of Blackness across mid-twentieth century British Columbia indicates a specific cartographic white out.

Histories of Black people in British Columbia tend to focus on Vancouver Island and the goldfields of the central interior (Winks 1977, 272–87; Pilton 1951; Kilian 2008), where there has been significant migration since the 1850s, and on settlement in the erased Hogan's Alley in Vancouver (Hudson 1996–97). Crawford Kilian's and James William Pilton's histories provide triumphant narratives of Black settlement. Winks (1977, 292) claims that, from the 1870s to the 1930s, white attitudes towards Black people degenerated from "mere neglect to active dislike" as various pseudo-scientific racist beliefs proliferated. He suggests that, in the early twentieth century, "a once vague mythology" had taken hold about "the Negro's inability to adapt to the North, of his love of pleasure, of his sexual appetites, his unreliability, laziness, and odour" (298). The Canadian government at this time restricted immigration of Others with "blacks ... informally denied entry after 1910" (Poulter 2009, 333). By 1908, when Chapman and his friends worked in Summerland, concentrated Black settlement in the region was not an option. In this era, the Okanagan was promoted to white British settlers as an exclusive white man's Eden (Koroscil 2003, 62–66, 94, 103–6; Bennett 1998).

A sense of how this space is promoted as a British Eden for white settlers is offered by the 1907 real estate pamphlet *Naramata Possibilities* (1982 [1907], 8), which frames the region as a space for well-heeled settlers from eastern Canada and "the Old World" that privileges domestic leisure over back-breaking Prairie farming, which is more suited to Eastern European types:

> They are people of means who can afford to pay handsome prices for what suits them. It is not easy to find a place where the climate conspires with man to produce comfort, culture, beauty, health, and profit in one combination ... There is a difference between a home and roost ... The kind of neighbors you have and the general tone of the community have much to do with the making of that boy of yours, and your happiness generally ... The class of people coming to Naramata is ... the very best Canadian stuff.

Being "the very best Canadian" here is implicitly defined as being masculine, white, of English origin, and capable of replicating those values in the next generation of men (Barman 1984, 1981; and Koroscil 2003 provide further documentation on this class of Anglo settler). The Okanagan is marketed as *heimlich* and as a healthy settlement unsuitable for Others who clearly live in "roosts" and might "unmake" one's son. In using the term *heimlich,* I am invoking Homi Bhabha (1990, 2), who works with Freud's sense of the uncanny, or *unheimlich*, in terms of a discourse of nationhood that sustains the following binary: "the *heimlich* pleasures of the hearth, the *unheimlich* terror of the space or race of the Other." The ad is selling comfort by selling a space well suited to Anglo settlers. This mixture of class and race is echoed by J.M. Sutherland, the developer of the South Okanagan towns of Naramata, Peachland, and Summerland, who boasts that the Okanagan is "a Canadian California" that served to stem the tide of "many of the best [Winnipeg] settlers, [who] year after year, sell out their belongings and go with their families and capital to California" (Mitchell and Duffey 1979, 56). The 1907 ad's attractive trope of the Okanagan's pleasing weather, "comfort, culture, beauty, health and profit" (*Naramata Possibilities* 1982 [1907], 8) plays with the notion of a region uniquely suited to a gentle class of settlers, the subtext being that it is somehow unsuitable for immigrants not originally from the British Isles.

The unsuitability of Canada and the Okanagan for non-British Others is revealed in an editorial published in the *Summerland Times* three months after the men's death. This editorial mused on how African American boxer Jack Johnson and his white wife were denied a hotel room in Vancouver, asserting that Canada is not fraught by racism as is the United States because "in the coolness of the north … colour problems are not an issue" ("The Miseries of Miscegenation" 1909, 7). The Okanagan as a pastoral Eden would seem to "naturally" attract the right sort of white people while discouraging the wrong sort of people, unless they are willing to work as part of the servant class.

TRACING BLAIR, CHAPMAN, AND WILSON

As already mentioned, Chapman and Blair died in December 1908. I have been unable to locate any reference to them in Canadian immigration files, which did not collect data prior to April 1908. The *Summerland Review* article on their deaths states: "Blair, Wilson and Chapman had only resided in Summerland for a few months" ("A Sad Fatality" 1909, 1). Arthur Wilson testified at the inquest into Arthur Chapman's death that he had been in Summerland for the last five months working as the second cook with Chapman, who was the waiter, having been in Summerland for six months. Wilson had known Chapman for eight years in Pittsburgh, Pennsylvania (Inquest into Death of Arthur Chapman 1909, 12). Beyond Wilson's testimony at the inquest, I have been unable to locate any evidence that he remained in Summerland or moved elsewhere following the incident.

The appearance of these men as workers at the Summerland Hotel (the hotel burned down sometime after the First World War [Two Town Sites n.d.]) does not seem to be part of a wider immigration movement to the Okanagan, although traces of Black migration exist and suggest that upper-class British settlers employed Black people in the services and trades. A prominent doctor in the region, B.F. Boyce, following a trip to the Barbados around 1909 or 1910, "arranged for the transport and employment to Kelowna of its first Negro family. Julian and Louise worked for the Doctor, Julian on the farm and Louise in the house" (Schoenfeld 1973, 53). That the last names of Louise and Julian are not included in this account while Dr. Boyce's name is reiterates the pattern of privileging the exalted Anglo colonial figure while making the Others anonymous. Another puzzling and parallel narrative of Black migration exists in a 1951 *Okanagan Historical Society* (*OHS*) report:

> There were a few Negro settlers in the valley. There was Proper at Deep Creek, near Hullcar, Alex Clark at Irish Creek and Big Tom. Big Tom came from Alabama ... He often complained on the warmest days, of being cold. He was a fine husky fellow and did a two-man job on the straw stack when we were threshing at the O'Keefe ranch ... Later it was reported he was shot in Washington during the course of a poker game. (Kneller 1951, 76)

The figure of the Black man as doomed labourer, who is not at ease with the climate and comes to a sticky end, seems a recurrent trope that mid-twentieth-century local white historians use repeatedly in memorializing Black people's presences in the Okanagan. This view is consistent with

Wink's view that, in the early twentieth century, settlers used the harsh Canadian climate as an alibi for "natural" white privilege. In this naming of N–toe Mountain, it is not settlers who are implicated in being unwelcoming or hostile towards Black men: it is Nature.

This notion of the Okanagan as a providential blessing for whites resonates with other strains of early twentieth-century environmental determinism. The intellectual origins of environmental determinism can be located in Yale University geographer Ellsworth Huntington's theory that mental activities were weakened by higher temperatures and that places like "Britain, northern Europe, New Zealand, and the Pacific Coast of the United States had ideal climates for civilizations," while tropical places did not foster or sustain "white energy" (Anderson 2005, 181). Canadian variants of this approach to natural racial zones are articulated by novelist and nationalist R.G. Haliburton, "founding member of the nationalist Canada First movement" (Sandlos 2001, 7), who proclaimed in 1869 on the Nordic character of Canada: "As long as the north wind blows, and the snow and the sleet drive over the forests and fields, we may be poor, but we must be a hardy, a virtuous, a daring, and if we are worthy of our ancestors, a dominant race … Let us revive the grand old name of Norland, [']the Land of the North'; We are the North men of the New World" (8). Thus, Canada becomes a place for Nordic-born European settlers to excel and embrace their environmental destiny. Nancy Stepan (1985, 98) asserts that mid-nineteenth-century science, working in the context of African American slavery and eventual emancipation, is a "science of boundaries between groups," with the "'proper' place of the white race … now defined as the temperate, 'civilized' world of Europe" (99), while Black people are "made by biological definition a tropical 'species' … Their movement out of the tropics cause[s] a degeneration from type" (ibid.). Thus the culture of science and national belonging naturalizes the fate of Black people, who degenerate in the Great White North. In the case of the reports on the deaths of these Black men, we might say that a sense of racial environmental inevitability is hardwired into the narrative.

The Okanagan's sunshine version of environmental determinism operates to ensure that this region is a *heimlich* space of belonging for whites that naturally excludes Others. Frenkel (1992, 144) notes that, for the academic geographical community, in the late nineteenth and early twentieth centuries environmental determinism held sway as a way of scientifically supporting the manifest destiny of the colonial project, though "by the mid-1920s, these ideas had lost much of their academic currency; outside universities and colleges, however, they retained considerable influence, perhaps as a result of their apparent commonsensical nature." As is demonstrated below, local historians in the region reify environmental determinism in their retelling of the N–toe narrative in a way that enforces a spatial logic that maintains the Okanagan as a naturally white space.

AMBIVALENT LOSS

The report on the Black men's deaths in the 1909 *Penticton Press* begins, "[a] sad wave of feeling went over the community when it became known that two of the three negroes who were seen in town on Christmas morning had been found dead near the road between Penticton and Summerland" ("A Christmas Tragedy" 1909, 1). The coverage of their deaths in the *Summerland Review* resonates with this sense of loss ("A Sad Fatality" 1909, 1). I do not mean to equate this sense of sadness with Freud's notion of melancholy, but I think these news reports offer a sense of these deaths as losses of Others: the men are *from* the community of Summerland but not *of* it.

Chapman's death triggered an inquiry since he had "a small bruise" on his right cheekbone (Inquest into Death of Arthur Chapman 1909, 5) indicating that foul play may have occurred, while Blair clearly died of exposure. Chapman's inquest concluded, based on the testimony of various witnesses and the autopsy, that he died of exposure, and it noted that all three men had been drinking. The *Penticton Press*'s account notes that, on Christmas Day, Chapman purchased from the Penticton druggist Henry Main "a perfume atomizer and lady's work case" ("A Christmas Tragedy" 1909, 1), which varies slightly from Main's testimony at the inquest, where he said that Chapman called at this house and asked him to sell him "a couple of presents" (Inquest into Death of Arthur Chapman 1909, 15) but did not say what they were. The purchase of these gifts, which I assume were intended for a woman, is excluded from the official inquiry and does not appear in the *Summerland Review*'s account, which does mention Mrs. MacDowell, who managed these men at the hotel ("A Sad Fatality" 1909,

1; "Change in Management" 1909, 7; Mrs. MacDowell Honoured 1909, 1). The purchase of these gifts hint that Chapman, after living for six months in the Okanagan, may have been accepted by at least one person – to whom he sought to offer these gifts. The *Summerland Review* reports: "of the two unfortunates, Chapman was better known to the citizens of Summerland, and was of a jovial disposition and a general favourite" ("A Sad Fatality" 1909, 1). Both articles use an elevated style to narrate the deaths and to confirm the inquest's conclusion that Chapman, although sober, died due to a wild horse and less than sober companions in what constituted a "natural" tragedy. Based on testimony from the inquest about the various foot- and hoofprints found in the snow, the Summerland newspaper claimed: "thoroughly exhausted in his endeavours to catch the horses, [he] sat down under the tree and fell to sleep, from which he never wakened" ("A Sad Fatality" 1909, 1). Thus freezing to death is euphemized as repose. If the community mourned these deaths, there might have been a less poetic and more forceful attempt to account for them. I am intrigued by how these accounts of the deaths hint that there might be another narrative of settlement for Chapman. For whom were these gifts purchased on Christmas Day? Why did the soberest of the three men die? There is no entirely satisfying answer to these questions, but perhaps a more apt question to pose is how the narrative of these deaths resonated throughout the valley's mid-twentieth-century history and place name making.

1948–55: WHO NAMES N–TOE MOUNTAIN?

In the 1950s, seven places names in British Columbia contained the n-word. In the 1930s, these places were likely so named to reflect the popular names locals had given the geographic feature in question as a result of the influx of Black migrants into interior towns like Rossland, Barkerville, Cranbrook, and Telegraph Creek during the gold rush. N–toe Mountain's naming in 1955 seems an odd exception to this sweeping adoption of the pejorative, and it likely reflects the involvement of the *OHS*, with Harvey's 1948 article titled "Okanagan Place Names" providing the initial historical gloss on the deaths of Chapman and Blair (Harvey 1948, 196). The reliance on the n-word rather than the surnames of Black settlers to name Black settlements seems to indicate the need to mark an absent presence: the lost Black men in the

Great White North. Thus, this naming operates, as Mukherjee (1981, 36) explains, to render "people of colour 'simultaneously invisible and over exposed'" (cited in Peake and Ray 2001, 180). The toponym "N–toe Mountain" is clearly consistent with this logic, which ensures that Chapman's and Blair's names and specific lives are lost to history while the place of their deaths is marked by a pejorative. This pejorative operates under a type of colonial white melancholia, articulated by Gilroy (2003, 2005), that retrieves not the lost object (any specifics about the dead Black men, which might suggest their active roles in colonization) but "preserves" a sad but oddly comforting narrative for white people regarding the unsuitability of white spaces for Black men. Implied in this failed attempt to retrieve the lost object of the lives of these particular Black men with the place naming is the notion that Anglo-settlers thrive and render the Okanagan prolific while these doomed Others appear as a quirky historical footnote.

Clearly, diverse populations and communities were part of the Okanagan in the early twentieth century. Huyskamp (2010, 3), in his 2010 report to the city of Kelowna, estimates that, in 1909, 15 percent ("roughly 250") of Kelowna's citizens were of Chinese descent, with the community reaching a peak population in the 1930s and then diminishing by the 1960s to sixty people (5). His report to the city of Kelowna, while mentioning the migration of the Chinese community to larger cities in Canada or back to China as well as its lack of women (5), fails to mention the federal Head Taxes of 1884 and 1905 and the Exclusion Act, 1923 (Harris 2000, 269) as forces that helped ensure this community faded away. Based on this report, it would seem that the narration of Other local histories in the Okanagan continues to operate in a melancholic mode to obscure the material conditions that resulted in the region becoming less diverse by the mid-twentieth century. There is evidence to the contrary. For example, an article from the 1946 *Kelowna Courier* records the dispute between an Indo Canadian woman and white homeowners over her buying a home in the city, with an alderman claiming: "[the] city has always followed a policy of keeping the Orchard City free of Orientals as much as possible … We have a town composed of Anglo-Saxons and it should continue as so. It just so happens the Occidentals and the Orientals do not mix" ("Tax Payers Object" 1946, 1). This article records that a number of citizens, along with the young Asian woman, eloquently opposed this type of local exclusion, yet it also documents that local government acted to ensure Anglo-white spatial privilege.

As previously mentioned, the traces for the origins of N–toe Mountain's naming in 1 December 1955 relies on Harvey's 1948 *Okanagan Historical Association Report* on toponyms in the Okanagan. Since its inception, this annual report has primarily operated as a regional heritage project for whites eager to record their history of place and a general scientific record of the Okanagan's geology and history (Okanagan Historical Society 2021). Harvey's toponymic project reveals that many geographical features bear the names of the original British settlers. These men pre-empted up to 160 acres of "Crown Land" for agricultural development (Pre-emption Regulations 1987, 10). A few other toponyms explained by Harvey bear the names of Others, who are remarkable in less celebrated and more quirky ways. The first and third entry in his alphabetic list offer examples of how the narratives behind toponyms enforce a racial hierarchy: the triumphant and objective specifics of British white settlement are given with the Aberdeen Lake entry: "Lord Aberdeen (1847–1934) Governor General of Canada 1893–98 who bought the Coldstream ranch nearby, 13, 261 acres in 1891 from Forbes George Vernon for €549,000, in conveyance" (Harvey 1948, 196). Racialized Others have more mythic and often comic references: "Little Aeneas, a wizened old Indian[,] lived alone at the south end of the lake and died about 1946 aged over 100" (ibid.), and polygamist chief Kalamalka, who renounced his four wives to be baptized and then took "in their place a comely young maiden" (207). Counter to this levity, British settlers like Richard Lowe Cawston are celebrated for vaccinating "Indians en masse during a small pox epidemic" (200). Thus, Indigenous people, like the land, are those whom settler history acts upon, or, in the case of the toponym for Chopaka Mountain, First Nations peoples are consigned to a mythic past where they cease to be human and become part of the land, with the details of this transformation being in dispute: "Name of Legendary Okanagan Indian hunter who was turned into stone by Coyote (A. Walsh), a transformed Indian Maiden (Parham 40)" (ibid.). Toponyms like Long Joe Creek, which memorializes "a tall, good looking Indian rancher ... drowned in Okanagan River" (ibid.) and McDougall Creek, which memorializes a Métis who also drowned in the lake (211), suggest that Indigenous people succumbed to natural forces rather than to the inhospitality of settlers. The history of pre-emption and the privileging of white settlers over Others is not given credence in these mid-twentieth-century explanations of toponyms. Black and Indigenous bodies, as signified by toponyms like "N–toe" and "Nkwala," serve to fill an imaginative space that white privilege is able to name, master, and contain.

Harvey's populist histories assume that there are "two kinds of bodies produced in Western society: normal and abnormal bodies. Alternatively, we can understand these as 'respectable' and 'degenerate bodies,' both of which are imprinted with particular (differing) gendered, racial, cultural, and other meanings" (Nelson 2008, 17). In *Razing Africville*, Nelson draws attention to how "racialized people are marked, managed, observed, and perceived by the dominant group," while for the dominant group "the dominant body remains unmarked" (ibid.). Toponyms in the Okanagan operate via this regulated version of race, where Others' bodies are excessive, mythic, prone to natural accidents, and often animal-like, while proper and productive white bodies, like Cawston and Aberdeen, inform the dominant culture as respectable exalted human subjects whose actions embody benevolent modernity in terms of looking after the medical needs of Indigenous people or simply developing the land. The narrative around N–toe and the two dead Black men whose bodies are represented via this strange case of synecdoche as a "toe" is consistent with how whites name spaces with traces or, in this case, fragments of Black bodies.

It is unclear if this synecdoche refers to the aerial topography of the entire mountain or whether the men were found at the proverbial toe of the mountain, thus transforming the "toe" into n–toe. The mountain's profile does not resemble a human toe. Nor does Google's topographic map give a sense of its looking like a toe. Thus, the toponym operates as part of a hazy oral narrative in which the exact origins of who names this feature is lost: all that remains is a sense of the toponym operating as a stage for these curious, yet environmentally inevitable, deaths. The only traces of their bodies are destined to become a "curious" toponym referring more to a legend than a historical event that might record early Black settlement.

Harvey's 1948 version draws on the 1909 Summerland newspaper account to reinforce the sense of colonial melancholy: "Chapman fell asleep from exhaustion and Blair from his liquor – never to awaken – their bodies being found near the foot of the mountain [the] next day … Officially, the mountain is unnamed" (Harvey 1948, 213). Throughout the 1950s, the story of the deaths of Chapman and Blair resonate in *OHS* reports: a report three years later notes the deaths without offering the names of the men (Higgins 1951, 92). Surprisingly, the 1958 *Okanagan Historical Report*, published three years after the official naming, states "when or by whom this name (unofficial) was given is not on record," and it offers the standard account of Blair's and Chapman's demise (N–toe Mountain 1958, 137), which seems like an odd case of amnesia, given that the same journal has reported the tale twice in the last ten years. It would almost seem that the white historians mentioned in the *Okanagan Historical Report* are not willing to take responsibility for the naming. They are never able to adequately explain the arbitrary linkage between "N–toe" and these men's death and, instead, repeat the sad cryptic facts. Thus, no settler is credited with inventing this peculiar naming, which literally functions to reduce Black bodies to lost parts. This naming operates as an act of benevolent white desire to partially admit traces of "failed" Black settlement as a lost historical fragment rather than as an integral part of the larger exalted white toponymic project that names the Okanagan.

Another perplexing example of "N–toe" memorialization as colonial melancholy occurs in an interview by oral historian Imbert Orchard with Alice Thompson, daughter of Val Haynes, who was "a stock manager for the South Okanagan Lands Co" ("A Christmas Tragedy" 1909, 1) and son of judge and land commissioner J.C. Haynes, who was responsible in the 1860s for the shrinking of Indigenous land reserves (Running Horse 1999, 16–17). According to Val Haynes's 1909 testimony at Chapman's inquest, on the morning of 26 December 1908, Haynes located the body of Charles Blair, and the following morning he tracked Arthur Chapman's body (Inquest into Death of Arthur Chapman 1909, 16), but he clearly did not save Arthur Wilson. However, some fifty-six years later, his daughter Alice Thompson provides a recollection replete with benevolence: about 1905 (not 1908) Haynes, riding his horse to Summerland one evening "between Christmas and New Year's," discovers and saves a drunken Black man who was part of a party of five Black men "on their way to serve New Year's Dinner in Summerland" (Mitchell and Duffy 1979, 6). Like a bad joke that uses exaggeration and repetition to build the narrative tension, according to his daughter, Haynes discovers one dead Black man after another until he "saves" the final man, who he throws on the back of his horse: "This coloured man was always grateful to my father for saving his life … he guessed that they just weren't accustomed to the climate" (6). This myth that Black men cannot withstand the Okanagan winter while white settlers like Haynes find the Okanagan to be a "Canadian California" (Robinson 1979, 56) is echoed in Harvey's populist history of the place, which insists that the Okanagan is a place that Black men are simply not able to safely inhabit and where even the most capable and benevolent of white men is only able to save one Black man. The linkage between Blackness and Indigeneity, which occurs with the transfer of the toponyms N–toe to Nkwala, occurs in the reminisces of Val Haynes in a book in which another settler, Carl McNaughton, insists that Haynes was well respected: "As far as I know, he got along very well with the Indians; and the Indians respected him. I can remember that at his funeral – Indians don't usually attend white people's funerals – but there was a delegation there and they walked up to the grave before it was filled and acknowledged Val" (Mitchell and Duffey 1979, 6). The point of both these narratives is to exalt the benevolent settler Haynes whose contact with racialized Others is based on mutual respect and benevolence. Alice Thompson's recollection suggests that, for settlers, N–toe Mountain persists as colonial melancholic fantasy of white benevolence while frozen Black bodies are stacked up like firewood.

Harvey's narrative appears to be the basis upon which the mountain was named N–toe (N–toe 2012). As mentioned, it echoes the *Summerland Review* coverage: "Chapman … sat down under a tree and fell to sleep, from which he never awakened" ("A Sad Fatality" 1909, 1) with the phrase "never to awaken" (Harvey 1948, 213). On one key point, Harvey's account differs from both the 1909 Summerland and Penticton newspaper versions: he places their bodies together "near the foot of the mountain" (ibid.), which is at variance with Chapman's inquest, which offers a hand-drawn map indicating that Chapman and Blair died quite a distance apart from each other (Inquest into Death of Arthur Chapman 1909, 17). Constable Tooth, with the help of Haynes, finds Blair's body on 26 December 1908 at 2:15 p.m. in a gully (not a mountain), and they locate Chapman's body the next day "against a pine tree." Tooth makes no mention of either body being found at the base of the mountain or side by side (16). Blair's body is located on the morning of 27 December "following up on tracks" (1). One of the men may have died at the "foot" of the mountain but not both, unless one is operating under a very generous definition of the foot of the mountain. I am not certain whether Harvey blurs the facts as reported in the newspaper accounts with the aim of calling the mountain N–toe or whether local folklore informs his account and thus the naming of the geographical feature.

Harvey does not track down the ancestors of Summerland's Mrs. MacDowell either to ask about her relationship with Chapman or to provide the reader with an account of what happened to the survivor, Arthur Wilson. Instead, his account is riddled with gaps. His entry fails to unpack the relationship between the pejorative signifier "N–toe," usually used to denote a Brazil nut or a variety of potato (N-word Toe 2021), and the signified: "the death of two black men." It strikes me that if two Irish settlers were to die of exposure in 1908 that the mountain would not be called "mick fingerling mountain" but might bear their names. Curiously, in the 1965 seesaw battle over the renaming of the mountain, no local, federal, or provincial government official suggested calling the mountain after Chapman or Blair. Nor did anyone rush to defend or provide a logical gloss for N–toe, suggesting that they all knew it was pejorative but no one took responsibility for the process that, only eleven years earlier, had seen the geographical feature dubbed "N–toe."

Kennedy's sociological and etymological study of the n-word claims that how and when the term became pejorative is unclear; however, "by the end of the first third of the nineteenth century, *n-word* had already become a familiar and influential insult" (Kennedy 2002, 4). He provides ample evidence from literature by prominent African Americans Frederick Douglass, Richard Wright, Malcolm X, and so on to indicate that, while the term may have seemed innocent to many white Americans, it operates to terrorize Blacks (13–18).

In the British context, the linkage to the n-word as a pejorative is much less clear in the 1950s. Gilroy (2005, xii) speaks of the triumphant British Second World War film released in 1955 *The Dam Busters*, which has "Richard Todd, in the role of Wing Commander Guy Gibson, with his faithful dog 'n-word' at heel, readying the heroes of the 617 squadron to go and bomb 'the Gerries.' … 'n-word,' [is] … the bombers code word for a successful strike on the Nazi dam Perhaps in "British" Columbia and in the Okanagan in the post-Second World War period the term would seem to have a neutral connotation for Anglo-white local historians like Harvey, who simply fuzzily drew from the local lore, ignoring the specifics of African Canadian settlement in the region to frame a quirky, generic melancholic name that obscures the lives of Arthur Chapman and Charles Blair. As explored in the next chapter, following a sweep in the United States to reform such names in little over a decade, the Canadian government initiates the overhaul of toponyms that use the n-word and thus N–toe becomes Nkwala Mountain.

REFERENCES

Note: as discussed in the introduction to practice cultural safety, I have redacted the use of n-word and N–toe in the references.

Anderson, W.P. 2005. *The Cultivation of Whiteness: Science, Health, and Racial Destiny.* Melbourne: Melbourne University Press.

Atwood, B. 2007. "The Australian Patient: Traumatic Pasts and the Work of History." In *The Geography of Meanings: Psychoanalytic Perspectives on Place, Space, Land and Dislocation*, ed. M. Teresa, S. Hook, and S. Akhtar. 63–78. London: International Psychoanalytical Association.

Barman J. 1981. "The World that British Settlers Made: Class, Ethnicity and Private Education in the Okanagan Valley." In *British Columbia: Historical Readings*, ed. W. Peter Ward and Robert A.J. McDonald, 600–26.Vancouver: Douglas and McIntyre.

–. 1984. *Growing up British in British Columbia: Boys in Private School.* Vancouver: UBC Press.

Benjamin, Walter. 1969. "Theses on the Philosophy of History." In *Illuminations*, ed. H. Arendt, trans. H. Zohn, 253–64. New York: Schochen Books.

Bennett, Jason Patrick. 1998. "Apple of the Empire: Landscape and Imperial Identity in Turn-of-the-Century British Columbia." *Journal of the Canadian Historical Association / Revue de la Société historique du Canada* 9 (1): 63–92.

Berg, Lawrence, and J. Vuolteenaho, ed. 2009. *Critical Toponymies: The Contested Politics of Place* Naming. Burlington, VT: Ashgate.

Berg, Laurence. 2011. "Banal Names, Neoliberalism, and Landscapes of Dispossession." In *The Politics of Spatial Inscription*, ed. Derek Alderman and Reuben Rose-Redwood, Special Issue of *ACME: An International E-Journal for Critical Geographies* 10 (1): 13–22.

Bhabha, Homi, K., ed. 1990. *Nation and Narration*. London: Routledge.

Bristow, P., D. Brand, L. Cart, A.P. Cooper, S. Hamilton, S., and A. Shadd. 1994. *We're Rooted Here and They Can't Pull Us Up: Essays in African Canadian Women's History*, Toronto: University of Toronto Press.

Canadian Genealogy Centre. 2012. Library and Archives Canada. Accessed July 19. http://www.collectionscanada.gc.ca/genealogy/022–908.005-e.html.

"Change in Management."1909. *Summerland Review* 1 (39): 7.

"A Christmas Tragedy." 1909. *Penticton Press*. 2 January.

Clarke, George E. 1997. "Honouring African-Canadian Geography." *Border/lines*. 45: 35–38.

Crayke Creek. 2021. *GEOBC*. Accessed June 8. http://archive.ilmb.gov.bc.ca/bcgn-bin/bcg10?name=4820.

Eng, D.L., and D. Kazanjian, eds. 2002. "Introduction: Mourning Remains." In *Loss: The Politics of Mourning*. Berkeley, CA: University of California Press. ProQuest ebrary.

Foster, C. 1996. *A Place Called Heaven: The Meaning of Being Black in Canada*. Toronto: HarperCollins.

Frenkel, S. 1992. "Geography, Empire, and Environmental Determinism." *Geographical Review* 82 (2): 143–53.

Freud, Sigmund. 1999 [1917]. "Mourning and Melancholia." In *Standard Edition*, 14th. ed., ed. J. Strachey, 243–58. London: Hogarth Press.

Gilroy, Paul. 2003. "Race Is Ordinary: Britain's Post-Colonial Melancholia." *Philosophia Africana* 6 (1): 31–45. *Academic Search Complete*, EBSCO*host*.

–. 2005. *Postcolonial Melancholia*. New York: Columbia University Press.

Goodeve Creek. 2021. BC Geographical Names. Accessed June 8, https://apps.gov.bc.ca/pub/bcgnws/names/40607.html.

Hage, Ghassan. 2000. *White Nation: Fantasies of White Supremacy in a Multicultural Society*. New York: Routledge.

Harris, C. 2000. *The Resettlement of British Columbia: Essays on Colonialism and Geographical Change*. Vancouver: UBC Press.

Harvey, A.G. 1948. "Okanagan Place Names: Their Origin and Meaning." *Okanagan Historical Society* 12: 193–223.

Higgins, C.N. 1951. "The Summerland-Naramata Ferry." *Okanagan Historical Society* 15: 90–95.

Hudson, Peter. 1996–97. "Disappearing Histories of the Black Pacific." *Mix* 22 (3): 48–56.

Huyskamp, R. 2010. *Report on Kelowna's Chinatown Sites*. City of Kelowna Community Heritage Commission. 5 August. Accessed August 8. http://www.kelowna.ca/CityPage/Docs/PDFs%5C%5CCouncil%5CMeetings%5CCouncil%20Meetings%20 2010%5C2010-10-04%5CItem%206.5%20-%20Heritage%20Interpretation%20 and%20Recognition.pdf.

Inquest into Death of Arthur Chapman. 1908. British Columbia Archives, GR 1327, vol. 12, 1901–18, reel BO2383 (233: 1907–5:1909), microfilm, 28 December.

Kennedy, R. 2002. *N-word: The Strange Career of a Troublesome Word*. New York: Pantheon, 2002.

Kneller, J. 1951. "Memories of My Early Days in the Okanagan." *Okanagan Historical Society* 15: 73–76.

Kilian, Crawford. 2008. *Go Do Great Things: The Black Pioneers of British Columbia*. Burnaby: Commodore Books.

Koroscil, Paul. 2003. *The British Garden of Eden: Settlement History of the Okanagan Valley, British Columbia.* Burnaby: Simon Fraser University Press.

McKittrick, K. 2002. "'Their Blood Is There, and They Can't Throw It Out': Honouring Black Geographies." *Topia* 7: 27–37.

"The Miseries of Miscegenation." 1909. In *The Summerland Review: Devoted to the Interests of Summerland, Peachland, and Naramata* 1, no. 34 (27 March): 7.

Mitchell, D., and D. Duffy, D. ed. 1979. *Bright Sunshine and a Brand New Country: Recollections of the Okanagan Valley, 1890–1914.* Victoria: Aural History Program, Ministry of Provincial Secretary and Government Services.

Mitscherlich, Alexander.1974. *Inability to Mourn: Principles of Collective Behavior.* Trans. Eric Mosbachs. New York: Grove.

Mohanram, R. 2007. *Imperial White: Race, Diaspora, and the British Empire.* Minneapolis: University of Minnesota Press.

Mount Nkwala. 2018. GeoBC. http://apps.gov.bc.ca/pub/bcgnws/names/18642.html.

Mrs. MacDowell Honoured. 1909. *Summerland Times* 1, no. 40 (6 May): 1.

Mukherjee, Arun. 1981. "An Invisible Woman." *Saturday Night* 96 (March): 36–40.

Naramata Possibilities. 1982 [1907]. *Smile of the Manitou*, ed. Don Salting and B. Wilson. 8–15. Penticton: Skookum Publications.

National Archives Microfilm Publications Relating to Canadian Admissions and Border Crossings. 2000. *Prologue Magazine* (updated 25 June 2007). http://www.archives.gov/publications/prologue/2000/fall/us-canada-immigration-records-2.html.

Negro Creek. 2021. *BC Geographical Names.* Accessed June 8. https://apps.gov.bc.ca/pub/bcgnws/names/13476.html.

Nelson, J. 2008. *Razing Africville: A Geography of Racism.* Toronto: University of Toronto Press.

N– Bar Creek. 2021. *BC Geographical Names.* Accessed June 8. https://apps.gov.bc.ca/pub/bcgnws/names/49562.html.

N– Creeka. *Geographical Names* 2021. Accessed June 8. https://apps.gov.bc.ca/pub/bcgnws/names/49219.html.

N– Creekb. *Geographical Names* 2021. Accessed June 8. https://apps.gov.bc.ca/pub/bcgnws/names/44146.html.

N– Creekc. 2021. BC Geographical Names. Accessed June 8. https://apps.gov.bc.ca/pub/bcgnws/names/42321.html.

N– Lake. 2021. *BC Geographical Names.* Accessed June 8. https://apps.gov.bc.ca/pub/bcgnws/names/44147.html.

N–toe Mountain. 2018. Natural Resources Canada. Accessed August 8. http://www4.rncan.gc.ca/search-place-names/unique/JAZPP.

N-word toe. 2021. *Oxford English Dictionary.* https://tinyurl.com/upw5yuea.

–. 2021 "N–toe Mountain." BC Geographic Names. https://apps.gov.bc.ca/pub/bcgnws/names/45296.html.

Okanagan Historical Society. 1958. "N–toe Mountain." In *The Twenty-Second Report of the Okanagan Historical Society 1958* (a historical gazetteer of Okanagan -Similkameen), 137. https://tinyurl.com/s55n64v8.

–. 1966. "A Mountain Renamed." *The Thirteenth Report of the Okanagan Historical Association.* 144. https://tinyurl.com/p9f7z64p.

–. 2021. http://www.okanaganhistoricalsociety.org/index.html. Accessed June 8. https://www.okanaganhistoricalsociety.org/reports_index.php.

Oxford English Dictionary. 2021. "N–toe." Accessed June 8. https://tinyurl.com/upw5yuea.

Peake, L., and B. Ray. 2001. "Racializing the Canadian Landscape: Whiteness, Uneven Geographies and Social Justice." *Canadian Geographer / Le Geographe canadien* 45 (1): 180–86.

Pilton, J. 1951. "Negro Settlement in BC, 1858–1871." MA thesis, University of British Columbia.

Poulter, G. 2009. *Becoming Native in a Foreign Land: Sport, Visual Culture, and Identity in Montreal, 1840–85*. Vancouver: UBC Press.

Pre-emption Regulations. 1987. *Kelowna, British Columbia, Canada: A Pictorial History*. 3rd ed. Kelowna: Kelowna Museum.

Ripmeester, M.R. 1990. "Everyday Life in the Golden City: a Historical Geography of Rossland, British Columbia." MA thesis, University of British Columbia. https://circle.ubc.ca/handle/2429/29146.

Robinson, J.M. 1979. "The Transition of the Okanagan as Told by J.M. Robinson, a Circular, 1926." In *Bright Sunshine and a Brand New Country: Recollections of the Okanagan Valley 1890–1914*, ed. D. Mitchell and D. Duffy, 57–59. Aural History Program Victoria, BC: Ministry of Provincial Secretary and Government Services.

Running Horse, A.E., and A. Artz. 1999. *Okanagan Nation Fisheries Commission Dam Research*. Okanagan Fisheries Commission. Vernon, BC: Summit Environmental Consulting. Accessed 12 July 2021. http://www.obwb.ca/obwrid/docs/019_1999_Ok_Nation_Fisheries_Commission_Dam.pdf.

"A Sad Fatality." 1909. *The Summerland Review: Devoted to the Interests of Summerland, Peachland, and Naramata*. 1 (22): 1.

Sandlos, J. 2001. "From the Outside Looking In: Aesthetics, Politics, and Wildlife Conservation in the Canadian North." *Environmental History* 6 (1): 6–31.

Schoenfeld, R. 1973. "Dr. B.F. Boyce." *Okanagan Historical Society* 37: 52–55.

Sharp, E.L. 1958. *Nkwala*. Illustrator William Winter. Boston and Toronto: Little Brown and Company.

Sim, K.C. 2001. "Victoria: The African-American Challenge to Public Spaces in Colonial British Columbia." Honours thesis, University of British Columbia.

Stepan, N. 1985. "Biology and Degeneration: Race and Proper Places." In *Degeneration: The Dark Side of Progress*, ed. J.E. Chamberlin and S.L. Gilman, 97–121. New York: Columbia University Press, 1985.

Tennant, Paul. 1990. *Aboriginal Peoples and Politics: The Indian Land Question in British Columbia, 1849–1989*.Vancouver: UBC Press.

"Tax Payers Object to Hindu Girl Buying House, But Girl Openly Defies All Protests." 1946. *Kelowna Courier*, 22 August, 1, 12.

Thobani, S. 2007. *Exalted Subjects: Studies in the Making of Race and Nation in Canada*. Toronto: University of Toronto Press, Scholarly Publishing Division, 2007. eBook Collection (EBSCOhost).

Two Townsites: Summerland Brows. n.d. *Summerland Museum: Virtual Exhibit.* Accessed June 8, 2012. http://summerlandmuseum.org/virtualexhibits/Two Townsites.html.

Walcott, Rinaldo. 2003. *Black Like Who?* 2nd ed. Toronto: Insomniac Press.

Winks, R.W. 1977. *The Blacks in Canada: A History*. 2nd ed. Montreal and Kingston: McGill-Queen's University Press.

CHAPTER 3

NKWALA

Colouring Hinterland Fantasies with the Indigenous

Daniel J. Keyes

The previous chapter discusses how N–toe Mountain, near Penticton, came into existence in 1955 under what local historians regard as mysterious circumstances, despite, mid-twentieth century, the Okanagan Historical Society's (OHS) having had a hand in recollecting the 1908 deaths of the two Black Summerland hotel workers, Arthur Chapman and Charles Blair, as a fuzzy origin for this mountain's naming. This chapter considers the federal government's replacement of the name "N–toe Mountain" with "Mount Nkwala" in 1966 in two subsections that leverage the previous chapter's discussion of the distinction between blocked colonial melancholy and potentially progressive mourning, drawing on the works of Atwood (2007), Eng and Kazanjian (2002), Gilroy (2005), and Mohanram (2007).

The first section details the specific politics of the name shift from N–toe to Nkwala to argue that lingering traces of colonial melancholy are erased with a name shift that, on the surface, would seem to celebrate Okanagan First Nations culture while also celebrating the name of a white writer's novel (Mount Nkwala 2018). As a toponym, "Nkwala" aims to exalt a settler nationalist identity that is made "native" rather than position Indigenous knowledge as fundamental to being in the Okanagan (Ahluwalia 2001). The second section of the chapter describes and analyzes the novel *Nkwala*, which, on the literal level, may appear to be consistent with the exalted colonial project that renames the mountain but that, on closer inspection, reveals how its plot has a subversive strand that indicates it is a "blocked" form of colonial melancholy. It is unable to confront the violence of colonialism to properly mourn the violence of dispossession and to find a way out of its benevolent white fantasy.

The Canadian government officially assigns toponyms in consultation with the provincial topography branch, but local settlers have a hand in shaping official naming. Kerfoot (1999) and Kerfoot and Rayburn (1990) detail celebratory histories of how the Canadian government has managed toponyms in a progressive manner. Kerfoot (1999, 272) notes that, by the mid-1950s, the Canadian Board of Geographical Names approved policy resisting the translation of First Nations names into English, although it suggested that "the use of Indian and Eskimo names should be avoided unless the Native name is short and euphonious." The management of this mountain's new Indigenous-sounding toponym balances the needs of the federal government for reform with the advice from local white business and heritage groups. In Canada, by 1965 the influence of the civil rights movement in the United States, which saw the removal of toponyms using the n-word (Monmonier 2006, 45), began to influence Canadian government naming practices. The 18 October 1965 minutes from the Canadian Permanent Committee on Geographical Names recorded: "The committee unanimously recommended that the word 'n-word' in Canadian topography by replaced by unobjectionable names" (Minutes 1965, 36). Later notes in these minutes indicate the replacement of the n-word as a toponym was to be a top-down change that locals could not resist; however, local community group were free to suggest alternative names (Minutes 1965). I sense this drive to change names was influenced by the United States toponym expert Dr. M.F. Burrill, who attended the Canadian committee meeting as a very active observer (Minutes 1965).

LORD BADEN POWELL OR NKWALA?

The 18 October 1965 minutes for the Canadian Permanent Committee on Geographical Names record "the committee unanimously recommended that the word 'n-word' in Canadian topography be replaced by unobjectionable names" (Minutes 1965, 36). The committee's work, while laudable in terms of replacing the pejorative, offers a glimpse of white benevolence, where the process is guided by good intentions but fails to consult African

Canadians or Indigenous who might be directly injured by pejoratives like the n-word or "s-word" that designates "An offensive term for an Indigenous woman" (Younging 2018, n.p.), ("Objectionable Names" 1965, 7). Evidence of Indigenous folks resisting terms like s-word appears in *The Native Voice* that suggests this work of reformation was a long project for Indigenous folks (White Owl 1955). Writing in 2018 Akwesasne Mohawk writer Schilling indicates that some feminist Indigenous scholars want to reclaim the term while in America in 2008 "the U.S. Board on Geographic Names renamed 16 valleys creeks and other sites omitting the name." He notes that these renaming included using the names of indigenous women; for example, the Phoenix S-word Peak was renamed Piestewa Peak: "The peak was renamed to honor Lori Piestewa, a Hopi/Hispanic soldier from Arizona who was killed in Iraq in 2003" (Schilling 2018). This slightly more enlightened approach to renaming in 2008 was not followed in the United States or Canada in the 1960s. The process adopted mirrors that first adopted by the American version of this committee and is guided by the aforementioned Dr. Burrill, the American observer on the Canadian committee, who suggested

> that when names of this nature come up for consideration by the United States Board on Geographic Names, the practice is to make representations to the local residents, stating that when this name was applied there was likely no derogatory implication, but due to changed circumstances it is now considered by many people to be objectionable, and to ask if they would like to propose another of local choosing, not that of the Board, and puts the Board in the position of approving a local decision. (Minutes 1965, 44)

Burrill's use of the passive voice with the phrase "when names come up" obscures the political nature of renaming within the context of the 1960s civil rights movement in the United States and Canada's revision of the Immigration Act in the 1960s, which was more inclusive of people emigrating from outside Northern Europe (Delisle 2010, 12). It carefully balances the interests of the state to provide a corrective against local interests.

Via the province of British Columbia, R.W. Young, chief of its geographic division responsible for surveys and mapping, coordinated efforts with local groups for the Canadian Geographical Names Committee. The method of consultation for this committee involved working with provincial representatives, the local Chambers of Commerce, and the Okanagan Historical Society. No correspondence with local First Nations appears to have occurred. Additionally, nowhere in the extensive record of letters from various community members and organizations is there an acknowledgment of "N–toe" as a placeholder for memorializing the deaths of Chapman and Blair.

This erasure is consistent with the larger movement across the province to regularize names as part of a federal effort to rename "derogatory names" in the 1960s (Minutes 1965, 44). The timing and nature of the alterations of these new toponyms is significant. In May 1961, the adjoining N–Creek and N–Lake in the Kootenays were redubbed "negro," keeping intact the traces of anonymous Black settlement (Negro Lake 2021; Negro Creek 2021). In the cases of the five other British Columbian n-word toponyms changed in the mid-1960s, it would appear, based on the minutes, that Burrill's process for "local choosing" (Minutes 1965, 44) resulted in deriving the replacement names from exalted settlers. Examples of this are Goodeve Creek (Goodeve Creek 2018), Crayke Creek (Crayke Creek 2018), and Mount Jeldeness (Mount Jeldeness 2018), or, as in one case just outside of Vernon in the North Okanagan, the company name, Pine Creek Mining Company (Pine Creek 2018), erases the pejorative and the fact of Black settlement.

With the renaming of N–toe Mountain, the provincial representative R.S. Young is tasked with consulting with white locals. On 5 November 1965, C.W. Nash, the provincial commissioner of the Boy Scouts of Canada, asks the British Columbia Centennial chairman Laurie Wallace if the mountain could be named "Jamboree" to anticipate a large Boy Scout Jamboree that was to occur in the region as part of the 1966 provincial centennial celebrations. A. Butler, representing Summerland's Chamber of Commerce, supports this suggestion in a letter to Young dated 7 January 1966. In a letter to Young dated 15 December 1965, John H. Ratel "feels the name Jamboree Mountain would be a most suitable substitute." On 14 January 1966, Reverend E.S. Fleming, secretary for the OHS, after consulting with members of the society replied to Young, indicating that he disapproved of the toponym "Jamboree"; he suggested that "the name of the

Founder, Lord Baden-Powell, would seem to have more significance. Since most of us in this area do not know the mountain, nor why it was given its present name" (Fleming 1966). As stated in the previous chapter, Young's professed lack of knowledge about the origins of the toponym is peculiar, given that the OHS had been reporting on N–toe in various forms throughout the 1950s. However, Fleming's suggestion that the pejorative be replaced with Lord Baden-Powell is an extreme attempt to whiteout local history. Given Wilson's and Chapman's deaths from exposure, it is ironic that Young would suggest Baden-Powell, given Baden-Powell's legacy as a British imperial figurehead and the leader of a movement designed to give British boys proto-militaristic outdoor survival skills (Voeltz 1997; Bailey 1982).

A letter dated 24 January 1966, from Kathleen Dewdney, secretary of the Penticton Branch of the OHS, to Young makes the case that Nkwala is the preferred name. She cites Sharp's 1958 novel and its fame. Additionally, the letter suggests a link to Indigenous people beyond the novel:

> There were two or three related chiefs at different times in this area whose names were Nkwala. The record of one in the Archives of the Smithsonian Institute says that he wore the medals the King and the Queen had presented to "him." We of the Penticton branch of the Okanagan Historical Society would like to suggest that native names be used wherever possible. Certainly our Indian names are among the most beautiful and distinctive wherever they are used in British Columbia. (Dewdney 1966, 1–2)

These two assertions – one, that Nkwala signals an Indigenous equivalent of royalty, and two, that Okanagan names are aesthetically beautiful – signify an attempt to domesticate the racialized Other for use as part of the local and national sense of being Canadian. The use of the phrase "our Indian names" signals how whites make themselves Indigenous via superficial respect for linguistic heritage (Ahluwalia 2001). The deaths of Wilson and Chapman, as the signified of a place, are to be replaced by a sense of Indigenous peoples removed from colonial history and domesticated for use within an imperial logic guided by the archaeological gaze of the Smithsonian. Dewdney's argument mirrors a modernist fascination with the symbols of Indigenous culture that clearly challenges the logic of assimilation offered in residential schools in the 1960s (Chrisjohn, Young, and Maraun 2006). Glenn Willmott (2005) sees early twentieth-century BC painter Emily Carr and Métis poet Pauline Johnson recoiling from European modernity to embrace "Aboriginal modernity" as a utopian alternative to colonial capitalism. Neither Dewdney's letter suggesting Nkwala nor the work of the federal committee to rename the mountain can be said to embrace this radical sense of using images of Indigenous culture to challenge modernity. Keyes (2011) documents how theatre in the Okanagan and British Columbia in the 1950s was powered by Anglo-white Canadian writing that saw white actors performing in redface as a way of locating authentic Canadian identity. Redface as an appropriative performance tradition is linked to blackface (in the American context), whereby issues of race, gender, and power are expressed in theatrical form for white audiences. In the instance of Dewdney's letter and the federal committee's renaming using Indigenous names furthers the authenticity of building the legacy of a modern nation based on the flattened whitening of safe symbols of Indigenous culture. This act of naming allows Anglo whites to become "Native" by adopting this toponym in a manner that fails to trouble how white privilege came to name, let alone own, the Okanagan. To reiterate, the adoption of Nkwala cannot be framed as a positive sense of tethering toponyms to Indigenous history; given the circumstances of this name swapping, the name seems like a radical move away from discomfort with colonialism – a move that might be dubbed colonial melancholy (see the preceding chapter for a discussion of Gilroy's sense of the colonial mentality being psychically stuck) and that instills an exalted sense of place by incorporating the signifier of the Other. The very real and tragic deaths of Charles Blair and Arthur Chapman, which are obscurely signalled by the toponym N–toe Mountain, are erased to be replaced by a fictional character, Nkwala, who signals a fictive precolonial past informed by modern anthropology. The white fantasy shapeshifts its symbols, but it maintains white hegemony.

NKWALA: EDUCATING SETTLERS

As the winner of the 1958 Governor General's Award for children's fiction, *Nkwala* is enshrined in the BC school curriculum as a way of teaching a universal coming-of-age story set in the pre-European contact period. The BC Department of Education designates the novel a "school text" (Sharp 1985, 406), thus ensuring that young schoolchildren learn about a "safe" precolonial Native experience. Thus, "being Canadian" operates for a few generations of schoolchildren as a way of understanding a particular anthropological version of historical Indigeneity removed from active resistance on the part of contemporary Indigenous people and the harm being done by the Indian residential school system (Chrisjohn, Young, and Maraun 2006). The novel, was originally published in 1958 and republished in 1974. Kevin Barlow's (1970) *Study of the Novel and Related Ideas* and Allan and Dyck's (1982) *Transitions: a Developmental Curriculum for "Growing Up"* both provide materials for teaching the novel, which suggest the novel was widely read in schools in British Columbia. Today, UBC's library system has twelve copies of the novel in its system and just one copy of the 1947 much taught Anglo Canadian classic coming of age novel *Who Has Seen the Wind* by W.O. Mitchell, which suggests *Nkwala* was widely studied in British Columbia schools from the 1960s to the 1980s (*Nkwala* 2021; *Who Has Seen the Wind* 2021). Not surprisingly, both these curriculum manuals for BC teachers use *Nkwala* to teach "universal" literary values for juvenile readers rather than to trouble the narrative's convenient focus on pre-contact Indigenous people.

The novel's plot offers a coming-of-age narrative as a hero's journey. The hero and novel's namesake is a young boy who, to escape a drought, moves with his tribe from what is now Washington State to the south end of Okanagan Lake. As mentioned, it imagines a precolonial contact experience for its characters. Thus the novel operates as a safe text for packaging Indigenous people as "primitives" from the past rather than as a people actively resisting modernity and agitating for rights and land. Textual evidence of resistance to colonialism on the part of First Nations in British Columbia can be found in the archive for the newspaper *Native Voice*, which was operated by the Native Brotherhood of British Columbia. See http://nativevoice.ca for issues of this journal from 1950 to 1955 that offer a "Pan-Indian" perspective on resisting colonialism. Additionally, see "Does This Mean Liquidation of Indian Lands in BC" (1955, 4) for an example of explicit Indigenous resistance to the ongoing colonialism related to land issues (O'Donnell 1985).

The main characters in the narrative are not grappling with colonialism, but again, like the narrative constructed for Chapman and Blair in the naming of N–toe discussed in the previous chapter, Nkwala and his tribe struggle against the climate, which, in this narrative, rather than being too cold is too hot. Nkwala and his tribe, the Spokans, live south of the Okanagan and are driven by drought into the region. In both these narratives, Others – whether Chapman and Blair or the fictional Nkwala – lack the skills to adapt and thus are at the mercy of the harsh Okanagan climate.

Nkwala's narrative can be read postcolonially as a sublimation of the terror of European settlement that would not neatly fit the provincial government's approach to an exalted nation-building curriculum that advances the project of modernity in the hinterland. Freud (1930, 79–80) uses the concept of sublimation to describe how a person might incorporate a negative into a positive as a form of repression that helps to complete the self. I deploy the term "sublimated" here not to suggest that an authentic First Nations Okanagan narrative is embedded as subtext in *Nkwala*; rather, I use it to designate how a colonial melancholic perspective has yet to come to terms with settlement and thus turns this pre-contact narrative to its own use, leaving traces of what Mohanram (2007, 123) might term being "psychically stuck." Thus, in this exalted anthropological narrative, the indigene continues to operate as a "lost" and ambivalent object (ibid.; Goldie 1989). From this perspective – that is, seeing the text as a redface rehearsal by its settler author –the character Nkwala, as a member of the Spokan tribe to the south, travels with his tribe to the Okanagan and offers what could be construed as a critique of European settlement that is sublimated by an anthropological framework in which, as yet, no Europeans exist. Evidence for this reading is presented in the novel's climax, when an Okanagon (American spelling) warrior declares: "The hunting territories of the Okanagan have been invaded ... Death to invaders!" (Sharp 1958, 107). This type of imagined resistance to invasion can only occur within the context of an inter-tribal conflict and cannot possibly be imagined in terms of how contemporary First Nations might resist colonization. In the next paragraph, the possibility for violent resistance to invasion is placated when the Spokan chief Running-Elk declares "invasion" is natural (111). The chief appeals to a universal law of *Amotqen* to imagine a pan-Salish alliance based on reciprocity. Implicitly, the message is that invasion or colonialism in whatever form it takes is a natural process. The dénouement imagines the tribes merging to capture "wicked ones who strike and run and stay hidden" (119) and thus imagines a pan-Okanagan alliance standing against these ghostly invaders. If these ghostly invaders operate as metaphors for white settlement that the Okanagan alliance will resist, then this reading of the novel would certainly not be offered in BC schools since it might trouble the imperative of reading an Indigenous culture as safely belonging to a pre-European contact era. Like the naming and unnaming of N–toe Mountain, the institutionalization of this novel in the curriculum to teach Indigenous culture suggests ruptures in the exalted, melancholy, mid-twentieth-century imperial settler project but not a progressive move towards mourning and addressing the damage done by ongoing colonialism.

This chapter argues that the erasure of N–toe and the creation of Nkwala should not be taken as a linear progression from a bad racist toponym to the more enlightened toponym Nkwala, which reflects white Okanagans' commitment to facing a landscape framed by dispossession. Rather, it contends that these toponymic shifts have occurred to conceal the complexity that informs this landscape of dispossession. These shifts offer examples of the colonial melancholic who cannot ever quite face the lost object of racialized Others that might trouble the ongoing colonial project and white privilege. One might be inclined to read this name swap as a quaint historical footnote regarding Okanagan toponyms, but I am inclined to read such toponymic shifts as indicative of ruptures in the hegemonic project. These ruptures gesture towards an Okanagan that might be able to face and constructively mourn rather than to exalt its colonial heritage.

In May 2015, the provincial government announced it was going to use Nsyilxcən, the language spoken by the Okanagan people, in the renaming of two parks that had been named after settlers (First Voices: Nsyilxcən 2018). Haynes Point Park, named after the British Columbia interior's first judge who, as mentioned in the preceding chapter, was responsible for the dramatic shrinking of Indigenous land reserves in the 1860a (Running Horse and Artz 1999, 16–17), was renamed "sw?iw?s park" (pronounced "swee-yous)" (sw?iw?s 2018). The word "sw?iw?s means place where it is shallow or narrow in the middle of the lake," and refers to the area's traditional use by "members of the Osoyoos Indian band" as a spot to cross Osoyoos Lake (Moore 2015). Coverage of this naming and responses to it online suggest that it threatened settler heritage. Mikey Arcand, one writer who used the online newsgathering website *Castanet* posted: "What about our heritage as settlers? You know the settlers who built what we have today. I'm all for history[,] but it is not mine. Not to my knowledge has the nsyilxc[ə]n tribe [sic] ever erected signs before we got here and erected ours. Let[']s keep our names and our maps and if the [N]syilxc[ə]n want to by all means do so as well but on their dime" (ibid.). His comments reflect a wider discomfort echoed throughout the online forum and in an editorial in the *Kelowna Daily Courier* (2015). This editorial expressed outrage and astonishment that the pro-business Osoyoos band chief Clarence Louis, in addressing the renaming at a Rotary luncheon, would tell the Rotarians to "suck it [the naming] up" and declare Judge John Haynes "a land thief" ("Louis Should've Known Better" 2015). The article does not engage with the chief's accusation about Haynes's status but wonders how Chief Louis, who is well loved by the business community, could make such outrageous statements. The article omits checking Louis's claim against Judge Haynes's record. Louis's claim is corroborated by Ormsby's (1982) biography of the judge, in which she notes: "in 1865 he [Judge Haynes] obtained permission to reduce the size of the two large Indian reserves at the head and foot of Okanagan Lake, thus making meadow and range lands available for white settlement." Clearly, resistance to addressing the issue of land dispossession dredged up by these relatively innocuous renamings is alive and well in the South Okanagan.

Berg's (2011, 20) critique of the contemporary practice of the banal naming of resort communities in the North Okanagan, without controversy, to legitimize land development on land over which the Okanagan Nation Alliance continues to assert claims suggests that this naming operates as a dialectic of "remembering and forgetting." The development in the South Okanagan, involving the province's erasing toponyms associated with exalted settlers and offering Nsyilxcən names, suggests a turning away from this banal naming practice to more productively challenge what, in Chapter 1 of this volume, Cohen and Chambers refer to as the whiteout. Redress for this toponymic whiteout might help not only to address Indigenous and Syilx identity, language, and the issue of land dispossession but also to trace forms of non-British migration to the valley – migration that might memorialize not just Chapman and Blair but Others who came to the Okanagan in its colonial period and who found the region unwelcoming. This might serve as a way of pointing towards a more diverse and inclusive future for the Okanagan.

REFERENCES

Note: as discussed in the introduction to practice cultural safety, I have redacted the use of s-word in the references.

Ahluwalia, Pal. 2001. "When Does a Settler Become a Native? Citizenship and Identity in a Settler Society." *Pretexts: Literary and Cultural Studies* 10 (1): 64–73.

Allan, J., and P. Dyck. 1982. *Transition: A Developmental Curriculum for "Growing Up."* Vancouver: Department of Counselling Psychology, University of British Columbia.

Atwood, B. 2007. "The Australian Patient: Traumatic Pasts and the Work of History." In *The Geography of Meanings: Psychoanalytic Perspectives on Place, Space, Land and Dislocation*, ed. M. Teresa, S. Hook, and S. Akhtar, 63–78. London: International Psychoanalytical Association.

Bailey, Victor. 1982. "Scouting for Empire." *History Today* 32 (6): 5.

Barlow, K. 1970. *Study of the Novel and Related Ideas*. Vancouver: BC Teachers' Federation Lesson Aids Service.

Berg, L. 2011. "Banal Names, Neoliberalism, and Landscapes of Dispossession." In *The Politics of Spatial Inscription*, ed. Derek Alderman and Reuben Rose-Redwood, special issue of *ACME: An International E-Journal for Critical Geographies* 10 (1): 13–22.

Chrisjohn, Roland David, Sherri Lynn Young, and Michael Maraun. 2006. *The Circle Game: Shadows and Substance in the Indian Residential School Experience in Canada*. Penticton: Theytus.

Crayke Creek. 2018. GeoBC. http://apps.gov.bc.ca/pub/bcgnws/names/4820.html.

Delisle, Jennifer Bowering. 2010. "'A Bruise Still Tender': David Chariandy's Soucouyant and Cultural Memory." *ARIEL: A Review of International English Literature* 41 (2): 1.

Dewdney, Kathleen. 1966. Letter to R.W. Young, Chief of BC Geographic Division, on behalf of OHS Penticton Branch, 24 January, Royal British Columbia Archives. BC government file K-1-55.

"Does This Mean Liquidation of Indian Lands in BC?" 1955. *Native Voice* 9 (12): 4. Accessed June 8, 2021. http://nativevoice.ca/wp-content/uploads/2018/07/5512v09n12.pdf. http://nativevoice.bc.ca/wp-content/uploads/2011/08/5512v09n12.pdf.

Eng, D.L., and D. Kazanjian, eds. 2002. "Introduction: Mourning Remains." In *Loss: The Politics of Mourning*. Berkeley: University of California Press. ProQuest ebrary.

First Voices: Nsyilxcən. 2018. https://www.firstvoices.com/explore/FV/sections/Data/nsyilxc%C9%99n/nsyilxc%C9%99n/nsyilxc%C9%99n.

Fleming, Samuel. 1966. Letter to R.W. Young, Chief of BC Geographic Division, on behalf of OHS, Kelowna Branch, Royal British Columbia Archives, 3 February, BC government file K-1–55.

Freud, Sigmund.1930. "Civilisation and Its Discontents." In *Standard Edition of the Complete Psychological Works of Sigmund Freud: The Future of an Illusion, Civilization and Its Discontents, and Other Works*, ed. J. Strachey. 64–149. 24 vols., vol 21. London: Hogarth Press.

Gilroy, Paul. 2005. *Postcolonial Melancholia*. New York: Columbia University Press.

Goldie, Terry. 1989. *Fear and Temptation: The Image of the Indigene in Canadian, Australian, and New Zealand Literatures*. Montreal and Kingston: McGill-Queen's University Press.

Goodeve Creek. 2018. GeoBC. http://apps.gov.bc.ca/pub/bcgnws/names/40607.html.

Kerfoot, H. 1999."Official Recognition of Canada's Aboriginal Toponymy: An Historical Perspective." *Names* 47 (3): 269–79.

Kerfoot, H., and A. Rayburn. 1990. "The Roots and Development of the Canadian Permanent Committee on Geographical Names." *Names* 38 (3): 183–92.

Keyes, Daniel. 2011. "Whites Singing *Red Face* in British Columbia in the 1950s." *Theatre Research in Canada* 32 (1): 30–63.

"Louie Should've Known Better." 2015. *Kelowna Daily Courier*. 3 May. Accessed June 8, 2018. http://www.kelownadailycourier.ca/opinion/article_610faa14-f086–11e4–9189–8b1401cc2180.html.

Minutes. 1965. The Canadian Permanent Committee on Geographical Names, 18 October 1965, files related to the Canadian Permanent Committee on Geographical Names (textual record), Library and Archives Canada, Ottawa, reference R1185–23–2-E. 36.

Mohanram, R. 2007. *Imperial White: Race, Diaspora, and the British Empire*. Minneapolis: University of Minnesota Press.

Monmonier, M.S. 2006. *From S-word Tit to Whorehouse Meadow: How Maps Name, Claim, and Inflame*. Chicago: University of Chicago Press.

Moore, Wayne. 2015. "Parks Take Native Names." *Castanet*. 22 May. http://www.castanet.net/news/Penticton/140517/Parks-take-native-names.

Mount Jeldenss. GeoBC. 2018. http://apps.gov.bc.ca/pub/bcgnws/names/10081.html.

Mount Nkwala. 2018 GeoBC. http://apps.gov.bc.ca/pub/bcgnws/names/18642.html.

Negro Creek. 2021. *BC Geographical Names*. Accessed June 8. https://apps.gov.bc.ca/pub/bcgnws/names/13476.html.

Negro Lake. 2021. GeoBC. Accessed June 7, 2021. http://archive.ilmb.gov.bc.ca/bcgn-bin/bcg10?name=13479.

"Nkwala by Edith Lambert Sharp; with Illustrations by William Winter." 2021. *UBC Library*. Accessed June 8. https://webcat.library.ubc.ca/vwebv/holdingsInfo?bibId=88923

"'Objectionable Names' Facing Extinction." 1965. *Prince George Citizen*, 21 October, 7.

O'Donnell, J.P. 1985. "The Native Brotherhood of British Columbia 1931–1950: A New Phase in Native Political Organization." MA thesis, University of British Columbia. Accessed June 7, 2021. http://circle.ubc.ca/handle/2429/25501.

Ormsby, M.A. 1982. "Haynes, John Carmichael." *Dictionary of Canadian Biography*. Vol. 11 (1880–90). Accessed June 7, 2015. http://www.biographi.ca/en/bio.php?id_nbr=5573.

Pine Creek. 2018. GeoBC. http://apps.gov.bc.ca/pub/bcgnws/names/16816.html.

Running Horse, A.E., and A. Artz. 1999. *Okanagan Nation Fisheries Commission Dam Research*. Okanagan Fisheries Commission. Vernon, BC: Summit Environmental Consulting. Accessed June 7, 2021. https://www.obwb.ca/obwrid/docs/019_1999_Ok_Nation_Fisheries_Commission_Dam.pdf.

Sharp, E.L. 1958. *Nkwala*. Illustrator William Winter. Boston: Little Brown and Company.

–. 1985. "Biography." In *Writers of the Okanagan Mainline*. Kelowna: Okanagan Mainline Senior Writers and Publishers' Association, 406–8.

Schilling, Vincent. 2018. "The Word S-word: Offensive or Not?" *Indian Country Today*. Sept. 13. Accessed June 9, 2021. https://indiancountrytoday.com/archive/the-word-squaw-offensive-or-not.

sw?iw?s Provincial Park (Haynes Point). 2018. http://www.env.gov.bc.ca/bcparks/explore/parkpgs/swiws/.

White Owl, Big.1955. "Those Reprehensible and Derogatory Terms." *The Native Voice* 4. Accessed June 7, 2021. 9 (12): 4. http://nativevoice.ca/wp-content/uploads/2018/07/5512v09n12.pdf.

"Who Has Seen the Wind /by W.O. Mitchell." 2021. UBC Library. Accessed June 8. https://webcat.library.ubc.ca/vwebv/holdingsInfo?searchId=33938&recCount=100&recPointer=2&bibId=3698311.

Willmott G. 2005. "Modernism and Aboriginal Modernity: The Appropriation of Products of West Coast Native Heritage as National Goods." *Essays in Canada* 83: 75–139.

Voeltz, R.A. 1997. "Reflections on Baden-Powell, the British Boy Scouts and Girl Guides, Racism, Militarism, and Feminism." *Weber: The Contemporary West* 14 (2). Accessed July 7, 2012. https://www.weber.edu/weberjournal/Journal_Archives/Archive_B/Vol_14_2/RVoeltzEss.html.

Younging, Greg. 2018. *Elements of Indigenous Style: A Guide for Writing by and about Indigenous Peoples*. E-book. Edmonton, Brush Press.

CHAPTER 4

THE RHETORIC OF ABSENCE

Susan Allison's Racial Melancholia

Janet MacArthur

Susan Moir Allison (1845–1937) was a British settler, born in Ceylon (Sri Lanka since 1972) and educated in England, who immigrated to the Colony of British Columbia in 1860. In 1868, she married John Fall Allison (1825–97), originally from Yorkshire, and moved with him to his ranch and trading post called "Allison's" near present-day Princeton, British Columbia. Given her demanding life as a stock raiser, storekeeper, and parent of fourteen children, she was a prolific writer. Allison's published and unpublished work is replete with individualized and sympathetic accounts of Indigenous people, their epistemology and lifeways, and direct (in unpublished work) and subtextual (in published material) criticism of white policy and practice. Allison published her recollections and other newspaper articles, essays in the *Okanagan Historical Society* and a British journal, and two long narrative poems as a book titled *In-Cow-Mas-Ket*. Here I read the ambivalences and ambiguities that I locate in her published writing as evidence of what has been called "settler melancholy" (Sugars 2006, 693; Turner 1999, 23), an impossible attempt to come to terms with the colonial legacy, in particular her secondary witnessing of trauma endured by the Similkameen and Okanagan people. My work therefore participates in postcolonial studies of the "unsettled" (Carter et al. 2005; Lawson 1995, 2000; Slemon 1990) position of the "invader-settler" (Brydon 1995, para.4).

John Fall Allison "pre-empted" uncultivated Crown land in the Similkameen River area (near what is now Princeton), first arriving there in

1860 after heading a prospecting and trailblazing expedition commissioned by Governor James Douglas. The Allisons ranched here and in the area of West Kelowna near Lake Okanagan (1873–80) for many decades. Susan Allison wrote her memoirs of these times while in her eighties in Depression-era Vancouver, where she had retired from Princeton in 1926. These recollections, as she called them, initially appeared as a series of Vancouver *Province* newspaper articles in the early 1930s. They were later published as an edited book: *A Pioneer Gentlewoman in British Columbia: The Recollections of Susan Allison* (Ormsby 1976). In this work, Allison begins her account of her move to the interior in 1868 – where she had very little white community – with an exuberant tribute to her life there: "Then began my camping days and the wild, free life I ever loved till age and infirmity put an end to it" (21). Literal depictions of "camping days" in the recollections are always associated with portraits of her Syilx "friends" (a term she often uses), observations of their customs, and with the narratives they shared with her.

From the 1860s on, many aspects of her work reveal her "transculturation" (Pratt 1992, 8) and "empathic unsettlement" (LaCapra 1998, 699) in a "contact zone" (Pratt 1992, 4), something unusual for a white woman. She developed "epistemological humility" (Kelm and Townsend 2006, 6) – or a decentring of white values – in her close contact with Indigenous people in the early settlement period in the interior (ca. 1850s-80s). Historian Robin Fisher (1977, 49) identifies 1849 to 1858 as the years of transition on Vancouver Island, in the Lower Mainland, and in parts of the interior, when the fur trade was displaced by mining and settler colonization. Widespread white settlement did not occur in the Syilx traditional territories until later. In her unpublished introduction (ca. late 1890s) and in her long poems published as *In-Cow-Mas-Ket* (1900), Allison identifies what I call the early period as the "sixties, seventies, and eighties" before the Similkameen people became "a downtrodden remnant." Her ability to speak Chinook (Ormsby 1976, xxx) and her relationships with Indigenous people placed her in what Homi K. Bhabha (1983, 204) famously names the "in-between" space of ambivalence for the colonial subject. Thus, her writing expresses the "repertoire of conflictual positions that constitute the subject in colonial discourse."

In unpublished writing, she is less ambivalent, expressing negative conceptions of the Eurocentrism of her time, based as it was on biologist racism and notions of white supremacy that install, encourage, and practise "segregation, white colonialism, moral superiority, assimilation" (Baldwin 2009, 429). Rattansi (2007, 31) asserts that biologist racism is based on nineteenth-century race science (among other discourses), which divided "humankind into distinct and permanent races"; it constructed a racial hierarchy with "whites at the top and blacks at the bottom." Thus "white" is sometimes used negatively in Allison's later writing (1890s–1930s), and she loses faith in the racial, gendered, and settler contracts endorsed by so many white British Columbians.

Since contact, what "white" signifies to white people in British Columbia has undergone some shifts in meaning:

> Until recent decades BC Whites openly identified themselves as "Whites" or "white people." The fourteen early treaties, for example, state that the purchased Indian lands are to become the "property of White people forever." Until the late 1940s Whites in the province were eager to distinguish themselves from non-whites and to protect white political interests, as they did in denying Indian claims, curbing Asian immigration, and prohibiting non-white groups from voting. (Tennant 1990, xi)

With the emergence of Enlightenment humanism and European race theories in modernity, whiteness became universalized as the good, the civil, the fully human, and so on (Coleman 2001, 13–16). Since the end of the Second World War, this notion of "whiteness" has been decentred. In recent studies of "race," "white" has accrued an ethnic specificity and a racial profile (long recognized by many of those defined as non-white) and is no longer the racially invisible signifier of full human essence. Discussions of post-Enlightenment whiteness in the West frame it as a value system linked with capitalism (Garner 2007, 14) and commodification; as constituted through propertied investment (Lipsitz as cited by Wiegman 1999, 116) and "the expectation or actuality of privilege" (Wiegman 1999, 134); and as geographically sited as sovereign over and defined by various "ethnoscapes" (Baldwin 2009, passim). Allison's writing indicates a growing ambivalence about and sometimes outright rejection of many features of this sovereign whiteness. Her developing awareness of the bad faith of the assimilative projects of her time and of the traumatic outcomes of a more strictly enforced Racial Contract (Mills 1997, passim) explains her shifting perspective. Making visible the racialization underlying long-standing iterations of the exalted moral and political concept of the social contract, Charles Mills (11) identifies the European Racial Contract instituted from the early modern period onward as one that designated certain people as "white" and others as "non-white," the latter bequeathed "a different and inferior moral status" that justified the exploitation of their "bodies, lands, and resources" and denied them "equal socioeconomic opportunities."

Incorporating Mills's work on the Racial Contract and extending her own earlier work on sexuality and gender in *The Sexual Contract*, Carole Pateman (2007b, 36) traces the foundations of what she calls the Settler Contract based on the European concept of terra nullius. "New World" lands were perceived as empty – as wilderness or wasteland in the "state of nature," not put to use, not owned, "unhusbanded," and therefore not civilized. She elaborates:

> Defenders of colonization in North America, including political theorists, frequently invoked two senses of *terra nullius*: first, they claimed that the lands were uncultivated wilderness, and thus were open to appropriation by virtue of what I shall call the *right of husbandry*; second, they argued that the inhabitants had no recognizable form of sovereign government. In short, North America was a state of nature. (36)

Both the Racial and Settler Contracts pivot on the perception of Indigenous people as animalized creatures without full human status and of their social organization and relation to the land as inadequate for any claim to sovereignty over it (or themselves). In other words, they are not en*titled* to (civil) subject status or land. Pateman also calls attention to the intersections of the Racial and Settler Contracts with patriarchal conceptions of gender (2007a, 154). Until recent decades, the roles of gender and sexuality were not central to mainstream accounts of the colonial project in Canada and elsewhere. Allison's written record, however, subtly reveals her growing awareness of how European notions of racial, gendered, and settler prerogatives create a traumatic impact on the lives of Indigenous men and women. The perspectives of many Canadians on race, ethnicity, land, and sovereignty were (and to some extent still are) shaped at the convergences of Western ideologies that structure concepts of race, gender difference, and land entitlement.

Susan Allison's experience in the early settlement years (from 1860 to the 1880s) was constructed by less oppressive contracts in British Columbia compared to what came later. Many white men had "country," or Indigenous, wives. Racial social organization was less rigidly demarcated and Indigenous mobility less restricted than it was later. For example, the destruction of wildlife and fisheries; the passage of the panoptical Indian Act, 1876, which "indelibly ordered how Native [and white] people think of things 'Indian'" (Lawrence 2003, 4); and encroachment upon and reduction of original reserve lands had a dramatic impact on Syilx quality of life. Moreover the Allison genealogy seems to affirm the conclusion that "colonies, as a spate of recent critical social histories have so eloquently attested, were hybrid, homespun places that constantly resisted efforts to render them compatible with ideals of racial hierarchy and separation" (Perry 2001, 118). For example, John Fall Allison fathered three children – Lily (1863–1943), Albert (Bertie) (1865–1919), and Charles (Charlie) (1868–1913) – with his Similkameen first wife Nora Yacumtecum before he married Susan. Lily is mentioned as part of the household many times in Susan's memoir, although she is not acknowledged as John's daughter. Moreover, Edgar Moir ("Ed") Allison (1869–1943) and Robert Wilfred ("Will") Allison (1871–1926), two of Susan's fourteen biological children, were eventually married to Indigenous women with whom they had children. At the Allison family reunion in 1999, the commentary on a slide show asserts these dates: "The early phase of his life with Nora Baptiste brought about three children; Lilly, Bertie, and Charley. All were born between 1863 or [sic] 1868. It was believed that Nora returned to the Chopaka Reserve. (BERNIE ALLISON_JEAN BAMAN [sic])" (Meldrum 1999).

An anxious letter written to her daughter Louisa Johnston (1874–1955) on 18 February 1930 seems to indicate that contractual shifts deeply affected family relations. Here Allison expresses concern about Will's nineteen-year-old daughter Mary:

> Louisa, I appreciate your goodness to Wills [sic] children – their [white] cousins who have had so much better chances and have done nothing with them, have the gaul [sic] to look down on *breeds* as they call them who have made the most of nothing. Wills [sic] children are like himself always dear to me – even if I can't help them as I wish to – I promised Will and Henry [Will's eldest son, born 1896] to do whatever I could for Mary [born 1913] and that seems to be nothing. I will write to her – I can do that any way [sic] ... Poor you must feel glad that your children are all settled down ... I think that I can understand my elder children better than the younger – Ed and Will, BJ, Rose, and You – seem to belong to another generation. (Allison 1930–33)

These elder children were all born between 1869 and 1875 and were racialized in closer association with Indigenous people and in a sparser white community than were their younger siblings.

Shifts in her own thinking are also implied in other places. The following passage from an unpublished "sketch" written in the 1870s conveys her sanguine perspective on race relations in the interior in her "camping days": "The Indians of British Columbia unlike their confreres in Oregon and interior Washington Territory and like the [sic] brethren the flat heads [sic] of the coast are as a rule peaceful and law abiding, and the reason is they have ever been justly and humanely treated both by the settlers and the various Governments that have existed in the country since the first great immigration of white men in -58-" (Allison 1870s). However, in her sequence of three long poems about the lives of two Similkameen chiefs whom she knew – "In-Cow-Mas-Ket [part one]," "In-Cow-Mas-Ket, second part," and "Quin-is-coe" – written in the 1890s, two of which were published in 1900, she indicts the "white man." In the narrative, white settlement is depicted as a catastrophe for the Similkameen, who experience community dissension and dissolution as a result of it. "Quin-is-coe" is a tribute to the continuing presence and power of Syilx religion. It respectfully details a Syilx exhumation rite, and its revenant chief chastises his people for straying. These poems were likely an attempt to honour the ancestors of her Indigenous grandchildren and to leave an account of "vanishing" Indigenous people and their life ways. This latter motive was shared with many other white people of her time, who subscribed to the "dominant ethnographic myth of [the] cultural demise of indigenous people" (Wickwire 2006, 299).

A variety of motives for writing emerge in Allison's introduction to these long poems. Most importantly, the piece reflects epistemological humility and empathic unsettlement from her secondary witnessing of the trauma endured by the Similkameen over thirty years or so. This introduction was cut from the published *In-Cow-Mas-Ket* (1900), probably for fear of alienating the white reader:

> This poem must be taken as part of my recollections, for it is an account of the lives, manners, and customs of the Similkameen Indians as I knew them in the sixties, seventies, and eighties, while they were still a people – I may say a passing people. Now they are nearly gone – just a down trodden remnant whose land is coveted and whose end is eagerly awaited for by most of their white neighbours.
>
> The first part shows them a free people – then they were in the majority; the second part, when they were coming under the influence of religion and civilization. They originally had their own beautiful religious ideas and their own manners and customs, which perhaps were not so beautiful from the white man's point of view, but they had no bestial sots, no maddening spirits. The white man has much to be ashamed of in his treatment of the rightful owners of the land. (Introduction to *In-Cow-Mas-Ket* n.d.)

This melancholic and unsettled piece registers the impact of personal and cultural trauma on someone who was a secondary witness to it, and such phenomena have been widely explored in academic and clinical studies over the last century or so. Important studies of cultural trauma by people such as Alexander and Margarete Mitscherlich (1967) on the German (FDR) Second World War generation's "inability to mourn"; Dominick LaCapra's (1998) multidirectional trauma studies founded on his work on the Holocaust; and Paul Gilroy's (2004, 99) identification of "postimperial melancholia" in contemporary Britain have all adapted some aspects of Sigmund Freud's (1917) distinction between mourning and melancholia, the latter defined as an incomplete, arrested, and prolonged mourning process. Instead of the satisfactory working through of loss, which Freud defines as a completed mourning process, melancholia is characterized by psychic "haunting" manifested in displacement, cathecting, and the acting out of conflicted and repressed psychic content. Stephen Slemon (1995, 110) notes that even settler writers whose work rejects colonialism's discourses have "always been complicit in colonialism's territorial appropriation of land, and voice, and agency, and this has been their inescapable condition even at those moments when they have promulgated their most strident and most spectacular gestures of post-colonial resistance." I argue that the settler's "ambivalence of emplacement" resulting in these "radically *compromised* literatures" (ibid.) is a sign of melancholia. Ambivalence and ambiguity in Allison's writing are symptomatic of the "melancholy condition of the settler" (Turner 1999, 23) as she struggles to find what Alan Lawson (1995, 168) calls a "usable past" (168).

Some responses to traumatic loss – individual or cultural – have been identified as forms of working through that can be put into the service of the attempt to establish a better present and future, such as confessional acts ("bearing witness"), reconciliatory or restitutional work, and activist work. While such mourning practices can never completely "cure" or transcend the wounds of trauma and of being a secondary witness of trauma, they can help embody the ghosts of the past and engage them in constructing the foundations of a better future. But when loss "is converted into (or encrypted in an indiscriminately generalized rhetoric of) absence, one faces the impasse of endless melancholy, impossible mourning, and interminable aporia in which any process of working through the past and its historical losses is foreclosed or prematurely aborted" (La Capra 1999, 698). Thus the gaps and omissions in Allison's published writing, which become evident when they are juxtaposed with unpublished accounts of her concerns about the treatment of Indigenous people and her Indigenous family members, constitute a (partial) foreclosure of the "urge to witness, to awaken those who sleep, and to reawaken them with a message of extremity" (Chambers 2009, x). Thus loss remains a haunting or melancholic absence because of some of the ways in which Allison evades responsibility for, does not/cannot understand, or avoids consciously acknowledging herself as an invader-settler. Hence what she is able to publish and what forms her historical discourse can take are limited, and loss is not converted into any significant participation in some form of "working through." The nostalgia for the "wild, free life" of the early settler period, then, is to some extent a consolatory fantasy (or white "redemption fantas[y]" [Thompson 2003, 17]) – an attempt to enable her to avoid confronting the fact of a white supremacist colonial motivation and its contracts, even in the early days, to disaffiliate herself from the power relations consolidated as BC whiteness and from the reality of invasion-settlement and its terrors. Like many white Canadians today, Allison uses strategies to avoid recognizing that "whiteness is a source of terror" (Garner 2007, 7) and that one is "part of the privileged structure regardless of what [one's] personal opinion may be and wherever [one lies] in the social hierarchy."

In the long unpublished passage cited above, she disaffiliates from "the white man" and expresses disaffection with white modernity. Disaffiliation is a common white strategy used to preserve the "safety, blamelessness, and certainty" that have come to be identified as features of white liberal discourse (to this day) on racial oppression (Thompson 2003, 8). Disaffiliation involves distancing oneself from those members of one's cohort whom one identifies as the perpetrators of terror and oppression from which one has nonetheless derived benefit, and trying to create impermeable boundaries between oneself and those easily identified as "perpetrators" of racism. However, recent studies have provided many compelling analyses of how white disaffiliation (Wiegman 1999; Baldwin 2009) often does little to decentre what Jacques Derrida has called the "white mythology" (Young 1990, 38) of Western metaphysics, to decentre whiteness from political and social agendas, or to significantly address oppression and mitigate the terms of oppressive contracts.

Moreover, the disaffiliation evident not only in the introduction to *In-Cow-Mas-Ket* but also in the decision not to publish it is likely related to audience considerations. Long-standing gendered constructions of women's writing as inferior, too affective and personal, and, therefore, not credible limit Allison's role as a public memoirist and may explain the decision to exclude this emotional passage. In addition, it was only her extraordinary experience as a first-wave "pioneer" that created a public readership for her, compelling her to celebrate and support the white and masculinist colonial identity from which she disaffiliates. Re-membering the past is therefore a struggle to bear secondary witness to white terrorism and its traumatic impact while exalting whiteness and refusing to become an overt "race traitor." The notion of the race traitor has been developed by Noel Ignatiev and John Garvey (1996, 10), who suggest that "the existence of the white race depends on the willingness of those assigned to it to place their racial interests above class, gender, or any other interests they hold. The defection of enough of its members to make it unreliable as a determinant of behaviour will set off tremors that will lead to its collapse." Such defection would permit a person defined as white to become a "race traitor." Susan Allison chose not to defect.

It is important to contextualize Allison's dilemma. There would have been little support from many family members or from the white community for public declarations of the cost of BC whiteness and settler colonialism to Indigenous people, and she would have lost the social capital accruing to the Allisons and their descendants as a "pioneer" family. Analyzing the cultural history of settlement whiteness in Canada, Daniel Coleman (2006, 5) uses the term "white civility" to describe the white Canadian normativity that was established in regions of English Canada where whiteness was conflated with civility, specifically with a "British model of civility." White civility in Canada has informed much of what has been constructed as BC history. Ironically, Allison's writing often betrays her misgivings about the white civility of which she has become a nostalgic symbol in BC studies, where she has been celebrated by Margaret A. Ormsby, a founding member of the Okanagan Historical Society, and others as the exemplary "pioneer gentlewoman."

Public expression of her anxiety and anger about the decline of her Indigenous family and friends in the later settlement period was problematic because Allison could not directly criticize the white British Columbians who were her primary reading public, nor could she forthrightly criticize the major brokers of the racial/gendered/settler contracts as they had developed in the province after extensive white settlement. Many of Susan Allison's relatives and friends of long-standing were of the "pioneer" Anglo-Celtic middle class who, by the time she was writing her memoirs, had been (or were to become) provincially and/or nationally prominent and powerful.

When Susan Allison, her sister Jane (who married Edgar Dewdney who became lieutenant-governor of the North-West Territories), her mother, and her stepfather arrived in the Lower Mainland in 1860, they were immediately welcomed by middle-class British professionals, administrators, and their families. Her recollections of her first eight years in British Columbia in the 1860s provide many reminiscences of her friendships with people whose names have "passed into provincial history" (Allison 1976, 19). Hence, the intersections of ethnicity, gender, race, kinship, and class in the formation of her identity produced many conflicting allegiances. This resulted in many silences, gaps, and indeterminacies in her writing that are symptomatic of an unsettled liminal position and ambivalence. Her writing is an attempt to come to terms with the loss of something that she encodes as "wild" and "free," which appears to be related to her conception of benign race relations and the well-being of the Syilx in the earlier as compared to the later settler period. The impossible task of publicly maintaining class solidarity and endorsing various contracts – after her witnessing of the destruction of the "passing people" she met in the 1860s – produces what David L. Eng and Shinhee Han (2000, 667) call "racial melancholia." They use this term to describe the failure of contemporary Asian Americans to resolve "conflicts and ambivalences" (670) stemming from the "everyday conflicts and struggles with experiences of immigration, assimilation, and racialization" (669) that result in the loss of whiteness as an ideal towards which they can strive. I locate a similar psychic struggle in Allison's work and see it as a constituent part of her melancholia.

One representation of this melancholia is Allsion's nostalgic reconstruction of Indigenous people and practice in the early days of settlement. Such depictions were a common symptom of white melancholia. The passage below expresses her elegiac respect for Indigenous practices as she recollects watching Similkameen gatherings in the 1870s:

> I had lots of fun watching Indian debates and doctors from my log at the fence ... Well, I watched the doctors and came to the conclusion that they used a force or power that we know little of. You may call it animal magnetism, telepathy, or give it any name, but it was something very real.
>
> I am afraid I have been mooning over my memories. I put in a good time one way and another in the early 70's. (Allison 1976, 39–40)

This is typical of her elliptical, unelaborated published writing about Indigenous people. Abrupt transitions, truncations of anecdotes, reluctance to elaborate, and the unpublished attempts to bear witness encode a repression of the urge to witness. Characteristically, in the paragraph that follows this confession of a melancholy "mooning" over the past, there is an abrupt transition to a completely different topic and a return to the progressivist narrative of the "pioneer" memoir.

From time to time, Allison (1976, 28) also extols Indigenous stoicism and gives non-judgemental accounts of the polygamous organization and reorganization of Similkameen families (Allison 1976, 39, 56). Furthermore, she takes the side of Indigenous people, for example, of the "wild" mixed-race McLean brothers, whom she depicts as having been driven to their infamous crime spree by the dishonouring of their sister Annie by prominent white official John Andrew Mara (1840–1920). Allan, Charles, and Archibald McLean – the "wild McLean boys" – were the sons of a white Hudson's Bay Company chief trader and his Indigenous wife Sophie Grant. Mara was a powerful and wealthy Kamloops politician and businessman. In the memoir, Allison recounts how one of the brothers, pursued by the authorities, came by her Sunny Side (West Kelowna) ranch in the late 1870s with his sister but was dissuaded by an Okanagan ranch hand from threatening her household. Allison (1976, 47) states: "His sister, a fair girl wearing a sunbonnet, passed riding a side saddle and carrying an infant. Poor girl, she was going to her mother's people! The Indians are good to those of kin to them." Here the writing seems to register Allison's awareness of how the BC racial and gender contracts, even in the "camping days" of the 1870s, constructed the abject position of a mixed-race woman like Annie McLean as no longer even on the margins of white civility. It also suggests Allison's awareness of how white notions of chastity worked to dehumanize Indigenous women and to exclude them from legitimate and "respectable" subject positions (Perry 2001, 48–56).

Allison also calls attention to the gendered contact zone in her commemorative tribute to an unnamed woman who, according to some of Allison's descendants, is Nora Yacumtecum. Just after Allison arrived in the interior:

> I had a visit from an Indian woman, a niece of Quinisco, the "Bear Hunter" and Chief of the Chu-chu-ewa Tribe. She was dressed for the

> occasion, of course, in mid-Victorian style, a Balmoral petticoat [woollen petticoat showing beneath a longer dress], red and gray, a man's stiff starched white shirt as a blouse, stiff high collar, earrings an inch long, and brass bracelets! I did not know my visitor seemed to think she ought to sit upright in her chair and fix her eyes on the opposite wall. I think "Cla-hi-ya" [a Chinook greeting] was the only word she spoke. I was not used to Indians then and knew very little Chinook. I felt very glad when her visit was over. I know now that I should have offered her a cigar and a cup of tea. (Allison 1976, 23–24)

Disclosure of a mixed-race background could jeopardize the treaty status and entitlements of Indigenous women and their descendants: "until 1985, the Indian Act removed the Indian status of all Native women who married individuals without Indian status (including non-status Canadian Indians and American Indians, as well as white men" (Lawrence 2003, 8). As settlement cultures grew, white men maintaining their marriages with Indigenous women risked social ostracism and "deracination" (Perry 2001, 1). Given the severe penalties for disclosing the existence of a mixed-race union or white paternity, Allison's decision to depict Nora at all invites speculation, given that the Indigenous wife was widely inveighed against in British Columbia as an affront to the civil and religious notion of (Christian) sacramental, life-long, monogamous marriage. Perhaps Allison's negotiation of various audiences, two in particular – white Vancouverites at their Sunday papers versus an "insider" white and/or Indigenous readership who knew the contact history between the Syilx and the Allisons – provides a clue. For her (white) newspaper audience, Allison provides an account of Nora's hybrid dress and of the culture shock experienced by the civil subject upon first contact with an Indigenous person as representing a threat to the creation of a white ethnoscape. On the other hand, insiders would likely find the passage a particularly amusing account of unsettlement in a new domestic contact zone but perhaps not view Nora as the interloper. Allison may also have wanted to leave a trace of what Jean Barman (1996, 8–20) terms the "lost history" of the "first families" (post-contact) of the southern interior. This occluded history has only recently been admitted to in popular and academic histories. In a slide presentation at an Allison family reunion in 1999 attended for the first time by white and Indigenous descendants, the presenter noted that John Fall Allison "left Hope on July 9th, 1860 a journey that would have consequences for all of us. On this trip he probably met Nora Baptiste [Yacumtecum] who was the leader of the trail. It is believed Nora was responsible for showing [him] the Hope-Skagit-Snass route" (Meldrum 1999, 2), now Allison Pass on Highway 3. Perhaps Nora's foundational role in establishing John Fall Allison's reputation as a "trailblazer" motivated this depiction. To this day, John Fall's fame (and Susan's, for that matter) for being among the first whites in the Similkameen and the Okanagan is still structured by the concept of terra nullius. Perhaps Susan Allison's depiction of Nora was meant to intervene in and unsettle this concept of an "imperial white male realm of rational economic exploitation" (Keyes 2011, 40). Allison is also careful to document Nora's genealogical pedigree (perhaps for the Indigenous grandchildren of both women) as a relation of Quinisco. Quinisco was also the grandfather of her son Will's ten children. Like many passages in the memoir, Nora's portrait is abruptly placed in the narrative without introduction and without any further elaboration.

Susan Allison also gives careful treatment in the memoir to what she knows about "Naaitka" (a phonetic approximation of the Syilx word) or what the Vernon Rotary and the Vernon Board of Trade dubbed "Ogopogo" in 1926 (Ormsby 1976, 109) in their appropriation of this mythical figure for tourism in the Okanagan Valley. In two essays respectively titled "The Monster" and "What I Know of Ogopogo," both, to my knowledge, unpublished, she gives more detailed accounts of it. These pieces confirm that she does not disclose all that she knows about Naaitka in her published recollections. All she says of Naaitka there is that her Indigenous friend, the packer Yacumtecum (Nora's brother), told her "yarns" about it when she first travelled to the interior: "The Indians did not call him that [Ogopogo] but spoke as if it were some supernatural entity and pointed out where it lived on an island in Okanagan Lake as we passed the spot. My husband always laughed at the Indian yarns but I did not, for I thought that there must be foundation for what they said. They told me more than they told most white people" (Allison 1976, 40–41). In the unpublished "What I Know of Ogopogo," she discloses more:

> I first heard of it by the camp fires on my first trip to the Similkameen and the Indians, I could see, were sincere in the awe with which they told their stories; I gathered from those stories that the creature was an amphibian. My husband told me the Whites spoke of it as "The Monster," but he said that none of the white men had seen it and though the Indians seemed terrified, he did not believe in it.
>
> Well, I listened to the stories of the Indians with an open mind – (and being Highland Scottish on my fathers [sic] side,) I partially believed in the monster. (Allison n.d., n.p.)

In the unpublished account, "The Monster," she bears witness to having seen the creature:

> The idea [that the creature was connected with strong winds] was certainly confirmed by the yarns told by Johnny McDougal as we sat round our camp fire on the first night of our arrival at Sunny Side. Perhaps I should not use the word yarns – that implies doubt, and who could doubt the truth of any story of Ogopogo, not I, for I saw the creature long years after. (Allison n.d., n.p.)

In a later paragraph in "The Monster," she says of her own sighting:

> It was not a bit like the serpent, since seen by others, but it might have been a big Saurian [amphibious "prehistoric" creature] and I am convinced it was one, however when my husband and boy returned from the [Okanagan] Mission, I told them what I had seen, they laughed at me and said that a fellow had come to the Mission and reported seeing the same thing from the other side of the lake, but they thought he had been drinking. The man's name was Smitheran, some one may still remember his story and I can bear witness to its truth. (Allison n.d., n.p.)

Fear of ridicule or accusations of "hysteria," or perhaps circumspection about providing another Ogopogo story for white cultural appropriation, may explain her decision not to discuss this sighting in her published memoir. More importantly, Allison's repeated references to the differences among white, Chinook, and Indigenous nomenclatures in all of her accounts; to Indigenous reverence for the creature; and to its being "not a bit like the [diabolical?] serpent" since seen by other whites provide strong evidence of transculturation. In "What I Know of Ogopogo," Allison states that the Syilx used the Chinook name when they spoke to her of it. She says that they referred to it as "'*Ook-ook mis-achie coupa lake*' (the wicked one in the lake) or as the '*hyas-hyas gust scaca cupa lake*' meaning the 'huge animal in the lake.' This creature they seemed to dread and spoke of it with lowered voices" (Allison n.d., n.p.). It is noteworthy that they did not use the Syilx name for it when they spoke of it to her and that she does not provide the Syilx name for it in the published memoir. Perhaps she understood Syilx views of language. Syilx Elder Jeannette Armstrong (1998, 176) has commented many times on the unity of land and language and living things in her culture as being central to Syilx language and epistemology:

> It is this *N'silxchn* [this unity] which embraces me and permeates my experience of the Okanagan land and is a constant voice within me that yearns for human speech. I am claimed and owned by this land, this Okanagan. Voices that move within as my experience of existence do not awaken as words. Instead they move within as the colours, patterns, and movements of a beautiful, kind Okanagan landscape. They are the Grandmother voices which speak ... The English term *grandmother* as a human experience is closest in meaning to the term *Tmixw* in Okanagan, meaning something like loving-ancestor-land-spirit.

In contrast to binary (subject/object) thinking in English, which underwrites the notion of signifier/signified, *N'silxchn*, the Okanagan language, does not signify white binary and hierarchical distinctions among land, people, animals, and so on. "Ogopogo" thus fixes, concretizes, and isolates while it appropriates, fragments, and degrades – put in Western terms, it is a kind of iconoclasm that threatens much more than Naaitka, as Allison's various discussions of it seem to imply.

As the above appeal to her "Highland Scottish" roots in conveying why she "partially believed" in the reality of Naaitka suggests, Allison attempts to explain her "Indigenized" perspective as a product of Celtic canniness, portrayed as an essentialized blood quantum at various places in her writing. White people often attempt to form alliances with Indigenous people and perspectives by identifying with someone or something from their personal or ancestral history whom they identify as having provided insight into First Nations people or the Indigeneity of the land itself. For a contemporary example, see Andrew Baldwin's (2009, 438) discussion of Canadian documentaries starring mostly white Canadian celebrities in which white environmentalism and Aboriginality are represented as "moral equivalents" in an act of white liberalism that ignores vast differences between white environmentalists and Indigenous people in terms of mobility, power, and other forms of privilege. For Allison, this is partly a strategy of representing her early settlement life as a form of "soft colonization" (Keyes 2011, 42), which thus creates an "alibi" (32) for her family's participation in white settlement by creating an Indigenized identity for them. For example, a convenient alibi still used by some white Canadians is the appeal to the sad diasporic history of their "prewhite ethnic" Scots and Irish ancestors – early victims of English racism and the English colonial enterprise – to deflect the gaze of racialized immigrant communities and Indigenous people who would hold them as responsible as any other white colonizer for the installation of white supremacy and the maintenance of white entitlement in Canada (Wiegman 1999, 136). This "alibi" is achieved by overlooking the ease with which many of these settlers and their descendants quickly *chose* whiteness and claimed a place within Canadian white civility. Critiquing the romance narratives that have developed around the Scottish experience in Canada, Daniel Coleman (2006, 5) indicates that the "Scots were the primary inventors of English Canada." He adds: "Scots, historically, were the primary inventors and promoters of the category of Britishness that is the conceptual foundation of the Canadian idea of civility" (6). In Allison's writing and elsewhere, Scots ethnicity functions as the foundational core of a Canadian identity based on white civility that relies on its American other for meaning.

Not surprisingly, then, Allison (1976, 1) creates ethnic distance between herself and the "English people" in the opening chapter of her memoir:

> In 1860, there was great talk in England of the Fraser River and its gold bearing sands. It had taken the place of California in the minds

> of English people. I say English people because I was living in London at that time. I am Scotch and I feel sure that my countrymen were there mining while we Londoners were talking about it.

Whereas many of her appeals to her "Scotch" identity are used in an attempt to be a non-signatory to various contracts in promoting herself and others of Scots descent as essentially more capable of understanding Indigenous ways of seeing or as "insiders" to whom Indigenous people "told more than they told other white people," here she represents the Scots (however tongue-in-cheek) as exceeding the English in their zeal to exploit land and resources. Thus, "Scotch" as both a pre-white ethnic identity and a white civil ("British") identity is useful in negotiating colonial ambivalence. It also enables her to project her white anxieties onto later settlers who seem to emerge as the real invader-settlers.

Similarly, her nostalgic recollections of early days in British Columbia often include laudatory accounts of Governor James Douglas, "a fine, far-seeing man" (Allison 1976, 13), whose Scots ethnicity is linked to the exceptionalism she constructs around the early settlers. While she lived as a young woman at Fort Hope in the early 1860s, Douglas visited on the way back from his trip to view the Similkameen area, telling the towns-people that it was a "paradise" and adding "with a Scotchman's pride 'there were thistles and heather growing in places'" (ibid.). She also describes him as "a genuine Douglas, kindly and urbane in manner – 'A glove of velvet in a hand of steel' – one of the wisest and best governors we ever had, if he was arbitrary" (6). Moreover, his understanding "of the Indian character" (35) is juxtaposed with the lack of vision of later administrations. In her account of "unrest" among the Similkameen in the 1870s, she states:

> There was great unrest stirring across the Line [Canada–United States border] and some [Indigenous people] were kinsmen of Quinisco, the late chief, and his brother, Incowmasket, the present one. Incowmasket had a loving memory of Governor Douglas and a great respect for the powers that be so kept his people from too open sympathy. And indeed the Indians on our side of the Line had little to complain of for the few whites there were in the country treated them honestly and fairly. (39–40)

Allison's assertion that the Indians had little to complain of is undermined by her own account of a visit from the Indian reserve commissioners to the Similkameen chief Saul in 1877: "The Indians were much quieter and more content after the visit of the Commissioners" (50). Historian Robin Fisher (1977, 178) writes of a "meeting of a large number of the tribes of the southern interior at Lytton [in 1879] ... from the Fraser and Thompson rivers, the Nicola Valley, and the Similkameen area" with Gilbert Sproat, the Indian reserve commissioner, to improve their condition. As they had been excluded from the political process, they were willing to engage in assimilative efforts to ameliorate their situation, but the white settlers were enraged at this attempt at organization and "were not interested in Indians improving their physical and social conditions" (179). Her respect for James Douglas may have been the product of a deeper identification with his life and work than just their shared Scots ancestry. Both Douglas and his wife Amelia were of mixed race. Douglas, raised in what is now Guyana, was a "Scotch West Indian" (Sir James Douglas), the son of a white father and a "free-coloured woman" (Sir James). Educated in Scotland, he later joined the Hudson's Bay Company. At Fort St. James, he met and married Amelia Connolly, whose father was a white Hudson's Bay Company chief factor there and whose mother was Cree. Like Allison, Douglas was biological kin to Indigenous people, something apparently comprehended in her deployment of the term "Scotch." For her, the fact of his investiture as governor with wife and family of mixed-race children in the upper echelons of early BC society likely signified a looser or unenforced racial contract in the early settlement period. Though debate is still alive about Douglas's role – for good or for ill in terms of its legacy for Indigenous people – in constructing (or not constructing) the treaties that created the foundations of the BC racial and settler contracts, he may have subscribed to assimilationist idealism. Adele Perry (2001, 119) summarizes his position: "James Douglas had been at best ambivalent about racial segregation. As Paul Tennant has argued, Douglas's policies assumed assimilation and the possibility of a biracial society." This may have been a notion that Allison shared and that had been quickly shattered by her witness to the genocidal outcomes of the intractable BC contracts in the late nineteenth and early twentieth centuries.

After the newspaper began to publish her recollections, Allison began to consider writing a more substantial book-length memoir, even though she had been originally reluctant to write the initial newspaper articles. In a letter to Louisa Johnston written during the time she was working on them, she indicates that her primary motive was to obtain money for the cash-strapped Depression household in which she resided: "It is only need that has made me write and I have left untold more than I have written" (Susan Allison to Louisa Johnston, 28 November 1930, in Allison 1930–33). An even longer life writing project would have meant further confrontation with the ghosts of the past and with her white status and the cultural capital it had accrued – compared to the sad legacies bequeathed to her Indigenous friends and relations. As Steve Garner (2007, 5) asserts – and as Allison's personal commentary on her struggles with writing suggests – "thinking about whiteness as a system of privilege is a huge source of anxiety for individuals who consider themselves white." The following haunted passage from the same letter to Louisa, in its uncanny juxtapositions, conveys ambivalence and the guilt and paralysis of melancholia:

> If Mr. Scott [editor of the Vancouver *Province* newspaper] would help with a Book it would I humbly think sell looking back on my past life with all its pleasures and pains. I seem like a spectator of the events instead of an actor – and when I think of my first trip out to the Similkameen with Tucktack [Tuc Tac] as bell boy, I grieve over poor old Yacumtecum – blind and helpless being mushed up by an Auto!! And the poor McLean boys hunted to death, because their mixed blood (wild highland and Indian) could not brook to see [John Andrew] Mara sitting in high places and their poor sister [Annie McLean] driven out an outcast from all but her Mothers [sic] people. I have of course not mentioned Maras [sic] name – I knew and liked the little girl he married[.] Dear old Joe McKay I love to think of but I have not told all I know of any thing [sic]. Well I have written more than enough about myself so will now proceed to discuss conditions in Vancouver – poverty and wealth cheek by jowl. I am sure that one of the surest cures would be a graded income tax – not to stop [sic] a small sum out of the poor mans [sic] slender wage – Oh about Mary [her deceased son Will's mixed-race granddaughter] I enquired about

> the Sacred Heart here and was told she could be received here for Fifty dollars per month and extras – make her bank her money – if I can I will come up in the Spring and try to figure out something. It is hard to be poor. I am sure that Alfs [sic] Gladys would be good to her if she visited her without belongings … (Susan Allison to Louisa Johnstone, 28 November 1930, in Allison 1930–33)

This passage conveys great tension induced by the narratives she knows and the narratives she can tell and on which she can capitalize. She must choose between the story of the destruction and degradation of the Similkameen or the highly marketable story of settlement inflected by the white race, class, and gender norms that structured cultural genocide.

Ambivalence is confirmed yet again in Allison's personal interpretation of the McLean story compared to that in her published memoir. Not mentioning John Andrew Mara or elaborating publicly on what he did suggests her unwillingness to cope with the repercussions of becoming a "class traitor." The "little girl" whom Mara married was Alice Barnard of the Victoria establishment, daughter of wealthy businessman Frank Barnard, who owned the very successful Barnard Express Company (BX), and sister of a lieutenant-governor. John Andrew Mara himself was an MLA and an MP. At the same time, the sympathetic depiction in the memoir of Annie McLean, with her baby presumably being taken in by her Indigenous kin (Allison 1976, 47), not only indicts Mara but also suggests that she may have had an inkling of how bereft white culture and many of her descendants were of any notion of what the Syilx describe as *T'mixw* – and therefore of how impossible it would be to try to convey it to a white readership.

The Allisons' lack of financial success, which emerges in this and other letters, figured largely in the kind of life Susan Allison led and where she lived, and thus in her remarkable experiences. The poverty and hardship in the households of her various children, including that of Alice Perkins Wright (1892–1971), the daughter with whom she resided in Vancouver at the time of her memoir writing during the Depression, are mentioned many times in her letters. John Fall and Susan Allison did not become wealthy, as did many early colonizers. Hard winters in which they lost much of their livestock, bad business partnerships, speculation in cattle in the 1870s based on anticipation of the railway mainline into Princeton (which did not happen until 1909), flooding, and grasshopper plagues account for this (Ormsby 1976, xxxvii-xl). Nevertheless, the Allisons' life story and livelihood is implicated in invasion-settlement and illustrates the contention that whiteness defines itself through "propertied investment." Though financial prosperity had eluded the Allisons, Susan Allison could not alienate herself from the other things the white family could rely on, such as the book-length autobiography (presumably a longer version of the recollections) with which she hoped the newspaper editor Mr. Scott might help her. The text of the letter in which she muses on this project suggests, yet again, her ambivalence: thinking about it seems to usher in a return of the repressed as traumatic memories of the elderly Yacumtecum "mushed" by a car on the highway (the trail purportedly "blazed" by John Fall) and of the McLean boys "hunted to death" – that is, a return of the biopolitical consequences for the Similkameen of the white ethnoscape achieved by settlement. Her awareness of what she owed to the agency of Indigenous people in her "camping days" – the Indigenous trail leaders, packers, cargodores, and bell boys – had to have haunted her as she witnessed not only their radically restricted mobility and agency but also their abjection and violent death.

Given some of my above assertions, the letter's observation "I seem like a spectator of events instead of an actor" (Susan Allison to Louisa Johnstone, 28 November 1930, in Allison 1930–33) could be read as yet another attempt at disaffiliation and the preservation of bystander status. But there are other possibilities. Perhaps it is produced by her awareness that, even in a more substantial book, she would still face the same limitations on her public narration – overwhelming discursive limitations in which personal reflection on and disclosure of her dialogical relations with Indigenous people would be impossible. In other words, the sense of futility conveyed in the letter suggests that, yet again, she knew that she could only represent herself as a "spectator." Or perhaps it is another nod to what she owes the Indigenous people in her life, people like Yacumtecum and Nora, who underwrote the Allisons' mobility and the heroic pioneer epic of their life but, more important, taught her things that altered her way of seeing – she as spectator or witness to their actions and agency in enabling invasion-settlement. Or perhaps her writing conveys the "wound of racism," the wound that Marty (1999, 52) suggests is so often manifested in the "white rhetoric," which, up to the present, "hides from white people's collective awareness the self-inflicted 'wound' that racism imposes on our moral integrity." All of these hypotheses are possible. My overall impression of her corpus – diverse and polyphonic as it is – is that it registers a transculturational process that called into question the grounds of her identity and that, without resolution, she grappled with to the end of her life.

One of her responses to the wound of racism may have been her interest in non-Christian spiritual practice. Some might read this as a retreat to the safety and detachment of liberal metaphysics and politics, a kind of compensatory or melancholic substitution for the work of mourning. She became "absorbed in studying Eastern religions" (Ormsby 1976, li) in her later years. Moreover she writes of her engagement with Jewish publications given to her by a Jewish neighbour and cites with approval how "liberal minded" (Susan Allison to Louisa Johnstone, 3 May 1932, in Allison 1930–33) the Jewish people were becoming, using as evidence an article defending Shakespeare's Shylock – "I really might of [sic] written it myself" (Allison 1932, in Allison 1930–33) – as more sinned against than sinning by the "fair" Venetians. She also relates going to Sir Oliver Lodge's (1851–1940) lectures in Vancouver (Allison 1930–33). Lodge was an English academic, scientist, inventor, and proponent of spiritualism, and an active member of the Fabian Society central to the British democratic socialist movement, which attracted many major writers and intellectuals from its founding in the late nineteenth century. At the time of her death, one person characterized Allison as someone who "sought a faith that was broader than creed" (Ormsby 1976, li). How much this spiritual liberalism was a product of the "something very real" that she acknowledged in her observations of Syilx spirituality and religious practice, or of her loss of faith in hegemonic BC whiteness, is hard to say. But it is possible to see many of these interests as a cathecting of the energies that might have gone into more public and authentic witnessing – that is, as symptoms of melancholia or "impossible mourning."

I would like to conclude by emphasizing Susan Allison's isolation from the small cultural movements and limited conversations that were taking place in (white) Canada during her time and that helped lay the foundation for post-Second World War critiques of imperialism and racism – in other words, her isolation from any significant (white) constituency that might have offered a venue for a collective process of facing up to the reality that empire building is "a violent, dirty, and immoral business" (Gilroy 2004, 94). These venues are still very small. Put in this context, it is remarkable that she left any trace of the history of suffering that was invasion-settlement in British Columbia or of her empathic unsettlement. For all its dodges, her work can be read as an early participant in the still tortuous process of unsettling and dismantling race thinking in Canada. Paul Gilroy (2004, 120) identifies a "conviviality" or "spontaneous tolerance and openness" (131) in multicultural urban life and popular culture in Britain that he hopes will move his society beyond its entrenchment in tired, centuries-old race thinking and point the way to a "planetary humanism" rather than to the "exclusionary humanisms of the past" (150). Though I have argued that Allison's commemorative projects were disabled and haunted by this latter exclusionary ideology, I also believe that her writing should be celebrated as the record of a settler who glimpsed something beyond sovereign whiteness.

REFERENCES

Allison, Susan. n.d. "Introduction to In-Cow-Mas-Ket." Unpublished manuscript. British Columbia Centennial '58 Centennial Anthology, 1862–1958 papers, microfilm MAL4, box 9771, British Columbia Archives, Victoria.

–. n.d. *The Monster.* Unpublished manuscript. BC Centennial '58 Committee Centennial Anthology, 1862–1958 papers, microfilm A1636, box 9771, British Columbia Archives, Victoria.

–. 1976. *A Pioneer Gentlewoman in British Columbia: The Recollections of Susan Allison,* ed. Margaret A. Ormsby. Vancouver: UBC Press.

–. ca. 1870s. *Sketches of Indian life.* Unpublished manuscript, I 4716, Penticton Museum, Penticton, BC.

–. n.d. "What I Know of Ogopogo." Unpublished manuscript. British Columbia Centennial '58 Committee Centennial Anthology, 1862–1958 papers, microfilm, A1636, box 9771, British Columbia Archives, Victoria.

–. 1930–33. Unpublished letters. Private collection.

Armstrong, Jeannette. 1998. "Land Speaking." In *Speaking for the Generations,* ed. Simon Ortiz, 174–94. Tucson: University of Arizona Press.

Baldwin, Andrew. 2009. "Ethnoscaping Canada's Boreal Forest: Liberal Whiteness and Its Disaffiliation from Colonial Space." *Canadian Geographer* 53 (4): 427–43.

Barman, Jean. 1996. "Lost Okanagan: In Search of the First Settler Families." *Okanagan Historical Society* 60: 8–20.

Bhabha, Homi K. 1983. "Difference, Discrimination, and the Discourse of Colonialism: The Politics of Theory." In *The Politics of Theory,* ed. Francis Barker, Peter Hulme, Margaret Iverson, and Diana Loxley, 194–211. Colchester: University of Essex.

–. 1984. "Of Mimicry and Man: The Ambivalence of Colonial Discourse." *October* 28: 125–33.

Brydon, Diana. 1995. "Introduction: Reading Postcoloniality, Reading Canada." *Essays in Canadian Writing* 95 (56). Accessed June 14, 2021. https://web.a.ebscohost.com/ehost/detail/detail?vid=6&sid=08d6d269-b5d7-411e-b4af-24c112e88d81%40sessionmgr4007&bdata=JkF1dGhUeXBlPXNoaWImc2loZT1laG9zdC1saXZlJnNjb3BlPXNpdGU%3d#AN=9602262146&db=aph.

Carter, Sarah, Lesley Erickson, and Patricia Roome. 2005. *Unsettled Pasts: Reconceiving the West through Women's History.* Calgary: University of Calgary Press.

Chambers, Ross. 2009. *Untimely Interventions: AIDS Writing, Testimonial, and the Rhetoric of Haunting.* Ann Arbor: University of Michigan Press.

Coleman, Daniel. 2006. *White Civility: The Literary Project of English Canada.* Toronto: University of Toronto Press.

Eng, David L., and Shinhee Han. 2000. "A Dialogue on Racial Melancholia." *Psychoanalytic Dialogues* 10 (4): 667–700.

Fisher, Robin. 1977. *Contact and Conflict: Indian-European Relations in British Columbia, 1774–1890.* Vancouver: UBC Press.

Freud, S. 1917. "Mourning and Melancholia." *The Standard Edition of the Complete Psychological Works of Sigmund Freud: Vol. 14 (1914–16)*, 237–58. London: Hogarth Press.

Garner, Steve. 2007. *Whiteness: An Introduction.* London: Routledge.

Gilroy, P. 2004. *Postcolonial Melancholia.* New York: Columbia University Press.

Ignatiev, Noel, and John Garvey, ed. 1996. *Race Traitor.* New York: Routledge.

Kelm, Mary Ellen, and Lorna Townsend, ed. 2006. *In the Days of Our Grandmothers: A Reader in Aboriginal Women's History in Canada.* Toronto: University of Toronto Press.

Keyes, Daniel. 2011. "Whites Singing Red Face in British Columbia in the 1950s." *TRiC/RTaC* 32 (1): 30–63.

LaCapra, Dominick. 1998. *History and Memory after Auschwitz.* Ithaca: Cornell University Press.

–. 1999. "Trauma, Absence, Loss." *Critical Inquiry* 25 (4): 696–727.

Lawrence, Bonita. 2003. "Gender, Race, and the Regulation of Native Identity in Canada and the United States: An Overview." *Hypatia* 18 (2): 3–31.

Lawson, Alan. 1995. "The Discovery of Nationality in Australian and Canadian literatures." In *The Post-Colonial Studies Reader,* ed. Bill Ashcroft, Gareth Griffiths, and Helen Tiffen, 167–79. London: Routledge.

–. 2000. "Proximities: From Asymptote to Zeugma." In *Postcolonizing the Commonwealth: Studies in Literature and Culture*, ed. Rowland Smith, 19–35. Waterloo, ON: Wilfrid Laurier University Press, 2000.

Marty, Debian. 1999. "White Antiracist Rhetoric as Apologia: Wendell Berry's *The Hidden Wound.*" In *Whiteness: The Communication of Social Identity*, ed. Thomas K. Nakayama and Judith N. Martin, 51–68. Thousand Oaks, CA: Sage.

Meldrum, Stu. 1999. "Slide Presentation for the Allison Family Reunion, July 30th to August 2, 1999 at Princeton BC." Unpublished manuscript, I-4716, Penticton Museum and Archives, Penticton, BC.

Mills, Charles W. 1997. *The Racial Contract*. Ithaca: Cornell University Press.

Mitscherlich, Alexandre, and Margarete Mitscherlich. 1967. *The Inability to Mourn: Principles of Collective Behaviour*. Trans. Eric Mosbachs, 1974. New York: Grove.

Ormsby, Margaret A., ed. 1976. *A Pioneer Gentlewoman in British Columbia: The Recollections of Susan Allison*. Vancouver: UBC Press.

Pateman, Carole. 2007a. "Race, Sex, and Indifference." In *Contract and Domination*, ed. Carole Pateman and Charles W. Mills, 134–64. Cambridge, UK: Polity Press.

–. 2007b. "The Settler Contract." *Contract and Domination*, ed. Carole Pateman and Charles W. Mills, 35–78. Cambridge, UK: Polity Press.

Perry, Adele. 2001. *On the Edge of Empire: Gender, Race and the Making of British Columbia*. Toronto: University of Toronto Press.

Pratt, Mary Louise. 1992. *Imperial Eyes: Travel Writing and Transculturation*. New York: Routledge.

Rattansi, Ali. 2007. *Racism: A Very Short Introduction*. Oxford: Oxford University Press.

"Sir James Douglas." 2008. *The Canadian Encyclopedia*. Accessed June 14, 2021. http://www.thecanadianencyclopedia.ca/en/article/sir-james-douglas/.

Slemon, Stephen. 1995. "Unsettling the Empire: Resistance Theory for the Second World." In *The Post-Colonial Studies Reader*, ed. Bill Ashcroft, Gareth Griffiths, and Helen Tiffen, 104–10. London: Routledge.

Sugars, Cynthia. 2006. "The Impossible Afterlife of George Cartwright: Settler Melancholy and Postcolonial Desire." *University of Toronto Quarterly* 75 (2): 693–717.

Tennant, Paul. 1990. *Aboriginal Peoples and Politics: The Indian Land Question in British Columbia, 1849–1989*. Vancouver: UBC Press.

Thompson, Audrey. 2003. "Tiffany, Friend of People of Color: White Investments in Antiracism." *Qualitative Studies in Education* 16 (1): 7–29.

Turner, Stephen. 1999. "Settlement as Forgetting." In *Quicksands: Foundational Histories in Australia and Aotearoa New Zealand*, ed. Klaus Neumann, Nicholas Thomas, and Hilary Erickson. 20–38. Sydney: University of New South Wales Press.

Wickwire, Wendy. 2006. "'They Wanted … Me to Help Them': James A. Teit and the Challenge of Ethnography in the Boasian Era." In *With Good Intentions: Euro-Canadian and Aboriginal Relations in Colonial Canada*, ed. Celia Haig-Brown and David A. Nock, 297–320. Vancouver: UBC Press.

Wiegman, Robyn. 1999. "Whiteness Studies and the Paradox of Particularity." *Boundary 2* 26 (3): 115–50.

Young, Robert J.C. 1990. *White Mythologies: Writing History and the West*. London: Routledge.

CHAPTER 5

CAMP ROAD

Audrey Kobayashi

A STORY OF A MURKY PAST

Camp Road winds through the middle of the Okanagan Valley, linking Okanagan Centre and Winfield. The road is named for a settlement established by my grandfather, Denbei Kobayashi, who received a contract from the Okanagan Land Company to clear and plant about eight hundred acres of land between 1910 and the First World War. Back in the day, the settlement was known as "Jap Camp" (Camp Road 2017; Fiwchuck 1993).

The spot is occupied today by Jack Seaton Park, which commemorates the life of Jack Seaton, who operated an orchard and packing house on nearby Seaton Road, and who chaired the Winfield and Okanagan Centre Irrigation District, from which the land to create the park was leased (Jack Seaton Park 2017). As one of the white pioneers of the region, Seaton's memory is etched into the contemporary landscape.

This chapter is a very personal, and somewhat impressionistic, attempt to describe the discursive atmosphere of whiteness that was the community that is now Lake Country, then known as Okanagan Centre and Winfield, when I was growing up in the 1950s and 1960s, about a kilometre northwest of the Camp. As an anti-racist scholar, I am aware that my account is unavoidably filtered by what I now understand as racialization, six decades later and more than a century after my grandfather established the camp. I make no apology for applying that filter, but I do recognize that it shapes fundamentally the ways in which I interpret events that at the time were seen as normal, and which I now understand to be normative, and very much a product of a society founded on whiteness.

First, some additional history: my grandfather arrived from Japan in 1906, worked at various low-paying jobs for which Asian labourers were typically hired, including a period at the Coldstream Ranch several kilometres to the north, near Vernon. In 1908, he moved to Okanagan Centre to work at the Grandview Hotel. As he tells the story (Kobayashi 1963; Lake Country Museum and Archives 2013), he felt that his English would improve more quickly in hotel service than it would if he remained in a primarily Japanese-speaking work gang at one of the large orchards in the area. It was at the Grandview that he learned of the Okanagan Valley Land Company's intention to develop eight hundred acres of fruit orchards in the Okanagan Centre area, and he managed to obtain a contract to do the clearing, fencing, and planting. He recruited labourers directly from Japan, some of whom later returned to Japan or moved on to other parts of British Columbia once the contract was complete; a few of whom stayed in the area and eventually bought and farmed their own orchards. They were part of one of the largest Japanese Canadian communities in the interior of British Columbia prior to the 1940s.

Those who became orchardists did well. My grandfather ended up purchasing much of the land that he had been contracted to clear. Most of the orchards that line Camp Road from Hare Road in Okanagan Centre to Seaton Road in Winfield, including the property that is now the home of the Grey Monks Winery, belonged to my grandfather and his brother, and eventually to their various sons and daughters. Imagine, then, the Kobayashi clan, spread out along the length of Camp Road by the 1950s, in a series of properties that produced apples, cherries, peaches, and pears, the mainstay products of the Okanagan Valley. None of us lives there now, the last having left by the 1980s (although a few still farm orchards not far away). The properties have been converted almost completely into vineyards and into some housing developments that command fantastic views of Lake Okanagan.

But this is not a story about the Kobayashi clan: it is a story about stories that merge and mingle and become real in the telling to create the identity of a community, stories that differ from one speaker to another yet converge on common, normative themes. It is not even a story about "truth," if by that term we mean facts that can be solidified, quantified, and verified by archival record. Even when such records are written (as I am doing now), they are usually created long after the fact, based on stories privileged by their telling. But nor is it a story based on fantasy.

The heritage of Okanagan Centre is written on the landscape in the names of the roads, representing the English (and a few other European) settlers who were known as the local pioneers. It was never a particularly wealthy community; status was conveyed by land ownership and a certain cultural superiority, which included membership in the United Church (or, in a few cases, the Anglican Church), involvement in the activities of the local school, and in organizing activities for children to instill a sense of English heritage through games, songs, and stories. In school, we memorized English poetry, read English children's books (I especially remember Enid Blyton), and learned English mannerisms. People in authority, such as the managers of the packing house and other representatives of the fruit industry, spoke with English accents. That my grandfather aspired to the same values, and indeed became one of the larger landowners in the area, made him the exception, not the rule. He moved between the worlds of white Canada and an alien and exotic Other. My grandmother did not share his social mobility; she never conquered the English language and, as far as I could tell, was seldom invited to the tea parties that were a major form of feminine socializing.

During the 1940s, Japanese Canadians within one hundred miles of the Pacific Coast were uprooted, dispossessed of all civil rights, and interned, sent to work or prison camps, or deported. My family already lived outside of the one-hundred-mile zone from the coast and was therefore among the few whose property was not confiscated by the government, although they were subject to the other measures: they were confined by a curfew, had to carry an ID card, could not travel without permission, and could not own prohibited items such as cameras. In fact, these provisions were rather difficult to enforce and seem to have been applied quite unevenly. There developed a curious term in this and other agricultural areas east of the restricted zone: "our Japanese" (or just "our Japs"), a patronizing and possessive term meant to distinguish established residents such as my grandfather from those expelled from the coastal areas. Indeed, my grandfather

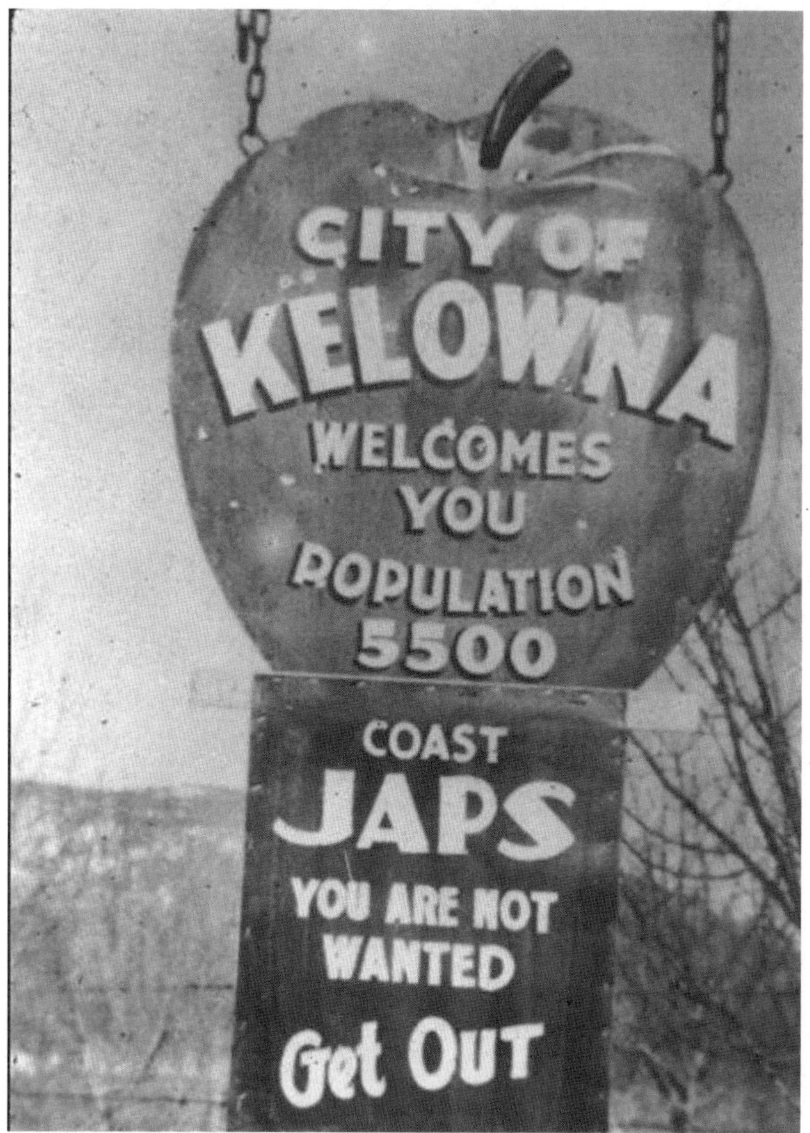

FIGURE 2 Sign posted outside Kelowna, British Columbia, in 1943. | Courtesy of Denbei Kobayashi

captured a photograph of the "Welcome to Kelowna" sign with a smaller sign attached reading "Coast Japs Get Out: You Are Not Wanted."

In the transition period, as people started being released from the camps in 1943 on the condition that they could find work on the outside, many came to work in orchards in the Okanagan Valley, some of which were owned by Japanese Canadians, including my family's. But the social divide, heightened by the events of the 1940s, remained. Adachi (1976), who thoroughly studied expressions of racism against Japanese Canadians throughout rural Canada, claims that Kelowna "symbolized the hostility" against the government's attempt to place people from the camps in agricultural and other jobs (see also Kyle 2016). The Kelowna City Council, and the local newspaper, the *Courier*, campaigned very hard:

> Kelowna refused to co-operate in a programme which was interpreted by the city as an attempt ... to "dump" upon them "potential saboteurs" or "undesirable enemy aliens." The city would take [them] only if they were placed in concentration camps and would allow them to work in the fields only if they were placed under armed guard. When 141 Japanese [sic] from the coast moved to the Okanagan Valley in April, 1942, the Kelowna City Council threatened to cut off electricity and water unless they moved out. (Adachi 1976, 255)

Adachi further quotes an editorial from the *Courier*: "Their presence is an insult and a stench to our nostrils and no technical, legal or economic considerations should be allowed to stand in the way of complete expulsion" (*Kelowna Courier*, 3 February 1944).

While the people of Kelowna may have reserved special hatred for Japanese Canadians, their venom was part of the larger picture of a society in which class and racial divides were seldom subtle. There were property owners and managers, as well as a small number of entrepreneurs, who formed the white ruling class; there were those who worked for others as labourers – in logging, construction, road maintenance; and there were the itinerants who occupied the margins. The latter included Indigenous peoples, some of the families who emigrated from Europe immediately after the Second World War, who were known colloquially as "DPs" (displaced persons) but who, if they were white, could shed that status by working hard and eventually buying their own orchards or taking up permanent employment. And there were "pickers," an itinerant population who moved through during the summer months and included migrants from Quebec or other "Eastern" places, Indigenous people (many of whom lived locally), young people of dubious but unspecified background, Roma, and small numbers of non-white immigrants (known as "Pakis") who were at the bottom of the scale. The pickers lived in "pickers' shacks" erected on most of the orchards, one-room buildings with minimal cooking facilities and outdoor privies. There was a tacit understanding that there were pickers for whom the itinerant life was temporary (young, white anglophones, especially students) and others who could never transcend the category. Although it was not openly acknowledged, the border was drawn along colour lines. And then there were the "bachelors," somewhat mysterious men who lived permanently in shacks scattered here and there, some of whom were workers on local orchards. The bachelors were not a part of established society, and one must never go alone into their shacks. A burden of unsaid innuendo about their sexual identity lurked in the air.

As in any place, the landscape of belonging and inclusion was complex and shifting. If Japanese immigrant workers were considered apart and alien during the early twentieth century, by mid-century they occupied a much more ambiguous space. Their presence needed to be reconciled both with those from the "coast," who were both alien and enemy, and those who had been accepted – albeit not entirely – as part of the community; hence the appellation of "our Japanese." Acceptance was not a recognition of multiculturalism, defined as a recognition that all people occupy a place on an equal basis, regardless of racialized background; rather, it was a recognition that there was room for Others who were able to operate within a white norm. There were discernible limits to that norm; the entry fee included being part of the agricultural community and the Christian church, sending children to schools run along anglophile lines, and participating in community activities built on white and Eurocentric traditions. When these criteria were met, "race" could almost, but never completely, be forgotten. But so could the names of those who actually occupied the camp on Camp Road.

KELOWNA TODAY

I recently returned to Kelowna to conduct research at the University of British Columbia Okanagan campus. The project is part of a national study of the experiences of faculty of colour and Indigenous faculty in Canadian universities. The project is funded by SSHRC Standard Research Grant 404252, held by Frances Henry (PI) and co-applicants Ena Dua, Carl James, Audrey Kobayashi, Peter Li, Howard Ramos, and Malinda Smith. The results are published in Henry et al. (2017). I conducted fourteen interviews among faculty from a range of departments. I will not discuss here their experiences on campus, but every one of them had something to say about Kelowna. The similarity of the responses was striking.

When I asked about their experiences in the wider community, nearly all of the respondents immediately gave an answer that referred to particular places: the mall, the super market, the gas station, a restaurant (they actually named the businesses, but I have not done so here). Several also mentioned experiences of their partners and children in schools. Typical experiences range from uncomfortable stares to outright challenges: a bank loan that was approved by telephone but retracted once the individual arrived at the bank in person, several cases of racial slurs in public, many questions asking at "which orchard" the individual was employed. Many of the labourers in the agricultural industry in Kelowna are part of the Temporary Agricultural Workers Program. They occupy a new kind of camp, still on the edges of white society, essential to but excluded from the local society. They are overwhelmingly racialized individuals from Latin America and the Caribbean (Aguiar, McKinnon, and Sookraj 2010–11).

Hurt tinged the voices of my informants as they told me about more serious experiences of partners and children: of highly qualified professional partners unable to find permanent employment and being subjected to barrages of questions about their ability to communicate in English instead of about their professional credentials; of children who were growing tough in response to the constant experiences of othering in the schoolyard. Several told me that they had been warned when they first arrived in Kelowna that they should dress formally so as not to be taken for an agricultural worker. One individual, however, asserted that he refused to change his presentation, especially since he was concerned about the racism experienced by agricultural workers and angry that people should treat him better because of his perceived class standing: that he was not a "picker."

Race intersects with class in a complex and nuanced manner. Respondents told me that they believed that white employees in the service industry (which is where most of the comments came from) have no difficulty with the presence in "their" community of racialized workers who are clearly in a subordinate socioeconomic position but that they have a very different attitude towards the increasing number of racialized university employees, whom they resent for their middle-class standing. These stories of the subtle expressions of class and race intersection are built upon a long history in Kelowna of whiteness, class positioning, and racial construction in which all Kelowna residents seek or are given a place.

SO, DO YOU HAVE TO BE WHITE TO BELONG?

Ghassan Hage (1998), drawing on Bourdieu's (1977) notion of "habitus," claims that whiteness gains power through the accumulation of cultural capital. It operates through a kind of spatial management that controls the organization of the landscape; the movement of people, things, and practices; the choreography of who belongs where doing what. The white fantasy is based on "contextually validated national symbolic capital" (Hage 1998, 54).

The Okanagan of my remembered childhood operated on a contextually validated *transnational* cultural capital, that of the English Canadian world in which cultural notions were drawn directly from an imperial imaginary. My anomalous grandfather managed to accumulate a fair amount of cultural capital through acquired language, land ownership, and a projected sense of dignity. He conveyed his own sense of belonging and entitlement by his bearing and attitude. In other words, he performed always under those imperial eyes and, in so doing, secured a precarious place in an otherwise hostile community.

Bearing, performance, "sense" of belonging: these are not easy concepts for the social scientist to capture in a manner that is intellectually convincing. It is also difficult for me to convey or make sense of how emotionally difficult it was for me to return to Kelowna for this particular research project. I had thought that my previous experience in the community would give me some insight into the experiences of those with whom I conducted interviews and that such insight would help to close the distance between myself and them. Indeed, I made that connection based on personal memories, but it was a troubling connection.

This question of connection goes far beyond my personal feelings or emotions, however, which are irrelevant to this story. It goes to an understanding that one route towards the anti-racist scholarship that I profess and practise is a link to the everyday experiences and relationships that constitute that slippery landscape of cultural capital in which the imperial fantasy is performed. As Philomena Essed (1991) argues so persuasively, everyday racism operates according to a heuristic system in which recognition, repetition, and context provide validation of lived experience. That validation, of course, is part of the everyday performance of identity of both the white and the racialized other. It is habitus made habitual.

And so I conclude with one of the strongest images that abides with me as a result of my recent research: that of a university professor casually donning his conservative sports coat as he exits his car to fill up at the self-serve pumps. "Oh, my," you may say, "how can she possibly infer racialization from *that?*" Just so. That seemingly banal action is part of the everyday, habitual set of actions through which he finds a place in a society in which his being is precarious, in which he is differentiated from the other other, the "picker" upon whose back so much of the Okanagan rests. The "picker" defines white society every bit as much as the other. It is a performance of a kind of invisibility against an imaginary in which difference is habitually made visible and invisible at the same time, in which the cultural capital of whiteness can be accumulated so that the presence of the Othered body can be made a little more absent. But there will always be Camp Road to remember.

REFERENCES

Adachi, Ken, and National Japanese Canadian Citizens Association. 1976. *The Enemy That Never Was: A History of the Japanese Canadians*. Toronto: McClelland and Stewart.

Aguiar, Luís L.M., Ann McKinnon, and Dixon Sookraj. 2010–11. "Repertoires of Racism: Reactions to Jamaicans in the Okanagan Valley." *BC Studies* 168: 65–79.

Bourdieu, P. 1977. *Outline of a Theory of Practice*. Cambridge: Cambridge University Press.

Camp Road. 2017. "1910 Japanese Camp," Lake Country Museum Archives. https://www.lakecountrymuseum.com/history/camproad-2/.

Essed, P. 1991. *Understanding Everyday Racism*. Newbury Park: Sage.

Fiwchuk, M. 1993. "The Japanese Pioneers of Lake Country." Lake Country Museum Archives, MS 25, binder 1.

Hage, G. 1998. *White Nation: Fantasies of White Supremacy in a Multicultural Society*. Annandale, NSW: Pluto Press

Henry, Frances, Ena Dua, Carl E. James, Audrey Kobayashi, Peter Li, Howard Ramos, and Malinda S. Smith. 2017. *The Equity Myth: Racialization and Indigeneity at Canadian Universities*. Vancouver: UBC Press.

"Jack Seaton Park" 2017. The Lake Country Museum Archives. https://www.lakecountrymuseum.com/history/jackseatonpark-2/.

Kobayashi D. 1963. *Kobayashi Denbei to sono ku*. Tokyo.

Kyle, Catherine. 2016. "Lost Landscapes of the Market Gardeners." PhD diss., University of British Columbia Okanagan.

Lake Country Museum and Archives. 2013. *Kakonosedai: A Century of Community*. Lake Country: Lake Country Heritage and Cultural Society.

Part 2
REVEALING AND CHALLENGING CONTEMPORARY WHITE FANTASIES

CHAPTER 6

MAPPING WHITE CONSUMER CULTURE

Kelowna's Tourist Maps, 1983–99

Jon Corbett and Donna M. Senese

Kelowna tourism maps from 1983 to 1999 operate within a visual discursive frame that attempts to fix identities and landscape for their readers. In the following analysis, we discuss the space of Kelowna, British Columbia, Canada, and its (re)presentation through the media tourist maps produced in the 1980s through to 1999. The Kelowna Public Archives of the Okanagan Heritage Museum's collection of thirty tourist maps date from 1951 to 1999. Maps dated prior to 1983 were devoid of pictorial landscape representation and were excluded from the analysis. This temporal range coincides with the process of deindustrialization and the shift to a tourism economy, where in Kelowna, as in other mid-sized Canadian cities, service employment more than doubled (Sands and Reese 2017). The 2008 closure of Western Star Trucks factory in Kelowna and its impact on the community mark a transition to a postindustrial local economy heavy on "services" (Aguiar and Marten 2010, 173–94). Through the reading of these tourist maps, we argue that they (re)present, (re)produce, and (re)inforce the dominant imagination of space in Kelowna – that is, as a place where race is consciously articulated with class, such that whiteness is secured as a privileged middle- and upper-class space of leisure. These maps follow the Western tradition of universalizing representations of place that are in fact very "specific to members of the hegemonic class" (Berg and Kearns 2009, 20). Furthermore, the idealization and aestheticization of the Kelowna landscape through tourist maps fetishizes landscape as a commodity that caters to white elite tastes and desires. The fetishization of the Kelowna landscape not only universalizes but also naturalizes elite class privilege over the landscape as the landscape becomes an essential marker of identity, race, and class (Walks 2006).

LOCATIONAL CONTEXT AND NEOLIBERALISM IN BRITISH COLUMBIA

The city of Kelowna is the regional centre of the Okanagan Valley. This chapter examines a set of Kelowna tourist maps and argues that these *mapspaces* – the represented landscape as space on a map – operate within a neoliberal discourse framework that imagines the whole Okanagan as a region of play, recreation, and affluent retirement. Relative to the rest of Canada, Kelowna's mild climate is used by the tourism industry to promote the city as a year-round playground (Aguiar, Tomic, and Trumper 2005) offering a variety of amenities, including ski hills, golf courses, wineries, and water sports on the many lakes throughout the valley. Kelowna has also become a favourable area to retire as white retirees are drawn to the region because of its mild climate and amenities (Teixeira 2009) .

Once home to a robust agricultural and manufacturing sector, as well as resource-based industries such as forestry and mining, Kelowna, like many other communities in interior British Columbia, now relies on post-productivist, or post-Fordist, amenity industries such as tourism, recreation, and retirement as an important part of its economy (Senese 2010). These industries and manufacturers went through a process of deindustrialization that coincided with the shift from Fordist and Keynesian type political economies to neoliberalism (Young 2008; Young and Matthews 2007). This process brought about deregulation, and the repositioning and relocation of industry within the province, which, in turn, threatened the economic viability of many communities.

Local agents of place promotion, such as regional governments, chambers of commerce, and tourism associations, have purposefully attempted to draw capital back to their regions through "place promotion" (Peck and Tickell 2002, 395). Mitchell (2001, 272) writes: "[the] lure of the local is more and more directed toward capital, seeking to lure it to the local, in hopes of staving off total decline for at least a little while longer." Especially as the value of resource industries to local economies and levels of employment has significantly dropped in the province through neoliberalization, it has become imperative for regions to promote themselves in ways they had not before (Carroll and Ratner 2005; Storey 2006).

Where local resources of a place were once harvested and sold as a commodity on the global market, now, through tourism, the largest industry in the world (Torres and Momsen 2004), it is "place" itself that becomes a commodity (Beilin 2001). "Commodification of the countryside can be understood as part of ... a cultural economy approach to ... development," whereby local knowledge is transformed into a local resource, and it becomes identified through a range of cultural markers such as "traditional foods, regional languages, crafts, folklore, local visual arts, and drama, literary references, historical and prehistoric sites, landscape systems, and their flora and fauna" (Kneafsey 2001, 764). In light of this turn, in British Columbia there has been a "growing shift away from what has been referred to as landscapes of production to landscapes of consumption as ... places are increasingly subjected to the tourist gaze" (Storey 2006, 1). Kelowna, as we show below, fits this development.

CRITICAL CARTOGRAPHY

Harley, in his influential articles "Deconstructing the Map" (1989) and "Cartography, Ethics and Social Theory" (1990), argues that we are often uncritical of maps and accept them at face value for what the mapmaker intended them to mean. Furthermore, he posits that "we often tend to work from the premise that mappers engage in an unquestionably 'scientific' or 'objective' form of knowledge creation" (Harley 1990, 1) and present no bias in the maps they produce and spaces they represent. Yet maps are situated within power relations as well as helping to position them, so they are not impartial documents (Bosak, Boley, and Zaret 2010; Crampton and Krygier 2006; Del Casino and Hanna 2000, 2006; Harley 1989, 1990; Sparke 1995). Maps themselves are powerful: they are not simply products of power; rather, they produce, reify, and reinforce power. Crampton and Krygier (2006) echo the same sentiments as Harley, arguing that, as instruments of power, maps conceptualize reality, emerging out of militaristic and political necessity as a means of representation that assists in policing and controlling space. Maps can, therefore, be understood as documents that not only represent hegemonic notions of space but also (re)produce them. They are political, economic, and social documents that are used to (re) inforce particular spatial representations.

Matthew Sparke (1995) provides a seminal critical analysis of mapping by discussing the map-making of Shawnadithit, the last survivor of the Beothuk in Newfoundland. By demythologizing and deconstructing the map, Sparke argues it is possible to recentre it as a document of contestation within the colonial process of (re)imagining space. He demonstrates that intricate relationships exist between maps and their representational spaces and, furthermore, discusses their contexts of social (re)production. Moreover, he emphasizes that deconstructing and demythologizing maps prevents individuals from claiming that any reading of a map as being complete, that its power relations have been exposed, or that the map is completely revealed. To make any such claim is problematic as readings of maps can shift based on context or subject position. Consequently, we are moved beyond a simple and emblematic concern with what cartographers intended and what their maps obscure. This type of analysis reveals a host of questions regarding the omissions and exclusions that produce maps in the first place.

Del Casino and Hanna (2000, 36) argue that maps are not simply "fixed at the moment of production, a result of the hegemonic authority embedded by the mapmaker in/on the representation," but that they should be conceived of as processes that are constantly modified and reversible. As much as these processes are modified and reversible, they are fluid and ambiguous, constantly changing with every examination and utilization of the map. A map's meanings are (re)produced with each reading and rereading, while the map and its meanings are constantly (re)produced *and* consumed.

Tourist maps are documents that (re)produce meaning about the landscape they represent. This process is achieved through a cyclical interchange of meaning that reinforces and superimposes itself onto the landscape through a discourse created by "production *and* consumption, authoring *and* reading, objectification *and* subjectification, representation *and* practice" (Del Casino and Hanna 2006, 36). In spite of this, most geographers have overlooked using tourism maps to undertake a critical analysis of space. Del Casino and Hanna (2000, 23) had earlier argued that this gap was due to a "reliance on positivistic assumptions" and that many geographers had "dismissed tourism maps because of their blatant biases as advertisements and/or their flagrant disregard of the cartographic rules for accurately modeling reality." Because of these factors, tourism maps have been increasingly critiqued for hiding reality rather than exposing it. Tourist maps produced by agents of place promotion provide insight into how the dominant neoliberal hegemony is reproduced and visualized in folk representations of cartography. Using these tourist maps, which rely heavily on inset photos and cartoon images, we explore how Kelowna has purposively mapped and marketed itself as a very specific kind of white leisure space.

LANDSCAPE OF LEISURE, THE *MAPSPACE* OF KELOWNA

Maps are not simple manuscripts. Their edges in the physical world are not defined by the map itself but are linked intrinsically to other spaces and other texts (Del Casino and Hanna 2000). In the case of tourism maps of Kelowna, they are intertextual to the many other media (including images and video) that are used to promote or create a discourse about the Okanagan tourism region. Together these texts frame a view of Kelowna for the tourist to see and, by implication, experience, with a fixed repertoire of recreating and exploring that fits into a reimagined post-Fordist city. Mutually, they create Kelowna through the discourse they impart. Furthermore, the discourses presented by these media influence the ways tourists perceive or gaze upon the landscape (Pritchard and Morgan 2000). As the tourists use the tourism map to navigate the landscape, their reading of the map is influenced by the perceptions created by the discourse of tourism while their reading of the landscape is influenced by the discourse of the map (Del Casino and Hanna 2006).

Through the use of symbols and images represented on the map, as well as the construction and appearance of its landscape in general, it is possible to understand the setting as a depiction. Furthermore, as Cosgrove and Jackson (1987, 96) identify, "landscape is a cultural image, a pictorial way of representing, structuring or symbolising surroundings." If we juxtapose this perspective with the *mapspace* of Kelowna, the city is represented and symbolized as a landscape of leisure, with labour having been erased from its image (Del Casino and Hanna 2000).

EVACUATION OF LABOUR IN THE *KELOWNA'S CHOICE MAP* (1996)

The background of *Kelowna's Choice Map* (1996) displays an oblique perspective of the city of Kelowna. The view is from the west looking towards the Rocky Mountains over the top of the city. The image is comprised of two main colours: green, representing land; and dark blue, representing Okanagan Lake. Throughout the green area on the map are pockets of trees, wild and domestic animals, hikers, grey lines marking roads, and the occasional cluster of cartoon-simplified residential buldings. The blue parts of the map contain boats, swimmers, and a comic representation of the mythical lake monster Ogopogo. At the top of the image, at the furthest point from the position of the viewer, are snow-capped mountains sprinkled with skiing infrastructure. It is the foreground of the image that captures the attention of the viewer. The map is dense with advertisments promoting local food outlets, banks, malls, recreational facilities, and restaurants. Small balloon-shaped marker pins contain information about local businesses. Strings attached at the bottom of the balloons anchor the advertisment to a specific location on the map. Combined, the content, cartoonish representation, and colour palette of the map represent an almost childlike frivolity. Kelowna is a place were people come to have fun. Labour is purely incidental and loosely associated with the people who will facilitate the presumed map users' leisure as they serve tourists in restaurants and shopping malls.

This spatial imaginary is an important distinction for tourists who seek to escape the everyday landscape of work to enter the unique landscape of leisure and enjoyment (Jansson 2002). Largely erased from the local landscape of Kelowna in this map are the many industrial sites. The bottom left-hand side of the map does show the Riverside plywood mill and Sun Rype juice factories. However, these choices suggest that Kelowna's industrial district is flattened into two local brands, and it further de-emphasizes working-class people performing unionized jobs in the factories throughout the city that contain manufacturing and natural resource-processing facilities. Therefore, erased along with the industrial zones is the working class of Kelowna. Grey, dirty, dusty, and noisy, the industrial zones are replaced with rolling green hills where tourists are able to explore the landscape unencumbered. *Kelowna's Choice Map* (1996) thus depicts Kelowna and its surrounding areas as a fantasyland designed simply for leisure. Moreover, an explicit comparison is made to Disneyland, the greatest fantasyland of all, with the bold white castle that assumes a prominent spot at the top of the map representing Scandia, a now aging mini-putt golf and video game park. The landscape of Kelowna is idealized, sanitized, and aestheticized, with its specific appeal being to a generic, homogenized American mode of leisure. Labour is erased from the landscape, as is the working class that lives there. Moreover, the erasure of workers from the landscape not only "denies the social relations of waged labor under capitalism" (Rose 1993, 91), it also denies the social relations of waged labour that is exploited to perpetuate tourism, which tends to employ non-unionized labour at or near the minimum wage (Okanagan Partnership 2008).

A pastoral ambiguity arises in this map, however, between work and leisure. Present on the map are icons representing ranches or farms. These are identified using images of contentedly grazing cows, industrious red tractors, and cute old-style settler farmhouses with white picket fences. These symbols seemingly imply that physical labour does in fact take place in this quaint landscape. However, there is no representation of individuals toiling on the landscape. This ambiguity manifests itself in part because "the very production of any leisure space is dependent on its Other, work, for its identity" (Del Casino and Hanna 2000, 38). We use the "Other" here as "a subject of difference that is almost the same but not quite" (Bhabha 1984, 126). Following Bhabha, we can say that the idea of work presented on the map is a mimic that disavows work and reinforces leisure. Kelowna is thus positioned as a place unencumbered by the drudgery of modern lifestyles, where visitors are able to step back to a time when life was less frenzied.

Moreover, these icons also imprint the social order onto the landscape of Kelowna by connecting this type of farm work to notions of heritage and culture. The heritage, culture, and ownership of the landscape is mapped by the use of these farm icons and attributed to European and English traditions of "work" in the landscape. Just as the icon of "work" strives to disavow the notion of work, it also renounces the colonial relations that made it possible for Europeans to "work" the landscape. Excluded and silenced from the landscape are the First Nations of the Okanagan, who, through colonialism, were removed from their traditional spaces, as well as the Latin American and Caribbean migrant workers who seasonally pick the fruit for minimum wage. The icon of "work" is a stark example of what Berg (2011, 16–17) argues are the "symbolic aspects of naming and the very material aspects of marginalization through capitalist accumulation by dispossession under neoliberalism." With the erasure of First Nations and migrant labour, or in both these cases, the Other from the landscape, and with notions of "work" and "leisure" introduced and reinforced by the "work" icon, this *mapspace* of Kelowna is identified and presented as an exclusive space.

DISCIPLINED SPACED IN *KELOWNA'S CHOICE MAP* (1997)

Another component of the *mapspace* that supports the notion that no one works in Kelowna is captured in the Okanagan lifestyle depicted on the cover of *Kelowna's Choice Map* (1997). The image shows ten wealthy middle-aged white people (both men and women) standing outside on a deck, wine glass in hand; behind them is a beautiful vista of the Okanagan Valley. The ambiguity of this image's meaning becomes apparent when we ask whether these people are locals or tourists. The question is left open to debate, for what really matters in the context of the map is that the people are performing their identities as affluent, white, and presumably heterosexual individuals. The effect of this image on the cover of the map is to inform and discipline the behaviour of readers as they read the *mapspace* of Kelowna and physically enter into that space. Yet it also disciplines identities, and "traces of the other are always hidden ... these disciplinary representations expose the presence of exclusions, margins and other ambiguities" (Del Casino and Hanna 2000, 30). By looking at the individuals on the cover of *Kelowna's Choice Map* (1997), one can infer that they represent the dominant imagination of Kelowna, the aspirations of those who live in the city as well as those who should visit it. Furthermore, the individuals represent class, where white Canadian identity is articulated as a middle-class identity – a perspective that is consistently reified throughout the *mapspace* of Kelowna. It is both in the *mapspace* as well as its physical space, where class and race intervene in determining for whom, and how, fun and outdoor activities become a "fundamental goal in life" (Aguiar, Tomic, and Trumper 2005, 130). *Kelowna's Choice Map* (1997) banally demonstrates how the landscape of leisure is thus represented and (re)created through the performance of middle-aged, white, bourgeois individuals on the landscape with the exclusion of the Other.

SEDUCTIVE ENCOUNTERS IN THE MAPS: *KELOWNA AND THE WESTSIDE* (N.D.) AND THE *NEW JAYCEES GUIDE MAP*

"Feminine landscapes abound in tourism imagery" (Pritchard and Morgan 2000, 126), and Kelowna tourism maps are no exception. Throughout the period from 1983 to 1999, the "feminine" is a prevalent image used to represent the landscape of Kelowna. On the cover of *The Map: Kelowna and the Westside* (n.d.) a young woman is dressed in a pastel blue leotard. She wears a pink head band to contain her faux scruffy blond hair. Beneath her is a basket of red apples, one of which is in her hand with a large bite taken out of it. In this case, the "feminine" symbolically disciplines the gaze of the tourist and informs the way in which the map should be understood and used once it is opened. The seductive pose, reminiscent of *Sports Illustrated* swimsuit issues or *Victoria's Secrets* catalogues, enacts an invitation of availability for sustenance or sex or both to the implied straight male viewer.

The manner by which landscape is represented, and thus viewed, (re) produces a particular sort of gendering (Setten 2003), and in the case of the Kelowna *mapspace*, the landscape is clearly gendered as female: "The female figure represents landscape, and landscape a female torso, visually in part through their pose: [photographs] of Woman and Nature often share the same topography of passivity and stillness" (Rose 1993, 96). Moreover, the visual discourse of the tourist maps covers from Kelowna create a feminine space – conceived as fertile and (re)productive – to the fertile and (re)productive capacity of white, often blonde, women displayed within, as well as representative of, landscape or nature. The model, a 1980s Jane Fonda-esque epitome of health, holds a half-eaten apple seductively enticing the male viewer not only to penetrate them with his gaze but also to take another bite and taste the fruit of their labour. Strangely out of place in the verdant green parkland, the leotard-clad woman appears to visually pleasure a presumed male viewer as a vision reminiscent of Eve offering the viewer a bit of Eden in Kelowna (Koroscil 2003).

Gendered depictions are not confined to women. On the back cover of *The Map: Kelowna and the Westside* (n.d.) a fit young man strides through an emblematic Kelowna orchard in bloom as he consumes the fruit of the landscape. At a moment's notice, he is ready to jump on his bicycle and ride off to his next adventure. This masculine representation is in stark contrast to the women represented in other parts of the publication, who are fixed within the landscape because they *are* the landscape. Because the women are immobilized (often sitting with legs crossed), just like the natural landscape, they become an object to be gazed upon and acted upon by the subject. The implied subject in the *mapspace* of Kelowna is a white, heterosexual male, whom Rose (1993, 6) terms "the master subject." As Pritchard and Morgan (2000, 120) argue, the "feminization of nature and landscape was accompanied by, indeed, was dependent on the existence of its binary opposite, 'the masculine gaze' – one which was construed as active in contrast to the passive landscape awaiting exploration."

Crouch (2005, 4) characterizes tourism as a "seductive encounter … where the tourist flirts with space in ongoing practice, [and] where space is performed." Furthermore, the gendered landscape of tourism offers "feminine seduction and masculine adventure – attractions which are constructed to appeal to a largely white, male heterosexual tourist gaze" (Pritchard and Morgan 2000, 122). Rose (1993, 97) argues that "the sensual topography of land and skin is mapped by a gaze, which is eroticized as masculine and heterosexual." In the *mapspace* of Kelowna, whiteness is also part of this sensual topography of landscape. The seductive looks from the women on the map covers are an attempt to draw the tourist into this "seductive encounter" with the landscape and *mapspace* of Kelowna, which is clearly identified as a white and heterosexual space. The 1990 version of *The Map: Kelowna and the Westside* displays a woman dressed as a princess. She again performs as landscape and nature while her implied desire is for a white, heterosexual male. It is evident, therefore, that the landscape and *mapspace* of Kelowna is represented as a space disciplined and named for the desires of white heterosexual masculinity.

However, these images and maps not only (re)present the space of white heterosexuality that is Kelowna but also reflect it. The title at the bottom of the princess cover image explains this point by telling the viewers they are looking at "reflections of Kelowna." The landscapes of tourism are named through discourses of patriarchy, white dominance, and heterosexuality that script an audience that is "Western, masculine, and white" (Pritchard and Morgan 2000). The reflection also "communicates who is uninvited, unwelcome in the city, since there are no representations [or reflections] of people who are 'different' and 'unfamiliar' to the landscape. Both white and non-white groups recognize these 'signs'" (Aguiar, Tomic, and Trumper 2005, 132). Hinterlands such as Kelowna "have been historically formed in such a way that today they constitute a place with a unique character, a unique 'quality,' a unique attraction; [yet] one that offers safety, familiarity and sameness" (124). Reflected in the maps is a landscape that is recognizable and safe to white heterosexual bourgeois tourists reinforced through the power of the masculine gaze constituted in its voyeuristic desire for the feminine.

Collectively the covers of Kelowna tourism maps overtly reinforce the disciplining force of the masculine gaze. This gaze not only has the power to commodify and transform places for the tourist experience but also to transform the people it depicts within these landscapes. These commodified bodies are often females, who are represented as eroticized and often "exoticized commodities" (Pritchard and Morgan 2000, 125) to be consumed by the masculine gaze.

Looking at *The Map: Kelowna and the Westside* (n.d.), further examples can be seen in which the "feminine" is inscribed onto the landscape, commodified for the consumption of the masculine gaze. These women are both examined by the masculine gaze and displayed for its consumption in a way that Laura Mulvey (1975) terms their "to-be-looked-at-ness." The landscape of the *mapspace* and material space contains the same "to-be-looked-at" quality. While the women and landscape are feminized in a way that renders them passive or present only to be looked at, alternatively the white masculine bodies represented in the *mapspace* of Kelowna are active and use the landscape to their liking. The feminization of what is gazed upon is important "because it … characterizes the dominant visual regime of white heterosexual masculinism [where] 'women appear' … but 'men act'" (Rose 1993, 88). This argument is demonstrated by the back cover of the *New Jaycees Guidemap 1988–1989* of Kelowna. The website for the

Kelowna Jaycees explains that this group consists of "a group of young male professionals and entrepreneurs, ages 18–40, that strive to grow as individuals while positively impacting our community, Kelowna, BC. Established in 1935, the Kelowna Jaycees have a rich history and are one of the city's oldest professional groups" ("About Us" 2020). On the most basic level of production, this map replicates this masculine entrepreneurial ideology. The passive and static woman appears on the beach while the man in an inset picture is windsurfing – he acts in the landscape by harnessing the landscape's natural elements. The woman appears simply to be looked at, while the man does not just stroll or roam through the landscape but "accelerates through ... [a] compressed and hyperinscribed space" (Bell and Lyall 2002, 21). Bell and Lyall describe this space as the "accelerated sublime," where the "passive viewing of nature has evolved to kinetic experiences within this accelerated nature" (ibid.).

A final image is again taken from the *New Jaycees Guide Map 1988–1989*. The front cover presents a busy cartoonish pastiche of Kelowna recreational activities. It is brash, colourful, heavy on illustration, and light on text. The large number of women, men, and children depicted on the cover are all smiling, carefree, and beautiful. Yet the cover further reinforces the case of women simply appearing and men acting in the accelerated sublime inscribed onto the landscape and space of Kelowna. Men are waterskiing, downhill skiing, fishing, windsurfing, and playing golf. Meanwhile, of the two most prominent women in the image, one is posing erotically on the beach while the other carries a child in one arm and a shopping bag in the other. Below the image of the woman and her child, there are two women who might also be construed as accelerating in the space; however, it is in the safe and protected space of a water park, not the "dangerous" space of "nature" in which men are able to act.

The *New Jaycees Guidemap* cover image is the definitive piece that ties all the themes of the separate images together into one reflection and/or (re)presentation of the physical and *mapspace* of Kelowna. First, all the individuals depicted on the image represent the face of whiteness – and not only whiteness but bourgeois whiteness. This being the case, it is again possible to consider the space of Kelowna as disciplined and named as a "white space" in which race, gender, and class are tightly intertwined. As Aguiar, Tomic, and Trumper (2005, 131) contend, the "history of the

Okanagan is of making space white and whiteness" that "is made 'real' on the ground through the maintenance of spatial boundaries." These "spatial boundaries" are made apparent and disciplined, in part, through the (re) presentations, reflections, and performances projected through these tourism maps.

CONCLUSION

By examining Kelowna's tourism maps and accompanying images, it is possible to recognize how the *mapspace* of the city, as well as its material space and the individuals within it, are disciplined and named through the performances of bodies and identities. The covers of the Kelowna tourism maps are perhaps more powerful than the map itself. Significantly, the images can be seen to be part of the map as it extends past its boundaries and becomes intertextual with other texts and representations (Del Casino and Hanna 2000, 2006). The intertextual images attempt to discipline the gaze that voyeuristically looks at the *mapspace*. These images in turn attempt to ascribe meaning to the material space, and the bodies and identities contained within that space are (re)presented as a space of white heterosexual masculinity. This ascribing function in turn maintains the view of a locality "in which tourism discourses privilege the gaze of the "'master subject' – white, male, heterosexual and bourgeois" (Pritchard and Morgan 2000, 132).

The images discussed in this chapter create a discourse that informs the gaze upon the *mapspace* of Kelowna and, therefore, its material space as well. Moreover, the discourse created by the images endeavours to discipline the performance of bodies within and on the landscape. Implicit symbols are provided that emphasize who is invited into the physical space of Kelowna as a tourist as well as the identities they should embody. Social relations have regularly been mapped, with symbols and places divining an insight regarding class and authority that attempts to claim ownership and to name landscapes while protecting the dominant imagination of space and place. Race and identity are realized through the production and protection of geographic margins (Aguiar, Tomic, and Trumper 2005), and tourism maps of Kelowna are but one device that (re)creates, reinforces, and reflects this spatial division. Finally, the chapter draws attention to the implication of gender in the whiteness of Kelowna. Straight white men are active, doers, impatient in place. Women are passive, immobile, mothers, and objects of desire for the white male gaze. Nature in Kelowna as framed in these maps is feminine. As such, Kelowna becomes a playground for straight males not only in terms of desire but also as a place to imprint themselves, free from an untamed, wild, unpredictable and otherwise bewildering nature.

REFERENCES

"About Us." 2020. Jaycees. https://jcikelowna.com/about.php.

Aguiar, L.L.M., and T. Marten. 2010. "Scripting Taste, Marking Distinction: Wine Tourism and Post-Fordist Restructuring in the Okanagan Valley." In *Interrogating the New Economy: Restructuring Work in the 21st Century*, ed. N. Pupo and M. Thomas, 173–94, Toronto: Garamond/University of Toronto Press.

Aguiar, L., P. Tomic, and R. Trumper. 2005. "Work Hard, Play Hard: Selling Kelowna, BC, as Year-Round Playground." *Canadian Geographer* 49 (2): 123–39.

Beilin, R. 2001. "Underlying It All: Faceless Landscapes and Commodified Views." *Rural Society* 11 (3): 147–61.

Bell, C., and J. Lyall. 2002. "The Accelerated Sublime: Thrill-Seeking Adventure Heroes in the Commodified Landscape." In *Tourism: Between Place and Performance*, ed. S. Coleman and M. Crang, 21–37. New York: Berghahn Books.

Berg, L.D. 2011. "Banal Naming, Neoliberalism, and Landscapes of Dispossession." *ACME: An International E-Journal for Critical Geographies* 10 (1): 13–22.

Berg, L.D., and R.A. Kearns. 2009. "Naming as Norming: 'Race,' Gender and Identity Politics of Naming Places in Aortearoa/New Zealand." In *Critical Toponymies: The Contested Politics of Place Naming*. ed. Lawrence D. Berg and Jani Vuolteenaho, 99–122. Burlington, VT: Ashgate.

Bhabha, H.K. 1984. "Of Mimicry and Man: The Ambivalence of Colonial Discourse." *October* 28: 125–33.

Bosak, K., B. Boley, and K. Zaret. 2010. "Deconstructing the 'Crown of the Continent': Power, Politics and the Process of Creating National Geographic's Geotourism Mapguides." *Tourism Geographies* 12 (3): 460–80.

Carroll W., and R.S. Ratner. 2005. *Challenges and Perils: Social Democracy in Neoliberal Times*. Halifax: Fernwood.

Cosgrove, D., and P. Jackson. 1987. "New Directions in Cultural Geography." *Area* 19 (2): 95–101.

Crampton, J.W., and J. Krygier. 2006. "An Introduction to Critical Cartography." *ACME: An International E-Journal for Critical Geographies* 4 (1): 11–33.

Crouch, D. 2005. "Flirting with Space: Tourism Geographies as Sensuous/expressive Practice." In *Seductions of Place: Geographical Perspectives on Globalization and Touristed Landscapes*, ed. C. Cartier and A.A. Lew, 23–35. New York: Routledge.

Del Casino, V.J., and S.P. Hanna. 2000. "Representations and Identities in Tourism Map Spaces." *Progress in Human Geography* 24 (1): 23–46.

–. 2006. "Beyond the 'Binaries': A Methodological Intervention for Interrogating Maps as Representational Practices." *ACME: An International E-Journal for Critical Geographies* 4 (1): 34–56.

Harley, J.B. 1989. "Deconstructing the Map." *Cartographica: The International Journal for Geographic Information and Geovisualization* 26 (2): 1–20.

–. 1990. "Cartography, Ethics and Social Theory." *Cartographica: The International Journal for Geographic Information and Geovisualization* 27 (2): 1–23.

Jansson, A. 2002. "Spatial Phantasmagoria: The Mediatization of Tourism Experience." *European Journal of Communication* 17 (4): 429–43.

Kneafsey, M. 2001. "Rural Cultural Economy Tourism and Social Relations." *Annals of Tourism Research* 28 (3): 762–83.

Koroscil, P.M. 2003. *The British Garden of Eden: Settlement History of the Okanagan Valley*. Burnaby, BC: Department of Geography, Simon Fraser University.

Mitchell, D. 2001. "The Lure of the Local: Landscape Studies at the End of a Troubled Century." *Progress in Human Geography* 25 (2): 269–81.

Mulvey, L. 1975. "Visual Pleasure and Narrative Cinema." *Screen* 16 (3): 6–18.

Okanagan Partnership. 2008. *Okanagan Tourism Labour Study 2008*. Kelowna: Okanagan Partnership.

Peck, J., and A. Tickell. 2002. "Neoliberalizing Space." *Antipode* 34 (3): 380–404.

Pritchard, A., and N. Morgan. 2000. "Constructing Tourism Landscapes – Gender, Sexuality and Space." *Tourism Geographies* 2: 115–39.

Rose, G. 1993. *Feminism and Geography*. Minneapolis: University of Minnesota Press.

Sands, G., and L.A. Reese. 2017. *Roads to Prosperity: Economic Development Lessons from Midsize Canadian Cities*. Michigan: Wayne State University Press.

Senese, D. 2010. "Amenity Resources and Rural Change in the Okanagan Valley of British Columbia." In *The Rural-Urban Fringe in Canada: Conflict and Controversy*, ed. K. Beesley, 158–75. Brandon, MB: Brandon University, Rural Development Institute.

Setten, G. 2003. "Landscapes of Gaze and Practice." *Norwegian Journal of Geography* 57 (3): 134–44.

Sparke, M. 1995. "Between Demythologizing and Deconstructing the Map: Shawnadithit's New-Found-Land and the Alienation of Canada." *Cartographica: The International Journal for Geographic Information and Geovisualization* 32 (1): 1–21.

Storey, D. 2006. "Images of Rurality: Commodification and Place Promotion." In *The Rural Citizen: Governance, Culture and Wellbeing in the 21st Century*. Presented at the Rural Futures Conference, University of Plymouth, 1–7, University of Plymouth, UK. Accessed May 26, 2021. http://eprints.worc.ac.uk/120/1/Storey.pdf.

Teixeira, C. 2009. "New Immigrant Settlement in a Mid-Sized City: A Case Study of Housing Barriers and Coping Strategies in Kelowna, British Columbia." *Canadian Geographer* 53 (3): 323–39.

Torres, R., and J.H. Momsen. 2004. "Challenges and Potential for Linking Tourism and Agriculture to Achieve Pro-Poor Tourism Objectives." *Progress in Development Studies* 4 (4): 294–318.

Walks, R.A. 2006. "Aestheticization and the Cultural Contradictions of Neoliberal (Sub)urbanism." *Cultural Geographies* 13 (3): 466–75.
Young, N. 2008. "Radical Neoliberalism in British Columbia: Remaking Rural Geographies." *Canadian Journal of Sociology* 33 (1): 1–36.
Young, N., and R. Matthews. 2007. "Resource Economies and Neoliberal Experimentation: The Reform of Industry and Community in Rural British Columbia." *Area* 39 (2): 176–85.

MAPS REFERENCED

Kelowna's Choice Map (1996)
Kelowna's Choice Map (1997)
The Map: Kelowna and the Westside (n.d.)
The Map: Kelowna and the Westside (1990)

CHAPTER 7

FANTASIES OF ENCORE WHITENESS IN THE CENTRAL OKANAGAN VALLEY

Luís L.M. Aguiar

This chapter argues that the Central Okanagan region persists in an encore whiteness sustained and encouraged by attitudes of smugness and niceness constrained by a discourse of anemic, neoliberal multiculturalism. Encore whiteness defines and pervades the region, smothering the voices of others who do not fit its smug and cozy configuration. Encore whiteness enforces these discourses in this contemporary moment characterized by economic disruption, vulnerability, and precariousness. This chapter analyzes federal and municipal government flyers, local slogans, billboards, and newspaper articles to delineate the ways encore whiteness represents and constitutes place and belonging, while intersecting with the neoliberalization of the valley. Neoliberalization refers to significant and disruptive economic changes in the last thirty years in the region. Three sections comprise the chapter: Section 1 locates encore whiteness; Section 2 unpacks local versions of neoliberalism that articulate with encore whiteness; and Section 3 elaborates on how neoliberalism inflects Canadian versions of multiculturalism in the valley.

LOCATING ENCORE WHITENESS IN THE CENTRAL OKANAGAN

The study of whiteness in Anglo settler societies in North America, the United Kingdom, Australia and New Zealand, and South Africa takes many forms in understanding the particularity of whiteness in nations and regions (see Bonnett 2008; Ignatiev 1995; McDermott and Samson 2005; Razack 2002; Shaw 2006; Yancy 2012). I am aware of the many criticisms levied at whiteness and its use and misuse by writers across the Global North (Satzewich 2007). Consequently, I tread carefully in understanding whiteness via analysis of place-making and representation in the southern interior of British Columbia. As elaborated in several chapters in this volume, white numerical superiority and economic and political power combine to continuously produce the Central Okanagan and the valley as a "whitopia." That is, as a place of self-segregating whites and their rationalizations for doing so, as documented by Benjamin (2009) trekking across the United States but also applicable in the Central Okanagan. Whitopia is useful in capturing places with significant white demographic numbers and cultural norms. Moreover, whitopia marks place in the contemporary Central Okanagan, as it does more generally in the ongoing exaltation of the Anglo history and future of the Okanagan and Canada (Koroscil 2008; Walcott 2019). The Central Okanagan's whitopia and encore whiteness underwrites the nature of whiteness in the region by reaffirming slogans, imagery, and attitudes that make this region a safe and comforting space of/for white people. This chapter examines these "soft" cultural expressions (e.g., billboards, slogans) to gain insight into place-making, representation, and economic change. Encore whiteness's self-assured sense of smugness and niceness affectively sustains the Central Okanagan as a whitopia; however, when encore whiteness is stressed, it can become combative.

With a population of approximately 195,000, only about 7 percent of residents in the Central Okanagan self-identify as visible minorities (Statistics Canada 2016; Areascore 2019). The latter statistic is startling and resistant to change, though Cohen and Chambers (Chapter 1, this volume) write that Indigenous peoples are in cultural and political ascendency in the region. But whiteness continues to matter despite some journalists' understating of this history (see *Vancouver Sun* 2007; MacNaull 2005), explaining it away by invoking the inevitability of history (e.g., historically, Kelowna has not attracted immigrants) or optimistically boasting that the city "is slowly becoming more diverse" (Kelowna Chamber of Commerce 2019, 28). Kelowna is the largest city in the Okanagan, and in 2016 it still retained the "lowest rate of immigrant population of any CMA [Census

Metropolitan Area] in the country" (27). In the second decade of the twenty-first century, whiteness grips Central Okanagan society no less than in the past. Despite the region's economic restructuring from Fordism to post-Fordism and a sprinkling of non-white faces gracing public posters, the statistical reality reflects a stubborn whitopia I document elsewhere (Aguiar, Tomic, and Trumper 2005a, 2005b; Whiteley, Aguiar, and Marten 2008).

While whitopia marks the geography and monoculture (Anglo) of the Central Okanagan, encore whiteness identifies white privilege's domination and reproduces and reasserts it through discourses of (whiteness) leadership in economic and political affairs (Aguiar, Tomic, and Trumper 2005a). Encore whiteness embodies the exalted monocultural Anglo heritage of whiteness in the Okanagan Valley, corresponding to economic leadership in the valley now and in the future. "Encore" implies more, and usually the same kind, of a given activity and practice. Much like a performer who dazzles an audience on stage and is then called back to the same stage to offer yet more of the same entertainment – to perform an "encore" – encore whiteness invokes more of what for generations whites have had and continue to control in the region. Encore whiteness is both the present and future of the valley as whiteness remains the mobilizing agent in defining place while nestled in the existing capitalist power structures of the Central Okanagan. It dazzles audiences with claims to its leadership in governing economic prosperity in the past and future of the Okanagan. Encore whiteness is common sense in that it is obvious and pre-empts alternatives (Walcott 2019, 401). This point is evident in the ideological articulation of the region's future. A prime example is a video produced in 2005 by the Okanagan Partnership (a coalition of the valley's bourgeoisie) imagining the Okanagan in the near future. In this video fantasy, the protagonist, a pre-teen white girl, imagines an idyllic future for the valley versus what the video's off-screen adult male narrator posits as a possible dystopia characterized by pollution, sprawl, and unctuous First Nations (Okanagan Partnership n.d.).

Encore whiteness can be flexible, adaptable, ambitious, and future looking despite its investment in an idyllic and exalted stable settler past. Beyond the cosmopolitanization of major Canadian cities, encore whiteness imagines flexibility and produces and reproduces whiteness. Yet, like the rest of

Canada, the Central Okanagan is subject to the forces of globalization, labour mobility, and global market competition. The agency of racialized Others is constrained in the region or recognized only when in the service of maintaining the place as white and aspirationally middle class. The preteen white girl in the aforementioned video embodies a figure of encore whiteness, untainted by the violence of colonialism or neoliberalism, who is seeking to maintain whiteness without accountability or regret. She embodies the aspiration of encore whiteness in seeing the next generation of settlers thriving in the valley with high-paying high-tech jobs, not scrabbling for existence picking fruit like the many Mexican temporary labourers who are pointedly not depicted in this video. As the valley economy restructures from its agricultural roots (Wagner 2009) to a post-Fordist and postindustrial economy, neoliberal multiculturalism (Melamed 2006) continues to racialize bodies and to co-opt many to serve the masters of the new economy (*Kelowna Now* 2019).

NEOLIBERAL RESTRUCTURING OF THE CENTRAL OKANAGAN

Globalization and the shift from Fordism to post-Fordism underline the push for new identities and reinventions in Western developed nations. Many municipalities and regions brand themselves in the same way as do companies (Harvey 1989a). Kelowna and the Central Okanagan both engage in smugness and niceness, rebranding from an industrial and agrarian economy to a city and region poised for the global knowledge economy (Kelowna Chamber of Commerce 2019). For example, Kelowna adopts a world city brand with world-class sporting venues, a world-class university, world-class wine and golf, and a cultural district rich in attractive venues and events (*Okanagan Life Magazine* 2008; Momer 2011). However, rebranding is not free of racialization, and whiteness remains central to the twenty-first-century economy of Kelowna and the wider valley. The pictures on the federal government pension flyer discussed below are examples of rebranding a city seeking to be cosmopolitan, world class, tolerant, and "diverse" (Momer 2011). The racial demographics cited above, with only 7 percent of residents classified as visible minorities, means the latter's presence does not jive with this region's aspirational rhetoric. In this time of globalization, neoliberalism, and place-making, diversity is cultural capital for a city marking place in the global cultural and economic landscapes. These features define a local neoliberalism combining with economic restructuring on a "more-than-local form[ation] … emergent rather than unilaterally imposed or 'top down,' and in its own way combinatorial, contradictory, and conjunctural" (Peck and Theodore 2019, 247). In the Central Okanagan, local neoliberal uniqueness interweaves economic restructuring with encore whiteness.

Abu-Laban and Gabriel (2002) show how the Canadian federal and provincial governments sought to attract global capital by recruiting diverse and skilled immigrant workforces for post-Fordist neoliberal Canada (see also Ameeriar 2017). In the Okanagan, an expanding postindustrial, post-Fordist economy replaces a previous hegemonic Fordist regime. The new economy focuses on tourism, wellness, retirement, high-tech, and luxury (Aguiar and Marten 2010). Computer geeks are the new "gentleman farmers" of the twenty-first-century Okanagan (Dunae 1981), and recent (im) migrants are the new servant class (Al-Solaylee 2016; Ameeriar 2017; Karjanen 2016). In reorganizing the economy (Aguiar and Marten 2010), most jobs are created at low pay scales to attract investment and companies who hire non-Canadian workforces without citizenship rights (see Kelowna Chamber of Commerce 2019). Companies pursue this strategy of numerical flexibility (Harvey 1989b) in a labour market in which temporary foreign workers are indentured, and locals earn low wages or accept work "in the bush" as fly-in-and-fly-out mercenaries in the punishing work of resource extraction in northern British Columbia and Alberta (Aguiar 2018). Having pushed into the bush local (mostly male) workers, capital and its representatives grow by recruiting foreign temporary migrant workers to take emerging jobs in the postindustrial economy (Tomlinson 2013; CBC News 2013; Wong and Trumper 2007) as well as jobs in traditional industries like agriculture (*Kelowna Now* 2019).

The foreign migrant workers are predominantly visible minorities who carry "identifiable" racialized identities and skills (James, Chapter 9, this volume; Aguiar, Mackinnon, and Sookraj 2010–11). They are here on a temporary basis and only fleetingly interact with locals. It was the presence of non-whites that led the Intercultural Society of the Central Okanagan (2008) to produce a report asking "Is Kelowna Ready for Demographic

Change?" This question exaggerates the change and implies resources and accommodations; it is also about the much larger issue of inclusion and citizenship in the city and region. This report does not mention the exploitation of Aboriginals and the suppression of their culture and identity, though Cohen and Chambers (Chapter 1, this volume) argue that this whiteout of First Nations lifestyles and cultures has been consistently resisted in the colonizing of the valley. The idea that whiteness is invisible and operates in some obscure consciousness is disingenuous in a region that is 93 percent white. It is its whiteness, and its recognition of such, that produces and reproduces the region over time as so monolithically white. However, the Other has been present all along in the Okanagan as the chapters in the first half of this collection attest.

The postindustrial and neoliberal economy of the valley persists in creating low-wage jobs, exacerbating the vulnerabilities of the local workforce, exploiting temporary migrant agricultural workers, and continuing to spike income inequality (*Kelowna Now* 2019; Kelowna Chamber of Commerce 2019). In 2013, the local online newspaper reported the living wage standard for a couple with two children increased for the third consecutive year to $18.01 per parent per hour (*Castanet* 2013a). This means that, according to a living wage calculations formula, $61,004.08 was required in 2013 as an annual income to meet a Central Okanagan family of four's basic needs (*Castanet* 2013a). A family of four needs a minimum income of $61,000 to purchase the basic needs of survival, and yet, in Kelowna, the median income per household is $60,360 per year (City of Kelowna 2014; AM1150 Radio 2019). Many locals are also trapped in exorbitant debt (Walks 2013). Symptomatic of this disparity between income and the living wage for many Kelowna families, the rate of demand for food at the Kelowna food banks is unprecedented and rising. For instance, the Kelowna food bank served 2,419 separate individuals in March 2013, which was a 1 percent increase over the same month in 2012. Children made up 38 percent of food bank users in Kelowna (*Castanet* 2013b). Poverty is also significant at the other end of age distribution as shelter use by seniors increased by 30 percent in 2013 (Szeto 2013). Kelowna ranks second (after Vancouver) in the country in total household debt as percentage of annual income (Walks 2013, Table 1, 166). Although these statistics are from 2013, they inform similar patterns of structural poverty that characterizes the sunny smug central Okanagan today. See recent news articles from the online local news service *Castanet* for evidence of how the entrepreneurial Okanagan is not a Garden of Eden for the working poor (Manchester 2018, Halpenny 2020, and Patel 2020a and 2020b).

The significance of these facts is that earned income gets used to service household debt, leaving less for family sustenance, while encore whiteness uses smugness and niceness to enhance its omnipresence in spite or because of the economic disruptions unfolding via local neoliberalism. The latter entails, in small- to medium-sized cities like Kelowna, cuts in "social progress," "cuts to income supports," "cuts to provisions of affordable housing," and downloading the governance of austerity to municipalities (Walmsley and Kadin 2018, 3). To make matters worse, Kelowna City Council recently invoked and enacted legislation to criminalize the poor: panhandlers are now prosecuted, as are those who give them money (Seymour 2018). A recent report by the Chartered Professional Accountants of British Columbia found that 7,700 workers left the local economy to find work in other regions; 3,200 of these were young workers. It concludes the 6.1 percent unemployment rate in Kelowna is misleading since this rate is a result of workers leaving the economy rather than of the economy creating new jobs (*Kelowna Now* 2019). Clearly, Kelowna's entrepreneurial reputation favours the few at the cost of the many (Kelowna Chamber of Commerce 2019, 21).

The above, then, is neoliberalism with Okanagan characteristics – or a local neoliberalism of economic niche-making with its own dynamics but tied to and impinged upon by larger forces of neoliberalism elsewhere (Peck and Theodore 2019, 247). Encore whiteness complements the economic restructuring of the valley by weaving local neoliberalism with whiteness and thus articulating a specific fantasy identity for the Central Okanagan. The cultural forms of encore whiteness perpetuate the smug fantasy of place despite the economic hardships generated by neoliberalism.

NEOLIBERAL MULTICULTURALISM

Neoliberal multiculturalism unites cultural diversity – most often applied to people racialized as "visible minorities" – with neoliberalism and the economic restructuring of twenty-first-century post-Fordist capitalism (Bannerjee 1995; Mitchell 2004). Neoliberal multiculturalism harnesses cultural identities and diverse features of a community for economic advantage in a global marketplace of mobile capital investment and flight. In Vancouver and in Canadian immigration offices abroad, such as in Hong Kong, Mitchell (2004) shows neoliberal multiculturalism taking shape in marketing ethnic identities and skills in global neoliberalism. She describes the value-added advantage of neoliberal multiculturalism in the global market. Melamed (2006, 3) views multiculturalism and global neoliberalism as complementary, with the former being an "alibi to neoliberalism." For her, neoliberal multiculturalism "manages racial contradictions" by obfuscating the structural forces of capitalism tied to racism and exploitation and, in doing so, "naturalizes inequality" (14). Rinaldo Walcott (2019, 396) further critiques multiculturalism configured as diversity; he argues that multiculturalism is a comforting lie for whites since it speaks of change, inclusion, and integration when in reality diversity does nothing except to reinforce the erroneous idea that whiteness is decentred in Canadians' lives: "we know collectively that the latter is not the case. The lie of multiculturalism then functions to produce a compact in which certain kinds of diversity can be celebrated as standing in for collective representation. To accede to these kinds of representational practices is to agree or at least become complicit with the lie" (397).

In the Okanagan case, neoliberal multiculturalism invokes representations of the "Other" in the neoliberal restructuring of the valley, bringing minority workers to farms, care work, construction, and even college apprenticeship programs. These people have few or no rights and lack routes to permanency residency status, thus having their vulnerability and precariousness exacerbated (Caxaj and Diaz 2018). It is, of course, this vulnerability (BCSAWP 2005; Fairey et al. 2008) that attracts employers since it disciplines workers to behave and to remain obedient and reliable (Wong and Trumper 2007), even if, occasionally, a rogue worker defies unacceptable working conditions and abuse (Nuttall 2015). The manoeuvring of recruitment and representation is inaccurate and deceptive since it obfuscates the mechanisms discriminating against visible minorities, who uphold, endure, and suffer economic restructuring while being expected to believe that encore whiteness will lead to prosperity and equality (Momer 2011; Alumni UBC 2018; Kelowna Chamber of Commerce 2019). Neoliberal multiculturalism operates as a facet of encore whiteness in conjunction with its other attributes, such as inclusion.

TEXTUAL ANALYSIS: INCLUSIVE FANTASIES OF ENCORE WHITENESS

During the government of Stephen Harper (2006–15), a Conservative member of Parliament distributed to thousands of householders in the Central Okanagan a flyer on Canadian retirement benefits and the risks to them in the current economic climate. It includes a statement from the then Conservative Government of Canada's plan to protect the future of seniors' pensions. The text in the flyer expresses familiar themes (e.g., cutting taxes, privatization) in the too often alarmist language of the then federal Conservative government's austerity program on social reform (Doern 2009; Albo and Evans 2008). What is striking about this flyer is the face of a distinguished-looking, grey-bearded Black man. He appears reassured and content, something that is evident in his satisfied smile. What is the meaning of a Black face on a flyer distributed throughout the Central Okanagan? The valley is in part a retirement space with its post-industrial and post-Fordist economy, and the distribution of such a flyer on retirement and pensions does make sense. But it would take some creative detective work to find elderly visible minorities retiring in the valley. In Kelowna, there are only 470 (35 Black) visible minorities between the ages of 64 and 74 (Statistics Canada 2011). So, why a Black face on a government flyer mailed to Central Okanagan residents? This representation is consistent with my argument that representations of diversity are gestures towards symbolic change with little anchorage in processes of real long-term change.

The Central Okanagan Foundation released a report called *Central Okanagan's Vital Signs 2009*. In it, the foundation evaluates eleven key issues, from safety to work to housing, for newcomers in the Okanagan (Central Okanagan Foundation 2009). The evaluation in school report card style assigns grades "A" to "F" to eleven issues and ascertains the likelihood of the region's meeting the criteria for quality of living and working in the Central Okanagan. The section on welcoming new immigrants and the issue of "getting started" receives a "C" grade, which translates into poor efforts to accommodate newcomers and to promote inclusion in the region (see also Teixeira 2009). As surprising as the findings in the report may be for some, with the poor showing of services, resources, and accommodation facilities, what is startling is the number of pictures of young Black faces in the pages of the report. Of five pictures in which faces are clearly visible, four are of young Black professionals. The faces are of models, with precise poses and perfect faces, standing in for the Central Okanagan's Black population. Historically, Blacks and other visible minorities have been effaced, rendered invisible, policed, surveilled, corralled, harassed, threatened, eroticized, exoticized, or made hyper-visible in the Okanagan (Aguiar, MacKinnon, and Sookraj 2010–11). No such pictures exist either in the more recent Chamber of Commerce's scorecard (Kelowna Chamber of Commerce 2019) or in the Central Okanagan Foundation's annual report (2018). Kelowna receives a "D" grade for the percentage of its population with post-secondary degrees who are visible minorities (seen as disadvantaging business), real GDP per capita, and disposable income per capita (Kelowna Chamber of Commerce 2019, 10). Ironically, the city receives an "A" grade in income inequality because "a high score indicates a high level of performance" (ibid.). There is, then, growing income inequality in the region as it is reimagined via diversity and inclusion.

In this context, the fantasy of neoliberal multiculturalism identifies diversity (as an economic asset) that is missing in the representation of the restructuring regional economy. But, as demonstrated above, the changes in the valley's facade are evidence of an encore whiteness that is flexible and oppressive, seeking to make a pre-emptive strike against potential reinterpretations of the presence of the Other in the valley. Neoliberal multiculturalism pushes surface over substance. It is an exercise in flat diversity, lacking authenticity and credibility (Depner and Teixeira 2012). The flat diversity neoliberal multiculturalism expresses in the Central Okanagan offers a superficial presentation lacking depth, integration, or agency in representations of the Other. It is smug in its omnipresence (and blindingly so to the white majority); it normalizes and fails to interrogate, explore, and deconstruct its domination. Flat diversity does not threaten and is often invoked to grow the cultural economy, paying lip service to tolerance and inclusion of the Other without acknowledging the history, presence, or experiences of racialized groups in the valley (Kelowna Chamber of Commerce 2019; Aguiar, Tomic, and Trumper 2005a).

When the Other is made visible, as in the sepia-tone photos of Chinese labourers from the early twentieth century in the international arrival area of the Kelowna airport, they are there not only to exalt the good will of white employers but also to serve as symbols of perpetual foreigners (Brown 2017; Kyle 2017; Seymour 2019). Whites, on the other hand, are represented throughout the airport. Sadly, even this tokenism pertaining to the history of racialized workers in the Okanagan was removed and put in storage in fall 2012 after the completion of the airport's expansion. Now posters advertising encore whiteness fill the "new" and "international" airport. Today, neoliberal multiculturalism is flat diversity depicted as broad, liberal, and inclusive but without its actually being so. In other words, whiteness reproduces its position of power and status through "economies of visibility" that "too often feature sanitized snapshots that promote 'integration without equality, representation without power, and presence without confining possibility of emancipation'" (Wiegman in McDonald 2005, 248). Representation is not "'detached from the continuing imperatives seeking dominance, privileges, and presumed superiority for white bodies'" (ibid.). Redclift (2014) argues that, as the racial make-up and landscapes in the UK change, some (including governments) assert that diversity dissolves racism. While I maintain that the Central Okanagan is unchanging in racial make-up, this does not preclude its power players and authoritative organizations from fantasizing that this is not the case. For instance, Kelowna elected its first-ever Sikh Canadian mayor for a second term in 2018 (*Global News* 2018). Consistent with the logic of postracial ideology (Da Costa 2015), Basran's 2014 and 2018 campaigns were free from issues of discrimination, white privilege, and racism; instead, he emphasized a pro-development regime, but with an endorsement from the LBGT community, thereby profiling a "progressive" angle in an otherwise pro-business approach to municipal politics (Michaels 2014; Munro 2019). But the mayor seems to practise a "progressiveness of convenience" since he recently refused to believe women's complaints that the local police force refused to take seriously their complaints of sexual harassment in the city (Rodriguez 2019a). He is also leading a campaign against the homeless in the city (Rodriguez 2019b). In other words, neoliberal multiculturalism unfolds its flexibility to reinforce encore whiteness in a valley "free" of "race," and phenotype racism thereby naturalizes inequality. By naturalizing inequality free of repertoires of racism, neither capital nor neoliberal multiculturalism are called into question (Melamed 2006, 14, 16), and only minimal gestures towards social justice are entertained (see Intercultural Society of the Central Okanagan 2008; and Alumni UBC 2018).

TEXTUAL ANALYSIS OF SMUG FANTASIES: "WE LOVE IT HERE"

The Free Online Dictionary defines smugness as an "offensive satisfaction with oneself or one's situation" ("Smugness" 2015). This definition reduces smugness to the individual. I, instead, follow Ahmed (2010) in paying attention to the social in viewing smugness as affect – that is, smugness not as what it is but as how it socially functions. In the Central Okanagan, smugness is an air of arrogance about place accepted and lived in the daily lives and interactions of locals. It hovers "outside" individuals, though very much ingrained in their habitus (lived experienced) (Bourdieu 1984). The aura of smugness reinforces encore whiteness as central to the Okanagan's dominant public culture. The smugness of the Central Okanagan is code for features of encore whiteness – safety, familiarity, self-segregating, free from the fear of the Other (Aguiar, Tomic and Trumper 2005a; Aguiar, Tomic, and Trumper 2005b). In addition, locals invoke and enact smugness through the recognition of clues and cues in social practices, imagery, and exaltations of place in their social milieu.

In the Central Okanagan an attitude of smugness as whiteness prevails in a lifestyle discourse whereby residents protect and reinforce this attitude, reprimanding anyone who objects and questions its promotion in/of the region. The discourses and practises of utopian fantasy ensure that whiteness is race-specific and advantageous to whites. Encore whiteness appears in plain sight in commercial publications (as opposed to the reports discussed in the last section) without a name, denying its oppressive smugness and preferring to interpret achievement and advancement through the capitalist values of personal worth, drive, dedication, and work ethic. This taken-for-granted appearance of whiteness involves what Lipsitz (2006) calls "a possessive investment in whiteness" but with a regional inflection in the Okanagan as a sanctuary of/for whiteness, so accurately captured in a tourist T-shirt purchased at the departure lounge in the souvenir shop at Kelowna airport. The T-shirt boasts of Kelowna as a "White Oasis ... Pure" and is an introduction to (or summation of) Kelowna's particular whiteness. "Pure" is placed on the back of the shirt (i.e., out of sight of the initial view of the shirt) as self-referential, with a twinkle in the eye for the "people in the know" since this may be interpreted as a joke or seen as a truism given how "delayed" and "late" the adjective "Pure" follows "White Oasis." And, if "Pure" refers to powdered snow on "Big White" mountain resort and ski hill, this is not exempt from unbearable whiteness (Coleman 1996). If neoliberal multicultural whiteness in the valley articulates as a type of flat notional aspiration for diversity, it has its corollary in a smug, sly celebration of white purity announced by this T-shirt and other cultural expressions explored below.

Writings on race and whiteness focus on the subtleties of racism and whiteness under the emergence of cultural racism (Balibar 2007). Discussing the latter unfolds with parallel effort to highlight and identify the harsh realities of racism by making the violence of whiteness visible (Clarke 1997; Stewart 2014). In the Okanagan, the violence of scientific racism (Lewontin, Rose, and Kamin 1985) creeps into the everyday and often operates alongside subtle racism in the form of white painless privileged racism (Aguiar, Mackinnon, and Sookraj 2010–11; Aguiar and Marten 2011; Lethbridge 1994; Munro 2019). The violence of racism (hooks 1982) operates alongside subtle racism, with whiteness described as a form of subtle racism. Vanderbeck (2006, 641), in studying whiteness in Vermont, argues that this rural landscape is defined by "political liberality/progressiveness," with notions of "rustic" and "tranquil" becoming code words for whiteness, exclusion, and racism. This kind of "unspoiled" ecologically "pure" whiteness is slippery for encore whiteness is flexible and combative when adaptability is required or the reassertion of its dominance necessary.

In the Central Okanagan, combative whiteness is spotty at best since opposition and resistance to its position and status is infrequent and isolated. For rare examples of combative whiteness, see James (Chapter 9, this volume), Svenson (Chapter 12, this volume), and Aguiar, MacKinnon, and Sookraj (2010–11). Encore whiteness's power is, in part, due to its flexibility in being "'translated into myriad forms; indeed, recognition of its adaptability, flexibility, and variability is essential to understand[ing] its power'" (Kobayashi quoted in Vanderbeck 2006, 644). The new codes of whiteness are like the old – intense, oppressive, and deeply felt despite encore whiteness appearing as adaptable and flexible to the Other. There are many examples in the Central Okanagan in which encore whiteness operates in explicitly oppressive forms (Aguiar, Tomic, and Trumper 2005a; Aguiar, Tomic, and Trumper 2005b). Encore whiteness is oppressive in its omnipresence and forced conformity. In the neoliberal Okanagan, explicit forms of white supremacy are reproduced in the local press as acts of "bad apple" racists, which rile the community but leave whiteness unexamined, as in the *Global News* (2021) report of neo-Nazi posters in the "Pandosy village" neighbourhood of the city. Thus, social issues like Indigenous women being discriminated against in their search for housing (see Lewis and Berg, Chapter 8, this volume) or multiple examples of hate crimes against Jewish and Sikh places of worship are seen as acts of deranged individuals rather than as the product of social milieux of exclusion (Aguiar, Tomic, and Trumper 2005a; Aguiar, Tomic, and Trumper 2005b; *CTV News* 2008; Singh 2018; Morton 2018). In the valley, as elsewhere in rural settler-spaces, whiteness is evident in the history of settlement narratives. It is also oppressive through the prevailing mood, sentiment (Fax 2012), aspiration, affect, and smugness (Ahmed 2010).

Quality-of-life discourses express the Central Okanagan Economic and Development Commission's tagline – "work where you play" (Community Futures Network of Canada 2015). This tagline carries both the desired aesthetic of the place and the oppressiveness of having to struggle to conform to this aesthetic. Lifestyle is oppressive in two ways: (1) as an agent of whiteness conformity and (2) as a measure of moral authority against which poor people fear to object lest they face shaming in the form of "what's-the-matter-with-you?" reprimands, regardless of their financial inability to "play." In other words, in the Okanagan Valley, whiteness has not receded but remains obvious in various spheres of social existence and experience. For example, Kelowna's Orchard Park Mall ran a smug promotional campaign called "We Love It Here!" The campaign focused on images of places and valley vistas, and hung sixty "We love it here" banners in the mall's corridors. The campaign did not stop there: the slogan was written on mall floor tiles, doors, buses, and benches. Finally, post-it notes were stuck on the front of the Saturday newspapers, bearing slogans like "Who wouldn't love it here?" and "Don't you love it here?" (*Tactics Magazine* 2003). While one has to recognize that this is a promotional campaign for a shopping mall, it is revealing that the campaign marries these promotions to the whiteness of the Okanagan and the smugness "everyone" feels, accepts, and shares in living in the valley.

An account of smugness as code for encore whiteness features in a 2015 editorial in the *Okanagan Home Magazine*. This free magazine is distributed to homes and workplaces across the Central Okanagan. It offers an array of real estate home investments in the region for affluent clients. A straight white couple who appear to be in their thirties edit the magazine. These editors boast: "This is one of our favourite times to be at home in the Okanagan. Brag worthy weather, loads of seasonal events and the buzz of never-ending supply of visitors to our region have us excited to be entering the summer months ... And as each long day of summer comes to an end, take some time to enjoy a perfect Okanagan sunset with a great glass of wine in your hand, from your favourite private – or public – outdoor living space. In the Okanagan, we know it will be hard to choose" (O'Connor and Hughes 2015, 15). Here, unlike elsewhere, the diffusion of smugness is uninhibited, there being little need to build consent since encore whiteness operates freely with little to no opposition. When and where opposition does emerge, it is individually expressed and so has little impact or consequence. Encore whiteness becomes separate from class and the economic challenges faced by most living within the smug aura of the Central Okanagan's self-inflated and self-absorbed version of itself.

LANDSCAPE OF NICENESS: DON'T YOU JUST LOVE IT HERE!

In the "The Happiness Turn," Sara Ahmed (2007–08) examines the rise of the "Happiness Industry." This industry relies on science to identify indicators and measurements for levels of contribution to happiness. The literature on the industry evokes classical definitions of happiness, harking back to ancient Greece, where happiness related to matters of the mind developed through virtuous activity during times of leisure, or to the English utilitarian theory of individual maximization through government initiatives (9). Both Eurocentric versions of happiness ask the same question: "What is happiness?" (7). This question assumes happiness as a given and as something we aspire to feel and to achieve, but Ahmed shifts the study of happiness from what it is to what it does and what it evokes. She asks different questions: "What does happiness do?" "What makes happiness appealing?" (ibid.). Happiness "generates effects, bringing a certain world into existence. Happiness can be understood as a promise or aspiration" (12). Happiness has agency and it "does things." Some of the things it does correlate "between happiness levels and social indicators, creating what [Ahmed] calls 'whiteness indicators'" (Ahmed 2010, 6). In the Central Okanagan, marketers recognize consumers' smug attention to place – in this case the whitopia of the Central Okanagan – as a "happy" place, and they seek to build an attachment to their products by relying on place indicators. Happiness is evident in Orchard Park's "we-love-it-here" campaign and the T-shirt blazingly proclaiming the valley as "White Oasis … Pure." These campaigns encourage residents to express a measure of self-satisfaction, either for a ski hill or for a shopping centre, that is symbolic of a desire to achieve an imagined state of happiness (Ahmed 2010). This state of happiness is another way of expressing the "sociability of happiness" in the Central Okanagan, whereby feeling good is enacted not only through social interactions but also through linguistic practices of smugness and niceness that enforce encore whiteness.

According to Setha Low (2009), niceness is another form of whiteness and white privilege. She writes that niceness is about constructing a place free of the Other by "keeping things clean, orderly, homogenous, and controlled so that housing and its values [for example] remain stable" (82). Niceness expressed through "cleanliness and orderliness indicate[s] the 'type of people' who live in a place and establish a norm of middle-class civility, masking the imposition of whiteness" (87). Thus, whiteness and the "reproduction of white privilege is generated in the absence of blatant racism" (Davis 2007, 354). It is through "banal ways," "ordinariness" that "things … are expressed but not stated; the routine and familiar forms of ideas that are sustained, but are often overlooked, precisely because they are mute" (ibid.). This ordinariness tends to "escape" detection, interrogation, and so deflects "racism, racializing and the absence of racial analysis" (356). This "muted racism" is symptomatic of twenty-first-century neoliberalism and is no less psychologically damaging than the blatant racism of the mid-twentieth century. Encore whiteness in the valley is oppressively omnipresent not only in sheer population numbers but also in the attitudes of smugness and niceness that discipline and reinforce residents and visitors regarding the place the Central Okanagan is and should remain.

Residents' claims about the niceness of living in the Okanagan Valley express whiteness as familiarity, safety, and security from non-whites. Page asserts that whiteness and white privilege are reinforced "through the circulation and manipulation of information, knowledge, and cultural symbols" (Page in Low 2009, 82). In other words, niceness is a cultural expression tied to whiteness. It also goes against the grain of the economic realities of many Kelownians who are vulnerable to a restructuring economy that is creating jobs with poor wages and benefits, coupled with a housing market whose rental vacancy rate (.2 percent) is the lowest in the country (*Global News* 2017) and in which the average home sells for approximately $700,000 (MacNaull 2017). Affordability and inequality are unprecedented (*Kelowna Now* 2019). Indeed, niceness is a form of "cruel optimism" in the hub city of the valley (Berlant 2007).

Niceness is another affective code word for encore whiteness and the happy feeling of living among those who look like you and are, therefore, more trustworthy than those who do not look like you and who practise different customs and activities from you (Ahmed 2010). In addition, niceness operates as a promise of being alone, free to contemplate landscapes that are long, large, and wide, and – most important – free of the Other (of all kinds) (Erickson 2013). Happiness is the Hotel Eldorado billboard "Life in a Postcard," "make[ing] things good" in the Okanagan (Ahmed 2007–08, 7). Found on a wall just prior to entering the arrival lounge in the Kelowna airport the billboard depicts a blond woman sitting on a couch with arms stretched along its back (I was denied permission to reproduce it here). Her gaze is fixed on the lake and the mountain across from the hotel. Serenity dominates the scene since no one else occupies space in the billboard – not even sailboats or swimmers. Perhaps it is here that a white "mom" can find peace and solace and time to relax by stretching out on the couch, absorbing and appreciating the landscape free from kids, husband, significant other, and the double day of labour. The billboard image conveys escapism and contemplation, with a hint of expectation and spontaneity assumed in the woman's arms stretched along the back of the couch. While she relaxes, she does not seem opposed to company – something that is evident in her "open"-arms pose. The whiteness in the billboard is evident in the image of the blond white woman and through coded visual cues like water, mountains, landscapes, and contemplation free of anyone who is non-white. In other words, white persons contemplate while Others labour to make this happen and obligingly remain outside the frame altogether. In this billboard image, the couch-sitting blond woman admires the landscape and, at the same time, through her eyes and the vantage point of the billboard, invites the viewer to do likewise. The billboard presents encore whiteness framed within the long history of Canadian landscape images of white figures in the "barren" landscapes of the nation (Erickson 2013). Here, smugness is white luxury exclusively consuming the landscape and inviting others like "herself" to do the same, free of interruptions and the presence of the un-belonging, of those who are not white and not wealthy – but who serve her in her postcard fantasy (see Corbett and Senese in this volume).

Setha Low expands and enhances our definition of whiteness by pinning it on middle-class civility and behaviour. She argues that, in addition to the fear of others: "signs, shop decor, and street furniture in suburban towns are subject to local scrutiny to prevent them from becoming disorganized and 'filthy' like nearby cities. Cleanliness and orderliness indicate the 'type of people' who live in a place and establish a norm of middle-class civility, masking the imposition of whiteness" (Low 2009, 87). However, "masking the imposition of whiteness" has never been the case in the Central Okanagan. Here encore whiteness is omnipresent, unquestioned, and oppressive in the power to demand conformity. What strikes me about the Central Okanagan is the visibility of its whiteness, even though its presence is only occasionally problematized, questioned, or opposed. Its oppressive impact is hyper-visible and asserted repeatedly through various ways, including landscape aesthetics, lifestyle devotions, and, frankly, the smugness of the life lived in the region. The niceness associated with living in the Okanagan exudes an oppressive smugness that exalts white forms of being. Low (2009, 81) captures this sense of how space is racialized in her concept of "nice" as defined by conforming to rituals of common definitions of what is nice and acceptable: "Landscape aesthetics function as a suburban politics of exclusion often referred to as making everything 'nice.'" Nice in the Central

Okanagan stands in for whiteness in the smugness that permeates the city and its aesthetics of playscapes and exclusive urban residences (Grant 2005). So, as it becomes increasingly difficult to restrict movement into white safe places like Kelowna and the Central Okanagan, the racialized other is disciplined, regulated, and instructed on whiteness via discourses of what is "nice" in and about this region. Its safety, pro-family environment, happiness, and smugness make it difficult to object to the "niceties" of Okanagan living.

An example of this smugness is evident in a few editorials in Kelowna's only daily newspaper – the *Daily Courier*. For instance, in one editorial on how the "business community shines," the managing editor begins with the following: "reasons why we love it here [Kelowna] No. 328" (*Daily Courier* 2009a). He confidently – and without irony – asserts the smugness of encore whiteness as a reprimand to readers who might not share in the Kelowna fantasy. The editorial confirms its readers belong to the 93 percent of the population who identify as white and for whom living in Kelowna is excellent. The editorial also implies that the business community is largely responsible for "us" liking it here as it juxtaposes reasons for why we love it with a story on the contribution of the business community. Clearly, without the business community, the laissez-faire business climate of the region, and the culture of whiteness, the Okanagan would not be as prosperous and as worth living in as it is today. No wonder some seek to keep it pristinely white (Aguiar, MacKinnon, and Sookraj 2010–11). In another editorial supporting freezing the wages for city hall workers, the writer concludes: "City workers are extremely well-paid, and have near iron-clad job security. *Plus, they get to live in Kelowna*" (*Daily Courier* 2009b, emphasis mine). The smugness of place revealed in this editorial reinforces the consensual fantasy of Kelowna as a region of whiteness for which indolent city workers should be grateful.

Niceness as encore whiteness is not only oppressive in its assumed conformity, it is patronizing in its symbolism for the "inclusion" of the racialized other. An example of this neoliberal multicultural dynamic may be found in a mural depicting racial harmony in the interlocked black and white hands on the side of one of the buildings (across from the BC Tree Fruits Building on Water Street) in downtown Kelowna. However, this image is a multicultural fantasy that does not exist in the Okanagan. The image of the locked hands in unison and harmony belies the barriers, obstacles (Stone 2001), and racisms that brown-skinned and mixed-raced people endure in the Okanagan Valley. The mural takes on an even more suspect tone when one considers the revanchist politics (Smith 1996) of the Downtown Kelowna Association (DKA). This group's goal is to sanitize the downtown core of graffiti and "undesirables" by staging several revanchist campaigns (*Capital News* 2007a; *Capital News* 2008; *Daily Courier* 2003). It employs a private security force that patrols and harasses and disciplines the homeless, panhandlers, and other "undesirables" in the tourist spaces of the downtown area. And it has gone so far as to campaign with local police to confiscate shopping carts from the homeless (*CBC News 2005*). The DKA also employs graffiti crews to remove all inscriptions on the walls and trash bins in the downtown area. Any possible markings on city walls will need the approval of the DKA; otherwise, they will be erased (Smith 2010). The DKA comprises downtown Kelowna's self-appointed civility police. The anonymous locked-hands mural is a manufactured and commissioned artistic rendition of racial unity that does not in fact exist. This fantasy is an example of a kind of pre-emptive revanchist whiteness strike against representation and spaces created by/for the Other. There is an attempt to pre-empt the agency of the Others or at least to coordinate, designate, and co-opt their agency. In this way, encore whiteness is not monolithic, though it is oppressive in its fluidity, making it hard to grasp identities and perspectives. As it happens, this mural no longer exists: it was bulldozed to "put up a parking lot."

On 27 June 2019, the city of Kelowna unveiled a mural paying tribute to the Chinese Canadian community of Kelowna, which, in the early twentieth century, constituted 15 percent of the city's population. The mural is in the courtyard of the Mission Gospel homeless shelter (Seymour 2019). This shelter is in the heart of downtown and is often under threat of removal from the city's prime real estate section to make way for profitable activities. And, while I support the initiative to recognize and memorialize the presence and contributions of the Chinese to Kelowna, I am perplexed by the decision to locate the mural next to a homeless shelter that locals avoid and that tourists have little interest in visiting. This is how neoliberal multiculturalism articulates the Other as invisible in plain sight. Recently, the mayor and city councillors enacted legislation to criminalize panhandling and sitting or sleeping on sidewalks. Fortunately, seventy people signed a petition against this law and presented it to council, and the group Homelessness in Kelowna organized a "sit down" to "stand for people without homes" (Wylie 2016). But this "gain" was short-lived since, in November 2019, pressured by downtown business capital, city council relocated a tent city of homeless Kelownians from Leon Street – a prominent downtown street and where the Gospel Mission sits – to a park on the periphery of the downtown business core. But homeless men and women are not wanted there either, as NIMBY residents organized to voice their displeasure with the city's choice of where to relocate the homeless (Rodriguez 2019b). In sum, the above shows that the municipal state is in cahoots with the local bourgeoisie to inscribe class and whiteness in the production and reproduction of place. This "coordination" of interests – business interests are *our* interests – is rarely contested since opposition is infrequent and atomized. And so, the fantasy of local entrepreneurial spirit persists even as the poor are dispossessed, displaced, and expelled from areas of the city by local elites.

Gramsci (1971) defined hegemony as the ongoing process of give-and-take between negotiating groups whereby all get something but leave intact the power of capital (and whiteness) in any given geography. However, in this place of encore whiteness, hegemony does not capture the quasi-totalizing presence of whiteness. There is little resistance to whiteness in the everydayness of the Okanagan; encore whiteness functions uninhibited by opposing forces or groups pushing for gains of their own. Whatever changes are made in the smugness and niceness of the Okanagan's landscape are shaped by the power structures of whiteness and not by some other internal/external force challenging the status and position of whiteness. In other words, challenges to Okanagan whiteness are shrugged off by attitudes of smugness and niceness that ensure encore whiteness perpetually repeats it self-assured fantasy. Here in the Okanagan, hegemony appears to be too soft a concept to capture, understand, and describe the stranglehold of whiteness. Here, encore whiteness is dominant and dominating. Here, encore whiteness is overwhelming albeit, in the Canadian way, nice and polite. And here, encore whiteness expresses its own momentum and internal dynamic by invoking multiculturalism and affect to perpetuate itself. Here, encore whiteness is authoritarian in its omnipresence.

REFERENCES

Abu-Laban, Yasmeen, and Christina Gabriel. 2002. *Selling Diversity: Immigration, Multiculturalism, Employment Equity and Globalization*. Peterborough, ON: Broadview Press.

Aguiar, L.L.M. 2018. "Sabotaged Bodies, Sacrifice, and Lost Youth under Punitive Neoliberalism." In *The Handbook on the Politics of Health*, ed. Richard Parker and Jonathan Garcia, 87–98. New York: Routledge.

Aguiar, L.L.M., Ann Marie McKinnon, and Dixon Sookraj. 2010–11 "Racialization and the Repertoires of Racism: Reaction to Jamaicans in the Okanagan Valley." *BC Studies* 168 (Winter 2010–11): 65–79.

Aguiar, L.L.M., and Tina Marten. 2010. "Wine Tourism and Post-Fordist Restructuring in the Okanagan Valley, British Columbia." In *Interrogating the New Economy*, ed. Norene Pupo and Mark Thomas, 173–93. Toronto: University of Toronto Press.

–. 2011. "Shimmering White Kelowna and the Examination of Painless White Privilege in the Hinterland of British Columbia." In *Rethinking the Great White North: Race, Nature and the Historical Geographies of Whiteness in Canada*, ed. Andrew Baldwin, L. Cameron, and A. Kobayashi, 127–45. Vancouver: UBC Press.

Aguiar, L.L.M., Patricia Tomic, and Ricardo Trumper. 2005a. "Work Hard, Play Hard: Re-Inventing the Okanagan Valley for the 'New Economy.'" *Canadian Geographer* 48 (2): 123–39.

–. 2005b. "The Letter: Racism, Hate and Monoculturalism in a Canadian Hinterland." In *Possibilities and Limitations: Multicultural Policies and Programs in Canada*, ed. Carl James, 163–74. Halifax: Fernwood.

Ahmed, Sara. 2007–08. "The Happiness Turn." *New Formations* 63: 7–15.

–. 2010. *The Promise of Happiness*. Durham, NC: Duke University Press.

Albo, Greg, and Bryan Evans. 2008. "Harper's Bunker: The Federal State, Neoliberalism and the Left." *Relay [21]: A Socialist Project Review*. http://www.yorku.ca/albo/docs/2008/relay23_albo.pdf.

Al-Solaylee, Kamel. 2016. *Brown: What Being Brown in the World Today Means (to Everyone)*. Toronto: HarperCollins.

Alumni UBC. 2018. "Okanagan: How Can We Make Kelowna a More Culturally Inclusive Community?" *UBC Dialogues*. 15 March. https://www.alumni.ubc.ca/event/kelowna-culturally-inclusive-community/.

Ameeriar, Lalie. 2017. *Downwardly Global: Women, Work, and Citizenship in the Pakistani Diaspora*. Durham, NC: Duke University Press.

AM1150 Radio. 2019. Iheartradio. http://www.iheartradio.ca/am-1150/news/household-income-in-kelowna-lowest-in-central-okanagan-1.3287433.

Areascore. 2019. http://areascore.ca/area/kelowna_bc/immigration_visible-minority-statistics.

Balibar, Étienne. 2007. "Is There a 'Neo-Racism?'" In *Race and Racialization: Essential Readings*, eds. Tania Das Gupta, Carl E. James, Chris Andersen, Grace-Edward Galabuzi and Roger C.A. Maaka, 83–88. Toronto: Canadian Scholars' Press.

Bannerji, Himani. 1995. *Thinking Through: Essays on Feminism, Marxism, and Anti-Racism*. Toronto: Women's Press.

BCSAWP. 2005. "Guidelines for the Provision of Seasonal Housing for Migrant Farm Workers in BC." Abbotsford, BC: Western Agricultural Labour Initiative. http://bcac.bc.ca/userfi les/fi le/wali/BCSAWP_Guidelines.pdf.

Benjamin, Rich. 2009. *Searching for Whitopia: An Improbable Journey into the Heart of White America*. New York: Hyperion Books.

Berlant, Lauren. 2007. "Cruel Optimism: On Marx, Loss and the Senses." *New Formations* 63: 33–51.

Bonnett, Alistair. 2008. "Review Article: White Studies Revisited." *Ethnic and Racial Studies* 31 (1): 185–96.

Bourdieu, Pierre. 1984. *Distinction*. Cambridge, MA: Harvard University Press.

Brown, Liz. 2017. "Okanagan Throwback: Chinatown." *Kelowna Now*. https://www.kelownanow.com/watercooler/news/news/Kelowna/17/04/13/Okanagan_Throwback_Chinatown/.

Capital News. 2007a. "City Wants to Crack Down on Beggars." 12 September, A1. http://proquest.umi.com/pqdweb?index=15&sid=3&vinst=PROD&fmt=3&s.

–. 2008. "Kelowna Security Patrolling with a Smile," 9 April, 18.

Castanet. 2013a. "Okanagan 'Living Wage' Rises Again." http://www.castanet.net/news/Central-Okanagan/95490/Okanagan-Living-Wage-rises-again.

–. 2013b. "Food Bank Use Remains High." http://www.castanet.net/news/Cast-A-Light/103408/Food-bank-use-remains-high.

Caxaj, Susana, and Luiz Diaz. 2018. "Migrant Workers' (Non)belonging in Rural British Columbia, Canada: Storied Experiences of Marginal Living." *International Journal of Migration, Health and Social Care* 14 (2): 208–20.

CBC News. 2005. "Kelowna RCMP Plan to Seize Shopping Carts from Homeless." 19 March. https://www.cbc.ca/news/canada/kelowna-rcmp-plan-to-seize-shopping-carts-from-homeless-1.531983?print.

–. 2013. "RBC Replaces Canadian Workers with Foreign Workers." http://www.cbc.ca/news/canada/british-columbia/rbc-replaces-canadian-staff-with- foreign-workers-1.1315008.

Central Okanagan Foundation. 2009. Vital Signs 2009. Kelowna: Central Okanagan Foundation.

City of Kelowna. 2014. *Exploring Our Community: 2014 Community Trend Report*. Kelowna, BC: City of Kelowna.

Clarke, George Elliot. 1997. "White like Canada." *Transition* 73: 98–109.

Coleman, Annie Gilbert. 1996. "The Unbearable Whiteness of Skiing." *Pacific Historical Review* 65 (4): 583–614.

Community Futures Network of Canada. 2015. Okanagan Valley Technology Sector Development Project. *Community Futures Network of Canada*. https://communityfuturescanada.ca/project/okanagan-valley-technology-sector-development-project/.

CTV News. 2008. "Okanagan Jewish Centre Targeted by Vandals." 21 June 2008. https://bc.ctvnews.ca/okanagan-jewish-centre-targeted-by-vandals-1.303828

Da Costa, Alexandre Emboaba. 2015. "Thinking `Post-Racial` Ideology Transnationally: The Contemporary Politics of Race and Indigeneity in the Americas." *Current Sociology* 42 (4–5): 475–90.

Daily Courier. 2009a. "Editorial: Business Community Shines." 15 October, A10.
–. 2009b. "Editorial: Time for Wage Freeze at City Hall." 13 October, A10.
–. 2003. "Kelowna's Biz Patrol on the Streets for Summer." 3 June, B7.
Davis, Dana-Ain. 2007. "Narrating the Mute: Racializing and Racism in a Neoliberal Moment." *Souls* 9 (4): 346–60.
Depner, Wolfgang, and Carlos Teixeira. 2012. "Welcoming Communities? An Assessment of Community Services in Attracting and Retaining Immigrants in the South Okanagan Valley (British Columbia, Canada), with Policy Recommendations." *Journal of Rural and Community Development* 7 (2): 72–97.
Doern, Bruce. 2009. "Evolving Budgetary Policies and Experiments: 1980 to 2009." In *How Ottawa Spends, 2009–2010*, ed. Allan M. Maslove, 14–43. Montreal and Kingston: McGill-Queen's University Press.
Dunae, Patrick. 1981. *Gentlemen Emigrants: From the British Public Schools to the Canadian Frontier*. Vancouver: Douglas and McIntyre.
Erickson, Bruce. 2013. *Canoe Nation: Nature, Race, and the Making of a Canadian Icon*. Vancouver: UBC Press.
Fairey, David, Christina Hanson, Glen MacInnes, Arlene Tiger McLaren, Gerardo Otero, Kerry Preibisch, and Mark Thompson. 2008. *Cultivating Farmworker Rights: Ending the Exploitation of Immigrant and Migrant Farmworkers in BC*. Vancouver: Canadian Centre for Policy Alternatives.
Fax, Joanna. 2012. "Vulnerability as Hegemony: Revisiting Gramsci in the Age of Neoliberalism and Tea Party Politics." *Culture, Theory and Critique* 53 (3): 323.
Global News. 2017. "Kelowna's Vacancy Rental Rate Lowest in Country." 28 November. https://globalnews.ca/news/3886556/kelownas-rental-vacancy-rate-lowest-in-the-country/.
–. 2018. https://globalnews.ca/news/4086775/diversity-discussion-part-of-ongoing-conversation-in-kelowna/.
Gramsci, Antonio. 1971. *Selections from the Prison Notebooks*. New York: International Publishers.
Grant, Jill. 2005. "Planning Responses to Gated Communities in Canada." *Housing Studies* 20 (2): 277–89.
Halpenny, Miriam. 2020. "Renters Being Squeezed: Report: Housing Unaffordable for Many Renters in Okanagan." *Castanet*. February 13. https://www.castanet.net/news/Kelowna/277040/Renters-being-squeezed.
Harvey, David. 1989a. From Managerialism to Entrepreneurialism: The Transformation in Urban Governance in Late Capitalism. *Geografiska Annaler: Series B, Human Geography* 71 (1): 3–17.
–. 1989b. *The Condition of Postmodernity*. Malden, MA: Blackwell.
hooks, bell. 1982. *Black Looks: Race and Representation*. Toronto: Between the Lines.
Ignatiev, Noel. 1995. *How the Irish Became White*. New York: Routledge.
Intercultural Society of the Central Okanagan. 2008. *The Changing Face of Kelowna: Are We Ready? Summary Report*. Ottawa: Canadian Heritage.

Karjanen, David J. 2016. *The Servant Class City: Urban Revitalization versus the Working Poor in San Diego*, ed. Susan E. Clarke. Minneapolis: University of Minnesota Press.

Kelowna Chamber of Commerce. 2019. "Kelowna Economic Scorecard 2019. https://www.kelownachamber.org/files/COK18-041_Economic%20Score%20Card_Single_web.pdf.

Kelowna Now. 2019. "Departure of Thompson-Okanagan's Young Workers 'Concerning' Says New Report." 12 June. https://www.kelownanow.com/watercooler/news/news/Provincial/Departure_of_Thompson_Okanagan_s_young_workers_concerning_says_new_report/.

Koroscil, Paul. 2008. *The British Garden of Eden: Settlement History of the Okanagan Valley, British Columbia.* Burnaby, BC: Department of Geography, Simon Fraser University Press.

Kyle, Catherine Jane. 2017. "Lost Landscapes of the Market Gardeners: A Qualitative Historical GIS Examination of the Demise of the Chinese and Japanese Market Gardening Industries in the North and Central Okanagan Valley, British Columbia, 1910s–1950s." PhD diss., University of British Columbia Okanagan.

Lethbridge, David. 1994. *SACAR Second Report: The Danger Is Real.* Salmon Arm, BC: Salmon Arm Coalition against Racism.

Lewontin, Rovjstf, Steven Rose, and Leon Kamin. 1985. *Not in Our Genes.* New York: Pantheon.

Lipsitz, George. 2006. *The Possessive Investment in Whiteness: How White People Profit from Identity Politics.* Philadelphia: Temple University Press.

Low, Setha. 2009. "Maintaining Whiteness: The Fear of Others and Niceness." *Transforming Anthropology* 17 (2): 79–92.

MacNaull, Steven. 2005. "Spat Settled over 'Censored' Video Project." *Okanagan Saturday* 18 June, A3.

–. 2017. "Average House Price in Kelowna Hits $700,000." *Daily Courier*, 9 June. https://www.kelownadailycourier.ca/business_news/article_a281243e-4d7a-11e7-85bb-439228f0493d.html.

Manchester, Jon. 2018, "40,000 Live in Poverty." *Castanet.* December 21. https://www.castanet.net/news/Kelowna/245099/40000-live-in-poverty.

McDermott, Monica, and Frank Samson. 2005. "White Racial and Ethnic Identity in the United States." *Annual Review in Sociology* 31: 245–61.

McDonald, Mary G. 2005. "Mapping Whiteness and Sport: An Introduction." *Sociology of Sport* 22 (3): 245–55.

Melamed, Jodi. 2006. "The Spirit of Neoliberalism: From Racial Liberalism to Neoliberal Multiculturalism." *Social Text* 24 (4): 1–24.

Michaels, Kathy. 2014. "Election 2014: Controversial UDI Forum-For-One Goes off without a Hitch or Differing Opinions." *Kelowna Capital News.* 30 October. http://kelownacapnews.com/news/280992782.html.

Mitchell, Kathryne. 2004. *Crossing the Neoliberal Line.* Philadelphia, PA: Temple University Press.

Momer, Bearnard. 2011. *Our City, Ourselves: A Cultural Landscape Assessment of Kelowna, BC.* Kelowna: City of Kelowna, Recreation and Cultural Services.

Morton, Sydney. 2018. "B.C. Sikh Temple Vandalized with Racist Graffiti." *Free Press*, 19 November. https://www.thefreepress.ca/news/b-c-sikh-temple-vandalized-with-racist-graffiti/.

Munro, Rob. 2019. "Update: Arrest Made in Online threat that Scared Kelowna Mayor." *Infotel*. https://infotel.ca/newsitem/kelowna-mayor-colin-basran-scared-and-angry-after-on-line-death-threat/it62193.

Nuttall, Jeremy J. 2015. "As Temp Workers Flow from Jamaica, Scammers Swoop." *Tyee*. http://www.thetyee.ca/News/2014/01/22/Scammers-Swoop/.

O'Connor, Justin, and Christy Hughes. 2015. "From the Publishers." *Okanagan Homes*, Summer, 15. https://issuu.com/okhome/docs/summer_2015.

Okanagan Life Magazine. 2008. "The Future of Our Valley – A Round Table Discussion." November.

Okanagan Partnership. n.d. "Two Tomorrows." http://www.altivero.com/okanagan/#.

Patel. Sarita. 2020a. "1 in 6 Kids Living in Poverty: One in Six Children Are Living in Poverty in the Central Okanagan." *Castanet*. January 24. https://www.castanet.net/news/Kelowna/275334/1-in-6-kids-living-in-poverty.

–. 2020b. Government Helps Food Bank: BC Announced More Funding to Help Food Banks across the Province." *Castanet*. May 29. https://www.castanet.net/news/BC/295829/Government-helps-food-bank.

Peck, Jamie, and Nik Theodore. 2019. "Still Neoliberalism?" *South Atlantic Quarterly* 118 (2): 245–65.

Razack, Sherene. ed. 2002. *Race, Space and the Law: Unmapping a White Settler Society*. Toronto: Between the Lines.

Redclift, Victoria. 2014. "New Racisms, New Racial Subjects? The Neo-Liberal Moment and the Racial Landscape of Contemporary Britain." *Ethnic and Racial Studies* 37 (4): 577–88.

Rodriguez, M. 2019a. "Homeless Encampment Moved." *Capital News*, 27 November, 1.

–. 2019b. "'City That Protects Racists': Sexual Assault Survivor Slams Kelowna Mayor for Defending RCMP." *Capital News*. https://www.thefreepress.ca/news/city-that-protects-rapists-sexual-assault-survivor-slams-kelowna-mayor-for-defending-rcmp/.

Satzewich, Vic. 2007. "Whiteness Studies: Race, Diversity and the New Essentialism." In *Race and Racism in 21st-Century Canada: Continuity, Complexity, and Change*, ed. Sean Hier and B. Singh Bolaria. 67–84. Peterborough, ON: Broadview Press.

Seymour, Ron. 2018. "Kelowna to Fine Those Who Donate Empties Near Depots or Give Cash to Intersection Panhandlers." https://vancouversun.com/news/local-news/kelowna-to-fine-those-who-donate-empties-near-depots-or-give-cash-to-intersection-panhandlers.

–. 2019. "New Mural Celebrates Kelowna's Vanished Chinatown." *Daily Courier*, 26 June. http://www.kelownadailycourier.ca /news/article_0546b4aa-9831–11e9–97c4–3f5669d7791a.html.

Shaw, Wendy S. 2006. "Decolonizing Geographies of Whiteness." *Antipode* 38 (4): 851–969.

Singh, Simran. 2018. "RCMP Investigate after BC Sikh Temple Vandalized with Racist Graffiti." *DH News* 22 November. https://dailyhive.com/vancouver/kelowna-sikh-temple-vandalized-racist-graffiti-2018.

Smith, Jennifer. 2010. "Bottle Depot Angers Neighbours." *Capital News*, 29 January, A10.

Smith, Neil 1996. *New Urban Frontier: Gentrification and the Revanchist City*. New York: Routledge.

"Smugness." 2015. *The Free Online Dictionary*. http://www.thefreedictionary.com/smugness.

Statistics Canada, 2011 National Household Survey, Statistics Canada Catalogue no. 99-010-X2011030, Accessed May 21, 2021. https://www12.statcan.gc.ca/nhs-enm/2011/dp-pd/dt-td/Rp-eng.cfm?LANG=E&APATH=5&DETAIL=0&DIM=0&FL=A&FREE=0&GC=915&GID=0&GK=10&GRP=0&PID=105392&PRID=0&PTYPE=105277&S=0&SHOWALL=0&SUB=0&Temporal=2013&THEME=95&VID=0&VNAMEE=&VNAMEF=.

–. 2016. https://www12.statcan.gc.ca/census-recensement/2016/dp-pd/prof/details/page.cfm?Lang=E&Geo1=CMACA&Code1=915&Geo2=PR&Code2=47 &Data=Count&SearchText=Kelowna&SearchType=Begins&SearchPR=01&B1=All.

Stewart, Anthony. 2014. *The Visitor: My Life in Canada*. Halifax: Fernwood.

Stone, Sharon Dale. 2001. "Lesbians, Gays and the Press: Covering Lesbian and Gay Pride Day in Kelowna, 1996." *Studies in Political Economy* 64 (1) (Spring): 59–81.

Szeto, Eric. 2013. "More Seniors Using Kelowna Shelters." Global News. 30 November. http://globalnews.ca/news/1000959/more-seniors-using-kelowna-shelter/BC.

Tactics Magazine. 2003. "We Love It Here." http://www.tacticsmagazine.com/2003/11/.

Teixeira, Carlos. 2009. "New Immigrant Settlement in a Mid-size City: A Case Study of Housing Barriers and Coping Strategies in Kelowna, British Columbia." *Canadian Geographer* (53): 323–39.

Tomlinson, Kathy. 2013. "RBC Replaces Canadian Staff with Foreign Workers." CBC News. 6 April. http://www.cbc.ca/news/canada/british-columbia/rbc-replaces-canadian-staff-with-foreign-workers-1.1315008.

Vancouver Sun. 2007. "Controversy Dogs Filmmaker's Choices." 14 June.

Vanderbeck, Robert M. 2006. "Vermont and the Imaginative Geographies of American Whiteness." *Annals of the Association of American Geographers* 96 (3): 641–59.

Wagner, John. 2009. "Water and Development in the Okanagan Valley of British Columbia." *Journal of Enterprising Communities: People and Places in the Global Economy* 3 (4): 378–92.

Walcott, Rinaldo. 2019. "The End of Diversity." *Public Culture* 31 (2): 393–408.

Walks, Alan. 2013. "Mapping the Urban Debtscape: The Geography of Household Debt in Canadian Cities." *Urban Geography* 34 (2): 153–87.

Walmsley, Christopher, and Terry Kading. 2018. "Introduction." In *Small Cities, Big Issues*, ed. Christopher Walmsley and Terry Kading, 3–20. Edmonton: Athabasca University Press.

Whiteley, Robert, L.L.M. Aguiar, and Tina Marten. 2008. "Neo-Liberal Transnational University: The Case of UBC Okanagan." *Capital and Class* (96): 115–42.

Wong, Lloyd, and Ricardo Trumper. 2007. "Canada's Guestworkers: Racialized, Gendered and Flexible." In *Race and Racism in 21st-Century Canada*, ed. Sean P. Hier and B. Singh Bolaria, 151–70. Peterborough, ON: Broadview Press.
Wylie, David. 2016. "Petition Targets Bylaw." *Castanet*, 5 December. https://www.castanet.net/news/Kelowna/182746/Petition-targets-bylaw.
Yancy, George. 2012. *Look, a White! Philosophical Essays on Whiteness*. Philadelphia: Temple University Press.

CHAPTER 8

WHITE SUPREMACY, SURVEILLANCE, AND URBAN INDIGENOUS WOMEN IN THE KELOWNA, BC, HOUSING MARKET

Sheila Lewis and Lawrence D. Berg

We outline in this chapter some of the key findings of a research project that examines the experiences of urban Indigenous women in the Kelowna housing market. In this case, we focus specifically on aspects of surveillance experienced by these women under conditions of white supremacy. The chapter is organized in the following manner. In the next section we discuss the concept of white supremacy as it has evolved in white studies. We argue that we need to think about the present racial formation in Canada – especially with respect to white-Indigenous relations – as one of white supremacy rather than of hegemonic whiteness. This is followed with a brief introduction to the long history of Indigenous Syilx inhabitance of what is now known as the Okanagan Valley, ending with the more recent history of the colonial production of "Native Space" through development of the reserve system. We argue (drawing on writers like Cole Harris 2002) that the production of such Native Space was intimately related to the production of white spaces through dispossession, especially white spaces like the Okanagan Valley. The subsequent section provides a brief description of the city of Kelowna, especially its demographic profile and its problematic relationship to urban Indigenous people. After this section we discuss the empirical findings of the research on surveillance and housing for urban Indigenous women, characterizing such surveillance as one of a number of ostensibly banal practices that underpin ongoing colonialism and operate to normalize (and naturalize) it in the minds of white Canadians (after Mbembe 2001). We end the chapter with a series of conclusions regarding the role of surveillance in the (re)production of colonial and white supremacist systems of control and violence in the lives in Indigenous women in Kelowna.

WHITE SUPREMACY

For at least three decades now, scholars have argued that we need to be more attendant to whiteness and, in particular, to the hegemonic character of whiteness (e.g., Bonnett 1996; Dyer 1997; Frankenberg 1993; McIntosh 1989), and these calls have played a key role in processes leading to the development of white studies as a formal focus of scholarship in the academy. White studies have helped us to better understand the many ways, including some of the more banal and prosaic processes by which, forms of whiteness are instantiated as the norm in white settler states such as Canada (e.g., Baldwin, Cameron, and Kobayashi 2011). Accordingly, hegemonic whiteness is now understood to have three interrelated components: first, whiteness can be seen as a location of structural advantage; second, whiteness is a standpoint from which white people understand the world and their position in it; and third, whiteness is a set of cultural practices that – in white settler societies such as the United States and Canada – are usually dominant but also unmarked and unnamed (Frankenberg 1997; see also Berg 2006).

These are important insights, but what is interesting is the way that, in this kind of thinking, hegemonic whiteness becomes structured as something akin to a space or a field of knowing from which some people can disaffiliate themselves. We think this is highly problematic. In making this problem visible, we need to ask: "For whom is whiteness hegemonic?" If we take Gramsci's (1971) theory of hegemony seriously, then we have to concede that whiteness is not hegemonic for most Indigenous people, people of colour, or other racially minoritized people (significant portions of the argument outlined here are taken from Berg 2012). These people have differing but, nonetheless, long-standing practices of studying white people as a survival strategy (see especially hooks 1989, 2005; see also Gilbert 1998). As bell hooks (2005, 19) argues: "Although there has never been any official body of black people in the United States who have gathered as anthropologists and/or ethnographers to study whiteness, black folks have, from slavery on, shared in conversations with one another 'special' knowledge of whiteness gleaned from close scrutiny of white people." So, the people who are marginalized by whiteness are not fooled into reproducing that marginalization because of the cultural arguments of the dominant social bloc (although they might reproduce white supremacy as a survival strategy itself [see hooks 1989]). Of course, marginalized populations aren't undifferentiated either. Accordingly, there are differences within groups as they relate to whiteness, and some people within these groups are more accommodating to whiteness than others (Satzewich 2000). Nevertheless, as Gramsci (1971) argues, hegemony is never complete but must always be worked at. Yet this is not an accurate description of the present racial formation under advanced capitalism in white settler societies like Canada; rather, the only people for whom whiteness is seemingly "invisible" is white people, and they clearly benefit from this set of conditions (see Hartmann, Gerteis, and Croll 2009; Pulido 2002; Thompson 2003; Wiegman 1999; Wilson-Gilmore 2002; and Svenson, Chapter 12, this collection). Sometimes the invisibility of whiteness is almost complete for white people, at other times – and particularly in the Okanagan Valley (see Aguiar, Tomic, and Trumper 2005a; Aguiar, McKinnon, and Sookraj 2010–11) – whiteness can become a very strong identity.

With that in mind, we argue the need to think of the power of whiteness not as arising within the social formation that Gramsci (1971) describes as "hegemony" but, rather, as a social formation that is much better described (in theoretical language at least) as "supremacy." This is the same conclusion that the Black feminist cultural critic bell hooks came to more than three decades ago. In 1989, she states: "As I write, I try to remember when the word racism ceased to be the term which best expressed for me exploitation of black people and other people of color in this society and when I began to understand that the most useful term was white supremacy" (hooks 1989, 84). We agree fully with hooks as she questions "racism" as a useful term for explaining race-based exploitation. While she was writing about the case of the United States, we think that her theorizing applies equally well to the Canadian situation, especially with regard to relations between white Canada and Indigenous peoples. We thus argue here that "white supremacy" is not some set of exceptional conditions but, rather, the phrase that best describes the *everyday state of racial affairs in Canada* and other similar white settler societies.

So how might we define the characteristics of white supremacy as it operates in Canada? Here, for inspiration, we are drawn to the work of African American scholars writing about the United States context. Obviously, the United States has a different historical geography of colonization and dispossession than does Canada, but we feel strongly that the arguments about whiteness that we are about to discuss apply to this country (albeit in historically and geographically contingent ways). In this regard, we argue that we need to think about Canadian race and colonial relations in terms of white supremacy rather than in terms of racism or hegemonic whiteness. We draw on the work of Charles W. Mills and how he defines white supremacy in *The Companion to African-American Philosophy*: white supremacy is "a political, economic, and cultural system in which whites overwhelmingly control power and material resources, conscious and unconscious ideas of white superiority and entitlement are widespread, and relations of white dominance and non-white subordination are daily re-enacted across a broad array of institutions and social settings" (Mills 2006, 269; see also Razack, Smith, and Thobani 2010). While it is always dangerous to import a theoretical argument about one geographical space unaltered into another, we nevertheless suggest (following Berg 2012; Razack, Smith, and Thobani 2010) that this definition accurately describes the present conditions in white settler societies like Australia, Canada, New Zealand, and the United States and that these conditions clearly obtain in Kelowna and the Okanagan Valley.

SYILX (OKANAGAN) PEOPLE IN THE COLONIZED OKANAGAN VALLEY

Kelowna is situated on the unceded territory of the Syilx people. Also known as the Okanagan, the Syilx are part of the Interior Salish ethnological and linguistic group. The Syilx describe their inhabitance of the Okanagan region in their own words:

> Okanagan (Syilx) people have been here since time immemorial, long before the arrival of the Settlers ... For thousands of years, the

> Okanagan people were self-reliant and well provided for through their own ingenuity and use of the land and nature. We lived united as a nation with a whole economy, travelling the breadth and depth of our territory, hunting and fishing, growing and harvesting, crafting and trading to meet our needs. Colonization divided us from one another and from our way of life. We were divided from the resources we relied upon, and our self-sufficient economy collapsed. (Okanagan Nation Alliance n.d., n.p.)

Indeed, Indigenous people have been forcibly removed from their lands in the Okanagan, and they have been restricted to small reserves located, for the most part, on the peripheries of the region (see Harris 2002).

The production of what Harris (2002) terms "Native Space," on reserves, was part of the wider production of white space in colonial British Columbia (and the Okanagan more specifically). Richard McBride, the first premier of British Columbia, argued that "British Columbia must be kept white" (McBride 1912 cited in Roy 1989, 229). McBride failed to acknowledge in such statements that early British Columbia was not completely white as a significant proportion of the population in the early colonial period was from China, Japan, Hawai'i, and other non-white spaces. Nonetheless, by 1921, over 60 percent of the population in British Columbia was from Britain or its colonial possessions (Barman 1996). This was the result of explicit policies designed to make British Columbia white (Anderson 1991; Ward 1972). A series of increasingly more prohibitive "head taxes" was put in place to stem the immigration of people from China in the late 1800s and early 1900s. Japanese Canadians were interned during the Second World War (Oikawa 2002), and Chinese Canadians were segregated in "Chinatowns" around the province (See Anderson 1987, 1991; Deer 2006) during the same period. In fact, Kelowna had an important Chinatown, located just off Bernard Avenue in its downtown, and it was destroyed through a combination of the head tax and white racism. Virtually no trace of this particular Chinatown remains (see Huyskamp 2010).

In the settlement era and through to today the Okanagan was a key space for the production of whiteness in British Columbia. A large number of British ex-military members and settlers created an enclave in the Okanagan Valley, where they (re)created race and "class-based institutions ranging from social clubs to private schools based on the British model" (Barman 1996, 140). The enclave performed the work of supporting white settlers who embarked on the development of agricultural capitalism in the Okanagan. The members of this early white enclave were effective in recruiting fellow whites to set up neighbouring orchards at the same time that they actively worked to exclude non-white migrant workers such as Japanese Canadians and Chinese Canadians from settling and operating their own orchards (see Bennett 1998; Koroscil 2003).

The work of (re)creating the landscape into something that reminded them of a familiar white homeland also became a social and cultural investment in the landscape. As a result, whites in the Okanagan worked hard to prevent non-whites, including both Indigenous people and people of colour, from living in or migrating to Kelowna (Aguiar, Tomic, and Trumper 2005; Aguiar and Marten 2011). With this in mind, we argue that there is a special form of white supremacy in operation in Kelowna, one that works in a more explicit and proactive way than the banal forms of white supremacy operating elsewhere, in order to produce and maintain Kelowna as a specific kind of white space. This operates in part because of the kind of whiteness that is produced in Kelowna and in part because of the many ways that Indigenous people are effaced from the white imaginary of urban space in Canada generally and in Kelowna specifically – in spite of the Syilx people's long history of living in the Okanagan region.

KELOWNA AND URBAN INDIGENOUS PEOPLE

At the 2011 census, the population of the Kelowna Census Metropolitan Area (CMA) was 176,435 persons (Statistics Canada 2013a), making it the third-largest urban agglomeration in BC after Vancouver and Victoria CMAs. The city is located approximately 470 kilometres by road east from Vancouver. That geographic distance is perhaps eclipsed by the epistemological and ontological differences between the two regions. Where just 52.5 percent of the population of Vancouver identified as white in the 2011 census (Statistics Canada 2013c), more than 89 percent of the population of Kelowna identified as white (Statistics Canada 2013a; compare this to 67.3 percent for the province of British Columbia as a whole [Statistics Canada 2013b]). Kelowna is surely one of the whitest spaces in British

Columbia (in the American context, Rich Benjamin [2009] refers to such spaces, including the very similar American city of Coeur d'Alene, Idaho, as "Whitopia").

As Aguiar, Tomic, and Trumper (2005) argue, Kelowna was not always a white space; rather, it was "made" white. Making Kelowna white started with an enclave of British settlers who developed successful land sale and agricultural industries that both symbolically and literally (re)created an English country landscape in the Okanagan Valley (Barman 1996; Bennett 1998; Koroscil 2003; Royal BC Museum 2002; Aguiar, Tomic, and Trumper 2005). The primary economic focus of the fledgling township that eventually became Kelowna was cattle ranching, but that quickly changed to other forms of more intensive agriculture, beginning with tobacco production and eventually shifting into a highly successful orchard industry focused on the production of cherries and apples. Settlers became both boosters and marketers for the community, emphasizing its close ties to Britain along with community leaders' commitment to British ideals (Barman 1996). Land sales and property "development" have long been a mainstay of the petite bourgeoisie in Kelowna, who initially marketed the city as a centre of agricultural capitalism then shifted its "brand" to that of an ideal retirement centre for white wealthy retirees from Calgary and Vancouver and, more recently, produced the city as a wonderful place for the (white) creative classes to "work hard and play hard" (Aguiar, Tomic, and Trumper 2005).

In addition to the kilometres upon kilometres of strip malls that blight the Kelowna landscape (another outcome of the significant influence that local land developers have exercised on the city until very recently), the geography of Kelowna is characterized by the highest per-capita number of houses situated in "gated communities" in all of Canada. These so-called "communities" were marketed in the 1980s and 1990s especially to white middle-class retirees, drawing specifically on their (irrational) fears of dangerous – read: non-white, working-class – Others (Lewis 2010; Marten 2009). More recently, as a result of the development of neoliberal forms of competitive urbanism, developers in Kelowna have shifted their focus to selling new housing to members of the white "creative class," with all the attendant problems that such simplistic responses to urban crises bring (Marten 2009; see also Peck 2005).

The landscape of whiteness in Kelowna is further (re)produced through place naming that reflects almost exclusively the white history of the city. Most of the street names and significant building names reflect the names of early white European settlers (or famous white historical figures from Britain). For example, street names, especially those of more highly utilized routes through the city – such as Abbott Street, Aberdeen Street, Benvoulin Road, Bernard Avenue, Ellis Street, Harvey Avenue, and Pandosy Street – are all named for early white settlers to the Okanagan. Other popular locations with names, such as Dilworth Mountain, Knox Mountain, The Mission, and Rutland, continue to reflect and (re)inforce Kelowna as an epistemologically white space, albeit one that is always under contestation as minoritized groups work to build safe spaces in the city (Kobayashi, Chapter 5, this collection; see also Berthiaume 2008) . Such naming operated early in the colonial period to help recreate Britain-in-the-Okanagan. More recently such naming practices work to erase the history of Indigenous peoples in Kelowna. They also elide the violence of the primitive accumulation of the early colonial period and the accumulation by dispossession of the contemporary period of ongoing colonialism (Berg 2011; for an overview of the politics of naming, see Berg and Vuolteenaho 2009).

Effectively, the Syilx people and their contributions to the space that is named Kelowna are rendered both silent and invisible to white settlers. The social and economic exclusion of the Okanagan people are achieved in part through historical narratives that are reified and legitimized through a hegemonic discourse of public remembering – and forgetting (Schein 1997; Dwyer 2000; Rose-Redwood 2008).

Notwithstanding the fact that Indigenous people's history and contributions in Kelowna are erased, urban Indigenous people make up a considerable proportion of the city's population – approximately 4.6 percent. Interestingly, citing census data regarding the proportion of the population of Kelowna who identify as Indigenous people operates to efface the importance of ongoing colonialism. In this regard, in reducing groups of peoples to proportions of a population, census data work to produce Indigenous people as having the same ontological status as that of settlers (English, Irish, German, Jamaican, etc.), even though Indigenous people have paid and continue to pay a heavy material price due to ongoing colonialism while, at the same time, most settler groups continue to benefit from being settlers on unceded Indigenous lands – even if some of them might be marginalized for being non-white.

While the figure of 4.6 percent is much smaller than Indigenous populations in other Canadian cities, such as Kamloops (7.6 percent), Saskatoon (9.3 percent), or Winnipeg (almost 11 percent), this population is nonetheless part of a long-standing movement of Indigenous people from the countryside to the city (for a wide overview, see Peters and Andersen 2013). More than 50 percent of all Indigenous people in Canada now live in cities. While white supremacy and ongoing colonialism ensure that Indigenous people experience marginalization across Canada, urban Indigenous people tend to experience this marginalization in particularly concentrated forms.

This situation exists in part because of the problematic way that the Indian Act instantiates an ongoing colonialism in Canada (Lawrence 2003). But it also exists because programs and services for Indigenous people continue to rely on a hegemonic discourse of Indigenous *rurality*, one that places Indigenous people in rural spaces, particularly on rural reserves, and in so doing ignores the facts of Indigenous urbanity (Berg et al. 2007; Evans et al. 2012; Peters 1996, 2002, 2005). Perhaps more insidiously, this hegemonic discourse of Indigenous rurality continues to operate powerfully in the social sciences in Canada, guiding the way that Indigeneity is imagined by social scientists and structuring research and research funding so that it often continues to elide Indigenous urbanity (Berg et al. 2007; Evans et al. 2012). This chapter is thus part of a wider movement to urbanize the white imaginary regarding what it means to be Indigenous in Canada as well as to contest the ways that white supremacy and colonialism come together in the production of that imaginary (see, e.g., Evans et al. 2012; Francis 2011; Peters 1996, 2005; Peters and Andersen 2013; Razack 2002; Razack, Smith, and Thobani 2010).

URBAN INDIGENOUS WOMEN AND THE HOUSING MARKET IN KELOWNA: SURVEILLANCE AS BANAL COLONIALISM

The following section is based on an analysis of interviews with twelve Indigenous women regarding their search for, and use of, rental housing in the city of Kelowna. The participants in this study were initially contacted with assistance from the Ki-Low-Na Friendship Centre, which was a partner in this research. The Ki-Low-Na Friendship Centre is operated by the Ki-Low-Na Friendship Society, a non-profit organization working with/for First Nations people and urban Indigenous people (although it also serves non-Indigenous people). It provides family services, counselling and support services, and some health and social services. The participants, all of whom have been given pseudonyms, were interviewed between February and August of 2009. The interviews were conducted at the Ki-Low-Na Friendship Centre. In what follows, we focus on the participants' experiences of surveillance in the housing market as an instantiation of white supremacy and ongoing colonialism.

The twelve Indigenous women that were interviewed for this study all had a strong sense of the way that white supremacy (although they might not use this terminology) and class position interlock to produce powerful divisions between themselves and white people in the city of Kelowna. Often, in their response to questions, they expressed how they feel the pressure of race and class, always pointing to what they called "the mainstream" as the racialized class position to which they were made to know that they did not belong, yet of which they were pressured to be a part in order to "get along" in the city. Rosa, for example, articulated what "mainstream" meant for her:

> Oh … mainstream to me means people who have grown up in a white culture and can only see white culture, have no understanding for a life with meaning. That meaning, to mainstream people, is … high-paying jobs, education, … which are things that would be good for all of us, right? But … having all your towels stacked in coloured order … you know, buying microwave food, having a fancy car, taking vacations to Bermuda but having that mind-set that if you don't have those things, you're not worth it. You're scum, you're white trash, you're trailer park trash, … you're an Indian. You're a dirty Indian. It's like having those things, to [mainstream people], is what life is all about and they don't see past that. That's what mainstream is to me. (Rosa: Interview transcript[1])

Rosa's comments point out the banal ways that race and class position are (re)produced in Kelowna among middle-class whites. They also point to the sophisticated (dare we say "theoretical") analysis of these banal, white, middle-class thoughts and practices on the part of the study participants, all of whom would likely be considered incapable of such sophisticated analysis by the very middle-class white people being analyzed here.

Even though the urban Indigenous women that were interviewed came from a range of backgrounds, their response to what they identified as the mainstream was the same. They understood that they were not part of any elite group in Kelowna. Despite the fact that some of them were professionals and highly educated, they were not afforded the same privileged positions that were open to white people. Drawing on the work of feminists of colour writing about interlocking analyses (e.g., Razack 2005; for an overview see Holmes 2012), we suggest that this points to the way that race and class interlock in the lives of Indigenous women living under white supremacy and middle-class hegemony.

The women understand such racialized class divisions because they are aware that their bodies are under constant surveillance in Kelowna. As one participant framed it, "Nowadays every little thing you do is, you know, under a magnifying glass, and they're watching you, right?" (Sandra, interview transcript). As the participants talked about the multiple ways and spaces in which they felt their bodies being surveilled, they also shared that they experienced a sense of worthlessness as a result of this surveillance. The women noted that they were acutely aware that stereotypes such as their being "dirty," "lazy," and "drunk" are often attributed to Indigenous people living in urban centres.

In addition, and in part because of the power of white supremacy and ongoing colonial practices, at least some of our participants reported avoiding what might be termed "Indigenous spaces" in order to fit in with white, middle-class expectations in Kelowna. The Okanagan Métis and Aboriginal Housing Society manages two subsidized rental properties: one located in West Kelowna and the other located in Rutland, an eastern suburb of Kelowna. These properties are specifically designed to meet Indigenous housing needs. Shelley, for example, admitted avoiding subsidized Indigenous housing in Kelowna because of the way that such spaces have been stigmatized: "For me it was like, okay ... I guess ... the downfall of this is I didn't apply for the low-income housing 'cause I just have my own, I guess, stereotypes in that I don't wanna be ghettoized, I don't want to be put in a bunch of houses where it's noticeably ... Native housing." (Shelley, interview transcript). Shelley expressed concern about the psychological and physical impacts of the negative stereotypes that white people have of Indigenous people in Canada. She points to this being her "downfall" as she carries some of these stereotypes herself and often has negative thoughts about what it means to be an Indigenous person.

Shelley was also concerned about how her son might "read" his landscape for what it means to be an Indigenous person. She feels: "You know, that there's ... the stereotypical drunken and homeless Indian man. You know, it's scary for me as a mother of a Native child and a Native son" (Shelley, interview transcript). The lack of positive representations of Indigenous people in the urban landscape of Kelowna is of much concern for Shelley as she strives to dissociate herself and her family from such negative ways of imagining Indigeneity. The question for her becomes: Where can she and her family live in Kelowna that would help her associate positively with being Indigenous? Her response, effectively, is that there is no escaping the power of white supremacy in Kelowna. As she says, in a way that sums up what all twelve of the research participants spoke about: "the stereotypes are very embedded in the society ... the [stereotype of the] worthlessness of being an Indian woman to me is an everyday occurrence. And I feel it constantly." (Shelley, interview transcript).

All of our participants reported that the everyday surveillance they experience in the rental housing market (and as house renters) creates a constant challenge to their sense of self. Almost all of them report being made to feel *worthless* as a result of this constant surveillance. Although they wouldn't use such terminology, this surveillance also provides a constant reminder to them that they are invited into white supremacy (i.e., that they must act like white people) but that they will never be allowed full membership in the "club." This kind of surveillance produces two kinds of bodies – "the normal and the abnormal body, the former belonging to a homogenous social body, the latter exiled and spatially separated" (Razack 2002, 11). The Indigenous women who participated in this study know this division well. As Sandra observed:

> it's rules for everybody, it's not just Aboriginal people but the experiences ... with Aboriginal people ... they're not looking at

> the person ... our First Nations people ... are so fuckin' worried about, you know, being judged ... they don't even look at themselves ... I get so frustrated sometimes, why can't you be who you are to find a home? (Sandra, interview transcript)

Sandra speaks about the way that Indigenous women have to navigate the urban housing rental market of Kelowna; how they have to dress up and present their bodies in a way that they perceive as *passing* for white, even if they know that they cannot pass for white. However, the attempt to do so, as Sandra identified, results in the women's experiencing how oppressive it is to have to act like someone other than who they are just to attempt to locate housing. Rosa articulates this feeling in terms of having to assume a "mainstream" appearance in order to be accepted:

> ... if you dress a certain way, it does open doors for you so ... I kind of [got] rid of them, but I used to have mainstream suits ... Blouses ... and high heels and things like that and make-up ... but it's like pretending to be something you're not. It wasn't comfortable, but I felt like I kind of gone to a few places, and I didn't get accepted, so when I went to that home I put, we all put on our best look ... So that somehow that instant impression would be that we were mainstream. (Rosa, interview transcript)

As Frantz Fanon (1967) so famously argues, colonialism produces in the colonial subject the impossibility of being a "normal," fully functional, well-adjusted individual. Colonization (or ongoing colonial relations) produces the colonial subject as a person who cannot be at one with the Self that is constituted in and through colonialism. Indian residential schools provided one of the key institutions for constituting white supremacy and colonialism in the bodies of Indigenous people in Canada. Alice, who identified as a survivor of the residential school system, is typical: "I was in ... a residential school and I ... from the time I was ten years old til' I was nineteen, I was supervised by nuns ... that's why I am so aware of it [the way we are suppose to look]" (Alice, interview transcript). The appearance of Indigeneity has real material consequences for Indigenous people in Canada. Accordingly, it became clear to us that the Indigenous women in our study had been made to feel that who they are is not something to be proud of, that their Self is not acceptable. Therefore, in their search for housing, and in their everyday interactions with landlords, these women strategically performed their allotted role in white supremacy in order to secure (and retain) rental housing.

CONCLUSION

As Michel Foucault (1977) argues, surveillance has important subject effects. Just as in Bentham's Panopticon, where prisoners begin to police themselves, the Indigenous women in this study report performing surveillance on their own bodies. Adopting particular strategies of both resistance and accommodation, many decide to fit into white supremacy and the normative bodily ideals that are produced under ongoing colonialism. They attempt to change their appearance in order to appear "less Indigenous" and thus avoid being stereotyped as "lazy" or "drunk." These women are surely exercising critical forms of agency, but because of the all-encompassing character of white supremacy, it is possible that some might interpret their actions as reinforcing the negative stereotypes about Indigenous women produced within white supremacy and colonialism. Surely, however, this is not the case. These women fully understand the many ways that colonialism operates in their lives, and they are fully self-reflexive about the choices they make. Instead, it might be much more appropriate to interpret their actions as critical responses to a set of poor options available to them under white supremacy and ongoing colonialism. These women are acutely aware of the consequences of making the "wrong" choice here: homelessness and even further marginalization.

We have presented some of the experiences of surveillance recounted by Indigenous women in the rental housing market in order to illustrate just one of the banal ways that white supremacy and ongoing colonialism are (re)produced in Kelowna, BC. As we argue, Kelowna is exceptional in relation to the rest of BC when we think about both the extent and the quality of whiteness in the city. At the same time, if we think of the province as a space of white supremacy, then perhaps this would force us to rethink the banal ways that such social relations are reproduced across the province. Be that as it may, there is something different about the character of white supremacy in Kelowna – something that operates to ensure that it remains so disproportionately white. As both the experiences of our research participants and other chapters in this book attest, white people in Kelowna have actively engaged in practices that operate to keep the city white. Sometimes, we might understand these practices as being of the "exceptional" variety: those that are not often found in other places in Canada. One example of this kind of "exceptional" white supremacy comes from Daylene van Ryswyk, New Democratic Party (NDP) candidate contesting the Kelowna-Mission riding in the 2013 provincial election, who was forced to resign as candidate by the party because of her racist comments on the local website, *Castanet*. There, she is recorded as saying about Indigenous people: "It's not the status cards, it's the fact that we have been paying out of the nose for generations for something that isn't our doing ... If their [Indigenous people's] ancestors sold out too cheap it's not my fault and I shouldn't have to be paying for any mistake or whatever you want to call it from my hard-earned money" (CBC News 2013, n.p.). Here van Ryswyk draws on a number of powerful tropes of white supremacy in Canada, including "colonialism as ancient history" and the "high cost of caring for Indigenous people." The former trope draws upon the idea that colonialism is something our ancestors engaged in but that present-day dominant members of Canadian society do not. The corollary of this kind of thinking is that dominant members of Canadian society are no longer benefitting from colonialism. The latter trope, regarding the high cost of caring for Indigenous people, is based on the notion that they never contributed anything to the Canadian economy and society. Over and above the erasure of the contribution that Indigenous people made and make as workers across the nation, this denies the important role that primitive accumulation via the theft of Indigenous lands played in the founding of Canada. It also denies the important contributions that Indigenous people in Canada continue to be forced to make to our economy through ongoing forms of accumulation by dispossession. The refusal of dominant Canadians to recognise such processes is made possible through the power of white supremacy and the banal practices whereby Indigenous perspectives are denied plausibility and Indigenous suffering is erased (except in instances where it is used to blame the victims for their own misfortune).

In many cases the practices that operate to keep Kelowna white are banal, such as Indigenous women having to "pass," – at the expense of their own sense of self – to dress and talk as white people when trying to negotiate rental housing in Kelowna. These kinds of practices might pass among whites as simply "looking out for one's neighbours," but their impact is so much more significant than this would suggest. Indeed, we argue that it is these banal practices that work so powerfully to ensure that white people continue to benefit disproportionately from white supremacy and ongoing colonialism in the city of Kelowna.

ACKNOWLEDGMENTS

Luís Aguiar and Daniel Keyes provided very constructive comments on earlier versions of this chapter. Two anonymous referees provided very helpful comments on the penultimate draft of this chapter. We are grateful to all of them for their assistance in improving it. All errors of both fact and interpretation remain our responsibility.

NOTE

1 In order to protect the confidentiality of our interview participants we do not provide dates for our interviews. Given the small number of interviewees, providing such dates would make it possible to identify participants.

REFERENCES

Aguiar, L.L.M., and T.I.L. Marten. 2011. "Shimmering White Kelowna and the Examination of Painless White Privilege in the Hinterland of British Columbia." In *Rethinking the Great White North: Race, Nature and the Historical Geographies of Whiteness in Canada*, ed. A. Baldwin, L. Cameron, and A. Kobayashi, 127–44. Vancouver: UBC Press.

Aguiar, L.L.M., A. McKinnon, and D. Sookraj. 2010–11. "Racialization and the Repertoires of Racism: Reaction to Jamaicans in the Okanagan Valley." *BC Studies* 168 (Winter): 65–79.

Aguiar, L.L.M., P. Tomic, and R. Trumper. 2005. "Work Hard, Play Hard: Selling Kelowna, BC, as Year-round Playground." *Canadian Geographer* 49 (2): 123–39.

Anderson, K.J. 1987. "The Idea of Chinatown: The Power of Place and Institutional Practice in the Making of a Racial Category." *Annals of the Association of American Geographers*. 77: 580–98.

–. 1991. *Vancouver's Chinatown. Racial Discourse in Canada, 1875–1980*. Montreal and Kingston: McGill-Queen's University Press.

Baldwin, A., L. Cameron, and A. Kobayashi, eds. 2011. *Rethinking the Great White North: Race, Nature and the Historical Geographies of Whiteness in Canada*. Vancouver: UBC Press.

Barman, J. 1996. *The West beyond the West: A History of British Columbia*. 2nd ed. Toronto: University of Toronto Press.

Benjamin, R. 2009. *Searching for Whitopia: An Improbable Journey to the Heart of White America*. New York: Hyperion.

Bennett, J.P. 1998. "Apple of the Empire: Landscape and Imperial Identity in Turn-of-the-Century British Columbia." *Journal of the Canadian Historical Association / Revue de la Société historique du Canada* 9 (1): 63–92.

Berg, L.D. 2006. "Whiteness." In *The Encyclopedia of Human Geography*, ed. B. Warf, A.J. Cravey, D. DeLyser, L. Knopp, D. Sui, and D. Wilson, 539–40. Thousand Oaks: Sage.

–. 2011. "Banal Names, Neoliberalism, and Landscapes of Dispossession." In *The Politics of Spatial Inscription*, ed. Derek Alderman and Reuben Rose-Redwood, special issue of *ACME: An International Journal for Critical Geographies* 10 (1): 13–22.

–. 2012. "Geography – (Neo)Liberalism – White Supremacy," *Progress in Human Geography* 36 (4): 508–17.

Berg, L.D., and R.A. Kearns. 1996. "Naming as Norming: 'Race,' Gender, and the Identity Politics of Naming Places in Aotearoa/New Zealand." *Environment and Planning D* 14: 99–122.

Berg, L.D., M. Evans, D. Fuller, and the Okanagan Urban Aboriginal Health Research Collective. 2007. "Ethics, Hegemonic Whiteness, and the Contested Imagination of Aboriginal Community in Social Science Research in Canada." In *Participatory Research Ethics*, special issue of *ACME: An International Journal for Critical Geographies* 6 (3): 395–410.

Berg, L.D., and J. Vuolteenaho, eds. 2009. *Critical Toponymies: Contested Politics of Place Naming*. Burlington, VT: Ashgate.

Berthiaume, M., dir. 2008. *Dragon Tracks: The Ben Lee Story*, video produced by the Kelowna Community Resources Society in collaboration with the Intercultural Society of the Central Okanagan.

Bonnett, A. 1996. "Anti-Racism and the Critique of 'White' Identities." *Journal of Ethnic and Migration Studies* 22 (1): 97–110.

CBC News. 2013. "BC NDP Candidate Quits over 'Hateful' Comments on 1st Campaign Day." CBC News British Columbia Online, 16 April. http://www.cbc.ca/news/canada/british-columbia/story/2013/04/16/bc-ndp-van-ryswyk-kelowna.html.

Deer, G. 2006. "The New Yellow Peril." In *Claiming Space: Racialization in Canadian Cities*, ed. C. Teelucksingh. 19–40. Waterloo: Wilfrid Laurier University Press.

Dwyer, O. 2000. "Interpreting the Civil Rights Movement: Place, Memory, and Conflict." *Professional Geographer* 52: 660–71.

Dyer, R. 1997. *White: Essays on Race and Culture*. London: Routledge.

Evans, M., C. Anderson, D. Dietrich, C. Bourassa, T. Logan, L.D. Berg, and B. DeVolder. 2012. "Funding and Ethics in Métis Community Based Research: The Complication of a Contemporary Context." *International Journal of Critical Indigenous Studies* 5 (1): 54–66.

Fanon, F. 1967. *Black Skin, White Mask*. New York: Grove Press.

Foucault, M. 1977. *Discipline and Punish*. New York: Vintage Books

Francis, M. 2011. *Creative Subversions: Whiteness, Indigeneity, and the National Imaginary*. Vancouver: UBC Press.

Frankenburg, R. 1993. *White Women, Race Matters*. London: Routledge.

–. 1997. *Displacing Whiteness*. Durham, NC: Duke University Press.

Gilbert M.R. 1998. "'Race,' Space and Power: The Survival Strategies of Working Poor Women." *Annals of the Association of American Geographers* 88 (4): 595–621.

Gramsci, A. 1971. *Selections from the Prison Notebooks*. Trans. Q. Hoare and G. Nowell-Smith. Moscow: International Publishers.

Harris, R.C. 2002. *Making Native Space: Colonialism, Resistance and Reserves in British Columbia*. Vancouver: UBC Press.

Hartmann, D., J. Gerteis, and P.R. Croll. 2009. "An Empirical Assessment of Whiteness Theory: Hidden from How Many?" *Social Problems* 56 (3): 403–24.

Holmes, C. 2012. *Violence Denied, Bodies Erased: Towards an Interlocking Spatial Framework for Queer Anti-Violence Organizing*. Kelowna, BC: PhD diss., University of British Columbia.

hooks, b. 1989. *Talking Back: Thinking Feminist, Thinking Black*. Boston, MA: South End Press.

–. 2005. "Representations of Whiteness in the Black Imagination." In *White Privilege: Essential Readings on the Other Side of Racism*, ed. O.S. Rothenberg, 19–24. New York: Worth Publishers.

Huyskamp, R. 2010. *Report on Kelowna's Chinatown Site*. Prepared for the City of Kelowna Community Heritage Commission. 5 August.

Koroscil, P.M. 2003. *The British Garden of Eden: Settlement History of the Okanagan Valley, British Columbia*. Burnaby, BC: Department of Geography, Simon Fraser University.

Lawrence, Bonita. 2003. "Gender, Race, and the Regulation of Native Identity in Canada and the United States: An Overview." *Hypatia* 18 (2): 3–31.

Lewis, S. 2010. "White Picket Fences: Whiteness, Urban Aboriginal Women and Housing Market Discrimination in Kelowna, British Columbia. Kelowna, BC." MA thesis, University of British Columbia.

Marten, T. 2009. "The Reconfiguration of Kelowna, British Columbia, Canada, 1980–2006, Kelowna, BC." MA thesis, University of British Columbia.

Mbembe, A. 2001. *On the Postcolony*. Berkeley: University of California Press

McIntosh, P. 1989. "White Privilege: Unpacking the Invisible Knapsack." *Peace and Freedom* (July/August): 10–12.

Mills, Charles, W. 2006. "White Supremacy." In *The Companion to African-American Philosophy*, ed. Tommy L. Lott and John P. Pittman, 269–81. Malden, MA: Wiley-Blackwell.

Oikawa, M. 2002. "Cartographies of Violence: Women, Memory, and the Subject(s) of the 'Internment,'" In *Race, Space and the Law: Unmapping a White Settler Society*, ed. Sherene Razack, 71–98. Toronto: Between the Lines.

Okanagan Nation Alliance. n.d. "Who We Are: The Syilx People." http://www.syilx.org/who-we-are/the-syilx-people/.

Peck, Jaime. 2005. "Struggling with the Creative Class." *International Journal of Urban and Regional Research* 29 (4): 740–70.

Peters, E. 1996. "'Urban' and 'Aboriginal': An Impossible Contradiction." In *City Lives and City Forms: Critical Research and Canadian Urbanism*, ed. J. Caulfield and L. Peake, 47–62. Toronto: University of Toronto Press.

–. 2002. "Aboriginal People in Urban Areas." In *Urban Affairs: Back on the Policy Agenda*, ed. C. Andrew, K.A.H. Graham, and S. Kingston Phillips, 45–70. Montreal and Kingston: McGill-Queen's University Press.

–. 2005. "Indigeneity and Marginalisation: Planning for and with Urban Aboriginal Communities in Canada." *Progress in Planning* 63 (4): 327–404.

Peters, E., and C. Andersen, eds. 2013. *Indigenous in the City: Contemporary Identities and Cultural Innovation*. Vancouver: UBC Press.

Pulido, L. 2002. "Reflections on a White Discipline." *Professional Geographer* 54 (1): 42–49.

Razack, S.H. 2002. *Race, Space and the Law: Unmapping a White Settler Society*. Toronto: Between the Lines.

–. 2005. "How Is White Supremacy Embodied? Sexualized Racial Violence at Abu Ghraib." *Canadian Journal of Women and the Law* 17: 341–63.

Razack, S.H., M. Smith, and S. Thobani, eds. 2010. *States of Race: Critical Race Feminism for the 21st Century*. Toronto: Between the Lines.

Rose-Redwood, R. 2008. "From Number to Name: Symbolic Capital, Places of Memory and the Politics of Street Renaming in New York City." *Social and Cultural Geography* 9 (4): 431–52.

Roy, P. 1989. *A White Man's Province: British Columbia Politicians and Chinese and Japanese Immigrants, 1858–1914*. Vancouver: UBC Press.

Royal BC Museum. 2002. "Ethnic Agriculture Labour in the Okanagan Valley: 1880s to 1960s – Living Landscapes." Accessed January 14, 2010. www.livinglandscapes.bc.ca.

Satzewich, V. 2000. "Whiteness Studies: Race Diversity, and the New Essentialism." In *Race and Racism in 21st-Century Canada: Continuity, Complexity and Change*, ed. Sean Hier and B. Singh Bolaria, 67–84. Peterborough, ON: Broadview Press.

Schein, R. 1997. "The Place of Landscape: A Conceptual Framework for Interpreting an American Scene." *Annals of the Association of American Geographers* 87: 660–80.

Statistics Canada. 2013a. Kelowna, CMA, British Columbia (Code 915) (table). National Household Survey (NHS) Profile. 2011 National Household Survey, Statistics Canada cat. no. 99–004-XWE, Ottawa. Released 8 May. http://www12.statcan.gc.ca/nhs-enm/2011/dp-pd/prof/index.cfm?Lang=E.

–. 2013b. British Columbia (Code 59) (table). National Household Survey (NHS) Profile. 2011 National Household Survey, Statistics Canada cat. no. 99–004-XWE, Ottawa. Released 8 May. http://www12.statcan.gc.ca/nhs-enm/2011/dp-pd/prof/index.cfm?Lang=E.

–. 2013c. Vancouver, CMA, British Columbia (Code 933) (table). National Household Survey (NHS) Profile. 2011 National Household Survey, Statistics Canada cat. no. 99–004-XWE, Ottawa. Released 8 May. http://www12.statcan.gc.ca/nhs-enm/2011/dp-pd/prof/index.cfm?Lang=E.

Thompson, A. 2003. "Tiffany, Friend of People of Color: White Investments in Antiracism." *Qualitative Studies in Education* 16 (1): 7–29.

Ward, P. 1972. *White Canada Forever: Popular Attitudes and Public Policy toward Orientals in BC.* Montreal and Kingston: McGill-Queen's University Press.

Wiegman, R. 1999. "Whiteness Studies and the Paradox of Particularity." *Boundary 2* 26 (3): 115–50.

Wilson-Gilmore, R. 2002. "Fatal Couplings of Power and Difference: Notes on Racism and Geography." *Professional Geographer* 54 (1): 15–24.

CHAPTER 9

"THE JAMAICANS ARE HERE AND WORKING"

Race and Community Responses to Black Presence

Carl E. James

"The Jamaicans Are Here and Working" declares the headline of Kelowna's *Daily Courier* newspaper of Saturday, 12 April 2008, C1. The article by Steve MacNaull tells of the arrival of Jamaican men in response to the identified need for skilled workers in Kelowna. But despite this need, the presence of Black people, and young Jamaican men in particular (age and gender are quite germane here), seems to generate ambivalence, caution, and unease among the members of the community, which number about 110,000 (Teixeira 2009) – a fairly homogeneous community of very few immigrants and racialized people. The responses to the Jamaican migrants say something about the readiness of the community to deal with the social and cultural changes that will inevitably occur when Black people are introduced into the community. But more to the point, as I argue in this chapter, the reactions to these Black Jamaican men, including the policies introduced to control their behaviours and movement, are reflective of Canada's anti-Black racism and the historical policies of controlled immigration of non-white immigrants, and the racial profile of Black Jamaicans. In making this argument, I reference newspaper reports about the Jamaican migrants that appear around the time of their arrival in the Kelowna community.

Scholars have suggested that media sources such as reports, editorials, news specials, and letters to the editor are relevant to the examination of the general tendency of a society on a given social issue. In all instances, we gain insights into the observations of editorial board members as well as those of letter writers and reports (Hynds 1991; Johnson-Carter 2005). Hynds (1991) also contends that media reports are a reliable and logical gauge from which researchers can make inferences about "public views" and feelings. But while media reports cannot be assumed to be representative of the public's sentiments (James 2009a), they nevertheless alert us to that which helps frame and delimit these sentiments (Hynds 1991). Indeed, as van Dijk (2000, 36) writes, the media play a powerful "discursive and symbolic" role in "modern information societies"; and together "with other powerful elite groups and institutions ... they have sometimes indirectly most influence on the lives of most people in society ... Media discourse is the main source of people's knowledge, attitudes and ideologies, both of other elites and of ordinary citizens." And, as Henry and Bjornson (1999, 17–18) point out, while it is not possible to accurately determine the extent to which media reporting influences attitudes, there is evidence to suggest that the media "re-enforce attitudes already held by members of the community" and that they do this through "agenda setting" – focusing on particular topics while ignoring others.

In this chapter, I examine the media's role in constructing and portraying particular images of Jamaican migrant workers in Kelowna through the use of "coded" words that identify them as foreign racial Others. These media portrayals invoke racialized representations, which are encoded in Canada's multicultural ethos of colour-blindness, which holds that race does not matter, does not inform immigration policies and practices, and hence has no bearing on individuals' interactions and position in society. But before launching into the discussion of the social, political, and economic concerns pertaining to the presence of Jamaicans in Kelowna, I set the context with a theorization of colour-blindness as embedded in and sustained through the hegemony of whiteness and its implication for migrants and racialized people in society. I continue with a brief review of Canada's contemporary immigration policies and practices pertaining to racialized people in general and Black people in particular. I then discuss the constructions of Jamaicans within the framework of whiteness, examining the ways in which Jamaican migrants in Kelowna are represented and discussed in newspaper reports. I conclude by suggesting that, despite the fact that these migrants are brought in to fill identified needs, they are, nevertheless, contributing to the regional as well as to the national economy.

Notwithstanding the likely benefits that Jamaicans will contribute to the local community, their status as guest workers and post-secondary education students will continue to be mitigated by age-old reservations about Black people in Canadian society. Such explicit and covert reservations could give rise to tensions and undue or undeserved hardships not faced by other migrants to Kelowna.

WHITENESS, COLOUR-BLINDNESS, AND BLACK PEOPLE

Notwithstanding Canada's claims to cultural freedom, equality, meritocracy, and respect for cultural differences as set out in its Multicultural Policy (1971) and Multicultural Act, 1988, generally, matters of race continue to mark how immigration and employment opportunities are established, governed, and legislated. In fact, racial distinctions play a fundamental role in how certain bodies are read and valued as belonging in Canada and, in particular, in Canadian communities (Ameeriar 2017). As Moras (2010, 244) states, "the politics of citizenship and migration have always been a discourse informed by race." In fact, the "keep-Canada-white" ideology, or whiteness, on which the Canadian state operates (Bashi 2004; James 2010; Ward 1990), has helped frame how Canadians live with and maintain racial differentiation. Seshadri-Crooks (2000, 3–4) refers to whiteness as a "master signifier that establishes a structure of relations, a signifying chain that through a process of inclusions and exclusions constitutes a pattern for organizing human difference. This chain provides subjects with certain symbolic positions such as 'black,' 'white,' 'Asian.'" In other words, through preserving and reinforcing cultural beliefs, racial bias, and the exclusion of racialized members of society, the hegemonic structure of whiteness serves to maintain the discourse for what constitutes human nature, moral character, ambition, and belonging. And, as Amanda Lewis (2004, 628) writes, while whites' access "to cultural capital and other resources may vary, all whites have access to the symbolic capital of whiteness or what DuBois (1962 [1935], 700) refers to as 'wages' of whiteness."

A major component of the contemporary ideology of whiteness is colour-blindness, a discursive shift from earlier explicit racist and discriminatory policies, programs, and practices to ones in which individuals claim to be "blind" to colour or race and hold to the notion that "we are all part of the human race" – often expressed as: "I don't see race. I see people as people." But, as scholars argue, such a claim reflects not only the goodness and innocence of individuals and the boundaries of whiteness (Schick and St. Denis 2003) but also their complicity in systems of oppression that makes them "blind to the effects of colo[u]r" and how colour continues to serve as an inherent element in maintaining dominant power relations (Lewis 2004, 636). Jiwani (2011, 40–41) asserts that, within contemporary discourses of race and racism, explicitly racist statements are verboten, replaced by an "inferential form of racism" in which racist assumptions and subtle articulations persist without ever being specifically invoked. In fact, whiteness-informed colour-blind discourse negates history, decontextualizes the experiences of racial minorities, leaves unacknowledged the significant role race plays in shaping identities, and sustains the "culture of privilege and contemporary White supremacy" (Ferber 2007, 15). As well, it determines the social location that individuals or group members come to occupy in the society and their resulting access to resources and opportunities. Ferber indicates that a colour-blind perspective is based on the assumption that racism "is a thing of the past and the playing field has been leveled," therefore, the circumstances in which individuals find themselves are of their own making (14).

In effect, cultural difference, and not racism, is used to justify differential treatments and maintenance of the racial status quo. Bonilla-Silva and Forman (2000, 69) refer to this "global justification" by whites as "colour-blind racism," which structures a "discourse of difference" in which racial minorities are represented as "Other" – "different, deviant, or a threat" to society. Other scholars refer to today's beliefs and differential treatment of racialized members as a product of "new racism" – "a racism whose dominant theme is not biological heredity but the insurmountability of cultural differences; a racism which, at first sight, does not postulate the superiority of certain groups or peoples in relation to others but 'only' the harmfulness of abolishing frontiers, the incompatibility of life-styles and traditions" (Balibar 2007, 84; see also Ferber 2007; Lewis 2004). In other words, the behaviours, values, and ideas or "cultural traits," which were once believed to be biologically determined, are now attributed to the "culture" of racialized groups; and the incompatibility of their cultures with that of the perceived "mainstream" (read: dominant group) is used to support, as Bashi (2004) notes, Western societies' preferences for "white immigrants."

The differences among the cultures of racialized or immigrant groups and the "mainstream" or host society is often evident in the news coverage. For instance, in Teun van Dijk's (2000, 23) chapter "New(s) Racism: A Discourse Analytical Approach," in which he examines media reports on immigrants and ethnic minorities in Britain, he found that the reports were riddled with negative portrayals and special "code-words." The reports tended to cover topics such as the social and economic problems of immigrants, especially illegal immigrants; their employment, housing, and welfare situation; and how they are different (culturally) and deviant in terms of their likelihood to engage in violence, crime, drugs, and prostitution. What is troubling, van Dijk argues, is how, through these portrayals, readers come to see and understand immigrants and minorities, particularly when "most white readers have few daily experiences with minorities ... have few alternative sources for information about minorities," and are exposed to problems that are "Threats to Us" (37). According to van Dijk, these issues provide positive but polarized identification for most white readers, in terms of Us and Them," thereby allowing white readers to maintain an everyday binary of a "positive self-presentation and negative other-presentation" (39).

In his examination of how people of different racial backgrounds were depicted in the Canadian media, Wortley (2008), using a sample of 1,932 crime stories appearing in two of Toronto's print media in 1997 and 1998, found that Black people were not only overrepresented but were also more likely to be depicted as criminal offenders than as crime victims. Wortley notes that over 80 percent of Black Torontonians are of Caribbean decent – either having emigrated or having parents from the region. Hence, the taken-for-granted notion in Toronto that "Black" people "have cultural roots in the Caribbean" (107). He writes:

> Indeed, about 90 percent of the stories involving Black subjects fall into sports, crime, or entertainment categories. Furthermore, almost half of the "serious" news stories (all stories excluding sports and entertainment) involving Blacks are related to criminal activity. Blacks are also much more likely to be associated with certain types of crimes

> (such as robbery and street crime) than are their counterparts from other racial groups. (121)

If, as Wortley concludes, this is frequently the information that whites receive about Black people, the news media will have had a "strong impact on the formation and maintenance of racial stereotypes" of Black people (126). Furthermore, in the multicultural context of colour-blindness, and in the absence of knowledge about, and direct experience with, Black Caribbean people, non-Black people will come to perceive Black Caribbean people as culturally homogenous. This essentialization is informed, in part, by the fact that the majority of Black people in Canada are of Jamaican descent (James 2008).

Before proceeding with the discussion, it is important to give attention to the immigration policies and practices that essentially account for the population of Canada apart from the First Nations peoples. My interest here is with contemporary immigration policies and practices of the late 1960s. As will become evident in the following section, today's immigration practices and policies have roots in "transnational anti-black immigration policy," which, as Bashi (2004, 585) explains, relies on "cultural and biological arguments" that justify "the unsuitability of Caribbean Blacks to the demands of regular employment" and their capacity to socially and culturally fit into society. In this regard, once those recruited fulfilled the labour demands, it was expected they return to their place of origin – "an expectation based on the certainty that black persons were inassimilable."

IMMIGRATION POLICIES AND PRACTICES IN CONTEMPORARY CANADA

In writing about the anti-Black orientation of Canada's immigration policies and practices, Bashi (2004, 585–86) indicates that

> Canada's anti-black immigration policy began officially in 1818 (well before the 1843 emancipation), with a law that "disallowed" voluntary black immigration (Marshall 1987). Two themes are evident in Canadian policy-makers' public and private statements at the time. First,

> they agreed that blacks from tropical regions could not survive or succeed in cold climates, and therefore should not be admitted. This argument was first promulgated in Canada in the late 1600s by the Governor Denonville but was used repeatedly throughout Canada's history. The second theme was the idea that admitting blacks meant the nation was just asking for problems (i.e., race riots) that Britain and the US had to bear for having black residents. (585–86)

However, since 1967, immigration policies have made it a requirement that independent (as opposed to family class) immigrants score 70 to 80 points out of a possible 100 based on, among other things, level of education, job skills, occupation demands, knowledge of English and French, and age. On the surface, this point system might be perceived as race and culture neutral, therefore affording Black Caribbeans the same chance of gaining entry into, and participating in, Canada as any other immigrant group. However, in reality, according to Razack (1999, 160), in the 1990s, the Canadian government initiated a variety of legislations and policies intended "to regulate more tightly the flow of immigrants and refugees to Canada" on the basis of trustworthiness. She observes that the racialized figure of "the criminal attempting to cross our borders" was a central feature of the type of individuals who cannot be trusted and, hence, must be monitored, managed, and kept out of the country. And as for those already in the country, specifically racialized people, they too were considered to be good or bad and, hence, needed to be policed. This policing of racialized people – Jamaicans in particular – is evident in how they are marked to be questioned not only about their status as a Canadian or immigrant (i.e. their right to be in the country) but also to ensure that they are not troublemakers or lawbreakers (James 2008).

An essential feature of the Canadian point system is not only to prescribe who are best able to socially and culturally "fit" into the society but also to ensure they are able to contribute to the economic development of the country through their educational and occupational skills and experiences. Bashi (2004, 587) writes that the point system has served to strengthen "the occupational orientation of the immigration policies." For this reason, although prospective family-class immigrants – those sponsored or nominated by husbands, wives, and fiancé(e)s – were not expected to meet these requirements, many of those gaining entry to the country tended to be professionals, skilled workers, and to have high levels of education. In the case of Caribbean immigrants, whether sponsored, nominated, or independent immigrants, many came with post-secondary education and professional credentials in the medical field, such as nurses and doctors, and in the field of education, mostly teachers (James, Plaza, and Jansen 1999). Indeed, Oreopoulos (2009, 8) makes the point that about 60 percent of recent immigrants to Canada entering under the point system, compared to 20 percent of Canadian-born individuals of similar age, had at least an undergraduate degree. Those without such credentials often came to Canada with the expectation of furthering their education, which they usually did (James 2009b).

Yet, policy-makers remain concerned that today's immigrants are not assimilating or integrating into the society as expected, particularly in the labour market. In investigating this concern, Oreopoulos (2009, 40) finds that employers tend to "discriminate by name and location of experience" with regard to job applicants because they believe that "these characteristics signal a greater chance of inadequate language and cultural skills for the job." In fact, based on his research on why "skilled immigrants struggle in the labor market," Oreopoulos establishes that, in a pool of interviewees, including applicants with foreign backgrounds, employers show preference for people with "English-sounding names" and value those with "Canadian experience far more than [those with] Canadian education" (38). Similarly, from her work on the employment situation of immigrants, Zikic (2009) concludes that their foreign credentials and experience are discounted, making it difficult for them to gain employment, especially in positions that suit them. Yet there are widespread feelings among many uninformed Canadians that immigrants take jobs away from Canadians (James 2010).

For years immigrants (or permanent residents) have been coming to Canada to fill its economic and labour needs, as have migrants or "guest workers" who are given short-term work permits with the expectation that they will return to their home country upon completion of their assignment. Most notable among the guest workers are farm workers from the Caribbean, Mexico, and elsewhere who have been entering Canada for decades to work from spring to the fall months. Migrant temporary agricultural workers from Mexico and elsewhere have been coming to British

Columbia and the Okanagan, in particular, via an organized program only since 2004 (Aguiar, Tomic, and Trumper 2011). But in recent years, labour shortages, especially in areas of construction, fast food service, and hotel cleaning in provinces such as British Columbia, Alberta, Saskatchewan, and Ontario, have driven provincial governments to request that the federal government bring in more migrant workers. This was the case in Ontario, which experienced labour shortages in the food industry – for instance, at Tim Hortons. L.C. Taylor ("Immigrants Sought to Fill Vacancies in Food Industry: Work Permits Seen as Way to Ease Ontario Shortage," *Toronto Star*, 29 October 2008, A20) writes with reference to Ontario that, because of the aging population, there will soon be relatively fewer young adults and teenagers. For this reason, the food industry will need some 200,000 workers in the coming years.

It is observed that, in some areas, short-term migrants are surpassing the number of individuals who enter as permanent residents through the points system, which has tended to privilege high-skilled immigrants such as doctors, scientists, and engineers (Taylor, "Immigrants Sought to Fill Vacancies in Food Industry," *Toronto Star*, 29 October 2008, A20). Critics of the guest worker programs charge that, in so far as the work permits tie these workers to a single employer, they are vulnerable to exploitation, "monitoring" or surveillance, and human rights abuses more generally, particularly when we take into account language differences, level of education, and unfamiliarity with Canada's labour laws (R. Brennan, "Immigration Changes Pose Risk Critics Say," *Toronto Star*, 15 March 2008, A19). Furthermore, advocates argue that such programs have the potential for workers to be treated more as commodities than as human beings, thereby ignoring the reality of their developing ties through conjugal relationships, which might produce children, and their participating in varying degrees in the broader Canadian society (D. Saunders, "Why Our Thinking about Immigration Remains Borderline," *Globe and Mail*, 3 November 2007, F3).

Essentially, over the years, Canadian immigration policies and practices have been premised on meeting the economic and labour needs of the country, as opposed to acknowledging how immigration has been a viable solution to population growth and economic sustainability. In this regard, determining who gains entry has been premised on determining who can best "fit in" socially and culturally. Early immigration policies opposed the admissibility of racialized people on the basis that they were unable to assimilate socially and culturally, and for Black people, added to this was their assumed inability to adapt to the climate. While in recent years the point system, the sponsored and nominated allowances, and guest worker programs have facilitated the entry of racialized people, the fact remains that the policies' predisposition towards a biological explanation of which people are best suited to become "good" productive Canadians continues to inform Canadians' perceptions of and experiences with immigrants. So, while an increasing number of racialized people, and Black Jamaicans in particular, are today entering Canada through existing immigration programs, even though this is a country with federal "multicultural" legislation, biological references remain hidden in the discourses of cultural "differences." Canadians have not been colour-blind after all, hence, any examination of the sentiments to be found in media reports must necessarily take into account the historical legacy of race in immigrant policies and in perceptions of Jamaicans.

CONSTRUCTS OF JAMAICANS IN CANADIANS' IMAGINATION

Elsewhere (James 2008), I have written about the "Jamaicanization" discourse that is related to the racialization and criminalization of Black-skinned people. I argue that the tendency to identify Black Caribbean people as Jamaicans not only has to do with the fact that well over one-third of Caribbean people in Canada are of Jamaican origin (Jamaica has the largest population of English-speaking Caribbean people) but also contributes to a homogeneous reading of all Caribbean people, thereby devaluing the complex, diverse, and transitory identities of people from the region. Further, "Canada's anti-black immigration policy" (Bashi 2004), combined with the increase in the number of Caribbean people entering the country since the 1970s, is conveniently used to explain some social problems – including illegal or criminal activities. Frances Henry and Carol Tator (2005, 54–55) write of the media's role in "the racialization and criminalization of Jamaican Canadians" constructing and maintaining their profile as belligerent, aggressive, violence-prone, and coming from a criminal culture. There are also media deportation stories of Jamaicans, portraying them as people who are in the country illegally and who engage in unlawful activities (James 2008).

Gwyn Morgan (2005), past president and chief executive officer of EnCana Corporation and a contributor to the *Globe and Mail*, in a speech to the Fraser Institute, commented: "our country needs more productive, competent workers," which could be provided through immigration. He argues that, apart from the economic aspect of immigration, there is the social cost, which is "all too evident with the run-away violence driven mainly by Jamaican immigrants in Toronto" and, in Calgary, "the all too frequent violence between Asian and other ethnic gangs." He goes on to make the point that "immigration groups blame 'poverty' or 'police discrimination' or 'lack of opportunity,'" but what they fail to acknowledge is that the "root cause" of the violence is the "violent tendencies" and "lawlessness" of the immigrants who "come from countries where the culture is dominated by violence and lawlessness. Jamaica has one of the world's highest crime rates driven mainly by the violence between gangs competing for dominance in the Caribbean drug trade. Why do we expect different behaviour in Toronto, Ontario[,] than in Kingston, Jamaica?" (10). This inference about Jamaica's reputation as a state with significant criminal activities can also be noted in an issue of *Maclean's* magazine (14 October 2010), in which it questions why Toronto, one of Canada's most populous cities, has the lowest crime rates in the country. The authors, Köhler and Treble (2010), write that Ontario's low reporting of crimes belies "the large numbers of new Canadians who have arrived from countries, like Jamaica, where police carry a reputation for corruption and abuse. That may be why York, Peel and Halton suburbs, part of the 905 donut surrounding Toronto and with a reputation for youth crime, come in so low on the crime-score totem pole" (15).

Morgan's assertion is a good example of new racism, in which the cultural "traits" (i.e., non-Western and non-white) of Jamaicans are seen as both "deficient" and "pathological" (see van Dijk 2000). This perception of Jamaicans as unable to escape their socialization both in terms of the environment in which they grew up and from which their ancestors migrated, is very much part of Canadians' understanding of "difference." In this case, difference is not merely a social construct: it also includes the conflation of a people's national, physical, and biological characteristics (James 2008, 389) as well as their "mental and emotional characteristics" (Comack 1999, 56). The supposedly innate features and capacities of

Jamaicans were taken seriously enough that, in February 2003, the then Toronto chief of police, Julian Fantino, went to Jamaica to learn how to deal with the issues of violence and crime in Toronto, and Jamaican police officers were, in turn, invited to Toronto (James 2008).

For decades, Caribbean people, and Jamaicans in particular, have been migrating to Canada as domestics, service and farm workers, care-givers, and health-care workers (including doctors and nurses), as undergraduate and graduate students. And, as permanent residents and citizens, they have been working in such roles as teachers, professors, pastors, lawyers, judges, civil servants, and police officers. Also, through tourism many Canadians have had opportunities to visit Jamaica (and other Caribbean islands), where they are able to experience that country's diversity. But despite the many service, occupational, and educational contexts in which Canadians have had opportunities to interact with Jamaicans – many of them educated – it seems these exposures or interactions have done little to challenge or dispel the preconceived notions and/or the existing racial profile of Jamaicans. Hence, it seems logical that governments and Canadians in general would want to put in place policies, or take pre-emptive actions, to deal with the problems that may arise when Jamaicans are part of society. It is possible that the coverage (June 2010) of Jamaican Christopher "Dudus" Coke in many of the world media might have helped to reinforce the perceptions of Jamaicans as lawless and violent. Coke, who was wanted by the United States on federal drug and weapon charges, was described as a "drug lord." He remained a fugitive for about five weeks in a west Kingston (Jamaica) neighbourhood, where he was protected from arrest by supporters, or, as some media described them, "his posse." Some seventy civilians and security officers died before he was arrested. The Canadian media told Canadians that Coke's posse also operated in Canada – at least in Ontario.

That Canadians tend not to see Jamaicans as embracing a similar work ethic and moral principles as those informed by Christian convictions, and tend not to see them as, like "us," racially, ethnically, and socially diverse, indicates not only ignorance about the diversity to be found among any given population of people but also the relentlessness of the historical legacy and media representation of Jamaicans that continues to restrict the imagination of many Canadians. So pretensions of colour-blindness seem not to apply to Jamaicans, and particularly not to Black Jamaicans. In what follows, I reflect on how that colour-blindness, a simultaneous disavowal of racism, and a fascination with Jamaican Black male bodies as spectacular sites of criminality are featured in media representations of Jamaican workers and students in Kelowna. But first I provide a profile of Kelowna.

JAMAICANS IN KELOWNA, BRITISH COLUMBIA

Kelowna – A Profile

In his examination of the barriers that minorities face in gaining access to housing in Kelowna, Teixeira (2009) writes that this mid-sized city was once portrayed by the local media as a "white-bread valley" with "older, caucasian, and English-speaking" residents as immigrants to Canada preferred to settle within larger, more multicultural cities. But, in recent years, Kelowna witnessed a rapid growth of migrants from other parts of British Columbia and other provinces. These migrants are mainly of European descent and, in many cases, are retirees with fairly comfortable incomes (Aguiar, Tomic, and Trumper 2005). And, as Teixeira (2009, 325) mentions: "Kelowna is a predominantly 'white' city. Visible minorities comprise only 6.2 percent of Kelowna's population, compared to approximately 25 percent of the BC population as a whole (Statistics Canada 2006). South Asians (28.8 percent), Chinese (19 percent), Japanese (13.6 percent) and Southeast Asians (9.5 percent) are the four most important visible minority groups in the city." From his research, Teixeira concludes that "it is significant that while the role of immigration as an important engine of economic growth has long been recognized by all levels of government in Canada's largest cities – Montréal, Toronto and Vancouver – less attention has been paid to this phenomenon in mid-sized urban areas such as Kelowna" (338; see also Central Okanagan Economic Development Commission 2010).

In their work about the reputation of Kelowna as a "conservative place intolerant of difference," Aguiar, Tomic, and Trumper (2005) write of the pervasiveness of "whiteness" and its "power to maintain its hegemony" without having to accommodate minorities and immigrants – the so-called "Others" who were not the expected migrants. In fact, as they write, "in a very telling way the dominant groups in the Okanagan hold up coded whiteness and monoculturalism as appealing cards to attract people, capital and businesses, to attract, for example, particular types of tourists, retirees and high-tech industries. In each and every case, the enticement is whiteness, and the target population whites" (167). Indicating that race and racism have historically structured the approach to populating the Okanagan, as in the case of the Japanese, Chinese, and First Nations people, Aguiar, Tomic, and Trumper declare, "Here, monoculturalism openly and shamelessly marks the space" (163; see also Plant 2007). Hence, it is consistent that the coming of Black Jamaican workers – mostly young men – and students to such a guarded "white space" would incite the unwanted or unwelcoming discourse to be found in both the media and the population. The reference to white space here is not so much about the visibility of racialized groups; rather, it calls attention to the spatial and cultural politics that maintain a quaint pastoral monoculture, untarnished by the influence of "unassimilable others" (Jiwani 2011, 41).

It is into this Canadian context that agricultural workers from Jamaica have been migrating for over a decade to work on farms in the Okanagan Valley. They have been coming through the Seasonal Agricultural Worker Program (SAWP) – a feature of Canada's Temporary Foreign Worker Program (RAMA 2016). The fact is, Jamaicans have been residing in Kelowna prior to 2007; however, as a result of the experimental program that was established at Okanagan College in 2007, the number of Jamaican migrants residing in Kelowna has grown considerably. As Wendy Leung (2008) writes in the *Globe and Mail*, the Jamaican students were recruited "to help fill a shortage of skilled workers in the Okanagan and the rest of the province." The "interprovincial refresher" program was expected "to train and find job placements for between 300 and 400 Jamaican students … in high-demand trades such as culinary arts, automotive collision repair and carpentry." From their position in the valley, Aguiar, McKinnon, and Sookraj (2010–11, 9) observe that "the racialization of the Jamaicans began prior to their arrival to the Okanagan Valley as 'residents'" and that their characterization as such was "culled not from experiences in the local setting or through personal interaction with Jamaicans, but through the infamous bedrock of Jamaican presence in Canada" and through the media representations of them in Toronto. Building on this assertion, in the following section, I examine how media reports and letters to the editor engaged with issues pertaining to Jamaican workers and students in Kelowna. In doing so, I focus on how reports prepared the community for the "colour that Jamaicans would add" to the community (A. Baldeo, "Jamaicans Will Add Colour to Kelowna," *Kelowna Capital News*, 19 September 2007, A29) and how the treatment of the workers and students were taken up by reporters and residents – as recounted in the local newspapers over a twenty-month period from April 2007 to December 2008.

MEETING THE LABOUR NEEDS OF THE OKANAGAN: BENEFITS, COSTS, AND ASSURANCES

A number of reporters have speculated that Jamaican workers might be the "solution" to the economic problems and employment needs of Kelowna. For instance, K. Michaels ("Hiring Foreign Workers May Be Answer to Labour Shortage," *Kelowna Capital News*, 19 September 2007, A23) writes: "It's no news to anyone that attracting and retaining skilled labour has been identified as the number one issue facing businesses in Kelowna. More and more employers have life-sized billboards outside their shops begging for workers, and few are getting the results they need which is stagnating growth, and threatening viability." The message is that, if Kelowna is to have a viable economy, then it is essential and urgent to get qualified, reliable, committed, and "much needed" workers to work in construction, car repair, window cleaning, and service and farming industries. Car repair was identified as one industry that "has been struggling to find enough local mechanics to hire," for, as the manager said: "We basically exhausted all of our efforts" (A. Nieoczym, "Transit Service Eager to Hire OC Grads," *Kelowna Capital News*, 10 December 2008). To this end, as reporter Don Plant ("Census Data Reveals White-Bread Valley," *Daily Courier*, 4 December 2007, A1, A4) writes, quoting the manager of the local Economic Development Commission: "We need to diversify this region, or we're in serious trouble. To compete globally, communities that are successful are more diverse and embrace different cultures."

As if to reassure the people of the region that Jamaican workers and students are fully qualified in the trades into which they were being recruited, reports repeatedly cited the migrants' education, training, qualifications, and years of experience working in the respective occupations: "Those workers will be skilled tradespeople, with three to 15 years experience," said the general manager of a construction company (A. Nieoczym,

"Jamaica Wants to Fill Jobs in the Region," *Kelowna Capital News*, 27 June 2007, A1). And noting that the workers would be paid the same as similarly qualified and experienced Canadians (a journeyman carpenter $20 to $30 an hour; and window cleaners $12.85 to $15 an hour – see A. Nieoczym, "Caribbean Workers 'the Solution to Our Employment Needs,'" *Kelowna Capital News*, 3 August 2007, A19), the agricultural support officer for the regional district's Economic Development Commission stated: "It's not really about cheap labour, it's about reliable labour" (ibid.). The migrants' reliability and experience were represented in reports that indicated that they were assessed and accepted into the program not once they came to Canada but through skill examinations and interviews in Jamaica, for which they "achieved acceptable scores." Further, it was noted that, in order for the migrants to obtain visas (usually for six months), they had to "qualify as journeymen," which meant that they had to have between five thousand and eight thousand hours experience in the particular trade; and for two-year visas, they were required to pass the national Red Seal certification, which in theory would enable them to apply for permanent residency while also securing employment outside of British Columbia (A. Nieoczym, "Testing the Labor Pool Waters," *Kelowna Capital News*, 4 November 2007, A3).

Readers were also assured that these Jamaican migrant workers were not taking jobs away from Canadians – a concern that is repeatedly expressed by Canadians with regard to immigration (James 2010). To this end, the idea that employers in the region have struggled to find enough local mechanics and window washers to hire in the face of labour shortage seemingly not only justified bringing in immigrants but also addressed the concerns of the people of the region. Indeed, S. MacNaull ("Caribbean Connection Could Ease Labour Crunch," *Okanagan Saturday*, 2 June 2007, A1) reminded readers that the Canadian government has policies in place to prevent migrants from taking away their jobs: "Any workers would first have to be approved by Service Canada's Labour Market Opinion process that a Canadian is not missing out on work if a Jamaican is hired. Jamaican workers then get a two-year temporary work permit." And it was emphasized that the workers were in Canada on a temporary basis and would return to Jamaica when the work was done – something that the Jamaica Liaison Office in Kelowna would ensure happened. A. Nieoczym ("Jamaica

Eager to Fill Need," *Kelowna Capital News*, 5 August 2007) also writes that many of those workers were expected to be in Canada "for short periods doing low-skilled farm jobs under the Seasonal Agricultural Worker Program and then returning to Jamaica." But others, like the construction workers who were skilled workers, were given temporary worker visas for up to two years.

The people of Kelowna were also assured that the Jamaican students who were enrolled in the Okanagan College's business, technical, and trade programs, and who were also assessed in Jamaica before coming to Canada, would not be taking jobs or college spaces from residents. In fact, comments seemed geared towards ensuring that community members understood the opportunities the students brought to the region and that they would not be a burden on the educational system or the economy. In this regard, media reports indicated that the students had to pay the full cost of their tuition – some two to three times the tuition of Canadian students, whose studies were subsidized by the provincial government. The extra money from foreign students, A. Nieoczym ("Jamaican, Okanagan Relationship Shaping up," *Kelowna Capital News*, 21 September 2007) writes, enabled the college to offer more courses, thereby "creating more access for Canadian students." Accordingly, as the college president is quoted as saying, "having foreign students at a college doesn't deny space to any Canadians. In fact, it's the other way around." On the question of students being able to meet their financial obligation, reports indicate that, before leaving Jamaica, students had to demonstrate to the Canadian Embassy there that their parents had a bank account of "at least $20,000," which was seen as the financial support they would need for about six months. And when a representative of the Jamaican government visited the region and announced that his government would be providing $200,000 in loans to students attending the college to help with their tuition as needed, it is understandable that this, too, was reassuring and encouraging news (M. Dann, "Come from Jamaica, and Feel All Right," *Globe and Mail*, 10 November 2008, B11; A. Nieoczym, "Jamaican Students a No-Risk Investment," *Kelowna Capital News*, 29 August 2008, A1). Essentially, the presence of Jamaican students in Kelowna was represented as an opportunity for the college to help meet "the training needs" of both the Okanagan and Jamaican communities. "It certainly drives home the College's understanding" said the chair of its Board of Governors, "that part of our role is to contribute to the region's social, cultural and economic development" (*Okanagan College News* 2007). And, as the college president also said, "I think it's fairly safe to say, little old Okanagan College has become the gateway to the Canadian labour force for an increasing number of students from the Caribbean" (A. Nieoczym, "Labour Agreement a Success for Okanagan College," *Kelowna Capital News*, 24 August 2008, A8).

It was also reported that, "Not only are Jamaican families dependent on money sent home from abroad, but so too is the government. Totaling approximately $1.6 billion a year, remittances from Jamaicans working overseas are the country's second biggest source of foreign exchange earning, next only to tourism" (A. Nieoczym, "Testing the Labor Pool Waters," *Kelowna Capital News*, 4 November 2007, A3; see also Mullings, Williams, and Lovell 2012). Such insights as well as the human interest stories of the Jamaican workers and students – stories that disclosed how they were taking responsibility for their children and families by sending money home – seemed to have played a role in the affirming experiences that the Jamaicans were receiving in Kelowna. There were expressions of appreciation for the friendly and "warm welcome" the migrants received from the members of the Kelowna community. And while some of them found the weather "a little cold," they nevertheless "loved the Okanagan," particularly with regard to the opportunity they were getting to work in Canada. According to one worker, "It's better paid, better working environment and more jobs." Another worker commented: "We like the work. I'm glad for the experience" (A. Flexhaug, "Jamaicans in Valley to Work Construction Trades," *Penticton Herald*, 9 November 2007, A4).

From most accounts, the workers were "well received" at their respective workplaces; as one employer put it, "the workers have been picking up each other's slang, becoming buddies and sharing their skills and tools. All the normal peer activities are going on" (A. Nieoczym, "Jamacain [sic] Workers Arrive in OK," *Kelowna Capital News*, 23 September 2007, A4). Another employer mentioned, "these guys are working out very, very well. They want to work[,] and you couldn't find a group of more enthusiastic, nice and hard-working guys" (S. MacNaull, "The Jamaicans are Here and Working," *Daily Courier*, 12 April 2008, C1). That these Jamaican workers showed gratitude, ambition, industriousness, friendliness, comradeship, and enthusiasm had as much to do with their interest in the work as with the fact that they took seriously their obligation to their fellow migrants and to the Jamaican community. One worker said to reporter A. Nieoczym that he "wanted people in the Okanagan to know he and the other Jamaican workers are here to work hard. 'We are here to do the work that you guys need, we're not here to step back.' He added he is aware that there are other Jamaicans who would like to have the opportunity he had to work in Canada, but that their chances depend on his being successful. 'We're ambassadors,' he said[,] 'We're representing Jamaica'" (A. Nieoczym, "No Sex, No Pot for Workers," *Kelowna Capital News*, 23 September 2007, A4). Thus, not only were the Jamaicans' technical skills affirmed by news reports but news readers were reassured that their values, work ethic, and character were consistent with the values of the region.

This idea of being an "ambassador" and a representative of a national and racial population of people no doubt underscores much of what the migrants said and did in Kelowna. Indeed, they understood the myths or stereotypes that they were up against, and it seems that they were making every effort to prove them wrong. This being the case, they used opportunities provided to them to address probable questions about their skills, training, qualifications, and experiences as well as about their being constructed as aggressive; as lawbreakers, drug-dealers, and pot-smokers; and as sexually promiscuous people from an "underdeveloped," laid-back, violence-prone culture. However, despite months of preparing the members of the community for a "sprinkling" – not a "saturation" – of skilled experienced workers and qualified students (A. Nieoczym, "Okanagan Employers Turning Their Attention to Jamaica," *Kelowna Capital News*, June 3, 2007, A9), residents of Kelowna still had their doubts (see Aguiar, McKinnon, and Sookraj 2010–11). These doubts persisted even though it had been communicated that all the Jamaican migrants had to pass a medical examination, criminal background checks, as well as the scrutiny of prospective employers, Canadian Consulate officials, and Jamaican government agents – a process that took almost three months. And the Jamaican migrants' stories of friendliness, gratitude, responsible parenting, commitment to work, industriousness, and their fitting in did not eliminate the age-old perceptions of them.

In fact, it was revealed that, in the summer of 2007, Kelowna City Council received a letter from a constituent warning that if they were not careful, Kelowna would become like Toronto, where people of Jamaican ancestry were believed to be responsible for the "majority of drug and violent crimes" (A. Nieoczym, "Crime Stereotype Raises Some Concern," *Kelowna Capital News*, 14 September 2007, A1). On the basis of this concern, the sponsors of the program subjected the Jamaican migrants to what a representative of the Jamaican Liaison Office termed "a series of stringent rules." Specifically, they were to abide by "an 11 p.m. curfew on work nights, … [and] refrain from drinking when they have to work the next morning." As well, they were given "a sheet," which stipulated that "the use of marijuana or any other non-prescription drug was illegal" and that "they [were] not allowed to have members of the opposite sex sleep over" (A. Nieoczym, "No Sex, No Pot for [Jamaican] Workers," *Kelowna Capital News*, 23 September 2007). News reports had earlier stated that workers who "breached their contract," "caused problems," or were "disruptive" would be sent home. These and other monitoring and surveillance measures to which the workers were subjected should have left little doubt that the Canadian and Jamaican sponsors of the program were highly sensitive to the concerns of the members of the Kelowna community and were doing everything in their power to "protect" that community through pre-emptive measures. To this end, representatives of the Jamaican Liaison Office also let it be known that, "once the work is done here, the liaison service will see that they return to Jamaica" (A. Nieoczym, "Caribbean Workers 'the Solution to Our Employment Needs,'" *Kelowna Capital News*, 3 August 2007, A19). And in the case of the seasonal agricultural workers, a Jamaican representative spelt out that the workers would be met at the airport, accompanied to their work site, and visited periodically at each farm by a representative of the Jamaican Liaison Office (ibid.).

In reacting to the media reports on the treatment of the Jamaican migrants, one community member, in his "letter to the editor," identified the contradictory, double-standard, and paternalistic approach to the migrants:

> My gosh! In a free country these are remarkable expectations and I wonder if they are even legally enforceable (aside from the drug use

> prohibition). Certainly, these rules might promote their effectiveness as labourers but to demand that they follow explicit codes of conduct which Canadian workers do not face, and which some local workers sometimes ignore is problematic. Obviously, if the new workers violate laws vis-a-vis illicit drug use or show up to work fatigued, intoxicated or "high" they should be subject to the same legal and other consequences as Canadian workers. I do not see, however, how they can be required to keep a "curfew" (these are adult men after all) or avoid social or sexual relations with the opposite sex when these are surely matters of personal morality. While the men may want to follow the rules, for a variety of reasons I fear that, in the long run, the rules may set them up for unnecessary problems over and above what our Canadian workers might experience. (G.W. Lea, "Canadian Freedoms Still Apply to Migrant Workers," *Kelowna Capital News*, 28 September 2007, A29)

Another citizen, who identified as a "Caribbean-Canadian," wrote:

> I was disappointed to read in *The Daily Courier* Sept 13 that the arrival of Jamaican students and skilled workers was making some people nervous in Kelowna. You can hardly call the arrival of 12 workers from Jamaica an influx. It is not fair to say that because of their arrival, drug trafficking and violence will suddenly increase. You would almost think that we will have to set up a "Jamaican Vigil" upon their arrival. It will be interesting to note that there is already a handful of Caribbean people living in Kelowna and they have not started any riots or revolution ... So we should not generalize that all Caribbean peoples or Jamaicans are here to create problems. Our fears are completely unfounded. (*Kelowna Capital News*, 19 September 2007, A29)

The writer ends his letter by reminding readers that the migrants were well screened and selected, and that they were probably "a group of people who are above average on their island" – a group of people that members of the community should get to know. And, appealing to the liberal sensitivities inspired by the multicultural discourse of the community members, he goes on to suggest: "indeed, these visitors can add a little colour to our city." The paper used this as the headline for the letter and, by doing so, reduced the migrants to mere bodies – bodies of "colour."

Apart from the few "letters to the editor" from community members expressing "disappointment" with the treatment of the migrants, there was no widespread community protest. One might, therefore, ask: What accounts for the tolerance, if not acceptance, of the treatment of the Jamaican workers and students? Would such measures and heightened media attention be tolerated or needed in another situation (e.g., with workers from Europe)? One interpretation might be that, sustained by the flurry of media reports, which seemed pre-occupied with preparing and reassuring community members of the economic and social benefits of the migrants, community members were concerned that "law and order" be maintained given the deeply entrenched profile of these migrants as troublemakers and misfits.

CONCLUSION

> *"Experts say, however, we have nothing to fear, and lots to gain, from the small Caribbean influx."*
>
> (A. NIEOCZYM, "CRIME STEREOTYPE RAISES SOME CONCERN," *KELOWNA CAPITAL NEWS*, 14 SEPTEMBER 2007, A1)

It is worth noting that one newspaper, the *Kelowna Capital News*, assigned a staff member, Adrian Nieoczym, to report on the program and related issues. Nieoczym even went to Jamaica as an all-expenses-paid guest of the organizers. So, building on their insights and experiences, reporters provided mostly positive representations of both the Jamaican migrants and the program in general. Nevertheless, there remained an underlying scepticism and fear among the people of Kelowna. The irony here is that, in trying to assuage this scepticism and fear, the media, through their extensive chronicling months before and after the arrival of the Jamaican workers and students, in all likelihood reinscribed these feelings – feelings rooted in whiteness and the "invisible" construct of white European people as Canadians (presumably, the rightful residents of Canada's land and opportunities) and people from Europe as logical migrants with cultural traits consistent with those of Canadians. The construct this sustains is the racialization in which the work ethic of Black people and their propensity for "sex, alcohol, and drugs" remain a concern; hence, the need to regulate their movement, time, and work habits.

While Kelowna residents might have appreciated the urgency to find qualified skilled workers to help address "stagnating growth" and alleviate looming economic and social problems, there seems to be a lingering question: Are these the best people to help us? In this regard, despite the human stories carried in the media, which attempted to show that these Jamaican men and women had lives like the rest of "us" and, according to a community member, some Caribbean people were already living and working among "us" as medical practitioners, artists, educators, and clergy – the fact remained that the social construct of Black people in general, and Jamaicans in particular, continued to make it difficult for them to have an "unqualified" welcome in the community. Consequently, they were regarded as unsuitable neighbours. Why else would there be the extensive media reports and policing of these particular migrants?

Amanda Lewis (2004, 641–2) writes that "part of the privilege associated with whiteness is, in fact, the ability not to think about race at all, not to take any notice whatsoever of its role in daily life ... The seriality of whiteness means that though whites do not necessarily take it up as an active identity, it still fundamentally shapes their lives, ... their feelings, goals and language. This colour-blind notion embedded in whiteness is evident in how the residents of Kelowna reacted towards the Jamaican migrants." While employers, college personnel, and some community members talked of these "highly qualified skilled workers" being able to satisfy the skill and economic needs of the region, there remained a passive acceptance of the migrants' temporary status. It is a paradox that the Jamaicans are important to the economic and social growth of the region but not good enough, or qualified enough, to become permanent residents or workers in Canada – unless they are able to pass the Red Seal certificate (and there is no guarantee of this). So the material situation of the Kelowna community does not change. In fact, even the community members who took time to write to the media voicing their disappointment with the way that the Jamaicans were treated said to their fellow community members, "Don't worry, be happy," for "in any case they are here on a mission, and on a temporary basis" (Letters to the Editor, *Kelowna Capital News*, 19 September 2007, A29). To only conceive of these Jamaicans as temporary workers – here today but gone tomorrow – does little to change how they continue to be conceptualized in the Canadian imagination. Furthermore, to use these Jamaicans only as a temporary solution to a labour shortage neither addresses nor rectifies the region's "prolonged period of decline [in immigration] for most of the last two decades" (Azmier 2005, 117).

ACKNOWLEDGMENTS

I am indebted to Krysta Pandolfi and Selom Chapman-Nyaho for the research assistance they provided; and to Luís Aguiar and Daniel Keyes for their editorial comments, research support, and invitation to contribute this chapter. As well, I thank the reviewers for their comments on earlier versions of this chapter. I remain appreciative.

REFERENCES

Aguiar, Luís L.M., A.M. McKinnon, and D. Sookraj. 2010–11. "Racialization and the Repertoires of Racism: Reaction to Jamaicans in the Okanagan Valley." *BC Studies* 168 (Winter): 65–79.

Aguiar, L.M., P. Tomic, R. Trumper. 2005. "The Letter: Racism, Hate and Monoculturalism in a Canadian Hinterland." In *Possibilities and Limitation: Multicultural Policies and Programs in Canada,* ed. Carl E. James, 163–73. Halifax: Fernwood.

–. 2011. "Mexican Migrant Agricultural Workers and Accommodations on Farms in the Okanagan Valley." *Metropolis British Columbia. Centre of Excellence for Research and Immigration and Diversity Working Series Papers*. 11.4. British Columbia.

Ameeriar, L. 2017. *Downwardly Global: Women, Work, and Citizenship in the Pakistani Diaspora*. Durham, NC: Duke University Press.

Azmier, J. 2005. "Western Canada's Unique Immigration Picture." *Canadian Issues* (Spring): 116–18.

Baldeo, A. 2007. "Don't Judge Jamaicans before You've Met Them." *Daily Courier*, 20 September, A11.

Balibar, E. 2007. "Is There a 'Neo-Racism?'" In *Race and Racialization: Essential Readings,* ed. Tanis Gupta, 88–83. Toronto: Canadian Scholars' Press.

Bashi, V. 2004. "Globalized Anti-Blackness: Transnationalizing Western Immigration Law, Policy, and Practice." *Ethnic and Racial Studies* 27 (4): 584–606.

Bonilla-Silva, E., and T.A. Forman. 2000. "'I'm Not a Racist, But...': Mapping White College Students' Racial Ideology in the USA." *Discourse and Society* 11 (1): 50–85.

Central Okanagan Economic Development Commission 2010. *2010 Economic Profile of Regional District of the Central Okanagan*. Kelowna: COEDC.

Comack, E. 1999. "Theoretical Excursions." In *Locating Law: Race, Class, Gender Connections*, ed. E. Comack, 19–68. Halifax: Fernwood.

DuBois, W.E.B. 1962 [1935]. *Black Reconstruction in America, 1860–1880*. New York: The Free Press.

Ferber, A. 2007. "The Construction of Black Masculinity: White Supremacy Now and Then." *Journal of Sport and Social Issues* 31: 11–24.

Henry, F. 1999. *The Caribbean Diaspora in Toronto: Learning to Live with Racism*. Toronto: University of Toronto Press.

Henry, F., and C. Tator. 2005. *Racial Profiling in Toronto: Discourses of Domination, Mediation, and Opposition*. Toronto: Canadian Race Relations Foundation (September). https://www.thestar.com/content/dam/thestar/static_images/racialprofilingintoronto_discourses.pdf.

Henry, F., and M. Bjornson, 1999. *The Racialization of Crime in Toronto's Print Media: A Research Project*. Toronto: School of Journalism, Ryerson University.

Hynds, E.C. 1991. "Editorial Page Editors Discuss Use of Letters." *Newspaper Research Journal* 1 (3): 124–36.

James, C.E. 2008. "'Armed and Dangerous'/'Known to Police': Racializing Suspects." In *Marginality and Condemnation: An Introduction to Criminology*. ed. B. Schissel and C. Brooks. 388–403. Halifax: Fernwood.

–. 2009a. "Media Accounts of the Integration and Settlement of 'Island' Immigrants in Anglophone Caribbean." *Journal of Eastern Caribbean Studies* 34 (1): 41–69.

–. 2009b. "African-Caribbean Canadians Working 'Harder' to Attain Their Immigrant Dreams: Context, Strategies, and Consequences." *Wadabagei* 12 (1): 92–108.

–. 2010. *Seeing Ourselves: Exploring Race, Ethnicity and Culture*. Toronto: Thompson Educational Publishing.

James, C., D. Plaza, and C. Jansen. 1999. "Issues of Race in Employment: Experiences of Caribbean Women in Toronto." *Canadian Women Studies* 19 (3): 129–37.

Jiwani, Y. 2011. "Mediations of Race and Crime: Racializing Crime, Criminalizing Race." In *Diversity, Crime, and Justice in Canada*. ed. B. Perry, 39–56. Don Mills, ON: Oxford University Press.

Johnson-Carter, K.S. 2005. *New Narratives and News Framing: Constructing Political Reality*. Lanham, MD: Rowman and Littlefield.

Köhler, N., and P. Treble. 2010. "Safety in Numbers? Why Do Canada's Most Populous Provinces – Quebec and Ontario – Boast So Many of Its Safest Cities?," *Maclean's*, 14 October. https://www.macleans.ca/news/canada/safety-in-numbers.

Leung, W. 2008. "Labour Shortage? Bring in the Jamaicans." *Globe and Mail*, 8 September. https://beta.theglobeandmail.com/life/labour-shortage-bring-in-the-jamaicans/article1060884/?.

Lewis, A. 2004. "'What Group?'" Studying Whites and Whiteness in the Era of 'Color-Blindness.'" *Sociological Theory* 22 (4): 623–46.

Moras, A. 2010. "Colour-Blind Discourses in Paid Domestic Work: Foreignness and the Delineation of Alternative Racial Markers." *Ethnic and Racial Studies* 33 (2): 233–52.

Morgan, G. 2005. "Getting beyond the Symptoms to Root Causes ... What Politicians Are Afraid to Say." *T.P. Boyle Founder's Lecture*, the Fraser Institute, 7 December. http://www.therxforum.com/showthread.php?t=377421.

Mullings, B., K-A. Williams, and A. Lovell. 2012. "Myths and Realities: The Challenge of Social Transformation through Canada/Jamaica Diasporic Exchange." In *Jamaica in the Canadian Experience: A Multiculturalizing Presence*, ed. C.E. James and A. Davis, 294–309. Halifax: Fernwood.

Okanagan College News. 2007. "Jamaican Minister of Labour and Social Security Announces Newservices for Okanagan Initiative" Media Release, 26 June.

Oreopoulos, P. 2009. "Why Do Skilled Immigrants Struggle in the Labor Market? A Field Experiment with Six Thousand Résumés." NBER Working Paper.

Radical Action with Migrants in Agriculture (RAMA). 2016. "Jamaican Farmworkers in the Okanagan Say Working in Canada Is 'Faster Money, Faster Death,'" *RAMA*. 26 May. http://www.ramaokanagan.org/jamaican-farmworkers-in-the-okanagan-say-working-in-canada-is-faster-money-faster-death/.

Razack, S. 1999. "Making Canada White: Law and the Policing of Bodies of Colour in the 1990s." *Journal of Law and Society* 14 (1): 159–84.

Schick, C., and V. St. Denis. 2003. "What Makes Anti-Racist Pedagogy in Teacher Education Difficult? Three Popular Ideological Assumptions." *Alberta Journal of Education Research* 49 (1): 55–69.

Seshadri-Crooks. K. 2000. *Desiring Whiteness: A Lacanian Analysis of Race*. London: Routledge.

Taylor, L.C. 2008. Immigrants Sought to Fill Vacancies in Food Industry. *Toronto Star*, October 29. https://www.thestar.com/news/canada/2008/10/29/immigrants_sought_to_fill_vacancies_in_food_industry.html?rf.

Teixeira, C. 2009. "New Immigrant Settlement in a Mid-Size City: A Case Study of Housing Barriers and Coping Strategies in Kelowna, British Columbia." *Canadian Geographer* 53: 323–39.

van Dijk, T.A. 2000. "New(s) Racism: A Discourse Analytical Approach." In *Ethnic Minorities and the Media*, ed. Simon Cottle, 33–49. Buckingham, UK: Open University Press.

Ward, W.P. 1990. *White Canada Forever: Popular Attitudes and Public Policy toward Orientals* in *BC*. Montreal and Kingston: McGill-Queen's University Press.

Wortley, S. 2008. "Misrepresentation or Reality? The Depiction of Race and Crime in the Toronto Print Media." In *Marginality and Condemnation: An Introduction to Criminology*, ed. B. Schissel and C. Brooks, 104–34. Halifax: Fernwood.

Zikic, J. 2009. "Breaking Down Barriers for Immigrant Professionals." *YFile: York's Daily Bulletin*. Online newsletter. 15 May.

CHAPTER 10

OKANAGAN IN PRINT

Exalting Typographical Heimlich *Fantasies of Entrepreneurial Whiteness*

Daniel J. Keyes

A 1907 pamphlet, created by the Okanagan Trust Company to lure settlers from Great Britain and eastern Canada to the Okanagan, claims that fruit is the type of produce grown by a certain class of gentleman orchardist, so one need not fear being "surrounded with garlic eating, foreign speaking neighbours, with whom you could have nothing in common socially" (Naramata Possibilities 1907 [1982], 8). Today this type of whitening media representation of the Okanagan subtly persists in untroubled promotional varieties of newspaper, glossy magazines, and websites. Indeed, an echo of this type of appeal to sophisticated tastes occurs in an advertising supplement in the *Globe and Mail*, which heralds the region as "an epicurean's nirvana" whose history begins with European settlement ("Kelowna," 24 March 2007, TK1). In this glossy promotional, the Okanagan's colonial past is constituted as a comfortable place for entrepreneurial-savvy white settlers and their descendants, whose hard work, guile, and inventiveness has resulted in the present moment, which embraces European modernity. The only reference to Indigenous culture in this tourism supplement is to the Turtle Island Gallery, "a purveyor of authentic Aboriginal Art and Wares" (ibid.). Heritage is constituted in this supplement as being available at the Laurel Packing House, where "you can learn about our wines and our heritage as a fruit-growing region" from citizens who are characterized as ranging from "trendy youths to hip boomers" (ibid.). Septuagenarian garlic eaters need not apply. That a tourist supplement for the *Globe and Mail* uses this sunny rhetoric is unsurprising, given that its sole purpose is to lure readers to the Okanagan. Perhaps what is surprising is that this sunny rhetoric is pervasive in the Okanagan's local print media.

This chapter analyzes a select corpus of print media from the contemporary Okanagan. It is informed by critical discourse analysis, which "studies the way social power abuse, dominance, and inequality are enacted, reproduced, and resisted by text" (Lorenzo-Dus and Garcés-Coneejo Blitvich 2013, 25). Drawing on the work of Thobani (2007) that sees Canadian white settler sovereignty as an exalted and dominant form, this chapter examines the persistence of exalted entrepreneurial white privilege in Okanagan journalism as reflected in traditional newsprint, glossy magazines, and internet representations of the region. It examines how the structure of ownership and distribution generate print content that reproduces a business-friendly press that tacitly champions white privilege and seldom faces the Okanagan's colonial past and neocolonial present. The adjective "neocolonial" resonates with neoliberal structures of governance, which are keen to disavow outstanding land claims, environmental, and social issues while championing the supposed level playing field of free market capitalism. See Hall, Massey, and Rustin's (2013) "After Neoliberalism: Analysing the Present" for a global overview of contemporary analyses of and resistance to neoliberalism. For a focus on neocolonialism in a Canadian context, see Razack (2013, 355), who contends "the state and corporations are enmeshed in ongoing battles over land and resources" that is structured by "settler colonialism, rather than the class system per se." Razack argues that the "violence of an ongoing colonialism" persists in the Canadian context (2013, 353).

Neocolonialism tends to relegate issues like the legacies of residential schooling and the general lack of treaties throughout British Columbia to a distant past rather than seeing them as urgently in need of contemporary redress. In the Okanagan, neocolonialism is embodied by an active denial of the violence of a persistent colonialism in favour of embracing the past in a celebration of pioneer pastoral heritage and an exalted entrepreneurial, implicitly Anglo white, present. Thus, small "c" capitalism as practised by an entrepreneurial class is the glue that holds community together and actively ignores and effaces Others who do not abide by its implicit rules. Under neoliberalism in the Okanagan, locally produced print journalism rarely deviates from presenting for its readers a white fantasy of *heimlich* belonging. Collectively, media help to shape and exalt a *heimlich* fantasy space for the Okanagan as a type of robust white man's middle-class Shangri-La. The use of *heimlich* here acknowledges postcolonial theorist Homi K. Bhabha's work on Freud's theorization of the distinction between the *unheimlich* and *heimlich* (Freud 1919 [1981]) as a way for the colonial self to securely relegate alterity to the uncanny, unsettling, and *unheimlich* (Bhabha 1994, 9). Bhabha's theories of the "homely" have been articulated throughout postcolonial studies. The anthropologist Ghassan Hage (2000, 37–46) describes how white Australians operate as "managers" of a homely, or *heimlich*, fantasy of nationalist practices that seeks to enforce and prescribe a proper sense of the homely national space. For Hage's nationalist manager of the white fantasy, the *unheimlich* appears as threats to this fantasy whether these threats are Indigenous people or more recent immigrants who refuse to play by the rules of the white fantasy. A similar fantasy of homely space operates in Okanagan print journalism to enforce a type of fit, white body that belongs in the natural beauty of the Okanagan. The persistent *heimlich* fantasy of Okanagan media operates for white readers via an unconscious and deeply familiar appeal to affect. In the Canadian context, and from a literary model, Sugar and Turcotte (2009, x–xii) assert that the sense of the settler as belonging to the land is perpetually vexed by gothic figures that haunt the homely fantasy of belonging in a land that is not quite terra nullius. They argue that the *heimlich* co-exists in an uneasy relationship with its *unheimlich* other. This chapter reads the invariably *heimlich* fantasies of contemporary print journalism in the Okanagan as a discourse invested in sustaining a particular white neoliberal version of that region. *Unheimlich* realities within the Okanagan that might speak to First Nations land claims or a lack of diversity tend to not fit within the dominant settler discourse that persists in contemporary local print and internet media.

This chapter excludes from its analysis discussion of television, radio, film, and national forms of print that, in relation to local media, exert complementary but different influences. No doubt these forms of media play a powerful role in hailing viewers and readers with a white form of affiliation that heeds the east-west pull of Canadian nationalism and the north-south pull of the American media. British sociologist John Gabriel

(1998, 97) asserts that "the ideology of 'white interests' has been built around and harnessed to ideas of economic security, prosperity, ontological security, and a sense of local and/or national belonging." Textual examples of how local media's *heimlich* imaginings of the Okanagan spill into national and international venues are offered by Wagner (2008), who documents how the Okanagan catchphrase, "the Napa of the North," "is particularly common in local BC media but also appears in national Canadian print media such as the *Globe and Mail* (2007) and in international media, including the *New York Times* (Tsui 2006)" (Wagner 2008, 33). By focusing on local print media, this chapter aims to document and analyze particular versions of white affiliation that complement these national and international imaginings of the region.

NEOLIBERALISM AND MEDIA CONCENTRATION IN CANADIAN NEWSPRINT

In the past thirty years, studies of Canadian print media have focused on the effects of the intensive conglomeration of daily newspapers in large urban centres and chains that own dailies in smaller urban areas, with little attention paid to the phenomenon of free community newspapers (Winter 1997; Hackett, Gruneau, and Gutstein 2000; Pitts 2002; Hackett and Uzelman 2003; Soderland et al. 2012). These studies challenge "the 'libertarian theory' of the press – that good decisions tend to emerge from stations where there is an abundance of competing information" (Soderland et al. 2012, 2); they argue that print media, when owned by a small group of investors, tend to reproduce a discursive frame that excludes challenges to neoliberal hegemony: "Canada's capitalist class had generally rallied ideologically around the neoliberal policies of trade liberalization, privatization, deregulation, public debt reduction, and social spending cutbacks since the 1980s" (Hackett and Uzelman 2003, 332). Soderland et al. document how increasingly concentrated ownership contributes to a narrow perspective offered (2012, 3) by mainstream print, which, via "agenda setting" and editorial "gate keeping," drive what counts as newsworthy.

Arguably the types of community papers in the Okanagan that arrive free to every homeowner's door stuffed with fliers have little resemblance to the types of big urban newspapers that Soderland et al. (2012) study.

Yet these papers are owned by large multinationals invested in a business model that cannot help but replicate a type of localized *heimlich*, exalted, neoliberal imaginary. Sawisky (2010, 32), expounding on the importance of "community newspapers" for small cities, idealistically asserts: "community newspapers are a vital form of media in a small town. The presence of a newspaper is a key component of maintaining quality of life in an isolated city, town, or village by promoting and increasing civic engagement in the community in addition to presenting readers with information on decisions affecting their community." The ethos for community papers he describes is admirable, but Sawisky ignores the evidence that many community papers and newsgathering websites in North America follow a neoliberal model that, while representing local events, relies on revenue not from dedicated readers buying subscriptions but from small and large businesses buying advertising. Thus community papers might appear to serve citizens, but their business model is one that serves advertisers first and treats citizens as customers. Bob Franklin (2005, 137–48) argues that, in England, conglomeration has gutted the democratic content of the small local free press with a managerial style akin to the McDonald's fast food model, which sees the diminishing of the public sphere in the service of faster, cheaper, and less thoughtful journalism that serves the advertiser first while deskilling journalists. Ward (2008) describes the free community paper model run by Black Press "as a sort of news/ink version of a Jehovah's Witness missionary" that arrives unwanted at homeowners' doors with the promise to advertisers that 80 to 90 percent of the target audience will read it. Newspapers in the Okanagan are produced on a lean journalistic standard that is becoming increasingly the norm for smaller communities as they struggle to compete with business models for news and information websites that rely on unpaid "citizen" journalists. The mandate for these community papers is to cover local events and to focus on where provincial or federal matters impinge on the local to provide a local perspective. Thus, Okanagan papers tend to offer "reports" from regional members of the provincial legislature and federal Parliament rather than offering analyses of policies or reports. Press releases from business, government, and community organizations provide much of the content. This approach to journalism does not risk proverbially biting the hand that feeds it – that hand being local businesses and political interests that provide advertising revenue – and thus it maintains an exalted hegemonic neoliberal whiteness as a value that is comfortable everywhere and largely unquestioned.

NEWSPRINT OWNERSHIP IN THE OKANAGAN

Alternative print media in British Columbia's interior is virtually non-existent. British Columbia's alternative print and online media is concentrated in the Lower Mainland. See the *Columbia Journal* (2015) and the online journal the *Tyee* (2018). The *Columbia Journal* published its last issue in September 2015. The interior of British Columbia rarely supports such initiatives, although arguably the e-newsletter *Fresh Sheet* and its spinoff, the irregularly printed *Next Okanagan*, aim to provide a voice for more progressive politics in the region. See the January 2012 edition of *Fresh Sheet* to see a range of social justice issues engaged in a pithy form that resists advertiser support. This journal published its last edition in April 2015, while *Next Okanagan* appears to only have one issue online. In May 2020, IndigiNews launch both an Okanagan and Vancouver Island online news website with three Indigenous Okanagan–based reporters and the support of APTN as a spin off from a Vancouver-based, community-based journalism initiative called *The Discourse* that suggests alternatives are possible using a social media donor driven business model (IndigiNews 2020; Miller 2021).

The Okanagan's dominant print media, like much of the province of British Columbia's print media, is published by two media conglomerates that tend to shape a neoliberal discourse whereas investigative journalism is muted. A portion of the remnants of former media baron and convicted white-collar criminal Conrad Black's empire is held by Horizon publications based in Illinois, which owns the *Penticton Herald* and the *Kelowna Daily Courier* with David Radler, former Conrad Black associate, as its CEO (*Fishwrap* 2018). Horizon has newspapers in small towns and cities across Canada and the United States, where they operate "the primary information sources for news and advertising in the communities that they serve" ("About Us" 2016a). The other print media conglomerate in the Okanagan is Black Press, owned by David Black. Black owns over forty local papers in BC's interior that tend to offer free bi- or tri-weekly editions (Black Press 2012). Hackett, Gruneau, and Gutstein (2000, 26) offer David Black as an example of the creeping direct corporate influence on editorial content: "in the fall of 1998 … David Black, the publisher of dozens of BC community newspapers, ordered his editors not to run any commentary supporting the land claim deal negotiated between BC's NDP government and the Nisga'a people." This one instance of influence suggests that Black Press has an investment in a neocolonial position that resists the treaty process as "bad for business"; however, in a 2008 interview, Black indicated he rarely, if ever, controls the message of his community newspapers (Ward 2008). He claims his focus is not on content but on sustaining a lucrative and lean business model. Thus, taking such an explicit neocolonial editorial stand is almost beside the point since the objective of a community paper is to serve readers' eyeballs to advertisers who invariably sustain a discourse of exalted *heimlich* belonging.

If the business model for Radler's Horizon's papers appears lean, Black's model is anorexic. Beers (2010) details how Black Press, as it has outgrown its BC roots, has moved into small American cities where it has bought numerous local papers, lightened coverage, and fired journalists. In 2013, Black Press's holdings in the Okanagan included the *Vernon Morning Star*, the *Salmon Arm Observer*, the *Peachland View*, the *Kelowna Capital News*, the *Winfield Lake Country Calendar*, the *Summerland Review*, the *Penticton News*, the *Penticton Western Star*, the *Oliver Chronicle*, and the *Osoyoos Times* ("Get Connected" 2013, 7). In 2021, four of these ten Okanagan papers no longer circulated: the *Penticton Western Star* and *Penticton News* amalgamated into the *Penticton Western News* while *The Peachland View*, *Oliver Chronicle*, and *Osoyoos Times* are no longer listed by Black Press (Publications 2021). All these papers focus on local news, with some news items taken from around the province via Black's chain, but the striking element about a paper like the *Kelowna Capital News* is how it blurs the line between information and advertisement. Since it is "free" to the public, its business model demands that revenues be driven by advertisements. The staffing levels at this paper suggest that selling advertising takes priority over investigative reporting, with the paper listing four columnist/reporters, two editors, and seven advertising consultants on its staff ("About Us" 2016b).

CONTENT IN THE OKANAGAN: OPEN FOR BUSINESS!!!

Much of the *Kelowna Capital News*'s content is written by columnists who provide free content that advertises their entrepreneurial enterprises. These columnists are usually small businesspeople, like alternative health care practitioners, who dispense free advice while advertising their business. This form of laissez-faire content management often makes for lively debates in the letters-to-the-editor sections as readers more accustomed to the Western biomedical model paid for by public health care take exception to the alternative medical advice offered by columnists. It is noteworthy that none of the columnists for the newspaper seem engaged in social justice or issues of race and so on. It is not just the unpaid contributors to the *Kelowna Capital News* who tend to embrace this sunny perspective. UBC Okanagan sociologists Tomic and Trumper (2012, 236) document how the paper's reporter, Julie Steeves, who also contributes to the trade magazine *BC Fruit Grower*, skewed reports on a preliminary study of the working conditions of Mexican farm labours towards the interests of *BC Fruit Grower* while not admitting her conflict of interest. The *Kelowna Capital News* is invested in promoting the entrepreneurial ethos that underpins local variations of dominant consumer society while paying heed to elite interests.

A prime example of this hegemonic ethos is offered in Joel Young's *Kelowna Courier* column on entrepreneurism. This piece articulates the neoliberal fantasy whereby empowered individuals, regardless of structural inequities, are able to pull themselves up by their own bootstraps. His columns tend to blur the lines between business reporting and self-help as he extols the virtues of transformative entrepreneurship while celebrating and promoting the efforts of local entrepreneurs. Young offers a sense of New Age capitalism whereby individuals create fortunes without exploiting labour or degrading the environment: "Entrepreneurship is the greatest vehicle we know to allow us to simultaneously envision, dream, analyze, create and profit" (Young 2010b). In his fantasy, entrepreneurs transform the world for the better and everyone is capable of succeeding if they can just become entrepreneurs, the new individualism of neoliberalism. For Young, all forms of state intervention have given way to caring capitalists who are able to make progressive changes by sheer force of will via social entrepreneurial activities that cure society's ills while making a profit. In an article targeting the disabled as an untapped resource for entrepreneurs, he expounds: "Just as economic entrepreneurs create and can transform whole industries, social entrepreneurs act as the 'change agents' for society, seizing opportunities others miss in order to improve the social order and its systems or lack thereof, invent and disseminate new approaches and advance sustainable solutions that give rise to creating a genuine social value in our lives" (ibid.). For Young, capitalism generates no problems or inequity; it can only provide creative solutions that governments, unions, and not-for-profits cannot. For him, regardless of race, gender, or ability, people must help themselves. He asserts the disabled are a "drain on the economy"; only entrepreneurship can "harness their abilities and channel them into avenues of prosperity" (ibid.). This utilitarian logic, which sees the disabled as raw material, is veiled in a discourse of benevolence. It ignores the range of socioeconomic and cultural barriers faced by the differently abled but assumes that they have the means and desire to embrace their inner entrepreneur.

In a similar manner, in an article focused on a future in which he champions immigrants and women who challenge the status quo profile of white male entrepreneurs, Young refuses to name "whiteness" as a problem. He writes of immigrants: "Although they bring education, professional experience and a developed network to their adopted Canadian landscape, often their professional assets do not always translate into value across cultural boundaries. However, immigrant entrepreneurs frequently have contacts in their native countries as well as Canada. This provides them with the opportunity to create entrepreneurial ventures that link markets" (Young 2012). Euphemisms like "adopted Canadian landscape" and "cultural boundaries" refuse to name white privilege, thus it is not the structure of Anglo-white society that impedes immigrants. This type of characterization is not unique to the Okanagan. Abu-Laban and Gabriel (2002, 29), in *Selling Diversity*, discuss how Canada in the 2000s tends to promote multiculturalism as an empty value detached from "substantive equality." See Tannock (2011) for a critique of Canada's immigration system that awards points for higher-educated immigrants. In Young's fantasy, "the Canadian landscape" that immigrants have "chosen" impedes them. In this benevolent fantasy, immigrants – like women, the disabled, and Others – bring a value added to the white-Anglo world. In another of his columns, relating to immigrant experiences, Young (2010a) introduces the case of "a gentleman in the UK" who is an information technology specialist "born of Indian parents in Fiji" looking to create a business in the Okanagan with his savings and family. After experiencing health setbacks, this highly qualified immigrant runs a successful Indian food restaurant. This story appears to say that the Okanagan is colour blind and that this family succeeded with the help of Young and supportive federal politicians. However, when read against another one of Young's (2010c) columns, in which he celebrates the success of Jason Richard (whom I assume is white), who comes from Victoria to the Okanagan after having worked for eight years in the American high-tech industry and is able to pursue and achieve his high-tech Okanagan dream rather than opening a successful "ethnic" restaurant, there is a nagging sense that the terms under which success occurs in the Okanagan are limited by notions of what types of businesses are "appropriate." Young's entrepreneurial fantasy is one in which all hardworking individuals succeed, yet the terms of success may be bounded by cultural stereotypes and white privilege. Young's column may not be representative of all editorial content in all Okanagan newspapers, but its entrepreneurial perspectives is paradigmatic as readers are hailed as entrepreneurs or nascent entrepreneurs.

GLOSSY WHITENESS

Glossy Okanagan magazines, like their newspaper counterparts, tend to be light on editorial content and are conspicuously structured by advertorial content that offers product placement for local entrepreneurs. Davis (2007, 357) explains how in the American context white privilege and the dominant neoliberal discourse "mute" resistance: "in this neoliberal moment, race-blindness prevails. White privilege shifts the ravages of racism to a market base and then explains inequality as the outcome of non-racial dynamics." These three glossy Okanagan magazines *Icon*, *Okanagan Life*, and *Okanagan Sun* work within this model, which constrains the limits of expression such that exalted forms of privileged whiteness can be celebrated while the "noise" of resistance to white progress is muted. *Icon*, which since 2011 offers four issues per year and is distributed to *Kelowna Daily Courier* subscribers and through a range of other outlets, provides the most unselfconscious exalted version of this celebration of hedonistic whiteness. *Icon* is a glossy magazine that has the feel of American men's magazines like *Maxim*. It is dedicated to the upwardly mobile consumers who engage in expensive leisure activities. Its website boasts: "at *Icon* Okanagan Magazine our mission is simple: [t]o get your ad in front of as many interested, qualified readers as possible" (*Advertise* 2012). *Icon* will not waste advertisers' dollars by putting ads in front of the unqualified and disinterested reader. More recently, *Icon*'s mandate has been revised "to produce a local publication with an international feel that appeals to a cosmopolitan audience. It is the ideal marketing tool for those wishing to access this lucrative market" (Advertise with Icon 2016). With *Icon* terms like "international" and "cosmopolitan" operate within a specifically Western framework that never leaves the mall. Whiteness is not constituted as an identifiable quality for *Icon*'s target readers, but certainly the magazine assumes its ideal reader has a propensity for conspicuous macho consumption. The Winter 2012 issue of *Icon* features "articles" on BMW's new SUVs, snowmobiling in the ultimate playground, a local celebrity chef, remote controls, a Tuscan villa mansion in the Okanagan, and a lingerie spread for the local fashion store.

Non-advertorial content is slight in this magazine. *Icon* supports the white fantasy of belonging and leisure that is the contemporary Okanagan as a mall wherein various entrepreneurs' businesses and personalities are swathed in glossy advertorial content. An example of this type of interwoven marketing is offered on page 45 in the Winter 2012 issue marked "advertisement" with the title "Are You Up for a Challenge," which features a health-nutrition scheme with Kimberley Stefanski promoting a product called the "Body by Vi Challenge," whereby in ninety days readers can transform their bodies into lean machines and, if they introduce friends to the challenge, they can enter their name in a lottery to win a BMW ("Are You Up for a Challenge" 2012, 45). Immediately following this is a two-page spread by a local lingerie store featuring slender young white female bodies in lingerie ("Hearts Aflame" 2012, 46–47), which suggests that female readers of *Icon* should be emulating these presentational soft core bodies by flipping back a page and taking the "Body by Vi Challenge" to "looser [sic] weight or just tone up for summer" (45). A few pages later, there is a "content" article titled "The Ultimate Health and Fitness 101" ("The Ultimate" 2012, 64–65), in which personal trainer and nutritional coach Stacey Lynn Zeman promises to whip readers into shape. This article features a picture of a young woman holding a hockey stick, wearing hockey gloves, a cropped "hockey" top, and short black shirt. The discourse of *Icon* ensures that white bodies are always striving to consume more within a muscular and masculine puritanical form in which the various contradictions of consumer society are glossed over.

Coleman's (2006) study of literary Canada from 1850 to 1950 theorizes whiteness in Anglo-Canadian literature as being formed around four allegorical figures, with one being the muscular Christian. I suspect *Icon* offers readers a more secular version of this super fit figure that reflects the notion of the Okanagan as "a year-round playground" for the super fit (Map of the Thompson Okanagan 2013). Beyond its service to local businesses, the look and content of this magazine makes it such that, with a few bits of local detail added, it could be transplanted into any wealthy predominantly white suburban North American community. *Icon* partakes of a sense that the Okanagan is a type of leisure mall wherein the best possibilities for young tanned well-muscled and coiffured consumers are presented.

Okanagan Life is a more community-minded magazine than *Icon*. Like *Icon* much of its content is advertorial in nature, with various merchants and local manufacturers spotlighted in its glossy pages in feature stories adjacent to their ads, and thus it assumes its readers are well-heeled white people. As with the community newspapers, there is a tension between serving the advertisers and serving the notional readers; thus, content reflects the white Okanagan back to itself by featuring stories on local history, events, and people. In some cases, content unrelated to advertising reflects multiculturalism and local First Nations with a view that tends not to question white Anglo privilege. *Okanagan Life Magazine* hints at the less sunny side of the Okanagan in Wilson's (2007) "Farming It Out," which explores the exploitation of migrant Mexican farm labourers, but for the majority of its reporting it sustains the fantasy of the Okanagan as a white playground.

The 2010 November-December issue titled "Best of the Okanagan" offers an example of how multiculturalism "fits" into the *Okanagan Life*'s discursive framework. This edition contains a variety of articles targeting the better life of white consumptions, with an article rating the best tourist attractions, local happenings, and businesses in the Okanagan (Best of the Okanagan 2010, 22–44); another article on local wines titled "Aging Is a Good Thing" (Botner 2010, 55–56); and a lavish pictorial on a four-thousand-square-foot home on a golf course (Carter 2010, 51–53). This edition features two "multicultural" articles. The first of these details the federal government's detention, under the War Measures Act, of Germans, Ukrainians, and other suspicious non-anglophones at the Vernon Internment Work Camp and other local work camps between 1914 and 1920. It documents a grim history of racism, exploitation, and deaths in these work camps and concludes with the following lament: "resentment has continued over the generations, but a call for atonement will never be heard. There is not a single notation in any historical publication in the interior of this shameful event" (Wilson 2010, 19). This *unheimlich* reporting of this local atrocity runs counter to another article, drawing from Koroscil's (2003) *Garden of Eden*, which exalts the current and historical roots of Anglo settlement. Rather than focusing on Koroscil's account of the robber baron mentality of land grabbing or linking to the previous article's discussion of the internment of Germans and Slavic-speakers during the First World War, this article offers an alibi for magazine readers: "many of the Valley's earliest settlers were of British stock and they established a thriving agricultural economy as well as community institutions that continue to this day" (Priegert 2010, 22). The article's *heimlich* linkage of contemporary British legacy to British settlement consists of naming businesses that cater to British customers and offering a list of British words that some Canadians might not recognize (23). Thus, it practises a type of white disaffiliation from atrocities committed during the colonization of the Okanagan. It celebrates a vertical multicultural "mosaic" where, implicitly, the Anglo identity is on top. With the sunny discourse of *Okanagan Life*, the persistence of the Anglo legacy in the valley is not a problem but simply another customer "choice" for those hankering for tea and crumpets and having an aversion to garlic. History is invoked to argue that the present is free of such things as racism and white privilege. Matt James (2009, 363), associate professor of political science at the University of Victoria, argues that, although "racist injustices have played a central role in shaping British Columbia," the province tends to embrace an "amnesiac culture of memory" that he characterizes as "reparation displacement," whereby the federal government, and not the province, is responsible for redress. These articles, which attempt to celebrate multiculturalism and even lightly mourn "historical" racism, participate in this form of reparation displacement.

Slivar's (2011) "Call of the Drumbeat," published as the cover story for the 2011 April edition of *Okanagan Life*, offers a white fantasy based on Indigenous spectacles as it offers a colourful pictorial on how Okanagan First Nations adopted the powwow. The article carefully explains how the powwow and dancing, in particular, has strengthened local Indigenous culture, but it also ties in these celebrations with an advertisement for the Turtle Island Gallery (the gallery closed 21 November 2015), which sells Indigenous art (23). The article does not discuss why the powwow has become important for local First Nations since that might entail mentioning the impact of the residential school system on Syilx culture. Its conclusion targets an implied white reader, who knows little of Indigenous culture yet can witness Indigenous performances: "For a lively immersion into First Nations culture, be sure to take in a powwow this summer" (Slivar 2011, 26). Thus, like multiculturalism, Indigenous culture in the pages of *Okanagan Life* operates as a non-threatening *heimlich* other that offers opportunities to consume without disturbing the white fantasy of belonging.

The closest *Okanagan Life* gets to questioning white privilege or signalling the Okanagan colonial past is a 2012 special issue, fittingly titled "Progress," which offers a post-Occupy Wall Street editorial by the magazine's publisher Paul Byrne that carefully negotiates resistance to capitalism in a way that does not attack the entrepreneurial spirit that defines the Okanagan fantasy:

> I don't dislike billionaires. I do dislike the way their brains work – or don't work if you like. And I don't like the way extreme inequality is threatening our quality of life and democracy. I do, however, really like millionaires. Millionaires are great for the economy, specifically because they do not stockpile their cash like billionaires do. They spend it and they expect to pay more taxes – because they make more. (Byrne 2012, 8)

In the 2011 edition of the magazine, titled "Best of the Okanagan," Byrne exhorts readers to embrace the millionaires of the Okanagan: "Patronize them! These entrepreneurs are our true heroes. Let's all shop [sic] the little guys ... and see if the billionaires even notice" (Byrne 2011, 9). As in Young's columns in the *Capital News*, local nimble entrepreneurial capitalism is offered as the solution to addressing society's structural inequities. The January–February 2012 Hockey Town issue, which focuses on hockey and curling as natural and historical "Okanagan" sports, ends with Gordon Hawkes's "Greed Redefined: An Occupy Movement Reality Check," in which he argues that the Occupy Wall Street movement, rather than being part of the 99 percent dispossessed, actually forms part of the First World's privileged set: "We need to stop taking the Occupy Wall Street Movement and its hypocritical brand of Marxism seriously. Instead, we need to wake up to our responsibility as the top 20 per cent to seek justice for the real poor in this world (Hint: it's not us)" (Hawkes 2012, 46). These two editorials are not tied to advertising. Hawkes clearly pokes at the journal's privilege as bound by developed First World thinking, yet the magazine's discursive limitation is bound by its mandate to sell the Okanagan "lifestyle," which entails golf courses, four-thousand-square-foot homes, thirty-dollar bottles of wine, and so on. The fantasy the magazine sustains does not jibe with the economic data uncovered by Walks (2013, 166), who indicates that in 2009 Kelowna's household debt, as a percentage of pre-tax income, is the highest in the country next to Vancouver's. Thus Hawkes's call to action to eschew Marxism and embrace a compassionate justice for those who do not belong to the developed world is fraught, especially when it is followed by an advertisement for a golf course and condo development asking readers to "Live the Good Life" (2012, 47) as offered by the Treegroup in its historic partnership with Westbank First Nations. This condo development may be a historic partnership, but the shape of the project is heavily weighted towards catering to golf, which tends to be the sport of upwardly mobile white people (Billings 2003, 30) unconcerned with addressing global inequities. *Okanagan Life*'s *heimlich* and exalted fantasy of white belonging thus glosses over the material contradictions of white entrepreneurial privilege despite its benevolent nods to multiculturalism, Indigenous people, and capitalism as practised by millionaires. Compared to *Icon*, one could argue that at least *Okanagan Life* gestures towards inclusion of alterity and attempts to trouble some elements of white entrepreneurial privilege, but my sense is that the magazine practises a strategy of containment that aims to avoid unsettling its audience members, who are assumed to be invested in white privilege.

Bernie Bates, the only self-identified Indigenous columnist in any Okanagan magazine, writes in the South Okanagan monthly *Okanagan Sun*, which tends to resemble Sawisky's ideal of community journalism by offering local features, stories, and less advertorial content than either *Icon* or *Okanagan Life*. Unlike *Icon*'s blunt claim to deliver consumers' eyeballs to advertisers, the *Okanagan Sun* favours readers over advertisers with its Oprahesque mandate to "celebrate human successes and focus on what is positive and unique about life in the South Okanagan" (*Okanagan Sun* 2012). This mandate precludes investigative journalism in favour of "feel-good" journalism and arguably limits Bates's expression of Indigenous culture to suit a "positive" white fantasy (See https://issuu.com/okanagan-sun for the archive of back issues). Bates last contributed to the magazine in June 2012. Since 2014, he has contributed to the humour section of the *First Nations Drum*, which bills itself as Canada's largest First Nations newspaper (Bates 2018). Bates (2011e, 17) supplements his columns with his own cartoons, which drive home the point of his humour. He writes in a populist manner, with his subject matter often being unrelated to his self-declared "Native heritage," and thus he more broadly addresses a white readership, who might laugh with him at his wife's excessive shopping habits in "Shopping Should Be Outlawed" (Bates 2011c, 17) or his modest proposal to create female-only roads in "And the Wheels Go Round" (Bates 2011b, 18). He uses references to Indigenous heritage with little overt political content, such as in "Thoughts on Groundhog Day," in which he plays with stereotypes: "You see we Natives, come from a long line of long winded ... I mean to say 'ancestral translators of factual information.' In other words[,] a Native Elder is like an elephant, they never forget" (Bates 2012a, 13). This populist move means that, in some articles, he downplays his Indigenous heritage; for example, in an article on the province of British Columbia's negotiations with the federal government to renew its contract for the supply of police services with the RCMP, he does not reference a critical Indigenous perspective on the RCMP (for such a perspective, see Ball 2011; Environics 2010; Mackey 2005; Razack 2002, 2011, 2012, 2013) but adheres to this populist argument: "This is the part that burns my buns. We often hear on the news that the suspect is 'known to the police': Which means they are repeat offenders. So instead of standing on the side of the road with a radar gun … would they [police resources] be better spent keeping surveillance on these career criminals?" (Bates 2011f, 17). A critical Indigenous and *unheimlich* perspective on the RCMP might speak to the police force's shortcomings with regard to investigating Indigenous missing and murdered women (Jiwani and Young 2006) and/or its reluctance to adopt civilian oversight (Bailey and Hunter 2011).

Bates's more politically inflected articles that deal with Indigenous issues tend to do so from either a general or a personal level, avoiding local issues. In "There's Good News and Bad News," he poses as a sly folk humorist educating his white audience:

> I think it is only fair that I should let you, the non-native population, know a little about us, the North American Indian, aboriginal, indigenous, First Nations, natives. If you cut us[,] do we not bleed? If you tickle us, do we not tickle? I thought I should use a little humour, because there is no way to express an entire race of people in a few paragraphs. (Bates 2011g, 13)

The reference to Shylock's "if-you-prick-us, do-we-not-bleed" speech from Shakespeare's *The Merchant of Venice* (Act 3, Scene 1) invokes an Anglo-humanist appeal while side stepping the ills of colonization. Humour wherein white readers and Bates chuckle together offers a *heimlich* amelioration of colonization, which is consistent with the *Okanagan Sun*'s feel-good mandate. Another example of his folksy approach to generalized racism occurs in "Fear of the Unknown," in which he cites both the reserve land system and residential schools as ills visited upon Indigenous people without indicating how settlers have historically supported and continue to benefit from these institutions (Bates 2012b, 13). In his account, the resurgence of Indigenous culture had been neither hindered nor helped by white Canadians: it has simply occurred. At the article's conclusion, he points to education in a way that speaks to his white reader, offering a limited call to action: "Only through the understanding of one and another will we come to just decisions. Only through accurate information will the masses realize the Bogeyman doesn't live on the Rez!" (ibid.). He replays a similar argument in "Knock, Knock, Who's There?," in which he simultaneously attacks "politically correct" humour and racial slurs. His educational approach tends to characterize racial slurs as derogatory language used by older, lower-class white people who have been raised on 1950s Hollywood B-Westerns:

> These "white hairs" love to tease me about my heritage. Just let it rain for more than three days in a row and I'll hear, "Stop doing that rain dance, you wagon burner." And I really do enjoy an innocent laugh with my old and wrinkled "white trash'" friends. You see, it's not so much what you say, but rather how you say it. If you look down your nose at me and snipe "hey chief," then you'd better circle your wagons because I don't think that's funny at all. But if you smile while you jest I'll play along with you "paleface." (Bates 2011e, 17)

This gesture towards accepting the "quaint" slurs of white trash and older people allows middle-class readers to disaffiliate from that particular type of "crass" racism, leaving untouched more systemic forms of racism. In "Breakfast with Church Ladies," he takes a more personal and local approach to racism. Specifically, he addresses his acceptance of "scientific atheism" and his rejection of organized religions due to his residential school experience: "Can you imagine being imprisoned, brainwashed, beaten, and threatened with a pitchfork and fire? I'm not talking about a poor criminal being tortured in some third world country; I'm talking about an eleven year old boy – me" (Bates 2011d, 17). Clearly, the joking humour of his other articles, which seek to align the reader with the Indigenous author, is broken here when he makes it clear that it was not a "third world country" but the Canadian government that was responsible for residential schools. Yet this tone is set aside as he admits to being invited to breakfast on Sunday after church by a group of elderly white women who are clearly not identified with the perpetrators of the residential schools because they "didn't preach, teach, or scold me" (ibid.). The "feel-good" ethos of the *Okanagan Sun* maintains a white fantasy of belonging. Its lone Indigenous columnist subverts this *unheimlich* appeal by the cartoon that appears below the "Breakfast with Church Ladies" article. This cartoon parodies Leonardo Da Vinci's *The Last Supper of Christ* by showing an Indigenous man, presumably the author, seated in the middle of a long table with his "apostles," the church ladies, on either side. The sun is directly behind the Indigenous man's head, giving the illusion of his being a classic Christian divinity. Bates comically challenges the exalted Christian bedrock of the Okanagan's fantasy.

Bates's final article for the magazine, "Are You Republican or Democrat?," moves away from his populist tendency to talk about Hollywood stereotypes and delves into the specifics of local First Nations-settler relations (Bates 2012c, 13). In this article, he ostensibly discusses American politics and identifies himself and readers as Canadians: "all we can do is cheer from the sidelines and hope they don't elect another rich, religious right-winger" (12). This nationalist affiliation shifts as the article veers into the local issue of the Westbank First Nation (WFN) reserve's rapid and expansive development. Bates elliptically refers to WFN's pro-business development under its then chief Robert Louie, who, via self-governance, had removed the WFN from the Indian Act to "move at the speed of business" with regard to leasing and developing land to generate wealth for the Westbank ("Westbank First Nation: Community. Pride. Leadership" 2012, 5):

> A lot of Westbank feel they don't have a voice in the community of West Kelowna. Not only is the highway of commerce divided, so too are the people of the west side.
>
> From a Native's point of view[,] I think it's pretty damned funny that it's now the white folks who are circling the Injins. I find it ironic that it's now the Indian who've become rich because of the non-native land owners. It's hilarious to see that it's the Natives who can boost self-government and laugh all the way to the bank. (Bates 2012c, 12)

Bates inverts stereotypes and indicates the hypocrisy of white politicians who are upset over Indigenous developments that threaten the environment. He is elliptically referring to the mayor of West Kelowna, Doug Findlater, who represented environmental interests opposed to the exchange of land between the province of British Columbia and the WFN (see "DWK Happy" 2012 for background information on the breakdown of this land exchange agreement). The article concludes, "personally, if I had a vote, I'd say give everything back to the Natives and start all over again" (Bates 2012c, 13). White readers may dismiss this "punch line" rather than accept it as a challenge to consider the historical roots of colonial settlement and First Nations land dispossession in the region. With Bates, like with Indigenous writers Thomas King (2013) and Drew Hayden Taylor (2005), humour operates to alert both Indigenous readers and non-Indigenous readers to the persistence of neocolonial practice. Bates only signals the privileged white fantasy of the Okanagan as slightly problematic, and he does so in comedic ways that white readers can easily chuckle over and dismiss; nevertheless, his comments challenge the typical viewpoints offered in glossy Okanagan magazines and print.

INTERNET JOURNALISM AND HYPERLOCAL WHITENESS

The next logical step in local media growth in the Okanagan is embodied by *Castanet*, an entirely web-based enterprise with a mission to "be the local online medium covering news, events, business, community, and shopping; including relevant links to the web and to connect local businesses to Kelowna customers so as to increase sales and reduce their advertising expenses" ("About *Castanet*" 2012). If *Castanet* sees local businesses as its main client, it sees its readers as potential "cowboy" contributors whom it "deputizes" to gather news ("News Tips" 2016). This "frontier" approach to lottery-style chequebook journalism pays a "reward of 25 dollars weekly to the top deputy" (ibid.). Thus *Castanet* operates as the mall rather than as a public not-for-profit community forum for the free exchange of ideas, despite empowering the potential of what cultural studies theorist Henry Jenkins refers to as "spreadable media," whereby sites like *Castanet* allow traditional newspaper readers to "think about the citizen as editor, determining which news matters to their community and passing it along in a more targeted way to their friends. We might think about the citizen as commentator" (Usher and Jenkins 2010). While Jenkins sees a democratic experiment taking place, with the Fifth Estate morphed by spreadable media, I assume that the Fifth Estate as composed in small community newspaper markets like the Okanagan will continue to edit and shape a white entrepreneurial world order for its readers and citizen journalists. Chris Kearney, the sales manager of *Castanet*, relates a business model that supports this entrepreneurial model:

> It's become a user-driven medium. A huge number of people provide free content through our columnists and written articles. It's just free content. The same is with pictures or videos. We just credit them to whomever took them. You don't always need a professional photographer to take a great picture. It also just shows we're a community-minded media as well. (Sawisky 2010, 54)

Unfortunately, the community that *Castanet* offers has its own virtual gates: The cover page and page 5 for *Castanet*'s advertising sales prospectus, titled "Embrace the Shift" (Castanet 2012), superimposes an image of a mix of young people of colour and other white people raising their arms onto the Kelowna backdrop, offering a white fantasy of the urban cosmopolitan. Despite this fantasy of *Castanet* delivering a young hip audience to advertisers, the document notes that 63 percent of its demographic resides in the very wide band of ages between 24 and 54, boasting that "Castanet has more +65 [year old] readers than the Internet average" (5). Few of the thirty-two columnists listed for *Castanet* have names that would suggest an origin other than European. Like the columnists for the *Capital News*, *Castanet*'s columnists belong to the entrepreneurial class that uses the column to bolster its professions in terms of money management, real estate, health and fitness, and so on. The public sphere as portrayed by *Castanet*'s columnists tends to reflect the white middle-class fantasy of home, health, security, and beauty.

Print content in the contemporary Okanagan is by no means as explicitly racist as the 1907 *Okanagan Trust Pamphlet* mentioned at the outset of this chapter. Yet, under the current business models for print and internet journalism, in which content is necessarily advertorial, it is hard to imagine the creation of a newspaper, magazine, or website that could challenge hegemonic entrepreneurial whiteness. Indeed *heimlich* neoliberal whiteness is a dominant value: *Icon*'s celebration of the good life of white consumption for fit bodies, Byrne's editorial for *Okanagan Life* celebrating millionaires while excoriating billionaires, and Young's entrepreneurial column in the *Capital News* all aim at sustaining an exalted *heimlich* space for white middle-class entrepreneurs. Despite an apparent "longing for diversity" that is evident in Young's entrepreneurial columns, attempts to redress ongoing and historical trauma by Wilson and Bates, and *Castanet*'s imagining of its young hip target audience, Okanagan journalism mutes challenges to white hegemony and free enterprise. The promise of spreadable media that would diversify or even challenge the Okanagan's white fantasy is one that, in practice, has not occurred under the neoliberal management of the free press – a management style that stifles investigative journalism and silences critical voices that might question entrenched interests. Perhaps IndigiNews may help nudge the region toward decolonization or at least provide alternative voices to the white mediated fantasy.

REFERENCES

"About *Castanet*." 2012. *Castanet.net*.

"About Us." 2016a. Horizon Publications. Accessed July 10, 2016. http://horizonpublicationsinc.com/about_us/aboutus.txt.

–. 2016b. *Kelowna Capital News*. Accessed July 10, 2016. http://www.kelownacapnews.com/about_us/.

Abu-Laban, Yasmeen, Christina Gabriel. 2002. *Selling Diversity: Immigration, Multiculturalism, Employment Equity, and Globalization*. Peterborough, ON: Broadview Press.

"Advertise with Icon." 2016. *Okanagan Life*. Accessed July 2016. http://www.icon-okanagan.com/advertise/.

"Are You Up for the Challenge?" 2012. *Icon*, Winter, 45. Accessed July 10, 2016. https://issuu.com/icon-okanagan/docs/icon.

Bailey, Ian, and Justine Hunter. 2011. "Province Announces Civilian Office to Probe Police." *Globe and Mail*, 18 May. S.2.

Ball, D.P. 2011. "Conference Confronts Police 'Culture of Oppression.'" *Windspeaker* 29 (6). http://www.ammsa.com/publications/windspeaker/conference-confronts-police-%E2%80%98culture-oppression%E2%80%99.

Bates, B.H. 2011a. "There's Good News and Bad News." *Okanagan Sun*, 13 May. https://issuu.com/okanagansun/docs/oksun_may_2011v5.

–. 2011b. "And the Wheels Go 'Round.'" *Okanagan Sun*, 18 June. https://issuu.com/okanagansun/docs/ok_sun_june_2012.

–. 2011c. "Shopping Should Be Outlawed." *Okanagan Sun*, 17 July. https://issuu.com/okanagansun/docs/oksun_july_2011.

–. 2011d. "Breakfast with Church Ladies." *Okanagan Sun*, 17 August. https://issuu.com/okanagansun/docs/oksun_august_2011.

–. 2011e. "Knock, Knock, Who's There?" *Okanagan Sun*, 17 September. https://issuu.com/okanagansun/docs/sept2011/17.

–. 2011g. "This Little Piggy Went to Market." *Okanagan Sun*, 17 November. https://issuu.com/okanagansun/docs/oksun_november_2011/17.
–. 2012a. "Thoughts on Groundhog Day." *Okanagan Sun*, 13 February. https://issuu.com/okanagansun/docs/ok_sun_feb_2012.
–. 2012b. "Fear of the Unknown." *Okanagan Sun*, 13 March. https://issuu.com/okanagansun/docs/ok_sun_-_march_2012.
–. 2012c. "Are You Republican or Democrat?" *Okanagan Sun*, 13 May. https://issuu.com/okanagansun/docs/ok_sun_-_may_2012.
–. 2018. "Humour." *First Nations Drum*. http://www.firstnationsdrum.com/humour/.
Beers, David. 2010. "Canwest Bidder David Black Has Record of Buying, Then Slashing." The *Hook: Political News Freshly Caught*, 14 March. http://thetyee.ca/Blogs/TheHook/Media/2010/03/14/DavidBlack/.
Bhabha, Homi. K. 1994. *The Location of Culture*. New York: Routledge.
Billings, Andrew C. 2003. "Portraying Tiger Woods: Characterizations of a 'Black' Athlete in a "White" Sport." *Howard Journal of Communication* 14: 29–37.
Black Press. 2012. http://www.blackpress.ca/division/index.php?divID=3.
Bottner, Michael. 2010. "Aging Is a Good Thing." *Okanagan Life*. November-December. Accessed June 11, 2021. https://issuu.com/okanaganlife/docs/nov-dec_2010.
Brydon, Diana. 1995. "Introduction: Reading Postcoloniality, Reading Canada (Introduction to Issue of *Essays on Canadian Writing* Entitled Testing the Limits: Postcolonial Theories and Canadian Literature)." *Essays on Canadian Writing* 56: 1–19.
Byrne, Paul. 2011. "Paul's Voice: Money Can Be Funny." *Okanagan Life*. November-December 8–9.
–. 2012 "Paul's Words: Spokes of Progress." Progress issue of *Okanagan Life (2012 Edition)* 8–9. Also published as a blog: *Spokes and Wheels of Progress*. http://okanaganlife.com/2012/03/spokes-and-wheels-of-progress/.
Carter, Laurie. 2010. "Fairway Views: Casually Elegant Lifestyle Fits Tower Ranch Home to a Tee." *Okanagan Life*. November/December. Accessed June 11, 2021. https://issuu.com/okanaganlife/docs/nov-dec_2010.
Castanet Media Kit. 2012. "Embrace the Shift." *Castanet*. Accessed July 5, 2013. https://www.castanet.net/advertise/images/2012-MediaKit-Kelowna-1d.pdf.
Coleman, Daniel. 2006. *White Civility: The Literary Project of English Canada*. Toronto: University of Toronto Press.
Columbia Journal. 2015. Accessed July 9, 2016. http://www.columbiajournal.ca/11–05/index.html.
"Columnists." 2012. Castanet.net. http://www.castanet.net/columnists.htm.
Davis, D. 2007. "Narrating the Mute: Racializing and Racism in a Neoliberal Moment." *Souls: A Critical Journal of Black Politics, Culture, and Society* 9 (4): 346–60. http://dx.doi.org/10.1080/10999940701703810.
"DWK Happy, WFN Disappointed with Land Swap Decision." 2012. *Kelowna Capital News*, 14 March. http://www.kelownacapnews.com/news/142589026.html.
Environics. 2010. *Urban Aboriginal Peoples Study: Main Report*. Toronto: Environics Institute.
Fishwrap. 2018. "Every Daily Newspaper in Canada." Fishwrap.ca http://fishwrap.ca/#bc.

Franklin, B. 2005. "McJournalism: The Local Press and the McDonaldization Thesis." *Journalism: Critical Issues*, ed. Stuart Allan. Maidenhead, UK: Open University Press.

Fresh Sheet. 2012. Accessed June 12, 2013. http://www.freshsheet.ca/jan2012.html.

Freud, Sigmund. 1919 [1981]. *The Standard Edition of the Complete Psychological Works of Sigmund Freud*. 21st ed., ed. James Strachey, Alix Strachey, Anna Freud, and Alan Tyson. London: Hogarth Press and the Institute of Psycho-Analysis.

Gabriel, John. 1998. *Whitewash: Racialized Politics and the Media*. London: Routledge.

"Get Connected with Us: 2013 Multimedia Kit." 2013. *Black Press: Community News Media*. Version 5. http://www.blackpress.ca/pdfdownload4nationalsales/2013BlackPressMediaKit.pdf.

Hackett, R.A., R. Gruneau, and D. Gutstein. 2000. *The Missing News: Filters and Blind Spots in Canada's Press*. Toronto: University of Toronto Press.

Hackett, R.A., and S. Uzelman. 2003. "Tracing Corporate Influence on Press Content: A Summary of Recent NewsWatch Canada Research. *Journalism Studies* 4 (2): 331–46.

Hage, Ghassan. 2000. *White Nation: Fantasies of White Supremacy in a Multicultural Society*. New York and London: Routledge.

Hall, Stuart, Doreen Massey, and M. Rustin. 2013. "After Neoliberalism: Analysing the Present." *Soundings* 53: 8–22. Academic Search Complete, EBSCOPetergfshost.

Hawkes, Gordon. 2012. "Greed Redefined: An Occupy Movement Reality Check." *Okanagan Life*, January–February, 46.

"Hearts Aflame: Not Just for Valentine's Day." 2012. *Icon*, Winter, 46–47. https://issuu.com/icon-okanagan/docs/icon.

IndigiNews Team. 2020. "IndigiNews: Where Your Stories Are Heard, Understood and Respected." E-mail. December 21.

James, Matt. 2009. "Scaling Memory: Reparation Displacement and the Case of BC." *Canadian Journal of Political Science / Revue canadienne de science politique* 42 (2): 363–86.

Jiwani, Yasmin, and Mary Lynn Young. 2006. "Missing and Murdered Women: Reproducing Marginality in News Discourse." *Canadian Journal of Communication* 31 (4): 895–918.

King, Thomas. 2013. *The Inconvenient Indian: A Curious Account of Native People in North America*. Toronto: Anchor.

Koroscil, Paul M. 2003. *The British Garden of Eden: Settlement History of the Okanagan Valley, British Columbia*. Burnaby: Simon Fraser University.

"Live the Good Life." 2012. *Okanagan Life*, January–February, 47.

Lorenzo,-Dus, and Pilar GarcEs-Conejos Blitvich. ed. 2013. *Real Talk: Reality Television and Discourse Analysis in Action*. Houndsmills, Basingstoke, Hampshire: Palgrave Macmillan.

Mackey, Eve. 2005. "Universal Rights in Conflict: 'Backlash' and 'Benevolent Resistance' to Indigenous Land Rights." *Anthropology Today* 21 (2): 14–20. http://www.jstor.org.ezproxy.library.ubc.ca/stable/3695191.

Map of Thompson Okanagan. 2013. http://www.gobc.ca/map/thompson-okanagan.

Miller, Erin. 2021. "Support Us." *The Discourse*. Accessed June 11, 2021. https://thediscourse.ca/support-us.

Naramata Possibilities. 1907 [1982]. *Smile of the Manitou*, ed. Don Salting and B. Wilson. 8–15. Penticton: Skookum Publications.

"News Tips." 2016. *Castanet.net*. http://www.castanet.net/contactus/news-tips.php.

Okanagan Life. 2010. "Best of the Okanagan." *Okanagan Life*. November-December. Accessed June 11, 2021. https://issuu.com/okanaganlife/docs/nov-dec_2010.

Publications. 2021. Black Press Community News Media. Accessed June 11, 2021. https://www.blackpress.ca/publications/.

Pitts, Gordon. 2002. *Kings of Convergence: The Fight for the Control of Canada's Media*. Toronto: Doubleday.

Priegert, Portia. 2010. "Mosaic: Joly Olde Ancestors – Early Settlers and Modern Immigrants, British Ties Still Strong in the Valley." *Okanagan Life*. November –December, 22–23.

Razack, Sherene. 2002. "Gendered Racial Violence and Spatialized Justice: The Murder of Pamela George" In *Race, Space, and the Law: Unmapping a White Settler Society, ed.* Sherene Razack, 121–56. *Toronto: Between the Lines.*

–. 2011. "The Space of Difference in Law: Inquests into Aboriginal Deaths in Custody." *Somatechnics* 1 (1): 87–123.

–. 2012. "Memorializing Colonial Power: The Death of Frank Paul." *Law and Social Inquiry*. 37 (4): 908–32.

–. 2013. "Timely Deaths: Medicalizing the Deaths of Aboriginal People in Police Custody." *Law, Culture and the Humanities* 9 (2): 352–74.

Sawisky, G. 2010. "Examining the Community Press in the Present and Future." *Small Cities Imprint* 2 (1): 31–60. http://smallcities.tru.ca/index.php/cura/article/view/13.

Shakespeare, William. 1988. *The Merchant of Venice*. Edited by A.M. Kinghorn. Basingstoke: Macmillan Education.

Slivar, K. 2011. "Call of the Drumbeat." *Okanagan Life*. April, 20–26.

Soderland, W.G., B. Colette, L. Miljan, and K. Hilderandt. 2012. *Cross-Media Ownership and Democratic Practice in Canada: Content Sharing and the Impact of New Media*. Edmonton: University of Alberta Press.

Sugar, Cynthia, and Greg Turcotte, eds. 2009. *Unsettled Remains: Canadian Literature and the Postcolonial Gothic*. Waterloo: Wilfrid Laurier University Press.

Tannock, Stuart. 2011. "Points of Prejudice: Education-Based Discrimination in Canada's Immigration System. *Antipode* 43 (4): 1330–56.

Taylor, Drew Hayden. 2005. *Me Funny*. Toronto: Douglas and McIntyre.

Thobani, Sunera. 2007. *Exalted Subjects: Studies in the Making of Race and Nation in Canada*. Toronto: University of Toronto Press.

Tomic, Patricia, and Ricardo Trumper. 2012. "Methodological Challenges Faced when Researching in Hostile Environments: The SAWP in a Canadian Hinterland." In *Researching amongst Elites: Challenges and Opportunities in Studying Up*, 233–52. Burlington, VT: Ashgate.

Tsui, B. 2006. "The Okanagan, a Napa of the North." *New York Times*, 6 October. http://travel2.nytimes.com/2006/10/06/travel/escapes/06okan.html.

Tyee. 2018. http://thetyee.ca/.

"The Ultimate Health and Fitness 101." 2012. *Icon*, Winter, 64–65. Accessed June 11, 2021. https://issuu.com/icon-okanagan/docs/icon_issue5.

Usher, Nikki, and Henry Jenkins. 2010. "Why Spreadable Doesn't Equal Viral: A Conversation with Henry Jenkins." NiemanLab, 23 November. https://www.niemanlab.org/2010/11/why-spreadable-doesnt-equal-viral-a-conversation-with-henry-jenkins/.

Wagner, J.R. 2008. "Landscape Aesthetics and Settler Colonialism." *Journal of Ecological Anthropology* 12: 22–38. Accessed June 11, 2021 from https://scholarcommons.usf.edu/cgi/viewcontent.cgi?referer=&httpsredir=1&article=1025&context=jea.

Walks, Alan. 2013. "Mapping the Urban Debtscape: The Geography of Household Debt in Canadian Cities." *Urban Geography* 34 (2): 153–87.

Ward, D. 2008. "Betting on David Black." *Seattle Times*, 15 July. Accessed June 2, 2011. http://www.seattleweekly.com/2008-07-16/news/betting-on-black/.

"Westbank First Nation: Community. Pride. Leadership." 2012. *Canadian Journal of Business*. August. Accessed June 2, 2013. https://www.cbj.ca/westbank_first_nation_community_leadership_pride/.

Wilson, B. 2010. "OK Archive: Shocking Secret." *Okanagan Life*. November–December: 16–19.

Wilson, Karin. 2007. "Farming It out." *Okanagan Life Magazine*, September, 40–47.

Winter, J. 1997. *Democracy's Oxygen: How Corporations Control the News*. Montreal: Black Rose.

Young, Joel. 2010a. "Kelowna Family Enterprises Help Build Valley's Economy." *Kelowna Capital News*, 27 April, b4.

–. 2010b. "The Disabled Can Thrive When Given a Taste of Entrepreneurship." *Kelowna Capital News*, 11 May, b4.

–. 2010c. "Entrepreneurial Leadership Normally Ends up Winning the Race." *Kelowna Capital News*, 17 August, b4.

–. 2012. "The Changing Face of the Entrepreneurial World." *Kelowna Capital News*, 5 April, A.1 http://www.bclocalnews.com/okanagan_similkameen/kelownabuzz/business/141797833.html?mobile=true.

CHAPTER 11

EMPLACING AND DISPLACING WHITENESS IN KELOWNA

Aporetic Urbanization and the Limits of Modern Politics

Delacey Tedesco

> *"A creative city is a competitive city in the global marketplace, and a welcoming, attractive home for a diverse population" – Kelowna cultural planning meeting*
>
> (MICHAELS 2010A)

> *"I was down at the beach this summer, and there were so many Chinese people I might as well have been in China, or Vancouver."*
>
> (OVERHEARD AT BUCKERFIELD'S, AN ANIMAL FEED, GARDEN, AND FARM SUPPLY STORE IN CENTRAL KELOWNA, SEPTEMBER 2012)

THE POLITICS OF WHITE URBANIZATION IN KELOWNA

Kelowna, the major population centre within the Okanagan, appears to be rapidly urbanizing (Simmons and McCann 2006, 62). Despite public and municipal debate about what sort of city Kelowna should become, there is a consistent desire to "enhance Kelowna's identity nationally and internationally" (Kelowna 2010, 304–5) by becoming "world-class," including streetscapes (Kelowna 2012, A-1), cultural and educational facilities (RCA n.d.; Squire 2013), and health care services (BC/IHA 2012). And yet, there is an apparent tension between Kelowna's stated desire to attract "newcomers from all over the world" in order to become "the best mid-sized city in North America" (Kelowna 2011b, 3, 19) and the pervasive construction of a colour-blind self-imaginary of whiteness (Bennett 1998; Aguiar, Tomic, and Trumper 2005; Aguiar and Martin 2011). This tension can be understood within the "creative cities" framework (Florida 2005) and the pressures on smaller cities to compete globally (Bell and Jayne 2006) and, thus, within the transformations and discontinuities of neoliberalism (Aguiar, Tomic, and Trumper 2005; Aguiar and Martin 2011).

However, Kelowna also counters a pervasive definition of cities as sites of "proximate diversity" (Jacobs 1992) and urbanization as a process of social and cultural diversification. This raises difficult questions about how definitions of urbanization rely on spatio-temporal and racialized assumptions about rural homogeneity and urban diversity and about how these assumptions constrain and enable Kelowna's ongoing whiteness. Understanding neoliberalism as an intensification of much older liberal modes of governance (Kataoka and Magnusson 2011, 279, 282) raises further questions about how the tension between urbanization and whiteness in Kelowna perpetuates the practices and discourses of "modern" Western politics. "Modern" politics is a contested, contingent, but remarkably persistent complex of ideas, practices, and institutions, centred on claims of sovereign authority. It arose in the West more than five hundred years ago, has undergone permutations that have refined but not challenged its sovereign core, and has been intensively and extensively internalized, universalized, and globalized through a range of techniques, including violence, (self-)discipline, and exclusions/inclusions. The challenge is to untangle this complicated relationship between urbanization and whiteness in Kelowna and to analyze how these productions support and undermine each other and the pervasive foundations of modern liberal politics.

This chapter sees the urbanization of Kelowna as a process of political production (Magnusson 2011, 41) of actual space and imaginaries of place that continually emplaces and displaces whiteness and its others. It focuses on how representations of "Kelowna" are generated from and respond to historically and geographically distantiated processes, and how they emplace and displace white and non-white subjectivities by claiming the authority to construct and segregate difference in time and space. It pays particular attention to the discourses of civilization that were used to justify displacing the Indigenous Syilx (Okanagan) peoples from their lands (Okanagan Nation Alliance 2019a) and to promote genocidal practices such as the removal of Syilx children into residential schools as far away as Kamloops and Cranbrook (Okanagan Nation Alliance 2019b). Representations of Kelowna's *urbanization* – from a rural, white, idyllic past to its dynamic present as an urbanizing regional centre to the claimed immanent future as a diverse world-class mid-sized city – enable its ongoing whiteness by mobilizing racialized and spatio-temporal imaginaries central to modern liberal politics. This production of Kelowna as a community of and for whiteness is embedded within a dominant form of Western liberal politics that uses "the city" (as particular place and pervasive imaginary) to help secure its claims to the sovereign authority to define modern political space as (appropriately) ordered and modern political subjectivity as (appropriately) white.

Through Kelowna, it becomes possible to identify the tensions and indeterminacies that bind the modern city to modern politics and that generate, sustain, and threaten the boundaries between white/non-white and rural/urban. By drawing attention to the ways that these boundaries have been challenged and resisted in Kelowna, this chapter aims to "disrupt those established attributes of place and the confining boundaries that have literally allowed whiteness to *take place*" (Kobayashi and Peake 2000, 393; emphasis in original). And the same time, this chapter offers an aporetic analysis that helps to explain why the efficacy and violence of these boundaries is so pervasive and ongoing. As such, this chapter also offers a caution to any optimistic belief that singular changes in representations of Kelowna as a city can, on their own, create sustained and systemic disruptions of the dominant political production of Kelowna as a place of and for whiteness.

APPROACHING KELOWNA: PUTTING DEFINITIONS OF URBANIZATION AND WHITENESS IN PLACE

Kelowna is a rapidly growing city whose predominantly white, English-speaking demographic is far out of proportion to the diversity of British

Columbia and cities of similar size within the province: "an urban location ... where racism and discrimination continue to exist" (Bahbahani 2008, 4–5). The city of Kelowna represents itself as an "anti-racist community" (Kelowna 2013, 78), while at the same time excising crucial anti-racist components from its Social Policy 360, claiming that these interventions are not what "cities" do (this policy revision is contained in the minutes of the January 2013 council meeting; see Kelowna 2013, 78–79). Moreover, in some population projections, visible minorities are increasing (Bahbahani 2008, 14), in others, they are decreasing or remaining stable (Michaels 2010b). Recognizing this tension between Kelowna's rapid growth and its shifting whiteness, *The Changing Face of Kelowna: Report on Ethnicity and Ethnic Relations* (Bahbahani 2008, 29) claims that "for Kelowna to continue to grow and thrive and ultimately survive as a city" it must not only "recognize the need for the growing stream of immigrants and the value that they bring to the city" but also recognize "how diversity strengthens rather than diminishes a city." The surprise that Kelowna is predominantly white, *despite its "urban" status*, and the imperative that Kelowna must diversify if it is going to survive *as a city* reinforce the common narrative that becoming a "real" city includes both a spatial transition from rural to urban and a demographic transition from homogeneity to diversity. This narrative grounds assumptions that increased diversity is necessarily *immanent* if Kelowna is to successfully urbanize.

Despite Kelowna's visible whiteness, whiteness is not an inherent set of characteristics derived from the colour of one's skin but "a form of racialization that is both historically specific and socially negotiated" (Satzewich 2007, 82). Whiteness is a set of claims and practices performed by complex, contingent, embodied subjectivities within shifting, multiple communities. As a technique of "identity formation and the formation and maintenance of group boundaries" (82), whiteness uses spatializations of difference to "*occup*[*y*] *space* within a segregated social landscape" and produce "landscapes that conform ... [to] values not immediately associated with 'race' but predicated upon whitened cultural practices" (Kobayashi and Peake 2000, 393–94, emphasis in original). Thus whiteness operates not only through the construction of subjectivities and communities but also through practices that emplace and displace racialized subjects in racialized spaces and times.

Similarly, cities are not simply geographic places of sufficient population but sites of ever-shifting social and economic linkages across vast distances (Wirth 1969; Sassen 1994; Dawson and Edwards 2004; Brenner and Schmid 2011). Kelowna is, therefore, not just a place but a *place-beyond-place* (Massey 2006, 181–87), shaped and defined through its distantiated links with the rest of the world (Amin and Thrift 2002, 13). Yet, despite academic shifts beyond the city as a simple object of analysis, debates about urbanization in Kelowna continue to invoke "the city" as an uncontested object of comparison. Kelowna's identity as a rapidly urbanizing but not yet definitively *urban* community is heavily debated in questions of whether Kelowna qualifies as a city, of what sort of city it should become, and of its ideal future form, as exemplified by residents' comments to a formal public planning process (Kelowna 2012, n.p.). In these practices, "the city" is less a place than an "imagined environment," an idealized or demonized imaginary of "the city" that is "above all, a representation" (Donald 1992, 427). To understand the tensions between Kelowna's urbanization and its continued whiteness, it becomes necessary to examine how *imaginaries* of the city – both generic imaginaries of "the city" and particular imaginaries that have developed over time in this place – operate here to emplace and displace whiteness and its others.

Two imaginaries of "the city" are particularly relevant to the tension between urbanization and whiteness in Kelowna due to their intersecting and contradictory racialized and spatial assumptions. First, the city has long been identified with the co-habitation of strangers (Simmel 1969; Sennett 1970) and with ethnic/cultural, economic, and gender differences (Jacobs 1992), invoking parallel imaginaries of the rural as a white, European, agrarian countryside. Second, imaginaries of "the city," as the modern European, industrialized "white" city also function as imaginaries of "the ideal city" and, thus, include powerful pressures towards ethnic, subjective, and representational homogeneity (Robinson 2006). Together, these make possible formulations of the suburb as an idealized balance of the rural and the urban (Bennett 1998; Kataoka 2009). The production and spatialization of whiteness holds a complicated relationship to the imaginaries of rural, traditional ways of life (Barraclough 2011) and urban complexity and diversity (Shaw 2007), and the transition narratives that have defined urbanization are linked to colonizing discourses of improvement, development, assimilation, and modernization (Barraclough 2011, 10–13).

These imaginaries are produced materially through segregations in lived spaces and times, often using discursive and aesthetic techniques. In Kelowna, as elsewhere, these imaginaries are produced through verbal and visual representations such as planning and policy statements, media language and pictures, official signage, heritage imagery, public art, and even academic engagements. Shields (1996, 227) suggests that representations can never get at the "real" of the city because "the city" is fundamentally *aporetic*, an indeterminate entity that cannot be a simple object of knowledge. This chapter shifts the aporetic analysis from *the city* as a complex of impossible imaginaries to *urbanization* as the production and destabilization of the boundaries that enable these imaginaries. On this aporetic understanding, representational claims about the urbanization of Kelowna produce boundaries of rural/urban and whiteness/otherness across spatial, temporal, and subjective registers, but they also produce vulnerabilities in these boundaries.

IMAGINARIES OF KELOWNA: URBANIZATION OR WHITENESS/URBANIZATION AND WHITENESS

Kelowna is clearly not a single homogenous entity, yet what I have sketched above suggests that a dominant fantasy of Kelowna is particularly concerned with its urbanization process and thinks explicitly about the city it hopes to become, emphasizing the need to become or remain a unique "place": "Culture is changing rapidly as global travel, immigration, and emigration increase. More and more communities are becoming 'nowhere places' as they fail to develop a unique sense of place, often accommodating a high number of national or international franchise-type businesses" (Kelowna 2008). While "place-making" can promote competitive commodification (Aguiar, Tomic, and Trumper 2005), it also recapitulates the tension under investigation here, simultaneously invoking the immanent diversification of Kelowna, emphasizing the need to become a unique "place" that can embody its imaginary of the ideal city, and suggesting a deep fear about the changes this diversity is assumed to bring. Thus "place-making" also demonstrates the complicated interplay between conflicting representations of Kelowna, materializations in spatio-temporal form and embodied subjective practices, and emplacements within more distantiated global processes.

Kelowna's contemporary place-making practices invoke and displace the history and geography of Kelowna's "resettlement" (Harris 1997) as a white township. Kelowna falls within the unceded territory of the Syilx (Okanagan) First Nation. Father Pandosy, a French Oblate missionary, established the first white settlement in 1859 at a site French Canadian fur traders called L'Anse au Sable ("Sandy Cove") (Kowrach 1992), and which had originally been called N'Wha-quisten ("Stone found there for shaping weapons of the chase and of war"). Soon after, incoming British settlers pre-empted the remaining land and displaced the Okanagan peoples onto reserve lands on both sides of Okanagan Lake. The members of the Westbank First Nation (WFN) are the most direct inhabitants of Pandosy Mission/Kelowna areas (WFN 2018). Early in its settlement, Kelowna became the site of a unique imaginary of a white community of British upper-middle-class families and young men (Bennett 1998). It was promoted as a place of orcharding – a leisure activity suitable for British gentlemen, distinguishable from farming as working-class labour – and it was explicitly linked to the British garden city movement, which proposed to solve urbanization by reclaiming elements of rural life (Bennett 1998). However, Kelowna was never an exclusively "white" settlement. Its reliance on visible minority labour, particularly in orchards, was at odds with its white imaginary, generating a tension between the need for, and fear of, non-white workers (Lanthier and Wong n.d., secs. 4 and 5). The predominance of whiteness in Kelowna is not neutral or inevitable; rather, it is a political production secured through extensive legal and social restrictions on non-white communities (Lanthier and Wong n.d.; Roy 1981) and ongoing representations of Kelowna as a place for whiteness (Bennett 1998; Aguiar, Tomic, and Trumper 2005).

This pervasive construction in Kelowna of an idealized self-image of white community contributes to the statistical whiteness of Kelowna, drawing predominantly white middle-class migrants, particularly retirees, primarily from within Canada (Steyn 2008, 3). Kelowna's contemporary urban aspirations lead it to promote social diversity as a necessary element of becoming a "real" city. The city of Kelowna's *Cultural Plan* states that "cities can only thrive if they are able to attract a diversity of people" and that Kelowna "appreciates and celebrates human diversity and is open and welcoming to newcomers from all over the world" (Kelowna 2011, 3, 19). Investments in the imaginary of a diversified, urban Kelowna lead to calls to leave Kelowna's rural (white) culture in the past, as is made clear by commentary in *Kelowna Capital News* (*KCN*) (see *KCN* 2007). Yet it also leads to "mixophiliac" (Bauman 2003, 33–34) desires to experience urban energy by intermingling with other (often exoticized) cultures: Kelowna is "boring" and its "lack of cultural diversity is snuffing out the valley's fun-factor" (Michaels 2008). Still, Kelowna exhibits less diversity and less openness to diversity than what characterizes imaginaries of a "real" city. There is a profound and ongoing "mixophobia" (Bauman 2003, 27–34), or the fear of intermingling with (racialized) strangers (Aguiar, McKinnon, and Sookraj 2010–11), and a strong current of fear that urbanization itself is the force that brings these racialized strangers to "our" (white) midst (Steyn 2008).

Therefore, while Kelowna is disproportionately homogenous for its size, the *imaginary* of white Kelowna is more pervasive than its reality: both a former mayor and the co-president of the Intercultural Society of the Central Okanagan emphasize that Kelowna has diversities that are not captured by statistical measures or white imaginaries (Michaels 2012; Teixeira 2009, 328–29). And yet, a resident can suggest that the positive promotion in her child's classroom of racialized cultural diversity is irrelevant (compared with socioeconomic difference) because the students are not only white but "blonde and blue-eyed" (*KCN* 2008). In other words, the *imaginary* of Kelowna as becoming a diverse world-class city is also much more pervasive than its reality. Thus, "place-making" in Kelowna displaces and emplaces contradictory but mutually reinforcing imaginaries of rural/urban and non-white/white. This complicated pattern derives, in part, from the way "the city" has been linked to civilization and to "modern," sovereign, liberal politics.

THE CITY, CIVILIZATION, AND MODERN EUROPEAN POLITICS: COLONIZATION, RACIALIZATION, URBANIZATION

Imaginaries of the city include two contradictory images: the city as a site, metonym, and imaginary of political possibility ("city of hope") and of a serious threat to politics ("city of fear") (Bauman 2003). The "city of hope" has roots in the mythology of a Western intellectual tradition, where "politics" is identified with the *polis*, the Greek city that is both a place and a self-governing body of people. Similarly, "civic" (public or municipal) and "citizen" (participant in politics and subject of governance) are derived from *civitas*, the Latin word for city and the root word of "civilization" (Lees 2004, 5). In this positive imaginary, urban social interactions, cultural developments, and economic productions identify the city with both politics and civilization and, thus, with civil, secure community (Mumford 1938; Wirth 1969; Jacobs 1992). Even critical engagements with the *polis* have argued that contestations over city life make becoming urban synonymous with becoming political (Isin 2002, 7). And yet, the modern, industrialized, metropolitan city has also amplified always-existing imaginaries of the "city of fear": fears about what sort of people live in cities (dissolute, self-indulgent, and corrupted by luxury; or lower-class masses, uneducated and irrational) and fears about the fragility of the "city of hope," the city as site of political possibility. Thus there developed an equally powerful imaginary of the city as a threat to pre-defined political life, particularly after the calcification of Western politics into the modern territorial sovereign state. The chaotic extremes of contemporary urban life only seem to intensify these threats.

The tension between urbanization and whiteness in Kelowna is rooted in these oppositional claims about the political possibility of the city, framed as the production and dissemination of (white/urban/modern) civilization, and the political threats of the city, framed as its chaotic destruction of (white/rural/traditional) order. In one telling example, promotional material produced by Kelowna's Board of Trade in 1908 argues that Kelowna must become *the right sort of city*: not a great "industrial" city, plagued with illness, poverty, difference, and *conflict*, but a "desirable" city, smaller in scale and wedded to elements of rural life (Bennett 1998, 75). In this vision of Kelowna, it is crucial to become a city, which confers the possibility of civilizing advancements, but it is just as crucial not to become the wrong sort of city, one in which the break from rural life is complete and its stabilizing and ordering influence lost.

While the language of civilization has a longer political history, it has been a key element in the articulation and imperial imposition of modern

Western politics as sovereignty, self-government, liberalism, democracy, and the state (Murphy 2009; Salter 2002; Brown 2006). This European definition of "civilization" was used to draw and naturalize a boundary between those who were part of a unified culture and identity of European modernity and those who were not (yet) (Salter 2002, 18; Brown 2006). The civilizational discourse aims to produce ordered subjects with the capacity to participate in the self-disciplining and self-authorizing practices required by (white) European institutions of modern liberal self-government (Mill 1991). Civilizationism within the West has, therefore, been a racializing, subjectifying discourse, producing "whiteness" as the sovereign subject of modern European politics. This process was considered a necessary precursor to living peacefully in modern conditions of urban density and difference (Freud 2004; Brown 2006). Indeed, urban planning as a discipline arose within "colonial practices of racialization and cultural difference" (Robinson 2006, 4) as a response to the dual challenges of imperialism: the socioeconomic changes wrought in the cities of imperial powers and the desire to construct new, modern, controlled cities in the colonies (King 1990; Davis 2004). As an "invader-settler" (Brydon 2005) state on Indigenous lands, Canada made use of the racialized discourse of civilization and the developing techniques of urban planning to institute municipal governance in the form of "the city as a corporation without citizens" (Isin 1992), which simultaneously displaced and disenfranchised Indigenous peoples and made settler communities subservient to the political authority of colonial governance and then the sovereign (provincial) state.

Reconnecting urbanization to "civilizationism" and the imperialist universalization of European sovereign politics as global "modern" politics problematizes imaginaries of urban diversity, which Kelowna uses to represent an idealized, immanent urban future, but it also problematizes imaginaries of an idyllic, homogenous rural past, which Kelowna uses to constrain and "civilize" its urban development. The development of Kelowna as a white orcharding settlement was an idealized response to the British experience of urbanization as corruption, and yet the process of developing Kelowna according to an imaginary of a rural, "white" Eden relied on networks of international (usually urban) capital (Koroscil 2003, 75), on the promotion of the orcharding lifestyle at agricultural fairs in

London and other urban centres (94–101), and on material practices, such as irrigation (Bennett 1998, 68) and architecture (Koroscil 2003, 63), that were refined in colonial British India. The incorporation of Kelowna in 1905 was seen as an inclusion into the law and order of Canada within the Empire, which "validated" the community politically, just as the establishment in 1906 of the Board of Trade ensured its economic viability (Bennett 1998, 71–72): "functioning in an imperial economy of images and finance, the establishment of [Kelowna as] an urban centre with its banks and financial houses was necessary to connect and market their ruralism to the wider imperial world." The imaginaries of Kelowna as a rural idyll were made possible by its urban imaginaries, and vice-versa.

Therefore, while one contemporary imaginary of urbanization in Kelowna emphasizes the process of becoming a heterogeneous city, another powerful imaginary of urbanization in Kelowna emphasizes the process of becoming a properly civilized (white) city. Kelowna is emplaced within imperializing Western discourses and racialized hierarchies of whiteness, urbanization, and civilization, and within the political hopes and fears that characterize the project of securing the modern sovereign state and its appropriate political subjects.

THE POLITICAL LOGIC OF APORETIC URBANIZATION

This account of Kelowna highlights the boundaries that support the colonizing narrative of a linear, progressive transition (Barraclough 2011) from Kelowna's white rural past, through a much-debated urbanizing present, to an (immanent) urban future as a "real" diverse city. These boundaries – between rural/urban, uncivilized/civilized, non-white/white, and their cognates – have been both pervasive and subject to continual reversals. At times, the rural is coded as a natural, normalized, white way of life that is authentic and traditional, while the urban is "other" (exotic, aberrant, non-white), modern, neurotic, or pathological. At others, the rural is natural, barbarian, or savage, driven by animal urges and thus non-white, while the urban represents white culture, advanced civilization, and the mature subject. Despite their powerful presence, these boundaries have been consistently experienced as fragile, always requiring further acts to secure them against perceived threats (Roy 1981; Bennett 1998). These boundaries are understood, in both whiteness studies and urban studies, as practices rather than as external, naturalized objects. However, it is necessary to develop a more rigorous analysis of how these boundaries are produced and how they can simultaneously seem so easily threatened and so difficult to destabilize.

One route is to understand these political productions as *aporetic* boundary practices. Derrida (1993) argues that aporetic boundary practices constitute the terms on either side of a boundary through the process of delineating each from the other. Rather than being oppositional or binary, the relevant terms are co-produced in the act of determining the line that separates them. Instead of producing the city as an aporetic *site* (Shields 1996), distinct from the rest of the world, *urbanization* as an aporetic boundary practice co-produces definitions of rural versus urban, just as *civilization* co-produces definitions of white versus non-white. The specific content of these definitions may shift over time, yet the pattern of their production and reproduction remains remarkably stable. Further, in so far as aporetic boundaries create and define these terms, they necessarily impose a limit (e.g., the limit of the city, the limit of whiteness) and create the inherent threat of the defining line being breached. Aporetic boundaries, therefore, are sites of limit experiences: not just the limits of the rural or the urban, of white or non-white, but the limits of security.

Analyzing urbanization as a complex of aporetic boundary practices that produce definitions of rural/urban, white/other, civilized/savage suggests that urbanization does not simply intensify encounters with the pre-constituted "strange(r)" (Bauman 2003), as the imaginary of an increasingly diverse, urban Kelowna suggests. It also exceeds the suggestion that cities are "difference machines": that the diversity of urban encounters constitutes and defines difference in sociological, ethnic/cultural, and political terms (Isin 2002, 51). Kelowna does not necessarily produce *more difference* because it has developed a *more urban* form, size, or complexity. Rather, urbanization, as an aporetic political production, defines and produces subjectivities as internally and externally estranged or familiar (such as non-white/white); designates appropriate spatial and temporal locations with which to segregate them (such as rural/urban, traditional/modern, past/present/future); and valuates and hierarchically orders various inclusions and exclusions (such as uncivilized/civilized). In this sense, to be embedded in a process of aporetic urbanization is to be the subject of and subject to the boundaries drawn between urban/rural and white/non-white, while necessarily revising and inflecting these boundaries. In so far as Kelowna has participated in the production of difference through techniques that mark, segregate, and exclude, it has been bound within global processes of aporetic urbanization from its first white settlement.

The politics of aporetic boundaries are not found solely in their *effects*, as serious, oppressive, or unequal as they may be, but in the naturalization and depoliticization of these boundaries. Aporetic boundary practices claim the authority to define acceptable and unacceptable spaces, forms, and practices of politics (Tedesco 2012b). However, the contingent foundation of aporetic boundaries makes them unstable and always vulnerable to threats and reconfigurations, such that they appear as unsolvable political problems (Derrida 1993, 11). Thus an aporetic boundary practice has the distinctive momentum of drawing a boundary that constitutes the terms on either side but also continually threatens to collapse; of idealizing a new boundary separation that is perceived to be more secure; and of confronting its ever-threatening instability, which generates an ongoing panic. Ultimately, aporetic boundaries simultaneously idealize and undermine an imaginary of stable politics, and the standard political response to aporetic instability is to look to the sovereign state or the sovereign individual to secure the non-securable (Tedesco 2012b). These claims to authority are central to modern liberal politics, and they are central to imaginaries of Kelowna that rely on spatialized and racialized boundaries of white/non-white and rural/urban.

APORETIC URBANIZATION IN KELOWNA: PRODUCING, SPATIALIZING, AND SECURING MODERN, SOVEREIGN, "WHITE" SUBJECTS

The representations that produce Kelowna as a place, through its self-imaginaries, also construct racialized spaces and times through historical accounts, public statements and artworks, and even academic interventions in these imaginaries. The tension between the city of hope and the city of fear frequently reappears in such representations of Kelowna in the connection between "whiteness," as a claim about political subjectivity, and the production and expected internalization of norms of "civilized" urban behaviour. In narratives of Kelowna's past, this moral ground is represented as primarily, if not exclusively, the terrain of feminine influence (Bennett 1998):

> As mining towns to the east did little to control gambling, drinking and prostitution, the towns in the Okanagan became more settled and seemed to adopt a valley-wide code of acceptable behavior. Women became increasingly active in improving the social fabric of their communities as they worked to establish schools and hospitals, to support appropriate cultural and artistic opportunities, and along with the churches, to provide moral and spiritual leadership. (Kelowna, Pioneer Pavilion, Knox Mountain 2003)

Kelowna, as a nascent (ideal) city, is supposed to "civilize" migrants (rural, non-white, and other "strangers") into urban order, yet there is a deep concern for the way that the "uncivilized" city threatens to upset urban order and requires constant control. This tension highlights that the political production of racialized and urbanized aporetic boundaries is embodied within particular subjectivities as much as particular built forms of community.

The boundaries that produce and normalize this idealized vision of white resident/white community, and simultaneously produce and displace forms of difference, have been materialized through spatial segregations (Bennett 1998; Aguiar, Tomic, and Trumper 2005; Aguiar and Marten 2011). Historically, this included racialized legal and discursive boundaries that segregated the Syilx (Okanagan) peoples onto reserves; that defined a spatially and racially segregated "Chinatown" in downtown Kelowna (Lanthier and Wong n.d., sec. 3); and that allowed non-whites to work on, but not buy, orchards (which closed economic doors and enforced social and spatial segregations as most non-white labourers inhabited orchards seasonally, in separate accommodation from orchard owners). There were also complex differentiations and spatial segregations within the "white" community, for instance with British-born residents on the south side of Mill Creek (near downtown) and Canadian-born residents on the north (Bennett 1998, 83–84). These early spatial boundaries set the groundwork for the later predominance of gated communities as a response to and generator of Kelowna's growth in the 1980s and 1990s.

More recently, the pervasive claims of the civilizing power of a controlled urban environment have enabled Kelowna's policies and planning processes to continue to produce and spatialize whiteness and its others, as one heavily-debated plan for a comprehensive redevelopment of Kelowna's downtown core demonstrates. The Comprehensive Development Zone (CD21 Plan), covering four blocks of downtown Kelowna, was approved in October 2008. It was cancelled in 2010 after the municipal election in November greatly reconfigured the council (Tedesco 2012a). As a spatio-temporal representation, downtown is identified as the historic core and urban future of Kelowna. Jane Jacobs was frequently invoked during the public hearings as a democratic urban theorist, particularly her claim that having diverse "eyes on the street" contributes to public safety. Yet Jacobs (1992, 29–30) also believed in "the drama of civilization versus barbarism in cities," which suggests that "eyes on the street" are a technique of the "civilizing," disciplining power of cities. This phrase, conjoined with imagery in the city's presentations, suggests that the redesign of downtown was not intended to encourage urban diversity; indeed, one presentation represented contemporary downtown Kelowna with images of graffiti, abandoned lots, and barbed-wire fences, while its urban future was represented by the glassy urban high-rises of "Vancouverism" (Kataoka 2009). Instead, the city attempted to use its provincially delegated authority over urban design and zoning bylaws to define and spatially segregate the strange, in this case those primarily street-involved inhabitants who do not manifest the appropriate "white" subjectivity of property-owning and consumption-oriented citizen-subjects. Thus Kelowna supports the suggestion that the fear of difference displayed in "mixophobic paranoia" (Bauman 2003, 34–35) is amplified, rather than reduced, by segregation. This insecurity and paranoia is exemplary of the logic of aporetic boundaries: it is impossible for the boundary, as drawn, to remain stable in space and over time, requiring constant restabilizations through new techniques of segregation.

These techniques are temporal as much as spatial, and these temporal segregations mobilize the civilizational discourse of urbanization as white, modern progress. For example, the information plaques on the top of Knox

Mountain Park suggest that Indigeneity is the irretrievable past, whiteness is the recent pioneer past that sowed the seeds of the present, and urban diversity is the (immanent) future that will be appropriately ordered due to the civilizing work of the white settlers (Kelowna, Pioneer Pavilion, Knox Mountain 2003). Such continual re-invocations of an image of the (desired, white) past in the present, particularly through the emphasis on the orcharding history of Kelowna, constrain imaginaries of Kelowna's possible urban futures. The historic apple box logos that cover Fortis electrical transformer boxes throughout the city are exemplary of this technique.

One distinctive image on these boxes – the logo for A1 grade, Empire variety "Occidental Apples" – emplaces all of Kelowna, now, within its colonial imaginary as a white Eden: the logo features a glorious sun setting behind snow-capped mountains, casting rays over an orderly orchard and a prim, white farmhouse, its imagery echoing the brand's hierarchical claims of white civilization. Another popular logo used on these utility boxes is the logo for C-grade Big Chief apples, which consigns Indigenous presence and presents to the past, figuratively removing them from the orcharding landscape by not representing Indigenous peoples in the image at all, despite their role as agricultural labourers (Lanthier and Wong, n.d., sec. 4). Both images displace subjectivities that do not fit within the progressivist imaginary of civilized white modernity. However, in so far as the primary policy function of these decorative wraps is to deter graffiti (Kelowna 2011c, 22), a paradigmatically urban practice of producing and marking space, the apple-box logos function as a doubled production and displacement of the non-(appropriately)white. The boundary between civilized and not can quickly exclude anyone with an "improper" respect for property and order, despite their visual "whiteness": precisely those whom the pioneers of Kelowna worked so hard to civilize (Kelowna, Pioneer Pavilion, Knox Mountain 2003). Therefore, Kelowna has relied not only on the emplacement of whiteness and the displacement of the non-white but also on the production of a very limited notion of whiteness.

Kelowna's vision of becoming a world-class mid-sized city would seem to depend on recognizing its historic minority communities, and supporting its contemporary ones, and yet Kelowna's promotion of "mixophilia" (Bauman 2003) is tightly constrained, such as in planning documents that segregate diversity conceptually to cultural issues and spatially to the cultural district as the core of Kelowna's "big city" experience (Kelowna 2011a, 2011b). There is a similar spatial and temporal segregation between permanent and temporary migrants. Landed immigrants, typically recruited from Western Europe (Kataoka and Magnusson 2011), become part of the imaginary of Kelowna's future, while short-term labourers (one of the most visible categories of minority newcomers) are housed in restricted locations in the city (common hotels, on-site farm accommodation), face curfews that establish temporal norms of encounter, and, as seasonal labourers, are generally confined to summer months when residents expect to encounter non-white visitors (Aguiar and Marten 2011; Lanthier and Wong n.d.; James, Chapter 9, this volume).

Whether despite or because of these pervasive segregations, representations of Kelowna abound with a profound sense of threat relating to actual or imaginary "encounters" with the "uncivilized," including non-white Indigenous and settler inhabitants and newly arrived migrants (Bennett 1998; Aguiar, McKinnon, and Sookraj 2010–11), as well as overly urban or rural subjective practices (*KCN* 2011; *KCN* 2007). An aporetic analysis emphasizes the subjectivizing and spatio-temporalizing boundary practices that produce "others," as in the case of defining "Black" Jamaican workers prior to their arrival in Kelowna (Aguiar, McKinnon, and Sookraj 2010–11). But it also suggests that the continual experience of threat – threats seemingly out of proportion to the predominance of white Kelowna statistically and in its imaginaries – derives from the fear that the "uncivilized" can destabilize the boundaries upon which "Kelowna" was founded. The common response to this experience of aporetic instability as threat is to invoke sovereign authority as the necessary stabilizing force, as seen in efforts to control, through curfews and other restrictions, the movements and activities of the incoming "Black" Jamaicans. These efforts to impose appropriately "civil" urban behaviour (which, in their inordinate restrictions, are actually inappropriate) attempt to produce subjects of sovereign politics until such time as they can be deemed "civilized" – that is, capable of internalizing and performing the codes of appropriate (white) behaviour. Yet the pattern in Kelowna suggests that the perceived threat never retreats and the dream of the "desirable" city – neither too big nor too small, neither too rural nor too urban, neither too white nor too diverse – is as impossible as the dream of incontestable sovereign authority (Magnusson 2011, 7). Further, these imaginaries of white citizen-subjects suggest that the stakes of Kelowna's complex boundaries of whiteness, continually re-secured through spatial and temporal segregations, are not only the ideal of a properly white, modern political community but also the boundaries of the self-legislating, "white," modern political subject: the subject with the authoritative capacity to draw definitive boundaries and govern itself (and subsequently others) by these ideals. Therefore, encounters with the "uncivilized" are encounters with the limits of dominant imaginaries of Kelowna and the limits of "modern" liberal politics that these imaginaries support.

APORETIC URBANIZATION AS DISPLACEMENT OF THE IDEALS OF MODERN (WHITE) POLITICS

Kelowna is founded on and maintained by a multiplicity of aporetic boundary practices that operate, through formal and informal representations of the past, present, and future of "Kelowna," to effect multiple displacements in order to emplace a white invader-settler community. These are powerful claims to authority, but the contingency of aporetic boundaries renders them insecure: the boundaries of "whiteness" and "the city," embedded in the imaginary of the "desirable" urban development of Kelowna, have constituted modern politics as sovereign communities and subjects, but the instability of these boundaries makes clear the constitutive impossibility of this "idealized" political imaginary.

It is possible to excavate other representations that emphasize the constitution of Kelowna in crossing and muddying the supposedly clear boundaries between white/non-white and rural/urban. For example, the initial "white" settlement, later imagined as a British upper-middle-class community, was founded by a French missionary and a French Canadian man with his First Nations wife, who were allowed by the Syilx people to settle only because of her family connection to an important chief in what is now Penticton (Cronin 1960). Kelowna remained a French-language settlement for many decades. Some accounts of the post-First World War period suggest that the necessary mixing of orchard owners and their "ethnic" workers led to greater acceptance (if not policy changes), while the fear of these workers was maintained primarily by those who had not crossed the constitutive boundaries of segregation (Lanthier and Wong n.d., secs. 4 and 5). The present lack of diverse visible minority communities in Kelowna, a seeming confirmation of the boundaries between white and non-white, can at times unsettle these boundaries: at the Ki-Low-Na (Aboriginal) Friendship Centre, which provides immigrant settlement services, newcomers have significant interaction with Kelowna's Indigenous population and learn about the colonial history of this place. This arrangement, unique to Kelowna (Kataoka and Magnusson 2011, 266), helps make explicit, and thus potentially denaturalizes, the white imaginaries of Kelowna and their displacements of Indigenous and minority communities. These boundary crossings are not instances of mixophilia, with its suggestion of pre-formed subjects seeking out the frisson of difference, but of generative encounters with the limits of the dominant imaginaries of Kelowna and their operative, but insecure, boundaries.

Such excavations highlight the multiplicity of boundaries – crossing, reversing, amplifying, undermining – that produce, emplace, displace, represent, and contest definitions of the spaces, forms, and practices of politics. As a gestural example, the early support for Indigenous land claims in the Okanagan by white "churchmen" (Bennett 1998, 86) represents this complicated interplay: pressures to secure land for the "appropriate" urban development of Kelowna (Koroscil 2003, 48–52); the "civilizing" imperialisms of Protestant and Catholic missionaries and their battles for influence over Indigenous communities (Blake 1998, 32); missionaries' first-hand knowledge of the negative effects of colonial land policies on Indigenous communities, gained by crossing dominant boundaries of segregation (29); threats to (provincial) state sovereignty posed not only by Indigenous nations but also by the very missionary system used to support colonization (43–44); and the commitment of the Syilx people to keep their land, language, and culture intact (see Okanagan Syilx websites cited above). These interplays are contestations not only between "white" modern politics and Indigenous modes of being political but also between the boundaries that define properly "civil" urban development and modern, sovereign politics (Blake 1998, 38). Blake argues that Oblate missionaries in British Columbia rejected the state's political land claims, which invoked "post-Reformation" Lockean property rights, and articulated a vision of

Indigenous land rights that used "an older Catholic tradition regarding natural law and property rights." To be clear, this is not to suggest that the Catholic missionaries were any less guilty of "civilizing" imperialisms, the genocidal violence of which was all too evident at the Catholic-run Kamloops Indian Residential School (Okanagan Nation Alliance 2021). Rather, it highlights that claims about the correct foundations of modern, white, secular sovereign politics were theologically-inflected and thus internally contested. However, Blake also states that the "threat" posed to the provincial state by the Oblate missionaries' position was negligible. This last contestation between "white" modern politics and Indigenous political rights to land and culture might demonstrate that the foundations for white displacements of Indigenous claims to and practices of politics have been contested internally as well as externally, and yet it also continues this colonial displacement by attempting to restrict political contestation to a debate over the authority to define the boundaries of "modern," white, sovereign politics and to restrict political participation in the debate to "white" subjects (Bennett 1998, 86).

Yet these alternative representations of Kelowna have the potential to produce alternative *political* imaginaries. They do not merely question individuals, groups, or institutions that currently exercise sovereign authority but potentially threaten the very imaginary of a securely modern, sovereign politics. These challenges to the dominant representations of Kelowna are experienced by those invested in that fantasy as a profound insecurity, a reaction to the constitutive impossibility of the dream of a pure white community. As such, the negotiations, contestations, and reconstructions of boundaries, which appear to have been present at many junctures, have been continually marginalized or internalized through practices that are central to the continuities of modern liberal politics: by restricting debates to the question of who has the authority to draw boundaries, which leaves the desire for sovereign authority intact (Magnusson 2011, 37); by replaying, in discourses of "progressive" politics, the spatio-temporal assumptions of improvement that are central to modern political imperialism; by finding new ways to inscribe representations of the superiority of white "civilization" and thus re-secure the limits of political possibilities. An aporetic analysis of whiteness and urbanization in Kelowna suggests that these practices are dominant yet insecure, raising questions about how representations might try to resist the enticements of sovereign security and the challenges they face in doing so.

REPRESENTING THE POLITICAL CHALLENGES OF APORETIC URBANIZATION IN KELOWNA

The intense challenges of producing representations that might engage such destabilizations are suggested by the public art project to commemorate 150th anniversary of Kelowna's mission settlement. The Okanagan-raised artist Crystal Przybille had lived in a small cabin on agricultural land across from the Pandosy Mission for some years, which led her to contemplate the role of Father Pandosy in creating contemporary Kelowna. She approached the Okanagan Historical Society with the idea of a bronze statue of Father Pandosy, and the approaching sesquicentennial anniversary and subsequent funding (including primary funding from the federal Canadian Heritage) made the project viable. In her research, Przybille found that Kelowna's settlement was more complicated and contentious than what was implied by the dominant narrative she had been taught. She became increasingly aware of how "much of the most directly accessible information regarding Pandosy was uncomfortably Euro-centric … I didn't want to create a piece of art that, like many of these books, tells only one side of a complicated story, or that perpetuates an idea that our current state of privilege is based on a kind of entitlement" (Przybille 2011, 89). Przybille approached the Westbank First Nation to discuss unsettling this narrative of white settlement and worked with Elder Delphine Armstrong and research curator Gayle Liman to conceptualize a statue that would include both settler and Syilx perspectives. Liman (2010) observed at an early stage in the project that inviting WFN participation was "a groundbreaking step … and it is my opinion that the final work created will, therefore, be a powerful depiction of the benefits of collaboration." The artistic focus shifted from the authority of a singular subject – either Father Pandosy or the artist herself – to a collaborative process that cut across the segregating boundaries of Kelowna's whiteness. The artist intervenes in a process that might simply exalt Pandosy as an exemplary missionary by developing a collaborative and consultative practice with Syilx-Okanagan peoples harmed by

FIGURE 3 Father Pandosy 150th Anniversary Sculpture. | Courtesy Crystal Przybille

missionary work. Developing a more collaborative process is a small gesture towards unsettling this very modern political assumption of individual subjectivity. The sculpture itself became both a "portrait" and "a contemplation on collective history, settlement, and preemption" (Przybille 2011, 90). For information on the statue, the artist, and the process, see Przybille (2012). The artist is a personal friend of the author.

The finished statue (Figure 3) is located at the Pandosy Mission site, a mix of preserved and relocated buildings. The statue shows Father Pandosy walking into a stiff wind. His left hand holds a branch staff that roots into the ground at his bare feet, capturing his role in Kelowna's agricultural heritage. The base of his cassock and blanket form a raised relief of images that the WFN felt best represented their ongoing Indigenous presence: the Food Chiefs – Spitlem (Bitterroot), Skmxist (Black Bear), Siya (Saskatoon or Service Berry), and Ntitiyix (Spring Salmon) – and resilient Senklip (Coyote). The wind "symbolizes several things: the challenges Pandosy faced internally, and also physically. The turbulence caused by the methods of European settlement, and the long-term turmoil that created for the Syilx" (Przybille 2011, 90). The accompanying plaque (unlike those at Knox Mountain Pioneer Pavilion) emphasizes this turmoil and makes it explicit that Euro-Canadian settlement was founded on the exclusion of Syilx people and culture and the pre-emption of their land.

The sculpture is a challenging representation of European colonization and the displacement of Indigenous peoples by white "pioneers." Some viewers see a celebration of European superiority and the linear path of Western "development" from Kelowna's Euro-Canadian settlement to its current urban status. Around the unveiling, local organizations and media celebrated this uncomplicated account of the (white) settlement and development of Kelowna. Despite efforts to publicize the work as a critical engagement with pre-emption, settlement, and cultural upheaval, these institutions saw the sculpture as part of Kelowna's dominant narrative of urbanization (Squire 2012; Waters 2012). Others, such as Liman (2010), saw an "acknowledg[ment] of Aboriginal voice, which has been adversely affected by colonization, residential schools, and trans-racial adoptions" and felt that such recognition "is a huge step in understanding and healing." To others still, such as Okanagan Nation Alliance member Dixon Terbasket, Father Pandosy was a "bully" and a figure of oppression, violence, and exclusion. The sculpture spoke to him, in painful ways, of "the untold story of the history of the Okanagan people," including how the Syilx people, including Terbasket's own grandfather, fed the settlers and helped them survive, only to be ignored, rejected, and dispossessed after the settlers became more established.

Przybille met Terbasket at the Ki-Low-Na Friendship Centre and invited him to view the statue and provide feedback. Terbasket was very open with the artist about the anger and negative feelings the statue of this "black robe" engendered, particularly regarding how the four Food Chiefs and Senklip were figured on the robe itself. Through conversation he learned that these images were suggested by Armstrong and incorporated with her approval; because he trusted that Elder Delphine Armstrong acted "out of the goodness in her heart," he came to understand this imagery as a powerful gift to the artist (personal communication with Dixon Terbasket, August 2014). Likewise, through these conversations Przybille understood that, despite her efforts at consultation, the effects of the sculpture on Syilx viewers were more powerful and, for some, more profoundly negative than she had anticipated (personal communication with Dixon Terbasket, August 2014). Terbasket's initial anger – openly shared and openly received by the artist in a joint willingness to venture across boundaries into difficult and unsettled terrain – has developed into an ongoing and wide-ranging conversation about what can be done to use the statue to tell "untold" and complicated stories.

The Father Pandosy sculpture fixes the complex personal and institutional processes and negotiations, which brought it into being, into a single material object, but this does not mean that its meaning is fixed and its emplacements and displacements predictable. As a representation of Kelowna's colonial past, it references multiple stories that are generally not told in Kelowna, including the history of Syilx dispossession, the role of Western Christian denominations, and the complicity of Kelowna's urbanization narratives in this history. Similarly, the multiple, cross-cutting responses destabilize the boundaries that have defined and segregated white and non-white communities as internally homogenous. By bringing these accounts into contention in one contentious place – the Mission grounds that previously made no mention of the Syilx people it displaced – this sculpture materially represents the challenges of engaging and destabilizing the dominant boundary practices that have produced "Kelowna" in its present form.

Further, the emplacement of this Father Pandosy sculpture led the WFN to commission Przybille to produce a bronze statue of Chief Swkncut, a contemporary of Father Pandosy. The Maquette, or

FIGURE 4 Chief Swkncut Maquette. | Courtesy Crystal Przybille

small-scale working model of the statue (Figure 4) was approved by the WFN in June 2015, and the full-sized cast-bronze statue was prominently installed in City Park in Kelowna on 21 June 2019 in collaboration with the city. This project was housed in a publicly accessible studio space and included a community discussion event on urbanization and colonization in the Okanagan (organized by the author and the artist in conjunction with the UBC-Okanagan AlterKnowledges Discussion Series, Alternator Gallery, 8 May 2015). At this event, Roxanne Lindley, a descendent of Chief Swkncut's sister, joined Liman, Armstrong, Terbasket, and others in articulating the lasting effects of colonization: segregation, disenfranchisement, and estrangement within families and between communities. They also spoke of the healing and regeneration represented by the Chief Swkncut statue: a recognizable likeness of a man whose descendants remain; a depiction, through the composition and imagery of the statue, of a strong, emplaced, living Syilx culture; an embodiment of the work of Przybille, a non-Indigenous artist, to immerse herself in Syilx culture and community. The statue now sits adjacent to the Tourist Centre in City Park, offering both visible recognition of unceded Syilx place on the land and contemporary cultural resilience, and also the consumption of Indigenous history and historical figures by visitors as an extension of place-making practices and urbanization narratives (Figure 5).

These efforts to represent the complexity of Kelowna open space and time to exceed the dominant narrative of secure white privilege in Kelowna, including ongoing conversations between the artist, the city, and the Syilx community, and critical interpretive conversations between students, scholars, and Indigenous- and settler-identified residents. Clearly, neither the Father Pandosy sculpture nor the Chief Swkncut sculpture can redraw narrative boundaries or produce new political communities: there is no direct line from idea to materialization, from intent to outcome, and to hope as much is to be seduced by modern assumptions of authority. However, the sculptures, and the practices they are embedded within and subsequently generate, engage the aporetic boundary practices that define, emplace, and displace Kelowna's colonial "past," its conflicted "present," and the complicated imaginaries of its urban "future." These practices suggest that other imaginaries of Kelowna's future are possible but that they can only take material shape through inclusive, proliferating engagements with the challenge of holding existing boundary determinations constantly to account.

FIGURE 5 Chief Swkncut Statue, Kelowna City Park. | Courtesy Luís L.M. Aguiar

INDETERMINATE CONCLUSIONS AND APORETIC POLITICS

This chapter locates the urbanization of Kelowna not in easy tropes of becoming a "real" city, with its dual imaginaries of hope and fear, but in the aporetic productions that constitute Kelowna as a particular place-beyond-place where whiteness is made to "take place" (Kobayashi and Peake 2000, 393). It suggests an alternate mode of engaging with the boundary practices that have constructed Kelowna according to this imaginary of whiteness: rather than succumb to the panicked urge to re-secure unstable aporetic boundaries by redrawing them again and again, it is possible to open these multiple practices to consideration and emphasize, rather than suppress, their contingency and instability. *Possible*, but as Kelowna makes clear, exceedingly difficult. Unlike the transition narratives that plague the colonizing, civilizing discourses of urbanization, aporetic urbanization makes no promise of progress towards a more equitable future, urban or otherwise. That outcome, it suggests, is fully reliant on the hard political work of negotiating and continually reconfiguring the contingent foundations exposed by this encounter with the limits of "modern" politics.

REFERENCES

Aguiar, L.L.M., A. McKinnon, and D. Sookraj. 2010/2011. Repertoires of Racism: Reactions to Jamaicans in the Okanagan Valley. *BC Studies* 168 (Winter): 65–79.

Aguiar, L.L.M., and T.M. Martin. 2011. "Shimmering White Kelowna and the Examination of Painless White Privilege in the Hinterland of British Columbia." In *Rethinking the Great White North: Race, Nature, and the Historical Geographies of Whiteness in Canada*, ed. A. Baldwin, L. Cameron, and A. Kobayashi, 127–44. Vancouver: UBC Press.

Aguiar, L.L.M., P. Tomic, and R. Trumper. 2005. "Work Hard, Play Hard: Selling Kelowna, BC, as Year-Round Playground." In *The Canadian Geographer / Le Géographe canadien* 49 (2): 123–39.

Amin, A., and N. Thrift. 2002. *Cities: Reimaging the Urban*. Cambridge: Polity Press.

Bahbahani, K. 2008. *The Changing Face of Kelowna: Report on Ethnicity and Ethnic Relations*. Kelowna: The Intercultural Society of the Central Okanagan (ISCO). Accessed June 13, 2018.

Barraclough, L.R. 2011. *Making the San Fernando Valley: Rural Landscapes, Urban Development, and White Privilege*. Athens: University of Georgia Press.

Bauman, Z. 2003. *City of Fears, City of Hopes*. London: Goldsmiths College, University of London.

Bell, D. and M. Jayne. 2006. *Small Cities: Urban Experience beyond the Metropolis*. London: Routledge.

Bennett, J.P. 1998. "Apple of the Empire: Landscape and Imperial Identity in Turn-of-the-Century British Columbia." *Journal of the Canadian Historical Association / Revue de la Société historique du Canada* 9 (1): 63–92.

Blake, L.A. 1998. "Oblate Missions and the Indian Land Question." *BC Studies* 119 (Autumn): 27–44.

Brenner, N., and C. Schmid. 2011. "Planetary Urbanization." In *Urban Constellations*, ed. M. Gandy, 10–13. Berlin: JOVIS Verlag.

British Columbia/Interior Health Authority (BC/IHA). 2012. *Interior Heart and Surgical Centre Moves Ahead*. Accessed June 8, 2018. https://news.gov.bc.ca/releases/2012HLTH0034-000440.

Brown, W. 2006. *Regulating Aversion: Tolerance in the Age of Identity and Empire*. Princeton, NJ: Princeton University Press.

Brydon, D. 2005. "Reading Postcoloniality, Reading Canada." In *Unhomely States: Theorizing English Canadian Postcoloniality*, ed. C. Sugars, 165–80. Peterborough, ON: Broadview Press.

Cronin, K. 1960. *Cross in the Wilderness*. Vancouver: Mitchell Press.

Davis, M. 2004. "The Urbanization of Empire: Megacities and the Laws of Chaos." *Social Text* 81, 22 (4): 9–15.

Dawson, A., and B.H. Edwards. 2004. "Global Cities of the South." *Social Text* 81, 22 (4): 1–7.

Derrida, J. 1993. *Aporias: Dying – Awaiting (One Another at) the "Limits of Truth."* Trans. Thomas Dutoit. Stanford: Stanford University Press.

Donald, J. 1992. "Metropolis: The City as Text." In *Social and Cultural Forms of Modernity*, ed. R. Bocock and K. Thompson, 417–61. Cambridge: Polity Press.

Florida, R. 2005. *Cities and the Creative Class*. New York and London: Routledge.

Freud, S. 2004. *Civilization and Its Discontents*. Trans. David McLintock. London: Penguin Books.

Harris, C. 1997. *The Resettlement of British Columbia: Essays on Colonialism and Geographical Change*. Vancouver: UBC Press.

Isin, E.F. 1992. *Cities without Citizens: The Modernity of the City as a Corporation*. Montreal: Black Rose Books.

–. 2002. *Being Political: Genealogies of Citizenship*. Minneapolis: University of Minnesota Press.

Jacobs, J. 1992. *The Death and Life of Great American Cities*. New York: Vintage Books.

Kataoka, S. 2009. "Vancouverism: Actualizing the Livable City Paradox." *Berkeley Planning Journal* 22 (1): 42–57.

Kataoka, S., and W. Magnusson. 2011. "Immigrant Settlement in British Columbia." In *Immigrant Settlement Policy in Canadian Municipalities*, ed. E. Tolley and R. Young, 241–94. Montreal and Kingston: McGill-Queen's University Press.

Kelowna Capital News (*KCN*). 2007. "Hill Climb a Throwback to the 1970s." Letters, 23 May. Accessed June 12, 2018. http://infoweb.newsbank.com.ezproxy.library.uvic.ca/iw-search/we/InfoWeb?p_product=AWNB&p_theme=aggregated5&p_action=doc&p_docid=11953B8429BD70A8&p_docnum=2&p_queryname=2.

–. 2008. "Hard to Embrace Something That's Not Here." Opinion-editorials, 17 February, C14. Accessed June 18, 2018. http://infoweb.newsbank.com.ezproxy.library.uvic.ca/iw-search/we/InfoWeb?p_product=AWNB&p_theme=aggregated5&p_action=doc&p_docid=11EE3BB60A12CBE0&p_docnum=7&p_queryname=1.

–. 2011. "Blame Crime on Urban Growth." Letters, 18 August. Accessed June 18, 2018. http://go.galegroup.com.ezproxy.library.uvic.ca/ps/i.do?id=GALE%7CA264596467&v=2.1&u=uvictoria&it=r&p=CPI&sw=w.

Kelowna. 2003. Pioneer Pavilion Historical Plaques, located at Knox Mountain. Dedicated by the City of Kelowna on July 14. Designed and produced by Quest for Success. Documentary photographs available from author on request.

–. 2008. *Welcome to Kelowna 2030: Greening Our Future.* Public Engagement Process Display Boards, 25 May. Accessed June 18, 2018. http://www.kelowna.ca/CityPage/Docs/PDFs//Community%20Planning/ kelowna2030/kelowna2030_OH1.pdf.

–. 2010. Council Meeting Minutes – 7 June. Accessed June 18, 2018. https://apps.kelowna.ca/citypage/docs/pdfs/Council/Meetings/Council%20Meetings%202010/2010-06-07/Minutes%20-%20June%207%20A.M.%20Regular%20Meeting.pdf.

–. 2011a. *Official Community Plan 2030: Greening Our Future.* Accessed June 18, 2018. https://apps.kelowna.ca/CityPage/Docs/PDFs/Bylaws/Official%20Community%20Plan%202030%20Bylaw%20No.%2010500/Official%20Community%20Plan%20-%20Full%20Bylaw.pdf?v=2CA72BDC45C455BB8944DE2A520FD77E.

–. 2011b. *Thriving, Engaging, Inspiring: 2012–2017 Cultural Plan.* Accessed June 18, 2018. https://www.kelowna.ca/sites/files/1/docs/community/culturalplan-web.pdf.

–. 2011c. *Your City. Your Voice. 2011 Annual Report.* Accessed June 18, 2018. https://www.yumpu.com/en/document/read/23802955/2011-annual-report-city-of-kelowna.

–. 2012. *My Downtown! – Downtown Plan.* Accessed June 18, 2018. https://www.kelowna.ca/sites/files/1/docs/2012-02-28_downtown_plan_report_final.pdf.

–. 2013. Council Meeting Minutes – January 14. Accessed June 18, 2018. https://apps.kelowna.ca/citypage/docs/pdfs/Council/Meetings/Council%20Meetings%202013/2013-01-14/Regular%20PM/Agenda%20Package%20-%20Regular%20PM%20Council%20Meeting_Jan14_2013.pdf.King, A.D. 1990. *Urbanism, Colonialism, and the World Economy: Cultural and Spatial Foundations of the World Urban System.* London: Routledge.

Kobayashi, A., and L. Peake. 2000. "Racism Out of Place: Thoughts on Whiteness and an Antiracist Geography in the New Millennium." *Annals of the Association of American Geographers* 90 (2): 392–403.

Koroscil, P.M. 2003. *The British Garden of Eden: Settlement History of the Okanagan Valley, British Columbia.* Burnaby: Department of Geography, Simon Fraser University.

Kowrach, E.J. 1992. *MIE. Charles Pandosy, O.M.I: A Missionary of the Northwest.* Fairfield, WA: Ye Galleon Press.

Lanthier, M., and L.L. Wong. n.d. "Ethnic Agricultural Labour in the Okanagan Valley: 1880s to 1960s." Accessed June 18, 2018. https://royalbcmuseum.bc.ca/exhibits/living-landscapes/thomp-ok/ethnic-agri/index.html.

Lees, L. 2004. "The Emancipatory City: Urban (Re)visions." In *The Emancipatory City? Paradoxes and Possibilities*, ed. Loretta Lees. 3–20. London: Sage.

Liman, G. 2010. "Westbank First Nation Letter of Support: Father Pandosy Mission 150th Anniversary Commemorative Sculpture." https://sites.google.com/site/pandosysculpture/letters-of-support/westbank-first-nation.

Magnusson, W. 2011. *Politics of Urbanism: Seeing Like a City*. London: Routledge.

Massey, D. 2006. *For Space*. Los Angeles: Sage.

Michaels, K. 2010a. "Cultural Concepts Thrashed Out." *Kelowna Capital News*, 2 December, A13.

–. 2010b. "Kelowna's Demographic Winter Predicted to Stay Awhile." Kelowna.com, 18 March. Accessed June 18, 2018 http://www.kelowna.com/2010/03/18/kelownas-demographic-winter-predicted-to-stay-awhile/.

–. 2012. "Census Shows Little Language Diversity in Kelowna." *Kelowna Capital News*, 25 October, A3.

Mill, J.S. 1991. "Considerations on Representative Government." In *On Liberty and Other Essays*, 203–467. Oxford: Oxford University Press.

Mumford, L. 1938. *The Culture of Cities*. San Diego: Harcourt Brace.

Murphy, M. 2009. "Civilization, Self-Determination, and Reconciliation." In *First Nations First Thoughts: The Impact of Indigenous Thought in Canada*, ed. A.M. Timpson, 251–78. Vancouver: UBC Press.

Okanagan Nation Alliance. 2019a. *Syilx Okanagan Nation Alliance – About Us*. https://www.syilx.org/about-us/.

–. 2019b. *Syilx Okanagan Nation Alliance – About Indian Residential Schools*. https://www.syilx.org/wellness/indian-residential-school/about-indian-residential-schools/.

–. 2021. *News – Spirit of Syilx Unity Run Makes an Emotional Journey to Kamloops Indian Residential School*. https://www.syilx.org/okanagan-nations-spirit-of-syilx-unity-run-makes-emotional-journey-to-kamloops-indian-residential-school-to-recognize-all-children-that-never-returned-home/

Przybille, C. 2011. "Crystal Przybille: Realizing a Dream." Interview. *Okanagan Art Works* 3 (2): 88–93.

–. 2012. "Father Pandosy Mission 150th Anniversary Commemorative Sculpture." https://sites.google.com/site/pandosysculpture/.

Robinson, J. 2006. *Ordinary Cities: Between Modernity and Development*. London: Routledge.

Rotary Centre for the Arts (RCA). n.d. http://www.rotarycentreforthearts.com/about/aboutus.html.

Roy, P.E. 1981. "British Columbia's Fear of Asians, 1900–1950." In *British Columbia: Historical Readings*, ed. W.P. Ward and R.A.J. McDonald, 657–70. Vancouver: Douglas & McIntyre Ltd.

Salter, M.B. 2002. *Barbarians and Civilization in International Relations*. London: Pluto Press.

Sassen, S. 1994. *Cities in a World Economy*. Thousand Oaks, CA: Pine Forge Press.

Satzewich, V. 2007. "Whiteness Studies: Race, Diversity, and the New Essentialism." In *Race and Racism in 21st-Century Canada: Continuity, Complexity, and Change*, ed. Sean P. Hier and B. Singh Bolaria, 67–84. Peterborough, ON: Broadview Press.

Sennett, R. 1970. *The Uses of Disorder: Personal Identity and City Life*. New York: Alfred A. Knopf.

Shaw, W.S. 2007. *Cities of Whiteness*. Malden, MA: Blackwell Publishing.

Simmel, G. 1969. "The Metropolis and Mental Life." In *Classic Essays on the Culture of Cities*, ed. Richard Sennett, 47–60. New York: Appleton Century Crofts.

Simmons, J., and L. McCann. 2006. "The Canadian Urban System: Growth and Transition." In *Canadian Cities in Transition: Local through Global Perspectives*, ed. Trudi Bunting and P. Filion, 40–64 . 3rd ed. Don Mills ON: Oxford University Press.

Shields. R. 1996. "Alternative Traditions of Urban Theory." In *Re-presenting the City: Ethnicity, Capital and Culture in the 21st Century Metropolis*, ed. Anthony D. King, 227–52. London: Macmillan.

Squire, J.P. 2012. "Father Pandosy Statue Unveiled at Mission Site." *Kelowna Daily Courier*, 27 May. Accessed June 18, 2018. http://www.kelownadailycourier.ca/news/article_0e82fc25-e10c-5d50–8b26–7ffe77d2bcd0.html?mode=jqm.

–. 2013. "New $68-million Building is Biggest One yet at UBCO." *Kelowna Daily Courier*, 31 January. Accessed June 18, 2018. http://www.kelownadailycourier.ca/front-page-news/new-$68-million-building-is-biggest-one-yet-at-ubco-2113.html.

Steyn, D. 2008. *The Changing Face of Kelowna: Are We Ready?* Kelowna: Intercultural Society of the Central Okanagan/Canadian Heritage.

Tedesco, D. 2012a. "Politicizing Urbanization: The Sustainable City Ideal in Kelowna, British Columbia." *Zeitschrift für Kanada-Studien* 32 (2): 84–106.

–. 2012b. "The Urbanization of Politics: Relational Ontologies or Aporetic Practices?" *Alternatives: Global, Local, Political* 37 (4): 331–47.

Teixeira, C. 2009. "New Immigrant Settlement in a Mid-Sized City: a Case Study of Housing Barriers and Coping Strategies in Kelowna, British Columbia." *Canadian Geographer / Le Geographe canadien* 53 (3): 323–39.

Waters, A. 2012. "Father Pandosy Sculpture Set for Kelowna's Pandosy Mission Site." *Kelowna Capital News*, 30 April. Accessed June 18, 2018. http://www.kelownacapnews.com/news/149581035.html?mobile=true.

Westbank First Nation (WFN). 2018. http://www.wfn.ca/.

Wirth, L. 1969. "Urbanism as a Way of Life." In *Classic Essays on the Culture of Cities*, ed. Richard Sennett, 143–64. New York: Appleton Century Crofts.

CHAPTER 12

THE IMAGINARY OF OKANAGAN REDNECK WHITENESS

A Sketch

Stephen Svenson

> *Odysseus now awoke from sleep on his native soil. After so long an absence, he failed to recognize it ... everything in Ithaca, the long hill-paths, the welcoming bays, the beetling rocks and the leafy trees, seemed unfamiliar. He leapt to his feet and stood staring at his native land. Then he groaned, and slapping his thighs with his hands cried out in dismay: "Oh no! Whose country have I come to this time? Are they some brutal tribe of uncivilized savages, or a kindly and god-fearing people?"*
>
> (HOMER – *THE ODYSSEY*)

The story of Odysseus can be the story of any person who returns home to find the place *strange*. My experience of being a "home-comer" (see Schuetz 1945) to the Okanagan Valley bears some resemblance to the tale told of Odysseus, who, after being placed sleeping on the shores of his home of Ithaca, awakes disoriented, the landscape cloaked in a fog that makes it unhomely to him. For me it is the culture of the Okanagan, not the landscape, that appears unhomely, uncanny. In both situations, both actors are out of place. Just as Athena disguises Odysseus as an old man to protect him from the people of Ithaca so that he may become "wise to things," I wear my own self-imposed disguise when I return "home": the version of myself that at times seems more cliché than real, my "redneck" persona. It allows me to navigate the strange and disorienting culture that once seemed as natural and familiar to me as the mountain trails I hiked; the fields, forests, and pastures that I hunted; and the sapphire lakes I fished. The fog in the story of my homecoming doesn't cover the natural landscape; it covers the cultural landscape, and the fog, unlike the fog of the story of Odysseus, is not meant to protect the homecomer but the native. This fog is "whiteness." Okanagan culture can often seem covered over by a white cloak of fog that provides residents with a sense of security and purpose, a cloak of white fantasies.

It wasn't until I had spent time away from the Okanagan for extended periods that I began to perceive the fog. The first time I perceived it was after I returned from a backpacking trip to New Zealand and Australia. Then, I experienced the fog as mild culture shock but nothing drastic as one of the reasons that I had chosen Australia in particular to travel to was the redneck fantasy it afforded. Yes, I *had* been induced to travel in part by the comfortably sexist, racist, homophobic, and transphobic film *Crocodile Dundee* (Buckmaster 2018). The time I returned after teaching English in Japan, though, it was much worse. I knew that Kansas had forever gone "bye-bye" when a friend tried to jokingly provoke me, using the harsh racist and sexist way of speaking to each other that was typical: "So how do you like fucking slopes?"

Each time I returned to the Okanagan, I understood a little more just what the fog was. I slowly realized just how embedded in the culture were racist, xenophobic, sexist, homophobic, and transphobic ideas. The development of my sociological imagination abroad, and then at university, began to allow me to make sense of what I was experiencing. My friendships with racialized others allowed me to vicariously experience the racism of the Okanagan, a racism in which I had formerly participated. One of my last experiences of racism before leaving the Okanagan for school in Ontario happened in the late 1990s. My friend Paul, a Sikh Canadian, and I went out with our girlfriends to Flashback's night club in Kelowna. We were having a great time rocking out on the dance floor to AC/DC's headbanging anthem "Thunderstruck," screaming out with everyone else the refrain "Thunder." The scene turned ugly very quickly as a young white couple dancing next to Paul and I turned towards us and began chanting "PAKI." We were escorted out of the bar by the bouncers after I "communicated" my displeasure to the couple. For Paul, it was not the first time that he had experienced harassment in a whitespace – and he chided me for making a scene.

I returned to the Okanagan in the fall of 2012 to teach at the University of British Columbia Okanagan (UBCO) after living in southern Ontario since the late 1990s. Kelowna's spaces hadn't changed much. There were now more strip malls along the highway going north to Vernon, but the demographic was still largely snow white, far from the multicultural cosmopolitan centre that some of its citizens may want to imagine it to be. The aspiring cosmopolitan university with its large residences on the outskirts of the city, where the shops ended, remained a slightly more diverse intellectual enclave, while the region's tourism brochures promoted Kelowna and the surrounding area as "shimmering white" (Aguiar and Marten 2011, 127). The population of the city's pubs and bars hadn't seemed to change either. I found them to be shockingly white, in contrast to my usual haunts in Kitchener-Waterloo. At a Kelowna Rockets hockey game in February 2012, with new friends from a working-class background, I related the story of my experience at Flashback's Nightclub many years ago. One friend's reply was a dismissive, "Hell, you see a lot of Pakis in there these days."

I decided to write for this volume after a piece in the digital *New York Times* landed in my inbox on 6 August 2012. The article concerned the shooting of six people at a Sikh temple in Wisconsin a day earlier. The shooter had deep ties to the white supremacist movement. He was described by officials as "a frustrated neo-Nazi who had been the leader of a racist white-power band ... in the thick of the white supremacist music scene, played with some of the best known racist bands in the country, [performing] incredibly violent [sets] about murdering Jews, black people, gay people and a whole host of other enemies" (Yaccino, Schwritz, and Santora 2012).

This Wisconsin story brought memories of the "redneck whiteness" I see cloaking the Okanagan to the fore of my consciousness: expressions of paranoia, fear, frustration, and white entitlement; a white working class that targets Sikh, Indigenous, and now Muslim populations with racist acts; a place where white supremacy is often expressed emotively and sometimes acted out violently against an imagined enemy. My intention here is not to tar all white Okanaganites or working-class people with the same brush but, rather, to indicate some of the problematic phenomena that the cloak of "redneck whiteness" hides. As the Oak Creek Wisconsin incident highlights, "white labour does not receive and resist racist ideas, but embraces adopts and, at times, murderously acts on those ideas. The problem is not just that the white working class is at critical junctures manipulated into racism, but that it comes to think of itself and its interests as white" (Roediger 1991, 5). Racial violence does not occur in a vacuum: it emerges from the fantasies that circulate in a culture, and so it is the culture and these fantasies about self and other that must be addressed.

The introduction to this volume asks: "How is the racialization of place sustained? How is whiteness secured today?" Part of the answer lies in the language practices and racial imaginings inherent in the Okanagan life-world, where a racially defined identity and imagined community is constructed and, crucially, sustained by practices and imaginings that speak to a need to belong. The sharing of slurs, jokes, adages, aphorisms, clichés, and stories (read: strategies, formulas, and attitudes) emerge as responses to this need and constitute "equipment for living" (Burke 1973). In the context of the Okanagan, these strategies, formulas, and attitudes have become colonized by a racialized discourse that limits our ability to reflectively engage our investment in the oppressive fog of white supremacy, a fog that keeps us from realizing our basic solidarity as human beings.

In this chapter, I use my ambivalent relation to the Okanagan as "home" as a resource to examine how white Okanagan Valley dwellers construct an image of themselves by grotesquely stereotyping non-whites. Schuetz's (1945) "homecomer type" is useful as an intervention here as homecomers are at some distance from their "home culture." These homecomers experience culture shock upon their return, where the once familiar has become strange, an aporia or puzzle. The figure of the homecomer also resonates with the research practice of autoethnography, which I employ to cultivate a distance from a culture that I am close to, allowing me to act as both interpreter and critic (Maréchal 2010). My membership in this culture is affirmed through a capacity to engage in shared practices (e.g., hunting and fishing) and shared language that take shape in the form of stories, jokes, and ideas about self and others. This cultural milieu is primarily working-class, male, and rural, and the discursive and social practices aggregate as "redneck whiteness" (O'Connell 2010). For the archetypal Okanagan "redneck," taken-for-granted understandings provide a source of identity, community, and accounts of difference. It is the social imaginary of the rural white working-class Okanagan Valley dweller with which I am familiar and that I will unfold here – a lifeworld that, while haunted by the spectre of white supremacy, is also structured by an emphasis on family, religion, hard work, and play.

In unfolding the imaginary of Okanagan redneck whiteness, I first locate myself, attempting to show reflexively how one is formed with regard to white rural Okanagan Valley culture, or how whiteness is accomplished as an everyday practical activity (Turner 1974). I detail my own lived experience of inhabiting the racialized environment of the Okanagan, demonstrating how racist discursive and social practices have a certain form and content, and function in particular ways to reinforce perceived differences that help legitimate white supremacy. Further, I analyze the rhetorical function of redneck talk, considering it a magic cloak that the Okanagan redneck dons in order to deflect deep fears and anxieties. I show how my own experience of Okanagan "redneck whiteness" relates to the political culture of the Okanagan, a culture that scapegoats non-whites as a solution to these collective fears and anxieties.

GROWING UP IN "ITHACA"

My feelings about the Okanagan are saturated with ambivalence, reflecting in part the conflict between the Okanagan's image as paradise and the real conditions of its social inequities and (especially working-class) struggles to make a living. Descriptions and images of the Okanagan's beauty, which one might find in a tourist brochure, evoke the civilized landscape and culture of ancient Ithaca described by Homer – a paradise. However, when we move beyond this postcard-perfect view of the valley to the "facts of life," the landscape becomes less welcoming. Homer's (2003, 174) "brutal tribe of uncivilized savages, or a kindly and god-fearing people," describes a tension in the redneck imaginary. Growing up, I learned how to be brutal and how to be civilized (kindly and god-fearing). The latter tendency was best represented in the figure of my paternal grandmother, the daughter of an Anglican minister and nurse. Born in China to missionary parents, her family left China for Vancouver in the wake of the Boxer Rebellion, a violent anti-foreign, anti-colonial, and anti-Christian uprising directed at imperial Britain's presence in China. Many missionaries and Chinese Christians were killed, the pacification of the "Indigenous" people having failed miserably in contrast to the "success" experienced by Britain and its missionaries in western Canada. A disciplined relationship to work and to the land was embodied in my paternal grandfather, the son a Swedish fisher turned Montana cowboy and a British nanny.

After my grandparents married, they moved to Tappen, BC, and then to Armstrong in the North Okanagan to try their hand at farming. For my grandparents that meant a small herd of jersey cows on the N1/2 of the NW1/4 of Section 12 just north of Armstrong in Spallumcheen Township (Svenson 1982). They struggled for most of their lives to make a living from farming until my grandfather, in his forties, tried his hand at real estate. His knowledge of farming and brusque "no-bullshit" working man's attitude served him well with people looking for farms and, later, recreational properties.

As a child, I lived in trailer parks in Penticton, Rutland, and Vernon, and then in a house on one acre in Lavington near the town of Lumby, BC, before my electrician father and homemaker mother bought some land from my grandparents. It was there we built a house and lived what I remember as a mostly idyllic existence, with my grandparents just a short hurdle of hay bales across the field. My mother and grandmother cultivated the "civilized" virtues of kindness, love of learning, cosmopolitanism, and, above all, *grace*, while my father and grandfather instilled the "manly" virtues of hard work, mental and physical toughness, and self-reliance through showing me how to work the soil and how to kill and process fish and game. We had a close relationship with the land, with family gatherings often focused on harvesting and processing food we had grown, foraged, hunted, fished, or purchased from our neighbours. I was to come to love the piece of land I lived on, publishing an article on the land's history in the *Okanagan Historical Society Journal* (Svenson 1982). I reread the piece recently and noted that there was no mention of Indigenous use of the area, even though my grandfather had found numerous arrowheads around the property's spring where people would have no doubt hunted for game. In my account of the history of the land, I was, in my "obliviocy," able to unproblematically exclude any mention of the people to whom the land originally and rightly belongs – the Splatsin or "Spallumcheen," the southernmost tribe of the Secwépemc (Shuswap Nation).

Most work activities had a gendered dimension, with the "men" heading out into the bush to drop snags to cut up for firewood while the women canned or baked. I recall blissful afternoons spent shelling peas on my grandparents' back deck, processing applesauce in the carport, or smashing through mountains of firewood with a splitting maul. Much of our leisure time was spent watching or playing hockey, fishing and hunting, playing in the field, or playing card and board games. We followed the Okanagan ethic of "work hard, play hard," identified by Aguiar, Tomic, and Trumper (2005) to a T.

When the 1980s recession and divorce hit my family, I became the "man" of the house. My farm boy physicality got put to use tilling and tending the large garden we relied on for much of our food, ensuring we had firewood for heating the house, and doing minor repairs. I carried flats of dirt around nearby Mariposa Greenhouses for extra money. My hardening attitude was put to the test dealing with the harsh realities of farm life, from putting down chickens that needed to be killed after being injured by a neighbour's dog to having to scrape up and bury the occasional farm cat that had been creamed by some truck. My identity as rural working-class male was forming, conditioned by my relationship to the land. This identity was also increasingly being conditioned by something else: the civilized brutality of farm life was increasingly integrated with the uncivil brutality of racism, sexism, and homophobia and its connection to an identity that relied unreflectively on the power and privilege that come with being a white heterosexual male. I had been raised with the maternal tools to resist brutal racist ideas and attitudes, but the toxically masculine culture to which I was increasingly exposed required me to play a more decidedly savage role.

WHITE FANTASIES: "COWBOYS, PAKIS, AND INDIANS" AT THE FRONTIER

As kids, one of our favourite role-playing games was "cowboys and Indians." Growing up in a rural area, with a landscape that had terrain elements that reminded us of some of the western movies we'd watched, lent the whole play fantasy a kind of realism. It was good fun. Through these games we internalized ideas of friends and enemies: insiders and outsiders. In dramatizing cowboys (ourselves) versus Indians (the other) we experienced that sense of purpose that can arise from a struggle against the other, the obstacle that (according to the story of the game) needed to be overcome or tamed. The played out cowboy-versus-Indian story stood both with and in contrast to the "redneck" myth of the Indians we encountered in everyday life: those allegedly overcome by their own laziness and love of alcohol. In both instances (child's play/redneck myth) the culture of the Original People appears as something to be ridiculed through play (as acting, as sarcasm) (see Keyes 2011). In both cases they remained the "other," they became the enemy of how to live. The cowboy/Indian imaginary allowed an unproblematic acceptance of the picture of "lazy and drunken Indians," a group to be more pitied than feared. What we knew about self and other was based on the ideology of a white supremacy closely tied to a frontier mentality.

This frontier mentality was reinforced by our almost daily encounter with the land, by practices of fishing and hunting, the collecting of firewood off Crown land, and of being able to play and freely wander through the landscape. There were few places that we couldn't go and that we didn't go. The local reserve was the only place that seemed off limits. With no desire to go there, the closest I ever got to putting foot on the reserve was the bus stop where the "Indian" kids got picked up.

I rode the bus with Frances, the FBI (Fucking Big Indian) as he was also known. He always sat at the back of the bus with the other kids from the reserve, often next to his cousin, whom white kids at the school had dubbed "Arrowhead." I remembered glimpses of Arrowhead's high school experience – on those rare occasions that he came to social studies class (the period before class started was always a time of play), he would have textbooks thrown at the back of his head. I remember in that same class, learning about the Indians but learning little about the reserve or residential school system and nothing about the damage that was done to the Original Peoples of this land because of these legacies of colonialism. Our "redneck education" took place both inside and outside the classroom.

Our parents drove us from Armstrong to Enderby to play hockey, where, as we passed through the Spallumcheen reserve observing the "run-down" houses and "ill-kempt" yards, we were taught about the parasitic nature of the "lazy and drunken Indian." As teens with our own wheels on our way through Enderby to do some paddling or swimming in the Shuswap River, we'd make the drive more amusing by trying to spot "No Legs" in his wheelchair. He was an Indian who, so the story went, had passed out on the railway tracks and lost his legs to a train. I shared the "No Legs" account recently with a friend I grew up with and his response was "Fuck man ... that's so true. Enderby was all about spot the legless Indian." General Herman's adage "the only good Indian is a dead Indian," which I often heard growing up, was reinforced with an added heaviness when a man from the local reserve passed out on a crest of Knob Hill Road below our house late one night and was run over by several vehicles and killed. People joked that it was "population control." Being oblivious to our part in alienating them, it appeared to us that "Indians" wanted to keep to themselves. As teens, the only time we had any issues with "them" was when we had to play hockey against a particularly rough "chug" team from Kamloops and we tried to avoid being "scalped," a reference to the way they used their hockey sticks. To Frances's credit, he pursued basketball and played for the high school basketball team, showing his courage in the face of racism and earning our respect. As for the "Pakis," they only presented us with a problem when we played the town of Merritt in basketball, and we had to check "stinky ragheads."

It wasn't until the late 1980s and early 1990s that "Pakis and Indians" became a "problem," a problem that threatened a "Canadian" way of life. The perception that "Pakis and Indians" posed a real threat to a white Canadian heritage manifested itself in reactions of suspicion and fear. "Pakis," for example, had begun to assert themselves beyond the basketball court. An echo of the current racist idiocy over the place of the *niqab* and *hijab* in Canadian culture, one reaction to the "threat" posed by Sikhs was the turban ban in Legions in Sparwood and Elkford in the 1990s (Swardson 1994) Canadians were angered by Sikhs who claimed their religious right to wear turbans and the symbolic kirpan while in an RCMP uniform (Ryan 2010). In rural and primary industry areas, fear and racism were fuelled by the fact that many Sikhs were working in the forest industry, particularly in sawmills, where, through collective entrepreneurship, they had secured ownership of several sawmills and were in direct competition for jobs with working-class white people (Johnston 1999).

At the same time this was occurring, "Indians" were beginning to "make noise," the Oka crisis in Quebec being the most obvious expression of rising dissent. In response to the changing legal landscape, the government of BC agreed to meet and discuss land claim issues with both the government of Canada and BC's Indigenous Peoples. Pub, coffee shop, and kitchen table talk often revolved around fears that white people were going to "lose *our* land" to the Indian. Often I heard the nauseating refrain, "the only thing we did wrong with the Indians was that we didn't finish the job."

Our parents' concerns gradually began to be reflected in our own political attitudes in an overt way. Our Grade 11 social studies mock Parliament exercise was fraught with racist overtones. The raucous and carnivalesque mock Parliament was true to its moniker. One of the bills tabled for debate by my friend the "Minister of Immigration" was to have all interior Indians "deported" to an island off the BC coast. His joking suggestion was an expression of what we had been informally taught for years: Indians were not citizens, not "true Canadians."

WHITE FANTASIES AND THE SOCIAL IMAGINARY

Thus far I have followed Ghassan Hage's (2000, 11) approach to working with white fantasies, an approach that privileges "the ethical importance of the intellectual art of listening and understanding even to the most unsavory views." As my tone thus far has no doubt indicated, I have not and will not pull any punches as I, like Hage, am tired of "worried whites." In furthering this analysis, I emphasize historical understanding, linking racial discourses and practices to a Western European social imaginary (Taylor 2004). The social imaginary of Okanagan redneck whiteness grows out of this Western social imaginary, a Euro-Canadian culture that is inflected by racial fantasies oriented by the ideology of white supremacy (Aguiar, Tomic, and Trumper 2005).

Our modern Western social imaginary is the product of a *disembedding* (Giddens 1990; Taylor 2004), a transformation beginning in medieval Europe that recast the social order, our relation to the cosmos, and our notions of human good. This disembedding, a legacy of modernity, has had profound implications for both the individual and society. While humans have been set free from the "shackles" of an old order, we are now tasked with the twin projects of identity and community (Taylor 2004, 62). Berger, Berger, and Kellner (1973, 196) aptly describe the unintended consequences of modernity as "homelessness," a homelessness that we seek to resolve in myriad ways. The narratives we embrace (myths, legends, stories) as a source of comfort are symptoms of our deep need to re-embed ourselves and are acted out in practices that reinforce feelings of belonging and community. In the context of the Okanagan Valley, redneck whiteness is part of the imaginary that allows people to re-embed themselves in a meaningful social order, a distorted aspiration for paradise anchored in the idea of race, where a sense of entitlement comes with the fantasy of a white supremacy stoked by threats to economic security and feelings of marginalization.

The fantasy of white supremacy is intimately linked to our Western modern social imaginary in that it provides a normative order that gives sense to white existence. When that supremacy is threatened, there is always the potential for scapegoating violence. It is in our times of leisure, in our leisure imaginary, that we most often can catch a glimpse of the potential of this violence, where in communal spaces such as festivals, sports events, dancing at a club, or participating in an online forum, attitudes are revealed, communities imagined, and occasionally violence erupts (Svenson 2015). Fantasies are present in jokes, myths, clichés, and so on, and comprise the affective and rhetorical structure of Okanagan redneck whiteness. In this section, I attempt to understand the fantasy structure that underlies the communal imagining of the Okanagan redneck – a communal imagining that engages in racial othering through employing white fantasies, fantasies that act as a kind of magic cloak for a delusional redneck Odysseus yet to leave his Ithaca.

Okanagan redneck whiteness relies on particular notions of a racialized self and others built on legends, myths, jokes, clichés, adages, and aphorisms. These speech acts, which we can broadly collect as stories because of their narrative structure, are, in Bormann's (1985, 5) terms, fantasies: the "creative and imaginative interpretation of events that fulfills a psychological or rhetorical need." This "equipment for living," this "magical cloak of redneck whiteness," provides the rhetorical resources, or strategies, that are used for dealing with concrete life situations (Burke 1973, 296–97). The practice of sharing these common fantasies or rhetorical resources transforms a collection of individuals into a cohesive group. Racist jokes and humour, the cliché of the redneck, and the frontier myth provide the fantasy structure for Okanagan redneck whiteness, its white supremacist social imaginary.

THE FRONTIER MYTH

The social imaginary is pre-given, existing before theoretical reflection, where action emerges from a shared consciousness of the social, the "intersubjectively shared lifeworld" (Habermas 1996, 322). This shared consciousness of the social is carried in the "way ordinary people 'imagine' their social surroundings and legitimate social practices, and is carried in images, stories legends, etc." (Taylor 2004, 172). Key here is that the social imaginary (1) is carried in stories, myths and legends, and (2) that it legitimates and makes possible common practices, including noxious racist ones.

The frontier mentality I discussed earlier is in dialogue with the frontier myth or narrative, the dominant myth that shapes the self-understandings and the social imaginary of Okanagan rednecks. It acts as a historical epistemology: "a way of knowing about history that provides a certain set of rules and assumptions that guide how 'truths' about the past, and by extension the present are to be created, understood, and conveyed" (Furniss 1999, 17). It is the story that many white settlers tell themselves about their relation to the land, a constituent element of white identity and white supremacy in the Okanagan. Furniss notes that "the idea of the frontier is ... evident in the way that Euro-Canadians construct a regional identity as a 'small town' on the periphery of mainstream society, a town surrounded by a natural wilderness offering an abundance of natural resources that are unowned and 'free' for the taking" (18). Furniss's description aptly captures the understanding of the Okanagan as a "playground" and place of abundance for whites, a paradise.

In my earlier account of growing up, I described how my life in the Okanagan was closely tied to my relationship to the land, where natural resources were imagined to be "free" for the taking. This is a widely shared sentiment reinforced by the frontier myth. This sense of entitlement has come increasingly under threat. In the redneck Okanagan, issues around gun control, environmental policy, immigration, and, in particular, Indigenous land claims, threaten this sense of entitlement and elicit strong reactions. For white settlers, paradise is under siege. Stories like "Indians are destroying the salmon fishery" are repeated in working-class white circles and are often reinforced in the BC media, setting whites against First Peoples (see, especially, Harding 2005, 2006; and Wilkes, Guppy, and Farris 2008). This contributes to white settlers conceiving of their relationship with Original Peoples in a binary manner, whereby "the categories of Indian and white are mutually exclusive and oppositional and in which Euro-Canadian cultural superiority, material privileges, and political authority are taken as unquestioned truths" (Furniss 1999, 18). O'Connell (2010, 538) observes that, in the frontier narrative, "the more 'homogenous' composition of rural areas re-enacts myths of white-European settlers as the natural and original inhabitants of the Canadian nation." This myth is so pervasive that we "naturally" forget that white settlers were not the first people in North America. I myself did this when working as a cultural assistant for Selkirk College. I had organized a campfire for new international students on the shores of Arrow Lake one evening, and as the fire crackled I noted to my newcomer friends that this was perhaps the first time they had had a real Canadian experience and, referring to myself, had "hung out" with a *true* Canadian. My friend George, a Nisga'a, who had accompanied us, quickly corrected me, "Hey man, I'm the true Canadian here." The response to Indigenous land claims displays the tenacity of the frontier myth. Statements like "the only thing we did wrong with the Indians is that we didn't finish the job," and mock solutions to the Indian "problem," such as having "all interior Indians *deported* to an island off the BC coast," demonstrate the complete sense of entitlement and lack of historical understanding that flow from the frontier narrative as a constituent element of Okanagan redneck whiteness.

RACIST JOKES AND HUMOUR

In the context of Okanagan redneck whiteness, the anxiety produced by the "uncanny" presence of the "Indian" or "Paki" is sublimated through jokes and humour. However, in addition to a coming to terms with the uncanny, these jokes also imply a "sly and malicious mischief" (Seshadri-Crooks 2000, 83). In the case of the Indigenous man tragically killed on the road beneath my childhood home, joking responses cordoned off the horror of the death as something that happened to and was perhaps reserved for "Indians." Seshadri-Crooks notes that racist jokes operate to enforce social boundaries and "usually emerge at the cusp of the inside and outside insofar as they seek to treat citizens as foreigners" (92). In the context of Okanagan redneck whiteness, racist jokes and humour work to delegitimize First Nations and Indo Canadian claims to equal treatment as citizens (a bill proposed in a high school mock Parliament session to deport Indians) and by dehumanizing them (referring to the tragic death of another human being as "population control"). This ongoing brutal caricaturization and delegitimization establishes the otherness of racialized groups and sets the stage for scapegoating violence. The adoption of a heroic "redneck" identity covers over this latent racism.

THE "REDNECK" AND THE POWER OF THE CLICHÉ

O'Connell (2010) argues that the term "redneck" has undergone a kind of renewal and a corresponding reversal. Once a component of a pollution ideology that served to separate working- and middle-class whites, the redneck identity is now celebrated in part due to its prevalence in popular culture. In the Canadian context, O'Connell writes:

> The redneck and its association with rural communities as a backward landscape and special source of racism no longer apply. Shame has shifted to celebration. In some cases, the redneck is cast as a minority identity and one injured by economic suffering, isolation, exclusion, and more specifically, marginality. The transformation of an earlier pejorative term into one that proudly expresses an identity, redneck is now used as a source of pride (547)

In the American context, Jarosz and Lawson (2002) argue that "rednecks" are a marginalized essentialized group, a cliché that acts as a foil for white liberal middle-class guilt. In the Canadian context, however, where the association with racism and poverty is de-emphasized, there are attempts to essentialize the redneck in a different way. Whites often try to capitalize on the positive aspects of that identity, without perhaps reflecting on the imaginary that underlies it and sustains the power of whiteness. For example, a high school friend currently has a band called the Redneck Rebels. I myself was pleased when one of the editors of this volume referred to me as a "redneck academic" in comments on an earlier draft of this chapter. The redneck that I identify with, in addition to being politically incorrect and a person of honour, embraces values of "hard work, practicality, and tenacity with little time for complaint or delay" best captured in the redneck phrase "Git-R Done" (O'Connell 2010, 552, 549). This identification allows the shame once associated with the label of "redneck" to be transformed into pride while bestowing a viable identity and imagined community. "Redneck pride" was put on display at a 2013 Okanagan festival. The town of Lumby in the North Okanagan themed its annual festival "High-Tech Redneck" (Knox 2013).

The term "redneck" has now, to a degree, become identified with a lifestyle that has been somewhat decontextualized from place, history, and class (Jarosz and Lawson 2002, 16). This demonstrates the term's appeal for helping to define a white identity, a free-floating signifier of white pride that is more global and perhaps more telling of a general sentiment or imaginary that transcends class and provides a vision of the future for worried whites. In the case of Lumby Days, a utopian vision is presented in which technology and redneckism go hand in hand in the pursuit of this future. This positive notion of the redneck as community strategy masks the insecurity that many whites feel in the new era of neoliberal globalization, where there is a sense of their being victimized by forces outside their control. The popular culture representation of the redneck captured in Lumby Days' high-tech redneck theme resonates with the notion of "class as a lifestyle, rather than on underlying political economic processes of changing opportunities and displacements," and references the notion that "all who work hard and move with the technological and consumptionist times can be successful and upwardly mobile" (Watkins in Jarosz and Lawson 2002, 14). Neoliberal globalization does not concern itself with "losers" and "whiners." It speaks of entrepreneurship, creativity, leadership, and winners who all fit snugly into the redneck white fantasy of the high-tech redneck theme.

The cliché of the high-tech redneck confers special status and provides a strategy of enhancement by linking the hard work and tenacity of the redneck to the promise of technology. The danger of any cliché as an element of ideology is that an actor absorbed in it can lose his capacity to reflect; the individual disappears because he is not oriented to anything other and is instead caught up in the flow. This has implications for society, "where society is marked by the absence of 'reflection,' of a perspective on itself" (Baudrillard in Blum 2010, 24). Hannah Arendt (1963) famously describes the danger of the unthought relation of society to itself, which comes with being submerged in an ideology (in this case, white supremacy), as the "banality of evil." In this context, the adoption of a clichéd redneck identity would appear to mask, excuse, and legitimize racist behaviour as part of a desirable "lifestyle."

THE FANTASY OF A WHITE PARADISE

As Berger, Berger, and Kellner (1973), Giddens (1990), and Taylor (2004) note, we now live in an age in which our meaning structures have become compromised. The unintended consequences of modernity, the homelessness and/or disembedding that have been described, elicit a reaction, one that can be discerned in social movements and ideologies that are oriented to repairing or rebuilding identity and community, to reclaiming or rebuilding "home." The version of home at stake for the Okanagan redneck is a white paradise, animated by a nostalgic yearning for an imagined past where whites were all powerful and unchallenged. This is an example of Berger, Berger, and Kellner's (1973, 195–96) *demodernizing impulse*, "which seeks a reversal of the modern trends that have left the individual feeling 'alienated' and beset with the threats of meaninglessness."

A recent example of the future-past orientation of the demodernizing impulse is captured in debate around the Idle No More movement. Postings about the Idle No More movement on my Facebook wall outline what's at stake in these contradictory attempts to reclaim "home." For sympathetic settlers the Idle No More movement captured the imagination, no doubt primed by the popular mythologies inherent in the films *Avatar* and *Fern*

Gully, and appeared to create an opportunity for solidarity across racial and economic lines by linking visions of a sustainable future to First Peoples' land ethic and spirituality. In contrast to the frontier narrative embraced by redneck whites, which orients towards a mythological past of white supremacy, a sympathetic settler reading of the Idle No More movement is that it offers a competing account of white settlement in Canada as one in which there was much more collaboration and mixing between Natives and settlers (see Saul 2008) and a vision of the future in which settlers and the Original Peoples of Canada collaborate, standing on an equal footing. The danger of this reading is that it hides within it a settler move to innocence, whereby settler guilt and complicity is overridden by a narrative that rescues settler futurity through a weak notion of allyship (Tuck and Yang 2012).

The redneck response to the Idle No More movement's forward-looking utopian aspirations invokes the backward-looking frontier narrative in the pursuit of paradise. Okanagan rednecks see the Idle No More movement and "Indians" as parasitic on Canadian life, the redneck narrative of "I work for my money and don't take government handouts" proclaimed loud and strong against a characterization of "Indians" as lazy and dependent. If I challenge redneck whiteness, I get lumped in with "Indians" as a parasite: "Have you ever made a living except from the taxpayer, Stephen? Just curios [sic]." Or, I am reminded of how my shared "white" heritage is one in which our "settler" grandparents came to the Okanagan Valley "without anything" and worked hard to build a life. This is contrasted with "Indians" who just "sit on their asses and expect to have everything handed to them," where all they do is "bitch and complain" and where white rights as "True Canadians" get trampled on by "Native rights." Idle No More can be imagined to create solidarity between settler and Native, while Okanagan redneck whiteness requires racial otherness and the fantasy of white supremacy to establish an exclusive solidarity with fellow whites, to continually re-establish an imaginary white paradise. Taylor (2004, 182) writes that, with any imaginary, "we have both a sense of security in believing that it really is in effect in our world and also a sense of our own superiority and goodness deriving in our participation in it and our upholding of it." Our belief in the superiority of our imaginary casts us as heroes in a fantasy defending the good and right: "This is why, in earlier times, we see people lashing out at such moments of threat with scapegoating violence against 'the enemy within,' meeting the threat to our security by finessing that to our integrity, deflecting it onto scapegoats" (ibid.). The redneck, delusional and imagining himself as a noble but beleaguered hero, is empowered by the fantasy of white supremacy. The magical cloak of Okanagan redneck whiteness, while protecting the redneck, works to "obscure the connections between past colonial crimes and current forms of racial violence" (O'Connell 2010, 538). Identifying and dealing with racism is extremely difficult in this context.

A public example of this difficulty is the Dayleen Van Ryswyk affair, in which Van Ryswyk is purported to have made anti-French and anti-Indigenous comments in an online forum. As a consequence of these statements becoming public, she was dumped from the NDP provincial ballot in the 14 May 2013 BC general election. Here is a snippet from one of her postings: "It's not the status cards, it's the fact that we have been paying out of the nose for generations for something that isn't our doing ... If their [Aboriginal] ancestors sold out too cheap it's not my fault and I shouldn't have to be paying for any mistake or whatever you want to call it from my hard-earned money" (*Huffington Post*, 16 April 2013). After her dismissal by the NDP, I was not surprised by the support that Van Ryswyk received. An online poll from the Okanagan's Castanet news agency asked the question: "Do you think Dayleen Van Ryswyk's comments were out of line?" In response, 1,769 people voted "No" and 534 voted "Yes" (Moore 2013). Letters of support for Van Ryswyk flooded in to the local newspapers, congratulating her for stating what "all of us are thinking" and, in one case, asking First Nations to "put on [their] big boy pants brush off and start fresh" while at the same time calling on "true Canadians" to "take our country back" from the "Indians" (Matotek 2013). Van Ryswyk's postings and the positive response to them fill out what is deeply disturbing, even nauseating, about Okanagan redneck whiteness: the sense of entitlement and feeling of supremacy summed up in the oft-repeated phrase "true Canadian."

The collected rhetoric above functions to cast the white Okanagan Valley dweller as victim, as a "true Canadian" hero, and imagines an enemy responsible for threatening that "true Canadian" identity and community. This same kind of talk is expressed in less politically correct language that can be overheard in coffee shops, pubs, around the kitchen table, or out hunting and fishing. Here's a paraphrased sample of such talk from "Uncle Reg."

> They say there might not be a salmon season. Stocks are down. I figure it's the damn Indians taking all the fish. It's pretty sad when you can't even fish in your own country. Pretty soon you won't be able to hunt either. Things keep going the way they are the Indians will own the whole damned place ... We should have finished the job when we had the chance.

Van Ryswyk's opinion, the letters to the editors, and the typical account from "Uncle Reg" are striking for several reasons. First, they cast whites as victims. Second, they both attribute the supposed offence to a racialized other. Finally, all are rhetorical attempts to create community and solidarity through the sharing of "white fantasies" of victimization aimed at persuading the conversational partner that there is a common enemy assailing their white paradise.

CONCLUSION: OVERCOMING DISCOURSES OF DENIAL AND UNPRODUCTIVE FICTIONS

> "What is yours and what is mine?
> 'Cause there is no more new frontier
> We have got to make it here"
>
> Eagles, *The Last Resort*

> "In many ways, home is an image for the power of stories. With both, we need to live in them if they are to take hold, and we need to stand back from them if we are to understand their power. But we do need them; when we don't have them, we become filled with deep sorrow. That's if we are lucky. If we're unlucky, we go mad."
>
> J. Edward Chamberlin, *If This Is Your Land, Where Are Your Stories?*

The imaginary I've laid out here is made more understandable in the context of an Okanagan culture that has undergone considerable change, particularly in terms of its economic base. The global forces of neoliberalism contribute to the breakdown in the cohesiveness of the Okanagan Valley lifeworld, which generates contradictory images of the valley either as playground and retirement destination for the wealthy or as economic backwater. The shift from a primary industry economy to a service industry economy renders a valley culture that has few prospects for upward mobility for young people who work in minimum-wage jobs in a service industry that largely services retirees and wealthy tourists (Aguiar, Tomic, and Trumper 2005). This shift has led to a "culture of defeat," as a friend and fellow ex-Okanaganite described it. It is in this feeling of being defeated and the general feelings of resentment or guilt over this "fall" that we can begin to understand the grounds of the racist, scapegoating speech acts in the Okanagan.

Kenneth Burke holds that the ultimate motivation of rhetorical speech acts is to rid ourselves of an oppressive sense of *guilt*, a catch-all term into which we can fold all manner of anxiety, feelings of inadequacy, lack, shame, and disgust (Griffin 2003, 316). The individual engaged in expiating guilt can take one of two pathways. Down one path is redemption through *self-mortification*, the act of purging guilt through blaming the self. This requires an admission of guilt and a request for forgiveness. Down the other path is a much more attractive option, redemption through *victimage*, the "process of designating an external enemy as the source of all our ills" (319). White fantasies as rhetorical acts not only purge guilt through scapegoating but also become a source of identity and community for working-class rural white people (rednecks) in the Okanagan experiencing a loss of economic and ontological security.

I've been in southwestern Ontario for about fifteen years. The Okanagan is a place where I now struggle to belong. Without my cloak of redneck whiteness, I can appear uncanny, unhomely, perhaps even a threat. That cloak now is the hair shirt I wear, a part of myself that I cannot leave behind and with which I must still try to make peace. My wearing of the cloak, as much as I find it suffocating, allows me to see what undergirds the white culture of the Okanagan Valley and, in particular, the working-class rural culture with which I am familiar. What is disturbing is that the racist rhetoric that was once more privately expressed is becoming more public. Online postings about the recent shooting death of Cree man Colten

Boushie by white farmer Gerald Stanley underscore this point. One individual wrote that Stanley "should have shot all five and [been] given a medal," while a rural councillor, Ben Kautz, and others posted that the only mistake the white shooter made was "leaving witnesses" (Canadian Press 2016). Social media has helped foster this culture of intolerance.

Just after the 2011 Canadian federal election, a debate erupted on my Facebook page where I had reposted a friend's disparaging comments about the Conservative election victory and the racist, redneck character of the people living in rural ridings. Naturally, most of my Facebook friends who lived in or had grown up in the Conservative stronghold of the Okanagan were on the defensive. Some were insulted and angrily took me to task for calling to their attention the widespread racism that inflects Okanagan Valley culture. The last comment on the thread ended the conversation. Daryl, a quiet and friendly guy in our high school days, had this to say:

> It's more than racism, there is an underlying bigotry as well, it wasn't until I moved away that I realized it, it is the worst kind of intolerance, it is not in your face like the KKK or some kind of movement, it is quiet and insidious, *teaching the young people to hate and shun others.* I love [the place] and my childhood was filled with great days, but I am glad my kids have grown up elsewhere. Some of the best people I know immigrated here [Vancouver] from Asia, and they would give the shirt off their back to help their neighbour! The next four years scare me, I think Canadians have had a huge lapse in judgment. (emphasis mine)

Daryl's words turned out to be prophetic as, under the Conservatives, the attitude towards minorities and First Peoples shifted dramatically. In the run-up to the 2015 election the Conservatives employed the politics of fear, crescendoing with the proposal of the hate-mongering Barbaric Cultural Practices Act. Both Daryl and I fired back at the increasing number of racist posts and memes circulated by our "friends." For my friend Daryl, the Okanagan, as it had for me, had become strange. It was the act of moving away for an extended period of time coupled with intimate exposure to culturally different others that made the problematic nature of Okanagan redneck whiteness apparent to us. Like Schuetz's (1945) homecomer, we can make strange the fantasy of a white homeland and begin to engage the other authentically, we can take the journey to make ourselves, like Odysseus, "wise to things." This will require courage.

White settlers need to be courageous enough to recognize that our "home" is on Indigenous land. The *Tsilhqot'in* decision established that Aboriginal title has not been extinguished. To quote a presentation my ancestor, Jim Williams (uncle, white settler, deacon in the Anglican Church of Canada, ally, returner of stolen artefacts to the Nisga'a from the Anglican Church, and one of the most kindly and god-fearing people I have had the pleasure to know), made in Victoria to the Select Standing Committee on Aboriginal Affairs, our dealings with the Original People must turn on the values of "FAIRNESS, JUSTICE, and HONOUR" (Williams 1997). We need to recognize that we are settlers and what this means as a responsibility, and that newcomers, arrivants, have the same claim to fairness, justice, and security as does anyone else. We need to start with acknowledging and making right the fundamental injustice done to the Original People. Rafe Mair (2014), referencing the ethical imperative of the Tsilhqot'in decision, argues that it's "time to grow up, Canada." He's right, it's time. The re-discovery of the 215 children buried at the Kamloops residential school and the rising numbers of bodies found at other residential schools across so-called Canada is a call to action we cannot ignore (Casmir 2021).

We need to gather the courage to throw aside the toxic cloak of redneck whiteness because, after all, it's a cloak woven of fear, hate, and lies – hardly an identity worth clothing ourselves in. I recognize that this is a task made more difficult in a climate of insecurity, in which the politics of fear and hate embarked on by the Harper government, and now bleeding up from the United States, is on the ascendant. This politics of fear and hate, economic insecurity, the resurgence of First Peoples, and the conflation of terrorism with Islam, and the exploitation of this for political purposes, has meant that anti new Canadian and anti-Indigenous sentiment is on the rise. This makes it even more imperative that we "Git-R Done," engaging in the hard work of attempting to see the other without distortion, as human. We can then, working together, fashion "narratives for a new belonging" (Bromley 2000) instead of perpetuating the chicken shit discourses of denial and the cowardly and unproductive fictions that lead to scapegoating violence.

In throwing aside the protective cloak of redneck whiteness, we open ourselves up to change. Taylor (2002, 295) writes that, "in coming to see the other correctly, we inescapably alter our understanding of ourselves. Taking in the other will involve an identity shift in us. That is why it is so often resisted and rejected. We have a deep identity investment in the distorted images we cherish of others." Our identity is bound up in the stories we tell about self and other. We need these stories, as without them we experience a deep sorrow or, worse, go mad (Chamberlin 2003, 77). We need to tell ourselves different stories, stories that can decolonize our minds and our hearts. The first step, as Chamberlin recommends, is to stand back and understand the power of the stories we tell ourselves. For example, we need to confront the self-serving and violent aspects of the frontier narrative and how it is buttressed by racist jokes/humour and the cliché of the redneck. Second, instead of perpetuating our own inward-looking imaginary we need to imagine something new. The Truth and Reconciliation Commission has set us on this trajectory. Initiatives like #NEXT 150 seek to put the recommendations of the TRC into action and invite participation. As we begin to live the story of reconciliation, we must be cautious. We must avoid the settler moves to innocence available in the Métis narrative (see Saul 2008) and in the appropriation of Indigenous cultural practices. We must start where we live to address the historical wrongs that have been committed. For the people living on the traditional territory of the Secwépemc, Nlaka'pamux, and Syilx peoples *The Memorial to Sir Wilfrid Laurier, Premier of the Dominion of Canada*, delivered by the chiefs of these nations to Sir Wilfrid Laurier on his visit to Kamloops in 1910, is a starting point. Here are a few of their good words.

> We have no grudge against the white race as a whole nor against the settlers, but we want to have an equal chance with them of making a living. We welcome them to this country. It is not in most cases their fault. They have taken up and improved and paid for their lands in good faith. It is their government that is to blame by heaping up injustice on us. But it is also their duty to see their government does right by us, and gives us a square deal. (*Memorial to Sir Wilfrid Laurier* n.d.)

In this short passage we see evidence of the patience and grace exercised by these people and their desire to live with the settlers in a harmonious but just way. There is a lesson here for us. In the coming months and years what we will need most is the redeeming and civilizing power of the grace expressed by these great chiefs, one that imagines a human community in which we affirm each other by being "patient and kind," by making "allowances" rather than being "vengeful or mean," and where we "look for the best and not the worst" in each other (Norris 1979, 179–80). Okanagan redneck whites need not behave like a "brutal tribe of uncivilized savages" (Homer 2003, 174). We have a duty to those who have been wronged to see justice done. It's high time redneck whites stopped being worried and afraid, and, taking our own advice, "put on our big boy pants brush off and start fresh." We need to take this opportunity, together with the Original Caretakers of this land and newcomers, to build something good here on Turtle Island – something fair, just, and honourable.

REFERENCES

Aguiar, L.L.M., A.M. McKinnon, D. Sookraj. 2010–11. "Racialization and the Repertoires of Racism: Reaction to Jamaicans in the Okanagan Valley." *BC Studies* 168 (Winter): 65–79.

Aguiar, L.L.M., and T. Marten. 2011. "Shimmering White Kelowna and the Examination of Painless White Privilege in the Hinterland of British Columbia." In *Rethinking the Great White North: Race, Nature and the Historical Geographies of Whiteness in Canada,* ed. A. Baldwin, L. Cameron and A. Kobayashi, 122–44. Vancouver: UBC Press.

Aguiar, L.L.M., Tomic, P., Trumper, R. 2005. "Work Hard, Play Hard: Selling Kelowna, BC, as Year-Round Playground." *Canadian Geographer* (49): 123–39.

Arendt, H. 1963. *Eichmann in Jerusalem: A Report on the Banality of Evil.* New York: Viking Press.

Berger, P., B. Berger, and H. Kellner. 1973. *The Homeless Mind: Modernization and Consciousness.* New York: Random House.

Blum, A. 2010. "The Imaginary of Self Satisfaction: Reflections on the Platitude of the 'Creative City.'" In *Circulation and the City: Essays on Urban Culture,* ed. A.S. Boutros, 64–98. Montreal and Kingston: McGill-Queens University Press.

Bormann, E.G. 1985. *The Force of Fantasy: Restoring the American Dream.* Carbondale: Southern Illinois University Press.

Bromley, R. 2000. *Narratives for a New Belonging.* Edinburgh: Edinburgh University Press.

Buckmaster, L. 2018. "Crocodile Dundee Was Sexist, Racist and Homophobic. Let's Not Bring That Back." *Guardian.* https://www.theguardian.com/film/2018/jan/23/crocodile-dundee-was-sexist-racist-and-homophobic-lets-not-bring-that-back.

Burke, K. 1973. *The Philosophy of Literary Form*, 3rd ed. Berkeley: University of California Press.

Canadian Press. 2016. Sask. "Councillor Regrets Social Media Post about Colten Boushie Shooting Death, Says Wife." CBC News. http://www.cbc.ca/news/canada/saskatoon/sask-councillor-social-media-colten-boushie-1.3730070.

Casmir, Rosanne. 2021. "Office of the Chief: for Immediate Release." *Tk'emlúps te Secwépemc/Kamloops Indian Band*. 27 May. https://tkemlups.ca/wp-content/uploads/05-May-27-2021-TteS-MEDIA-RELEASE.pdf.

Chamberlin, J.E. 2003. *If This Is Your Land, Where Are Your Stories? Finding Common Ground*. Toronto: Knopf.

Furniss, E. 1999. *The Burden of History: Colonialism and the Frontier Myth in a Rural Canadian Community*. Vancouver: UBC Press.

Giddens, A. 1990. *The Consequences of Modernity*. Cambridge: Polity.

Griffin, E.M. 2003. *A First Look at Communication Theory*. New York: McGraw Hill.

Habermas, J. 1996. *Between Facts and Norms*. Boston: MIT Press

Hage, G. 2000. *White Nation: Fantasies of White Supremacy in a Multicultural Society*. New York: Routledge.

Harding, R. 2005. "The Media, Aboriginal People and Common Sense." *Canadian Journal of Native Studies* (25): 311–35.

–. 2006. "Historical Representations of Aboriginal People in the Canadian News Media." *Discourse Society* (17): 205–31.

Homer. 2003. *The Odyssey*. Trans. E.V. Rieu. New York: Penguin Books Canada.

Huffington Post BC. 2013. "Dayleen Van Ryswyk, Kelowna NDP Candidate, Quits over Racist Comments." HuffPost British Columbia. http://www.huffingtonpost.ca/2013/04/16/dayleen-van-ryswyk-kelowna-ndp-racist_n_3093747.html.

Jarosz, L., and V. Lawson. 2002. "'Sophisticated People versus Rednecks': Economic Restructuring and the Class Difference in America's West." *Antipode* 34: 8–27.

Johnston, Hugh. 1999. "The Sikhs." In *Encyclopedia of Canadian Peoples*, ed. Paul Robert Magosci, 1148–64, Toronto/Buffalo: Multicultural History Society of Ontario and University of Toronto Press.

Keyes, D. 2011. "Whites Singing Red Face in British Columbia in the 1950's." *Theatre Research in Canada* 32 (1): 30–63.

Knox, R. 2013. "Lumby Days Offers Fun." *Vernon Morning Star*. http://www.vernonmorningstar.com/community/210114051.html.

Mair, Rafe. 2014. "Tsilhqot'in Decision: Time to Grow up, Canada. Gone Are Childish Notions Dismissive of Native Land Claims." *Tyee*. http://thetyee.ca/Opinion/2014/07/07/Tsilhqotin-Decision/.

Maréchal, G. 2010. "Autoethnography." In *Encyclopedia of Case Study Research*, vol. 2., ed. A.J. Mills, G. Durepos, and E. Wiebe, 43–45. Thousand Oaks, CA: Sage.

Matotek, Shelley. 2013. "Dayleen Van Ryswyk Resignation" (letters to the editor). http://www.castanet.net/news/Letters/90519/Dayleen-Van-Ryswyk-resignation.

Memorial to Sir Wilfrid Laurier, Premier of the Dominion of Canada. n.d. Accessed June 10, 2021. Kanaka Bar Band. https://www.kanakabarband.ca/files/memorial-to-sir-wilfred-laurier-pdf.pdf.

Moore, Wayne. 2013. "Would You Vote for Van Ryswyk?" *Castanet.* http://www.castanet.net/news/Poll/90575/Would-you-vote-for-Van-Ryswyk.

Norris, R.A. 1979. *Understanding the Faith of the Church.* New York: Seabury Press.

O'Connell, A. 2010. "An Exploration of Redneck Whiteness in Multicultural Canada." *Social Politics* 17 (4): 536–63.

Roediger, D.R. 1991. *The Wages of Whiteness: Race and the Making of the American Working Class.* New York and London: Verso.

Ryan, P. 2010. *Multicultiphobia.* Toronto: University of Toronto Press.

Saul, J.R. 2008. *A Fair Country: Telling Truths about Canada.* Toronto: Penguin.

Schuetz, A. 1945. "The Homecomer." *American Journal of Sociology* 50 (5): 369–76.

Seshadri-Crooks, K. 2000. *Desiring Whiteness: A Lacanian Analysis of Race.* London: Routledge.

Svenson, S. 1982. "The Saga of the N1/2 of NW1/4 of Section 12." *Okanagan Historical Journal: Forty-Sixth Report* (46): 83–88.

–. 2015. "Chasing Leisure: A Hermeneutic of Late Modernity." PhD diss., University of Waterloo.

Swardson, Anne. "Religious Headgear Banned." *The Washington Post.* https://www.washingtonpost.com/archive/politics/1994/06/07/religious-headgear-banned/621c9da5-b5dc-496f-80cf-bd0c689cf4e5/.

Taylor, C. 2002. "Understanding the Other: A Gadamerian View on Conceptual Schemes." In *Gadamer's Century: Essays in Honor of Hans-Georg Gadamer*, ed. Jeff Malpas, Ulrich Von Arnswald, and Jens Kertscher. 279–98. Cambridge, MA: MIT Press.

–. 2004. *Modern Social Imaginaries.* Durham, NC: Duke University Press.

Tuck, E., and K.W. Yang. 2012. "Decolonization Is Not a Metaphor." *Decolonization: Indigeneity, Education, and Society* 1 (1): 1–40.

Turner, R. 1974. *Ethnomethodology.* London: Hazell Watson and Viney.

Wilkes, R., N. Guppy, and L. Farris. 2008. "No Thanks, We're Full: Individual Characteristics, National Context and Changing Attitudes toward Immigration." *International Migration Review* (42): 203–329.

Williams, J. 1997. *Presentation to the Select Standing Committee on Aboriginal Affairs,* 18 February. Victoria: BC Legislature.

Yaccino, Stephen, Michael Schwirtz, and Marc Santora. 2012. "Gunman Kills 6 at a Sikh Temple Near Milwaukee." *New York Times.* 5 August. https://www.nytimes.com/2012/08/06/us/shooting-reported-at-temple-in-wisconsin.html.

CONTRIBUTORS

Luís L.M. Aguiar is an associate professor in sociology at the University of British Columbia and cofounder of the urban studies theme in graduate studies in the College of Graduate Studies at the same university. He teaches and researches on issues of "race," "the city," "the changing workplace," "globalization," "elites," "the sociology of the Okanagan," and qualitative methods. He has two previous coedited books: *Cleaners in the Global Economy* (Blackwell 2006) and *Researching amongst Elites* (Ashgate 2012).

Lawrence D. Berg is a professor of critical geography and coordinator of the Urban and Regional Studies Interdisciplinary Graduate Program at the Okanagan campus of UBC. His research focuses on wide-ranging issues of place and the politics of identity. Lawrence also has a keen research interest in issues of neoliberalism and white supremacy in academic knowledge production.

Natalie Chambers is a settler from London, England. For the last twenty years she has lived in the Okanagan Nation with her Syilx Okanagan husband and children, and she is a mother of two and stepmother of five children who have participated in community language immersion programs. For her PhD research, Natalie supported the development of Language Nest immersion programs for young children in the Okanagan Nation. She continues to support fund development for the Language Nest into the present day. For the last twenty-five years, Natalie has been a qualitative researcher in the areas of Indigenous education, health behaviour, and cross-cultural health. She is a Professor in the Interdisciplinary Studies Department at Okanagan College.

Bill Cohen is from the Okanagan Nation and specializes in the areas of Indigenous knowledge, education, and transforming pedagogy. He is an educator, artist, storyteller, and author. The focus of Bill's continuing research is to identify, understand, and theorize the transforming potential of Syilx Okanagan and Indigenous knowledge and pedagogy through organic language and cultural knowledge revitalization. As an educator, he has organized numerous community, school, arts, language, literacy, and numeracy projects involving Elders, fluent speakers, parents, and children. He lives in Nkmaplqs, Okanagan territory, with his wife Natalie and children Mary-Rose, Emma-Jane, Will, Dempsey, and Devon. He is Assistant Professor in the UBC Okanagan School of Education.

Jon Corbett is a professor in the Community, Culture and Global Studies Department at UBC Okanagan and is the director of the Institute for Community Engaged Research. He has two primary research interests: first, to explore how digital multimedia technologies can be combined with maps and used by communities to document, store, and communicate their spatial knowledge; second, to examine how geographic representation of this knowledge, using these technologies, can strengthen the community internally as well as externally through increasing their influence over decision making and their ability to become active agents in the process of social change. All aspects of his research incorporate a core community element.

Carl E. James, FRSC, teaches in the Faculty of Education and the Graduate Program in Sociology at York University where he is also the Jean Augustine Chair in Education Community and Diaspora, and Senior Advisor on Equity and Representation. His research interests include examination of the ways in which accessible and equitable opportunities in education and employment account for the lived experiences and social achievements of Black and other racialized and marginalized Canadians. His most recent publication includes: *"Colour Matters": Essays on the Experiences, Education and Pursuits of Black Youth* (2021).

Daniel J. Keyes was raised in southern Ontario on a farm on the perimeter of Camp Borden, a Canadian military base, on Treaty 18 land (1818) in southern Ontario with little consciousness of his status as a settler. He teaches English literature and cultural studies with an emphasis on media studies at both the graduate and undergraduate levels at UBC Okanagan. His research focuses on settler colonial privilege in media and space. He has published "Whites Singing Red Face in British Columbia in the 1950s" with *Theatre Research in Canada* (2011) and "Green and White Space Invaders: New Urbanism in the Okanagan, British Columbia" with *Home Culture* (2015).

Audrey Kobayashi, PhD, FRSC, is a professor and the Patricia Monture Distinguished University Professor and Queen's Research Chair at Queen's University, Kingston, Ontario. She was born in Kelowna. Her research involves questions of racism, multiculturalism, immigration, disability, and employment equity, and she has published widely in these areas. She is currently involved in a number of research projects that involve collaboration with community groups.

Sheila Lewis, MA, grew up and currently works in the Okanagan territory. She is from the Shushwap and Lilooet Nations. She specializes in the areas of housing and discrimination, research, knowledge translation and transfer, and radical activism. Sheila's work has brought her into the non-profit sector working directly with marginalized groups. As a result, she has been able to bring her experience and expertise to the sector and to help inform various processes of decolonization and destigmatization. More important, she has been able to address the ongoing exclusionary culture of whiteness in the Okanagan area.

Janet MacArthur is an Associate Professor Emeritus (English) in the Faculty of Creative and Critical Studies at the University of British Columbia Okanagan where she created and taught the first courses in women's literature, autobiography, and Holocaust Studies. She has published a monograph on the reception of early modern poetry as well as articles on women's writing, postcolonial literature, settler colonialism, and disability narrative. Recent conference presentations have been on relations among Syilx and settler women, and on Holocaust fiction and film. She is one of three authors of a forthcoming collection titled *Okanagan Women's Voices: Syilx and Settler Writing and Relations, 1870s–1930s.*

Donna M. Senese was born and raised in the Niagara region of Ontario. After obtaining a PhD in geography from the University of Waterloo, Donna moved to the Okanagan Valley, where she is now associate professor of geography at the University of British Columbia Okanagan. Her research and teaching interests are in rural sustainability, tourism, and wine, and she has most recently authored: "Wine Tourism" with Barbara Carmichael and "The Okanagan Wine Region" in *Wine Geography* (Springer Publishers 2011); and "Amenity Resources and Rural Change" in *The Canadian Rural Urban Fringe* (Brandon University Press 2010). Donna teaches a variety of geography courses at the undergraduate and graduate levels, including tourism planning and development, parks and recreation, and wine geographies.

Stephen Svenson is a precarious academic worker and community organizer on the Haldimand Tract in Kitchener-Waterloo active on issues of climate justice, food justice, and Indigenous sovereignty. He is a settler who comes from the traditional territory of the Splatsin (Spla-jeen) people in the North Okanagan where growing up as a fisher, farmer, and forager he gained a deep appreciation for the land. Currently, he teaches, among other subjects, sociology of education, sociology of youth, environmental sociology and research methods at Wilfrid Laurier University where he is working on the impossible problem of decolonizing education in an institutional setting. He is also cohost of the podcast, *Rights of Passage: A Reconciliation Podcast*.

Delacey Tedesco is a lecturer (assistant professor) in politics at the University of Exeter, UK, and director of the new combined honours undergraduate program in politics and geography that she established there. Her research addresses patterns of security and insecurity in contemporary politics and international relations, given the geopolitical uncertainties generated by global urbanization, global decolonization, and global ecological reconfiguration. This work has been developed in relation to the unstable aporetic boundaries of nature, the city, the subject, and sovereignty. Her more recent work investigates these problematics through global fashion and everyday dress practices, thus developing political fashion curation as innovative methodology for critical social science research. Prior to taking up her position at the University of

Exeter, she taught human and urban geography with Community, Culture and Global Studies at the University of British Columbia Okanagan. Originally from Vernon, BC, she lived and worked in Kelowna for close to a decade while writing her dissertation and several publications on the Okanagan Valley.

INDEX

Note: "(f)" after a page number indicates a figure or map